real stew

*300 Recipes for Authentic Home-Cooked Cassoulet,
Gumbo, Chili, Curry, Minestrone, Bouillabaisse,
Stroganoff, Goulash, Chowder, and Much More*

clifford a. wright

THE HARVARD COMMON PRESS
Boston, Massachusetts

For my darling daughter,
Dyala Katri Kattan–Wright

The Harvard Common Press
535 Albany Street
Boston, Massachusetts 02118
www.harvardcommonpress.com

Printed in the United States of America

Printed on acid-free paper

Library of Congress Cataloging-in-Publication Data

Wright, Clifford A.
    Real stew : 300 recipes for authentic home-cooked cassoulet, gumbo, chili, curry,
minestrone, bouillabaisse, stroganoff, goulash, chowder, and much more / Clifford A.
Wright.
        p. cm.
    Includes index.
    ISBN 1-55832-1985 (hc : alk. paper)—1-55832-1993 (pbk : alk. paper)
      1. Stews. I. Title.
TX693.W75 2002
641.8'23—dc21

            2002017290

Special bulk-order discounts are available on this and other Harvard Common Press books.
Companies and organizations may purchase books for premiums or resale,
or may arrange a custom edition, by contacting the Marketing Director at the address above.

10 9 8 7 6 5 4 3 2 1

COVER RECIPE: RAGOUT OF "CINNAMONY" VEAL WITH TOMATO AND CREAM, PAGE 66
COVER DESIGN BY NIGHT & DAY DESIGN
COVER PHOTOGRAPH BY MARK THOMAS PHOTOGRAPHY
ILLUSTRATIONS BY NEVERNE COVINGTON
BOOK DESIGN BY KATHLEEN HERLIHY-PAOLI, INKSTONE DESIGN

Contents

Acknowledgments

There are many people who have helped me with the recipes in this book, and they are usually mentioned in the recipe itself. But there was a steadfast group of people who would on a moment's notice help eat all these stews either by coming over to my house or by allowing me to arrive at their doorstep, stew in hand (or pot, I should say). Without Martha Rose Shulman and Bill Grantham, Barbara Shulgasser-Parker and Norman Parker, Russ and Kathy Parsons, Bill and Laurie Benenson, Heidi Mage Lloyd, Anne Troutman, Alex Istanbuli, Kimba Hills, Steve Monas and Maggie Megaw, Najwa al-Qattan, Liz Marx, Katina Shields, Simeon Pillich, Sarah Pillsbury, Stuart and Helen Garber, Pauline Lord and David Harlow, Lois Fishman, and my children, Ali, Dyala, and Seri, there would have been a lot of leftover stew. Once you read this book, you'll see that that is not a bad thing. Nevertheless, my freezer wasn't that big.

I would also like to thank Pam Hoenig, my editor, and Doe Coover, my agent, for once again providing the guidance and support that makes my books not only fun to write but, I hope, fun to read. Thanks also go to Bruce Shaw, publisher, Deborah Kops, copyeditor, and everyone else at The Harvard Common Press for making this book what it is. Special thanks go to Brian J. Maynard, Christopher E. Hubbach, and the KitchenAid Corporation for their assistance.

Introduction

As the crisp, cold New England air descends in late September, the rusty leaves fall, sweaters are donned, and you can see your breath, thoughts turn to the first stew of the cold days ahead. I lived in Massachusetts for fifteen years and those cold, enveloping winters gave birth to many a piping hot, rib-sticking stew chock-full of long-simmered meats, hearty root vegetables, and other flavorful foods. Stews gave rise to many a warming thought and an even warmer kitchen, whose aromas would entice us all day long.

Making stews is an enjoyable activity filled with great expectation. When you think of comfort food, when you think of hearth and home, when you think of good cookin', you are undoubtedly thinking of a stew. Every step of stew making is inviting, from tossing chopped onions and celery into the stewpot and listening to the sizzle, to dissolving the tomato paste in water and stirring in the red wine, and, of course, hearing someone in another room yell, "What's cookin'? It smells so good."

WHAT MAKES A STEW A STEW?

I have a broad conception of what a stew is and, technically, I suppose, some of the stews in this book are not stews. Perhaps they are ragouts and braises. But if there is one thing that distinguishes a stew, it is that it cooks gently for a long time and so do ragouts and braises and that's why I include them. One of the things I love most about stews, in addition to their taste, is the fact that the aromas permeate the house for hours. There is something else I love about them: you can never make too much because stews are wonderful the second time around. Many of the stews in this book actually ask you to cook them several times, because each new stage of cooking adds yet another level of flavor complexity. Not all stews cook gently, though; take, for instance, fish stews, which cook quickly in some cases.

I speak of braises, ragouts, and stews in the same breath. A braise involves cooking meat slowly in some fat in a covered pot with very little liquid, which then becomes the final sauce. A ragout also involves cooking well-seasoned meat and vegetables slowly, but with a thicker sauce, a gravy really. *Stew* is the catchall word to describe the process of cooking at a simmering heat, and for that reason I think it covers everything. Some people use the word *braise* to be that catchall phrase.

Stews are as old as the invention of the first pot. M.F.K. Fisher notes in *How to Cook a Wolf* that making stew is a "satisfying procedure and can give no harm to man or beast. There is a different recipe for everyone who has thought of making one, but in general the rules are simple." In culinary terms, one reason for stews, and there are many, is to break down the connective tissue in cheaper—that is, tougher—cuts of meat so that it is palatable. This can only be done through long simmering. For this reason, one would never stew filet mignon, because there is little connective tissue and the meat is already tender. On the other hand, one cannot quickly grill a brisket because it would not come out tender. The muscles of the animal that get a good workout, such as the foreleg or rump, are surrounded by very thick sheets of connective tissue. That is why these cuts of meat are tougher. But that slow cooking also make them moist and tender too. According to Russ Parsons, food editor of the *Los Angeles Times*, it takes extended moist heating to break down the connective tissue of tougher cuts of meat, typically raising the internal temperature of the meat to 180 to 185 degrees Fahrenheit, as opposed to most red meats, which are considered cooked at 130 to 140 degrees.

Stews begin in different ways. Some cooks like to brown the meat first by sautéing it in a little fat and then adding liquid and other ingredients. Other cooks start braising or stewing without the initial browning. These are called blanquettes and are often made with chicken or veal. In the initial browning of the meat you

Tureen

should remember that you're also cooking it, so don't overbrown it. The meat should be crispy golden brown on the outside, and that should be accomplished over not a very high heat but rather a medium-high heat.

Le Creuset casserole

CHOOSING A STEWPOT

What do you cook a stew in? Throughout the book I will almost always call for stewing in a stew pot or a casserole. When I say *casserole*, I mean the one I use very often, which is a large enameled cast-iron casserole made by Le Creuset that can be used on the stove top and in the oven. There are other kinds of stew pots and casseroles, including earthenware, which I recommend highly because it truly provides another level of flavor. There is the *marmite*, a French word for a potbellied stew pot with a tight lid, and the Dutch oven, a cast-iron stew pot with a domed cover that captures moisture very well and seals in flavor. They are sold in fine cookware stores such as Williams-Sonoma or Sur La Table. Although I think it would be great to have all of these various cooking vessels, you can stew in whatever you have or are used to.

OF TAGINES, COUSCOUSSIERS, AND OTHER COOKING VESSELS

Throughout the world cooks use their own special versions of stew pots. In Tunisia, a handleless earthenware casserole with a conical earthenware lid that is used for stewing is called a tagine (or *ṭājin* or *ṭājīn*), an Arabic word that derives from the Greek *teganon*, or "frying pan," which also gives us the modern Italian word for frying pan, *tegame*. One particular Tunisian stew, a *madarbal* (page 111), meaning "a stew cooked with vinegar," is traditionally made in a stew pot called a *ṭānjara*, a tin-lined cylindrical *marmite* with a cover. In North Africa,

Tajine

couscous is cooked in a *kiskis*, a two-piece vessel. The ragout cooks in the bottom part, a potbellied stew pot, steaming the couscous through the perforated top part, where the couscous sits. In this book I call the bottom part by the French name, *couscoussier*; it makes an excellent stew pot. On the Balearic Island of Menorca, they use an earthenware casserole called a *greixonera*. In Spain, a number of different stew pots and casseroles are used. Most common is the shallow earthenware casserole called a *cazuela*, which is either handleless or has two protruding knobs that act as handles. It is 8 to 12 inches in diameter and 3 inches high, with a flat bottom. It often has an earthenware lid. The Spanish also use an earthenware stew casserole called a *caldero*, which can also be an iron cauldron. And then, of course, there is the famous potbellied stew pot

called the *olla*, which appears in *Don Quixote*. In the Castellón region of Valencia, stews are traditionally cooked in a copper kettle called a *perol* or *peroles*. The Turks stew their foods in a very similar earthenware casserole. They call it a *güveç*, which also gives its name to the stew itself. The Turks also cook one of their most famous stews in a clay bowl called a *tas*, which gives its name to the lamb stew known as *tas kebabı* (page 128). In Greece, a *kakavia* is a three-legged cooking pot traditionally used to cook soup and stews; today it also gives its name to a fish stew (page 259). Even older traditional forms of Greek stew pots are the *kappamás*, a covered clay oven pot used for baking lamb and stewing, and the *kazáni*, a large copper pot used for

Couscoussier

heating water or cooking lamb trotter stews like *patsas* (see my book *A Mediterranean Feast*, pp. 689–90). The Greek *téntsero* is a deep, tin-lined copper stew pot, and the *tsoúka* is a clay stew pot. In Egypt cooks prepare *fūl*, the national dish of stewed fava beans, in large cauldrons called *qidra* or *qidr*, which are sometimes made of earthenware and usually pot-bellied. Two other kinds of stew pots used in Egypt are the *kift* and *ḥalla*.

Daubière

In Italy, a variety of stew pots, some old and traditional and some not, are used. The standard stew pot is simply called a casserole, or *casseruola*. In Apulia, a small, potbellied stew pot called a *caldariello* is used for a famous eponymous stew of lamb cooked in milk (page 93). Another version of this stew pot is the *calderotto*, an earthenware cauldron or *marmite* used for cooking stews. In Basilicata, stews are cooked in a *pigneti*, an earthenware *marmite* or "jug" that is used for cooking. The cook hermetically seals the earthenware jug with clay and then places the *pigneti* in the embers of a fire to cook. In France, cooks make daube (page 11) in a *daubière* and tripe in a *tripière*. The *daubière* is a large, heavy, tin-lined copper vessel and the *tripière* is a flat-bottomed, wide, round earthenware casserole. In Serbia, cooks use a *glineni lonac*, a pot-bellied stew pot made of soft terra-cotta with two handles and a tight-fitting lid. In Hungary, the famous goulash began as a kind of shepherd's soup in the ninth century, and was cooked in a heavy iron stew pot called a *bogrács*.

In the end, a good stew is a simple thing that cooks slowly for a long time. The idea is to take a variety of quality ingredients including meat, vegetables, herbs, and spices, and simmer them gently together so that the intensity of flavor is extracted and the final stew is a delectable amalgam of the interaction of all these ingredients. We think of stews as easy, and they can be, but sometimes stews are complex and you will encounter both in this book. There were countless ways for dividing up this book; I chose to separate the stew recipes into their chapters based on the way I, and I imagine everyone else, decides to eat a stew. You ask your family and yourself, "What do you want for dinner?" And the answer is usually simple: "beef" or "chicken," or whatever. So that's how the stews are grouped—those with beef, veal, pork, lamb, fowl, vegetables, and mixed meat stews.

This book is filled with easy stews, hard stews, long-simmering stews, quick fish stews, involved stews, and not so involved stews. There are stews from everywhere, including India, Yemen, Tunisia, France, Canada, Latin American countries, and the United States. This book has got something for everybody, but most especially, it's got exciting recipes that will permeate your home with wonderful aromas that will make everyone happy. So let's start stewing!

STEWS WITH BEEF

The range of stews you will encounter in this chapter is as varied as the Ragout of Meatballs Stuffed with Cauliflower from Tunisia (page 35), which consists of ground beef molded around florets of cauliflower, then braised in a tomato ragout seasoned with Tunisian-style spices, and a classic Braised Beef Short Ribs in Merlot (page 5), stewed ever so slowly in Merlot wine until the succulent pieces of meat are nearly falling off the ribs. Speaking of classic stews, you will find Beef Burgundy (page 10), Daube Provençale (page 11), and what can be called the very first American stew, Amelia Simmons's "Beef Alamode" from 1796 (page 45). Classic stews are not necessarily well-known stews, but they are classic in the culture in which they are made. For example, *sjömansbiffgryta*, or Swedish Sailor's Beef Stew (page 22), cooks in a 450°F oven for two hours and is one of the most typical family stews, one that every Swede knows. From Central Asia comes a stew from Kazakhstan called *Kuyrdak* (page 32), a beef stew with a copious amount of scallions, dill, parsley, and basil that is stewed in tomatoes and served with goat's milk yogurt; it is considered to be the national dish. You will find some great American stews, such as Beef Stew with Bourbon (page 46) and the standard but always satisfying Old-Fashioned American Beef Stew (page 48), not to mention one of the best chilis con carne (page 49) you'll ever taste (if I do say so myself). Hold onto your hat!

BEEF BROTH

THIS ITALIAN-STYLE BEEF BROTH IS AN all-purpose broth that can be used for any recipe calling for beef broth. A good broth is the foundation of sauces, soups, and many stews. Broth freezes well and can be made in advance. For recipes calling for veal broth, replace the beef with veal shoulder and other bones; for lamb broth, substitute lamb neck and shoulder; and for vegetable broth, omit the meat and add a bunch of spinach or Swiss chard and an additional cut-up leek. French cooks make the broth richer by first browning the bones in a skillet or roasting them in an oven. See the variation below for that method.

---

4 pounds cracked beef marrow, shin, and/or
   shank bones, with meat on them
1 large onion, cut into eighths
4 ripe plum tomatoes (optional), cut in half
1 carrot, cut up
1 celery stalk, cut into chunks
1 leek (white and light green parts only), washed
   well and cut into chunks
10 black peppercorns
1 bouquet garni, consisting of 3 sprigs fresh
   parsley, 1 sprig fresh thyme, 2 fresh sage
   leaves, and 1 bay leaf, tied in cheesecloth
4 quarts water
Salt and freshly ground black pepper to taste

---

1. Put all the ingredients, except the salt and pepper, in a stockpot. Bring to a boil, then reduce the heat to a simmer. Skim the surface of foam until no more appears. Partially cover and simmer over very low heat for no less than 6 hours.

2. Pour the broth through a strainer (a chinois, or conical strainer, would be ideal) and discard all the bones, meat, vegetables, and the bouquet garni. Now pour the broth through the same strainer, lined with cheesecloth. Season with salt and pepper.

3. To defat the broth, let it rest in a refrigerator until the fat congeals on the top and can be lifted off. The broth can be kept, refrigerated, for up to 2 weeks and frozen for up to 6 months.

Variation: To turn this broth into a *fond brun de veau* (rich brown veal stock), replace the beef with veal and start by browning the meat in hot clarified butter in a large skillet until golden brown, turning the pieces with tongs. Remove to the stockpot. Add the onion and 2 peeled carrots cut into rounds to the skillet. When the onions have yellowed, remove to the stockpot and continue with the recipe. Alternatively, place the meat bones in a roasting pan and roast at 425°F until well browned before using.

Makes 2 to 3 quarts

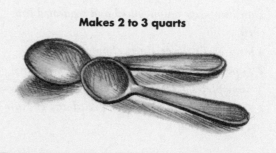

BEEF AND POTATO STEW WITH SAFFRON FROM LA MANCHA

SHEPHERDS ROAMED WITH THEIR FLOCKS through the summer pastures of the vast, empty plains of Extramadura, La Mancha, and Andalusia in Spain during the Middle Ages. Spanish sheep were crossbred with sheep imported from North Africa, and their offspring were more important to the Spanish economy than olives, grapes, copper, or even the treasures of Peru, the economic historian Roberto Lopez has argued. Cows, on the other hand, were rare and skinny during this time, probably not weighing more than 325 pounds. Once the potato arrived in Spain from the New World, sometime around 1570, it was grown in beautiful local gardens, which were irrigated with an old Arab invention called the *noria*, a kind of waterwheel.

The food of La Mancha is hearty, and this stew is simplicity itself. It is sometimes called *tojunto*, meaning "everything is thrown all together." Serve with crusty bread.

1/2 cup extra virgin olive oil
2 large green bell peppers, seeded and sliced
1 medium-size onion, sliced and separated into rings
6 large garlic cloves, finely chopped
2 1/4 pounds boneless stew beef, trimmed of any large pieces of fat and cut into irregular shapes
1 3/4 pounds boiling potatoes, peeled and cut into 1 1/2-inch chunks
1 tablespoon salt
1 teaspoon freshly ground black pepper
1/4 teaspoon freshly ground cloves
1 bay leaf
Good-size pinch of saffron threads, crumbled in a mortar
1 cup dry white wine

1. Put the olive oil, bell peppers, onion, garlic, and beef in the stew pot, in that order. Layer the potatoes on top of the beef. Add the salt, pepper, cloves, bay leaf, and saffron. Pour the wine over and add enough water to cover.

2. Bring to a boil, reduce the heat to low, cover, and cook until the meat is very tender, about 2 hours. Serve immediately.

Makes 4 servings

BEEF STEW WITH PARSNIPS AND WINE
IN THE STYLE OF A LANGUEDOC HOUSEWIFE

IN WINTER, LONG-SIMMERING BRAISES OF meat are everyone's favorite. There is not much work to be done for this stew once everything is going, and it's always very popular because a hungry family sniffing the aromas all day will come ravenous to the table. This *ragoût de boeuf à la ménagère* is typical of the housewife cookery of the rural Languedoc, in southwestern France. The parsnip, a wonderful root vegetable for wintertime, provides a natural sweetness to the preparation that makes it all the more luscious, as does the initial browning of the beef in both butter and olive oil.

———●———

2 tablespoons extra virgin olive oil

2 tablespoons unsalted butter

2 pounds boneless beef chuck, trimmed of any large pieces of fat and cut into 4 pieces

1 large onion, chopped

6 large garlic cloves, finely chopped

1 celery stalk, chopped

1 bouquet garni, consisting of 10 sprigs each fresh parsley and sage and 1 bay leaf, tied in cheesecloth

1 large parsnip, peeled and cut into chunks

1 large, ripe tomato, peeled, seeded, and chopped

2 cups dry red wine

1 cup water

Salt and freshly ground black pepper to taste

———●———

1. In a casserole, heat the olive oil with the butter over medium-high heat until the butter melts, then brown the beef on all sides, 6 to 7 minutes. Remove the beef and set aside.

2. Add the onion, garlic, and celery to the casserole and cook, stirring, until the onion is translucent, 4 to 5 minutes. Return the meat to the casserole, add the bouquet garni, parsnip, tomato, wine, and water. Reduce the heat to low, cover, and cook until the meat is very tender, 3 to 4 hours. Season with salt and pepper, discard the bouquet garni, and serve.

———●———

Makes 4 servings

PARING A PARSNIP

———●———

Parsnip, like carrot, is a biennial, cultivated for its fat, wedge-shaped white roots. When shopping for parsnips, look for ones that are relatively smooth skinned and straight (because you end up wasting a lot of the crooked ones when peeling). For larger parsnips, you can avoid the unpleasant woody texture and taste by cutting them in half lengthwise and cutting out the inner section, which is a slightly different color. Avoid parsnips that have a lot of hairy-looking rootlets, as well as ones that are limp.

BRAISED BEEF SHORT RIBS IN MERLOT

SHORT RIBS ARE A REALLY NICE CUT OF meat that comes from the short plate of the cow, the underside of the animal below where the rib roasts would be cut. They are sold in supermarkets as "beef short ribs," so they should be easily found.

This French recipe is quite a satisfying preparation when you want something to stave off hunger and cold. It's a good way to get rid of old green beans, but if you are using fresh ones (they will snap when bent), then put them in when there are only about 45 minutes of cooking time left. The short ribs cook a long time, until they are very tender and barely clinging to their bones. The pancetta in this recipe is not an authentic ingredient, but is meant to replace the traditional *petit salé*, a lean salt pork used in French country cooking. Because the wine is an important part of this stew, you should use a good Merlot, something you would be pleased to drink too. Serve with crusty bread and a light salad.

———————•———————

¹/4 cup (¹/2 stick) unsalted butter
2 slices pancetta (about 1 ounce)
3 pounds meaty beef short ribs
Unbleached all-purpose flour for dredging
1 large onion, coarsely chopped
6 large garlic cloves, finely chopped
2 large carrots, cut into small pieces
2 large parsnips, peeled and cut into small pieces
1¹/2 pounds small button mushrooms, brushed
  clean and left whole
³/4 pound old green beans (they should bend
  rather than snap), ends trimmed and cut into
  1-inch-long pieces
1 bottle Merlot wine
Salt and freshly ground black pepper to taste
1 tablespoon dried summer savory or oregano

———————•———————

1. In a large casserole or Dutch oven, melt the butter over medium-high heat with the pancetta. Meanwhile, dredge the beef short ribs in the flour, tapping off the excess. Once the pancetta is sizzling, add the short ribs to the casserole and cook until the beef is browned on all sides, then add the onion, garlic, carrots, and parsnips. Cook until slightly soft, about 10 minutes, stirring frequently. Add the mushrooms and cook for 5 minutes. Add the green beans and wine, season with salt and pepper, add the summer savory, and stir everything together.

2. Reduce the heat to very low and simmer, covered, until the beef is tender, about 2 hours. Remove the lid and continue to cook until the meat is falling off the bones and the sauce is syrupy, another 1 to 1¹/2 hours.

———————•———————

Makes 4 servings

TRIPE À LA MODE DE CAEN

T HIS IS AN EXTRAORDINARY STEW AND I want to tell you a lot about it because you haven't lived until you've eaten *tripe à la mode de Caen*. Caen is arguably the most important city in Normandy. It is the capital of the Calvados *département* and was the favorite residence of William the Conqueror in the eleventh century. In fact, the ancient Norman citadel that dominates and is the center of Caen still stands, especially the Abbaye aux Hommes with William's tomb, the Abbaye aux Dames, and the Church of St. Nicholas. All three are gems of eleventh-century Norman architecture. The more plebian guidebooks forget to mention that the Exchequer, a tenth-century Norman civil building, still stands. In the Abbaye des Hommes, built in the 1060s, the tomb of William the Conqueror is inscribed with the following epitaph: *Hic Sepultus est in victissimus Guillelmus conquestor Normanniae dux et angliae rex Hujus ce domus conditor qui obiit anno*

TRIPE TRIVIA

Tripe refers to the first, second, third, and fourth stomachs of the cow and other ruminant animals, animals that chew their cud. Ideally, in a dish such as *tripe à la mode de Caen,* you should have a mixture of the first three, the fourth not being used that much for cooking in France. The first stomach is known as the paunch or rumen in English or *gras-double* or *panse* in French. The paunch, a smooth-surfaced tripe, is sometimes sold in American supermarkets, although the second stomach, known as honeycomb or reticulum in English, is more common in American markets; it is known in French as *bonnet* or *feuillet.* The third stomach is called the manyplies, omasum, or psalterium in English, and must be special ordered from a good butcher (who is very unlikely to know it by these names). The fourth, or true stomach, is the absomasum or reed, called *caillette* or *millet* in French. All this tripe is best ordered through a butcher.

Tripe is highly perishable, so use it the day you get it, or freeze it if you are not going to use it immediately.

MLXXXVII ("Here is buried the victorious William, conqueror, duke of Normandy and King of England, builder and founder who died in the year 1087").

Norman and Normandy have resonance for me for two reasons. First, in the 1950s I lived in the Norman town of Beaumont-le-Roger, a tiny village where my father, then in the U.S. Air Force, decided to move his family in order to live with the local population rather than in base housing. Second, I wrote a book on Sicily in the early 1990s. If you remember your college history, you know that the final Norman conquest of Sicily was accomplished in 1091 by Roger Guiscard de Hauteville, the Great Count, a relative of William's, when Roger defeated the Arabs. He and his successors ruled Sicily with an enlightened government until the late twelfth century. I became quite enamored with Norman ingenuity during my research and travels. But now let us return to Caen and the most famous culinary preparation of this city.

I read somewhere that the traditional way to eat in Normandy is to have tripe in Caen, duck in Rouen, and an omelet in Mont St. Michel. The last time I was in Normandy, we never encountered any of these traditional preparations in the restaurants, although we ran across lots of apples, especially in the form of cider or Calvados. So, to get a recipe for tripe, I had to do a lot of research and a lot of fiddling with a million different ideas about how it should be cooked.

Tripe in the style of Caen has a history going back to the Vikings, or so claim the locals. William the Conqueror is said to have enjoyed tripe simmered in apple juice. *Tripe à la mode de Caen* is a classic dish of Normandy, and every year a competition is held for the Tripière d'Or, an award in the shape of the traditional earthenware casserole in which it is cooked—round and flat on the bottom, a design that ensures very little moisture is lost in the long cooking of the tripe, up to 12 hours.

The food writer and cooking teacher Anne Willan suggested that the excellence of this dish is probably due in equal measure to the quality of the local cattle and the method of cooking. The method varies from cook to cook. Some cooks make the dish over two days, letting the tripe rest and become a cold aspic before reheating it. This is the way I like it. The famous French chef Auguste Escoffier warned that a very common mistake is using calves' feet instead of oxen's. Calves' feet have too much gelatin for the tripe to absorb. Plus, they are more tender than oxen's feet and disintegrate before the tripe is cooked. He also reminds the cook that the tripe should always be cooked and served in an earthenware casserole.

Once the tripe is tender, the cooking liquid should be shiny and thick enough to form an aspic. The tripe itself should have the texture of perfectly cooked squid. This recipe requires an oversized earthenware casserole, described in step 2. If you don't have such a thing, then use two casseroles, earthenware or whatever you have.

If you decide to make this preparation, you will be confronted by three problems: First, it's a lot of work over several days. You will have some 20 pounds or more of food, and it all cooks down to yield enough servings for six people. But what servings they are! An unctuous, apple-flavored and enriched gravy coats the bits of now squid-like, tender tripe, which is the gustatory equivalent of being in the Sistine chapel alone. Second, you will need a quite large earthenware casserole, which I imagine you don't have, so you'll need to use two or three smaller ones instead, and you will have to carefully divide all the ingredients between them. Third, most Americans don't eat tripe, and you will be hard-pressed to justify all this work if no one is going to eat it. I usually use this recipe as an introduction to the way tripe should taste, and also mention that once upon a time Americans were so fond of tripe that it was a regular part of a New England clam bake. This preparation is a quite unique taste, and to pass it by, I believe, would be as ill advised as William passing up his chance at Hastings in 1066.

PORK SKIN AND BEEF FAT

Pork skin and beef fat are used as flavoring agents in stew cookery. The most common cut of pork with skin attached is pork butt, which you are likely to find in the supermarket. If you can't find pork skin, you will need to ask the butcher. Alternatively, some packaged salt pork still has the skin on, and you can use that. As for beef fat, it too is great for flavor. You can sometimes find fat on pieces of meat, but it is just as easy to ask the butcher for some fat. It may seem unnecessary to use pork skin and beef fat, but I assure you it's worth the effort.

7 pounds mixed beef tripe (see page 333)
2 cups cider vinegar (preferable) or white wine vinegar

2 cups water

4 large onions (about 2 pounds)

16 cloves

3 pounds carrots, split in half lengthwise

1 1/2 pounds leeks, halved crosswise, then split in half lengthwise and washed well

1 bouquet garni, consisting of 1 bunch fresh parsley, 5 sprigs fresh thyme, and 1 bay leaf, tied in cheesecloth

4 beef feet (about 10 pounds), preferably split

1/2 pound pork skin (see page 8)

1 garlic bouquet, consisting of 1 head garlic with first layer of peel rubbed off, 12 black peppercorns, and 2 cloves, tied in cheesecloth

Salt and freshly ground black pepper to taste

1/2 pound beef fat (ask your butcher for this), sliced

2 quarts apple cider

1 cup plus 1 jigger Calvados (preferably) or apple brandy

Flour paste rope (see below)

---

1. Soak the tripe in the vinegar and water overnight in the refrigerator. Drain. Cut the tripe into 2-inch squares. Pierce each of the 4 onions with 4 cloves each. Preheat the oven to 265°F.

2. Place the onions, carrots, leeks, and parsley bouquet garni on the bottom of a very large, round earthenware casserole about 16 inches in diameter and 6 inches deep or two smaller, but still large, casseroles, earthenware or otherwise. If you use two casseroles, you will have to divide the ingredients equally between them. Place the beef feet on top of the vegetables, along with the pork skin. Place the tripe on top of them, pushing it down into the spaces in between. Add the garlic bouquet, season with salt and pepper, then add the slices of beef fat, cider, and 1 cup of the Calvados. Cover and seal the lid with the flour paste rope, so no moisture escapes. If you don't have a lid for a very large casserole, you can use a large baking stone, or fashion a lid out of aluminum foil.

3. Place the casserole in the oven and bake, undisturbed, for 12 hours. Remove the casserole from the oven. Break open the flour seal and remove and discard the beef feet, vegetables, bouquet garni, and garlic bouquet. Since everything will have disintegrated, ladle out the items to be discarded carefully so you don't end up throwing out any tripe. Transfer the tripe to a deep bowl and pour the juice through a strainer to cover the tripe. Push the tripe down into the bowl so that when the dish cools, the fat congeals, and the aspic forms, none of the tripe is intermingled with the fat.

FLOUR PASTE ROPE

A number of recipes in this book call for a rope to be made out of flour and water, which then goes around the stewpot and lid, forming a seal while the stew cooks. This is very simple to do: Pour some flour into a bowl and add enough water to form a malleable dough. Roll out the dough like a snake or thick rope until it is the circumference of the lid you are sealing. Wrap the rope around the lid and the cooking vessel and pinch the seal tight. When the cooking time is over, break off the rope.

Refrigerate overnight, then skim the fat off the top and discard.

4. Preheat the oven to 300°F. Transfer the tripe and its aspic to a smaller, round, flat-bottomed earthenware casserole and reheat, covered, until the sauce is bubbling gently, about 30 minutes. Pour in the remaining jigger of Calvados and serve.

Makes 6 to 8 servings

BEEF BURGUNDY

EEF BURGUNDY IS A CLASSIC FRENCH stew from the Bourgogne region of France, home also to the great pinot noir grape, which makes Burgundy wines, the key ingredient in this preparation. Beef Burgundy is also one of the most bastardized of French dishes, and in Franco-American cooking, I believe it becomes quite disappointing. This recipe, though, is the traditional one from the Burgundy region, where it is known as *boeuf à la bourguignonne*. It is most often prepared by housewives and the cooks of small restaurants and bistros. Before you start making beef Burgundy, be aware that the marinating takes place over two days, before you even start cooking. The stew cooks for a long time and slowly. Because of this, you will want a rump steak or chuck or a similar cut of beef and, of course, a hearty red wine from Burgundy. In older times, cooks would lard the beef and cook it whole, but this method of cutting it up into chunks is a bit easier for contemporary American cooks. The aroma of the wine throughout the house during the cooking time is what makes this stew so delectable and such a sought-after favorite. For that reason, it makes sense to use a good quality wine, something you would enjoy drinking too. Nice accompaniments to beef Burgundy are boiled potatoes with butter and parsley and freshly steamed haricots verts, or thin green beans. A proper beef Burgundy is ever so slightly tricky, so read the recipe a couple of times before trying it.

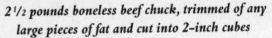

2 1/2 pounds boneless beef chuck, trimmed of any large pieces of fat and cut into 2-inch cubes

FOR THE MARINADE:

3 cups red Burgundy wine
1/2 cup brandy
2 tablespoons extra virgin olive oil
1 medium-size onion, sliced
1 carrot, sliced
1 bouquet garni, consisting of 5 sprigs fresh parsley, 2 sprigs each fresh thyme and tarragon, and 1 bay leaf, tied in cheesecloth
1 garlic clove, crushed
4 cloves
10 black peppercorns

FOR THE STEW:

1/4 cup extra virgin olive oil
6 ounces salt pork, cut into strips about 1/4 inch thick
Salt and freshly ground black pepper to taste
20 small white onions (about 1 3/4 pounds)
1 pound small button mushrooms, brushed clean

¹/₂ cup red Burgundy wine

3 tablespoons unsalted butter

3 tablespoons unbleached all-purpose flour

1 bouquet garni, consisting of 5 sprigs fresh parsley, 2 sprigs each fresh thyme and tarragon, and 1 bay leaf, tied in cheesecloth

1 cup Beef Broth (page 3) or water, as needed

———————●———————

1. To marinate the beef, place it in a glass or ceramic bowl with the marinade ingredients and marinate in the refrigerator for 2 days, covered with plastic wrap. Toss the marinating meat at least twice a day. Remove the meat and pat it dry with paper towels. Strain and save the marinade and the onions and carrots separately. Discard the bouquet garni. It is important to pat the meat dry, otherwise it will not brown well later.

2. To begin the stew, in a large casserole, heat the olive oil over medium heat, then brown the salt pork until crispy, 6 to 7 minutes. Add the beef, seasoned with salt and pepper, and brown on all sides, about 10 minutes. Remove the beef and salt pork from the casserole with a slotted spoon and set aside on a plate.

3. Add the whole onions and reserved sliced onions and carrots from the marinade to the casserole and cook over medium heat until the outer layer of the whole onions is translucent and the sliced onions are soft, about 15 minutes. Remove with a slotted spoon to another plate and set aside.

4. Add the mushrooms, season with salt and pepper, and cook until brown and a little softened, about 7 minutes, deglazing with a few tablespoons of the wine if the liquid has evaporated and the mushrooms are sticking. Remove the mushrooms and set aside with the onions.

5. Add the butter to the casserole and, once it has melted, add the flour and cook until a light brown roux is formed, stirring to make sure it doesn't burn. Pour in the strained marinade and wine and add a little salt and pepper and the bouquet garni. Return the meat and salt pork to the casserole, and bring to a boil. Reduce the heat to low, cover tightly, and simmer for 2¹/₂ hours.

6. Add the whole onions, cover tightly, and simmer until the meat is tender, about 1 more hour. If the gravy gets too thick at any time, dilute a little with some beef broth or water. Add the reserved mushrooms and sliced onions and carrots, continue to cook for another 30 minutes, and serve.

———————●———————

Makes 6 servings

DAUBE PROVENÇALE

⟨leaf⟩

DAUBE IS PROVENCE'S MOST FAMOUS meat stew. It has crossed the borders of provincial France and is found in other regions too, such as the Savoy, where cooks add the liqueur known as Marc, and Gascony, where they use Armagnac. The origin of a daube seems to be related to the Italian *addobbo* (which also gives us the Mexican *adobo*), meaning "seasoning" or "dressing." It is likely that the French incorporated this Italian concept sometime before the seventeenth century.

A daube is made of beef, although in Avignon they make it with lamb. A daube is traditionally cooked in a stew pot called a *daubière* and is eaten with *la macaronade*, flat macaroni cooked with a sauce made from the juices of the daube. The sauce is reduced and tossed with the pasta along with some Parmigiano cheese and a fresh grating of nutmeg. Some cooks insist that the beef come from two different parts of the cow, say rump and shoulder, to mix the flavors. Once the daube has cooled down after its long cooking, it can be reheated—and many people think it is even better that way—and it is then called by the Provençal a *nougat de boeuf*, "beef nougat."

———————

2 ounces slab bacon, cut into 2 slices, then diced
1/2 cup finely chopped fresh parsley leaves
5 large garlic cloves, finely chopped
3 tablespoons extra virgin olive oil
3/4 cup diced lean salt pork (about 2 ounces)
2 1/2 pounds boneless beef bottom round or chuck, trimmed of any large pieces of fat and cut into pieces the size of a small child's fist
3 medium-size onions, 2 quartered and 1 studded with 4 cloves
2 small carrots, quartered
3 pounds meaty beef short ribs or flanken
1 beef or veal foot (about 1 1/2 pounds; see page 39)

1 bay leaf
1 teaspoon dried thyme
1 teaspoon dried summer savory
2 large, ripe tomatoes, peeled, seeded, and quartered
2 shallots, coarsely chopped
2 sprigs fresh parsley
1/2 celery stalk, chopped
2 cups dry red wine
1 long piece orange zest
1/2 cinnamon stick
10 black peppercorns
Salt to taste
Flour paste rope (see page 9)
La Macaronade (optional; recipe follows)

———————

1. Dredge the bacon in the chopped parsley and garlic. In a stew pot or casserole, heat the olive oil with the salt pork over medium-high heat. When the fat starts to sizzle vigorously, brown the beef on all sides, about 12 minutes. Add the bacon and cook for 5 minutes, stirring and turning the meat. Add the quartered onions, the clove-studded onion, the carrots, beef ribs, beef foot, bay leaf, thyme, and savory. Toss well so everything is mixed, then cook for 3 minutes.

2. Add the tomatoes, shallots, parsley sprigs, and celery and stir to mix well. Cook until the mixture is well blended, about 3 minutes. Pour in the wine, add the orange zest, cinnamon stick, and peppercorns, and season with salt. Bring to a boil, then reduce the heat to very low, using a heat diffuser if necessary. Cover, seal the lid with the flour paste rope, and cook for 8 hours.

3. Remove from the heat, break the seal, and uncover. Remove 1 cup of the juice for La Macaronade, if making, or as much juice as you would like to pour on any accompanying pasta. Remove the bay leaf, beef foot, orange zest, cinnamon stick, and clove-studded onion and serve as soon as the pasta is done.

Makes 6 servings

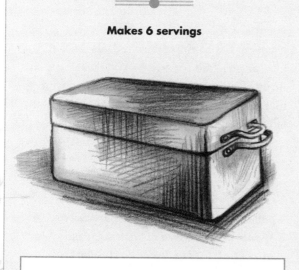

PEELING OR GRATING TOMATOES

Most recipes with tomatoes call for peeled and seeded tomatoes. For small plum tomatoes, it's best to drop them into boiling water for 1 minute to loosen their skins, which will then come right off. Larger tomatoes are best grated, rather than blanched and peeled. Cut a large tomato in half, then squeeze each half over a receptacle to remove all the seeds. Now, place a tomato half in your palm and, using the tomato skin to protect your skin, rub against the largest holes of a 4- or 6-sided grater, over a bowl, until all the pulp is removed.

LA MACARONADE

This macaroni dish is the traditional accompaniment to Daube Provençale.

2 tablespoons unsalted butter
2 tablespoons extra virgin olive oil
1 pound small button mushrooms, brushed clean
$^1/_2$ cup dry white wine
1 cup juice from Daube Provençale (page 11)
$^3/_4$ pound flat pasta, such as fettuccine or pappardelle
Freshly grated Parmigiano–Reggiano cheese for sprinkling
Freshly grated nutmeg for sprinkling

1. In a large skillet, heat the butter with the olive oil over medium heat until the butter melts. Cook the mushrooms until soft, about 15 minutes. Add the wine and cook until nearly evaporated, then add the juice from the daube and cook until the juices are reduced by half.

2. Meanwhile, bring a large pot of abundantly salted water to a rolling boil. Cook the pasta until *al dente*. Drain the pasta without rinsing it. Toss the pasta with the sauce from the skillet and sprinkle with some Parmigiano cheese and a fresh grating of nutmeg.

Makes 6 servings as a side dish

FRENCH FRY SECRETS

———●———

The trick to making crunchy golden French fries is to

• Use fresh potatoes such as Idaho russets, not frozen.

• Pat dry the cut fries thoroughly with a paper towel before frying.

• Fry the potatoes twice, the first time at 360°F until half cooked, about 4 minutes. Then let them cool completely and fry a second time at 375°F, until golden and crunchy. Never fry before the oil is the correct temperature.

• Use at least 1½ quarts of clean peanut or canola oil for frying. Ideally, instead of oil use animal fat, namely beef tallow, for an incredible-tasting (if less healthy) French fry.

• Never crowd the deep fryer: fry in batches a handful at a time.

• Let the fries drain for a few seconds.

• Salt immediately.

BULL STEW
IN THE STYLE OF THE CAMARGUE

THIS FAMOUS STEW FROM THE CAMARGUE region of Provence is known as *gardiane de taureau, taureau sauvage à la gardiane,* or simply *la gardiane. Gardiane* means "bull stew," but is also the word for the cowboys of the Camargue. The reason this stew tastes so good are fourfold. First, oxtail contains a lot of the gelatinous material that breaks down through slow cooking and flavors the resulting stew. Second, the homemade beef broth adds an important level of complexity to the taste of the stew. Third, the typical Provençal flavor combination of black and green olives and orange peel elevates the stew to its distinctive position as one of the great stews of Provence. Fourth, wine always makes a stew better.

This recipe comes from the seaside restaurant of A la Brise de Mer in the small coastal town of Les Saintes Maries-de-la-Mer in the Camargue. The road to Saintes Maries winds down from Arles through the Camargue, a marshy land of alluvial deposit, past grazing lands and horse farms. The stew is excellent accompanied by French fries (see left).

———●———

¼ cup extra virgin olive oil

4 pounds oxtail (bone-in) or 3 pounds beef shank, well trimmed of fat and cut into 2-inch pieces (ask the butcher to do this for you)

1 tablespoon lard

2 medium-size onions, finely chopped

1 pound boiling potatoes, peeled and diced

2 cups Beef Broth (page 3)

1 cup dry red wine

1 bouquet garni, consisting of 15 sprigs fresh thyme, 5 sprigs each fresh parsley and savory or tarragon, and 1 bay leaf, tied in cheesecloth

Zest of 1 orange in one long spiral

1 medium-size onion, peeled and studded with 1 clove

1 garlic clove, crushed

1 tablespoon tomato paste

¼ cup chopped imported pitted green olives

¼ cup chopped pitted black Niçoise olives

Salt and freshly ground black pepper to taste

1. In a large, heavy casserole, heat the olive oil over medium-high heat. Brown the oxtail on all sides, about 5 minutes. Remove the oxtail from the casserole and set aside, keeping it warm.

2. In the same casserole, melt the lard over medium-high heat. Cook the chopped onions and potatoes until the onions are golden, about 8 minutes, stirring frequently and adding small amounts of water to scrape the browned bits off the bottom of the casserole, if necessary.

3. Return the oxtail to the casserole. Pour in the beef broth and wine, and add the bouquet garni, orange zest, whole clove-studded onion, garlic, tomato paste, and olives. Season with salt and pepper.

4. Reduce the heat to low and simmer, uncovered, until the sauce is thick and the meat tender and falling off the bone, about 4 hours. Remove and discard the orange peel, bouquet garni, and whole onion. Serve immediately.

Makes 4 to 6 servings

STUFATO

I N ITALIAN *STUFATO* SIMPLY MEANS "STEW" or "stewed meat," and one encounters it in every region of Italy. In Lombardy, *stufato* has come to be identified with a stew made with a whole piece of beef rump marinated for a day in Barolo or Barbera wine. The famous twentieth-century Italian cookbook writer Ada Boni called Lombardy's version "one of the most important Italian dishes." It is important for historical as well as culinary reasons because the word, and perhaps the stew too, traveled and is known in Greece as *stifado* and Corsica as *stufatu*. My recipe is a traditional one that follows Boni's closely. To accompany this preparation, you'll want freshly made Polenta (page 188) sprinkled with Parmigiano cheese, and some of the gravy from the stew. For a vegetable, I think spinach or Swiss chard sautéed in butter and olive oil with garlic and mushrooms would be ideal. I ask you to lard the beef, which you will be unable to do if you don't have a larding needle. Go ahead and get one from a good kitchen supply store; larding large pieces of beef is actually quite fun if a little more work. Or you can try asking your butcher to do it for you, although there are few "real" butchers around anymore to do that. Before you leap into this recipe, remember that it takes two days to prepare.

One 3-pound beef rump roast
One ¼-pound slice pancetta, half of it cut into
  strips, half of it chopped
FOR THE MARINADE:
1 carrot, diced
1 small onion, thinly sliced
1 celery stalk, chopped
1 garlic clove, crushed
1 bay leaf
2 cloves
3 thin slices fresh nutmeg
2½ cups Barolo or Barbera wine
Salt and freshly ground black pepper to taste

FOR COOKING THE BEEF RUMP:
Unbleached all-purpose flour for dredging
6 tablespoons (¾ stick) unsalted butter
1 small onion, chopped
Salt and freshly ground black pepper to taste

1. Lard the piece of beef with the strips of pancetta by using a larding needle (see below). If you don't own one, you can ask the butcher to do it or you can cut the beef open (that is, butterfly it so it is still in one piece), layer the strips of pancetta, then close it up and tie it off in four places with kitchen twine. Place the beef in a large ceramic bowl and add all the marinade ingredients, turning the roast to coat it. Cover with plastic wrap and marinate for 18 to 24 hours in the refrigerator, turning it several times.

2. Remove the beef rump from the marinade and pat dry with paper towels. Strain the marinade through a fine mesh strainer, discarding the solids and saving the liquid. Dredge the meat thoroughly in the flour without tapping off any excess.

3. In a large casserole, melt the butter over medium-high heat, then cook the onion and chopped pancetta until the onion is translucent, about 4 minutes, stirring. Add the meat, season with salt and pepper, and brown on all sides, about 3 minutes. Add the reserved strained marinade. Bring to a boil, cover, and reduce the heat to low. Simmer until a fork run across the side of the rump shreds some of the meat, about 4 hours. The sauce should be fairly thick. Turn the heat off, cool for about 45 min-

utes, and refrigerate the meat in the casserole overnight.

4. The next day, begin to reheat the rump over low heat about 1½ hours before you want to eat.

5. Once it is heated through, remove the meat from the casserole, cut into thin slices, and arrange on a serving platter. Ladle some of the gravy over the meat slices and serve the remaining gravy in a sauceboat. If the gravy is liquidy, reduce it over high heat until syrupy.

Makes 6 servings

LARDING

Larding refers to the process of puncturing a tough piece of meat and interspersing strips of fat through it, which, when they cook and melt, tenderize and flavor the meat. Larding is not done very much anymore, but should you choose to lard a piece of meat, you will need a larding needle, a sharp needle, or ice pick type of device, to which the strip of fat is attached. The larding needle is then pushed through one side of the piece of meat and, when it comes out of the other side, the strip of fat is released and stays in the meat.

STRACOTTO

IN NORTHERN ITALY, THIS RICH, LIGURIAN-style stewed beef, called *stracotto*, is famed as a leftover too, chopped up and used as a stuffing for ravioli. They even know this delicious stew as *estoufado* over in neighboring Provence, where housewives make their own version. *Stracotto* means "overcooked," which is how you prepare the meat—for a very long time. As you can see by the ingredients list, there is a lot of flavor in this stew. I particularly like the result one gets by using prosciutto fat and garlic in the initial *soffritto*, an Italian word that refers to the frying of a finely chopped vegetable-and-fat mixture that is the foundation or beginning to a ragout or sauce. Ask for prosciutto fat from the deli counter of a supermarket or Italian market.

4 large garlic cloves, finely chopped
2 ounces prosciutto fat, ham fat, or pancetta, finely chopped
1 teaspoon freshly ground black pepper
One 2½-pound piece boneless beef rump or top side
3 tablespoons extra virgin olive oil
1 medium-size onion, finely chopped
1 large carrot, finely chopped
1 celery stalk, finely chopped
Salt to taste
¾ cup dry red wine
1 pound ripe tomatoes, peeled, seeded, and crushed
1 clove
1 cup Beef Broth (page 3)

1. In a small bowl, mix together the garlic, prosciutto fat, and pepper. Slice the meat in half without cutting all the way through and stuff it with this mixture. Close it up and tie off the meat tightly in four places with kitchen twine.

2. In a casserole, heat the olive oil over medium-high heat, then cook the onion, carrot, and celery until soft, stirring, 5 to 6 minutes. Add the meat and brown on all sides, about 4 minutes. Season with salt and add the wine, tomatoes, and clove. Cover and reduce the heat to very low, using a heat diffuser if necessary. Cook, always under a boil, until the meat can be shredded with a fork by gently tugging at it, 5 to 6 hours. Add some of the broth to the casserole occasionally to keep it moist.

3. Remove the beef and let rest while you reduce the sauce to about 2 cups over high heat. Slice the meat and cover with the sauce.

Makes 4 to 5 servings

BEEF AND CARDOON STEW FROM TUSCANY

THIS STEW IS POPULAR IN LOMBARDY and Tuscany, where it is called *stufatino*. It is traditionally made with vegetables from the celery family or celery-like vegetables, such

WHAT'S A CARDOON?

———●———

The cardoon (*Cynara cardunculus*) is a kind of thistle from which the artichoke was developed, and is probably native to the Mediterranean. The edible part is the cooked petiole and not, as in the artichoke, the flesh on the inside of the bracts of the flower head. The cardoon is a perennial, but it is usually grown as an annual for the fleshy, celery-looking leaf bases. These are formed by the basal rosette of huge leaves, which are tied up and blanched. The dried flowers can be used as a substitute for rennet in cheese making.

Cardoons usually appear in markets in December. They look like oversize celery bunches and are a dull, pale green color. Choose cardoon bunches with very firm stalks. Store them in the refrigerator unless you intend to cook them within two days. Cardoons are bitter, taste vaguely like artichokes, and require long cooking in salted and acidulated water. The water is acidulated using vinegar or lemon juice so the cardoons do not discolor.

To cook cardoons, begin by removing any remaining leaves. With a vegetable peeler, peel the tough, stringy part from the outside edge of the stalk. If you have a pot big enough, tie the loose stalks and head together with string and steam them whole, or break off individual stalks to cook. Alternatively, and more easily, cut the stalks into 2-, 3-, or 4-inch lengths. Boil the cardoons until completely tender in salted water with the juice of 1 lemon or 1/2 cup vinegar, about 3 hours. Drain and dry them. You can freeze them for later use.

as alexanders, lovage stalks, angelica, the wild green called *athamanta* (*Athamanta sicula*), celery, celeriac, or cardoons. *Stufatino* is the diminutive of *stufato* (page 15), a kind of stew in Italy made with beef. It is known in Corsica as *stufatu* and in Greece as *stifado* (page 28). This recipe calls for cardoons, which must first be cooked for a long time (see above). If you prefer, you can replace the cardoons with celery, which does not need any special preparation.

———●———

6 tablespoons lard
1 large onion, chopped

6 tablespoons finely chopped prosciutto or fat
   from a cooked ham
1 1/2 celery stalks, chopped
3 large garlic cloves, finely chopped
2 pounds boneless beef round, trimmed
   of any large pieces of fat and cut into bite-size
   pieces
2 teaspoons dried oregano or marjoram
1 1/2 cups dry red wine
Salt and freshly ground black pepper to taste
2 1/2 tablespoons tomato paste
2 cups Beef Broth (page 3)
2 pounds cooked cardoons,
   cut into chunks (see above)

1. In a large casserole or stew pot, melt the lard over medium heat. Cook the onion until soft, stirring, about 10 minutes. Add the prosciutto, celery, and garlic and cook until the celery is soft and the prosciutto is somewhat rendered, 6 to 7 minutes, stirring occasionally. Add the beef and oregano and brown on all sides, about 5 minutes. Pour in the wine and cook until it is nearly evaporated, about 25 minutes. Season with salt and pepper.

2. Dissolve the tomato paste in the broth and add to the beef along with the cardoons. Cover, reduce the heat to low, and cook until the meat is very tender, about 2 ¹/₂ hours. Serve immediately.

Makes 6 servings

HOME-STYLE BEEF AND TOMATO STEW FROM SICILY

ONE DOESN'T OFTEN THINK OF STEWS being cooked in Sicily because we associate this island in the sun with heat and aridity, and stews with cold weather. But winters in Sicily can be quite cold and a Sicilian family will be as amenable to a soul-warming stew as their northern compatriots. This Sicilian stew is called a *spezzatino*, which simply means "stew." It is a tomato-based preparation flavored with red wine and a little onion, garlic, and basil. It can also be made with chicken, and is known by every Sicilian family. Traditionally, the Sicilians would serve the meat as a second course and pour the sauce from the stew over some macaroni as a first course.

¹/₄ cup extra virgin olive oil
1 small onion, chopped
2 pounds boneless stew beef, trimmed of any
    large pieces of fat and cut into 1-inch pieces
Salt to taste
1 tablespoon tomato paste
¹/₂ cup dry red wine
1¹/₂ pounds ripe tomatoes, peeled, seeded, and
    chopped
2 large garlic cloves, sliced
2 tablespoons finely chopped fresh basil leaves
1 bay leaf
Freshly ground black pepper to taste

1. In a casserole, heat the olive oil over medium-high heat. Cook the onion until translucent, stirring, about 6 minutes. Add the beef, season with salt, and brown on all sides, about 6 minutes. Dilute the tomato paste in the wine and stir into the casserole. Cook until the wine is nearly evaporated, about 5 minutes.

2. Add the tomatoes, water to cover (about ¹/₂ cup), the garlic, basil, and bay leaf and season with pepper. Cover, reduce the heat to very low, and simmer until the meat is very tender, about 3 hours. Discard the bay leaf and serve immediately.

Makes 4 servings

CARBONNADES FLAMANDES

ONE OF THE GREAT CLASSICS OF FLEMISH cuisine is *carbonnades flamandes*, also called *boeuf à la flamande*, a Flemish-style beef and onion stew simmered in beer. They make this dish in northern France and the Franco-phone part of Belgium, where they serve it with bread spread with mustard. Use three pounds of beef if serving six people and four pounds if serving eight. It is best to use a Belgian beer such as a fruit-flavored lambic beer (see right).

3 or 4 pounds beef brisket, cut into 3-inch squares
Unbleached all-purpose flour for dredging
¼ cup (½ stick) unsalted butter
2 large onions, chopped
1 large carrot, finely chopped
2 cups Belgian-style lambic beer
1 tablespoon white wine vinegar
2 teaspoons salt
½ teaspoon freshly ground black pepper
2 bay leaves
½ teaspoon dried thyme
3 tablespoons finely chopped fresh parsley leaves
1 tablespoon firmly packed light brown sugar

1. Dredge the beef in the flour, tapping off any excess. In a large casserole, melt the butter over medium-high heat, then brown the meat on all sides, about 5 minutes. Add the onions

LAMBIC BEER

These Belgian beers are also known as wild beers because they rebel against the traditional method of brewing beer with yeast. These wheat beers are brewed without yeast and ferment sponta-neously. They are brewed in a small area to the west of Brussels called Payottenland. One can sample these beers in their native land in special cafes that buy their young lambic still fermenting in the barrel. Some cafes serve only old lambic, aged three to four years. The brewers insist that microorganisms in the atmosphere contribute to this yeastless fermentation, but research still has not solved the puzzle behind spontaneous fermentation.

and carrot and cook until the onions are golden, stirring, about 6 minutes. Add the beer, vinegar, salt, pepper, bay leaves, thyme, parsley, and sugar.

2. Bring to a boil, reduce the heat to low, and cover. Cook the stew so that it barely simmers until the meat is very tender, about 4 hours. After 3 hours, check the broth and, if it is very liquidy, uncover and reduce over medium-high heat until syrupy. Reduce the heat to low again and continue to gently simmer. Discard the bay leaves and serve.

Makes 6 to 8 servings

BEEF STEWED IN BEER AND VEGETABLES FROM AUSTRIA

THIS AUSTRIAN STEW, *RINDFLEISCH IN Bier*, "beef cooked in beer," is the kind of warming meal I remember fondly from the time I lived in Salzburg as a student in the 1970s. During a cold December, my fellow students and I would frequent a cozy local restaurant with lots of *Gemütlichkeit* and order a dish like this with some dumplings. This stew cooks for a long time, until the beef is falling apart. The vegetables flavor the broth and don't actually get eaten—you wouldn't want to either, since they are, by that time, totally demolished, having given up all their flavor to the stew.

---

6 thick slices bacon

2 large onions, sliced ¼ inch thick

3 medium-size carrots, sliced ¼ inch thick

1 leek, split in half lengthwise, washed well, and sliced ½ inch thick

2 medium-size turnips, peeled and sliced ¼ inch thick

12 black peppercorns

6 juniper berries, lightly crushed

6 leafy sprigs fresh parsley

2 bay leaves

Six 1-inch-long pieces lemon zest

One 4-pound piece boneless beef rump, trimmed of any large pieces of fat and cut into 8 pieces

Two 12-ounce bottles lager beer, preferably Austrian, Bavarian, or Czech

Salt and freshly ground black pepper to taste

2 tablespoons unsalted butter

2 tablespoons unbleached all-purpose flour

---

1. In a deep, heavy casserole, layer the bacon, onions, carrots, leek, and turnips, in that order, and sprinkle with peppercorns, juniper berries, parsley, bay leaves, and lemon zest. Lay the pieces of beef on top. Pour in enough of the beer so it reaches the top of the meat, but does not cover it. Season with salt and pepper. Bring to a boil, reduce the heat to low, and simmer until the beef is tender, 3 to 4 hours. Check by gently pulling on the beef with a fork; once it pulls apart very easily, it is done. If you have to cut it with a knife, it is not ready.

2. Remove the meat, keep it warm, and discard the vegetables. Strain the broth and set aside 2 cups of it. In a medium-size saucepan, melt the butter over medium-high heat. Once it has stopped sizzling and is turning light brown, add the flour and cook, stirring, until it begins to turn into a smooth, light brown roux, 2 to 3 minutes. Slowly add the reserved broth, stirring or whisking constantly, and simmer over low heat until it is a smooth gravy, about 30 minutes. Correct the seasoning if necessary, then pour over the beef and serve hot.

Makes 6 to 8 servings

EVERYDAY SWEDISH MEATBALL STEW

S WEDEN IN WINTERTIME IS SNOWY, white, and cold. A lot of activities take place indoors when the otherwise very outdoorsy Swedes are resting from their appetite-building cross-country skiing adventures. My friend and master Saab mechanic, Håken Wiberg, remembers fondly a stew his mother, and most Swedish mothers, would make during the winter when he was growing up outside Stockholm. It was called *köttbullsgryta till vardags*, which literally and simply means "meatball stew for every day." The kind of crackers you want to use are plain, Swedish-style crackers (not crispbread), or substitute Carr's plain water crackers. Swedish cooks often use cubes of concentrated beef bouillon when a recipe calls for bouillon.

1/2 cup crumbled crackers
1 cup whole milk
1 large egg
1 pound ground beef (not more than 15 percent fat)
1 teaspoon salt
1/2 teaspoon freshly ground black pepper
1/4 teaspoon freshly ground white pepper
3 tablespoons unsalted butter
1 1/2 pounds boiling potatoes, peeled and cubed
3 cups beef bouillon (homemade or from a concentrated cube) or canned low-sodium beef broth
1 teaspoon paprika
2 tablespoons finely chopped fresh parsley leaves

1. Soak the crackers for 10 minutes in the milk in a small bowl. Squeeze the milk out of the crackers. Place the egg in a food processor and run for 15 seconds. Add the crackers, beef, salt, and black and white pepper and process until pasty. Alternatively, everything can be mixed by hand in a bowl, but the meatballs will be more coarsely textured. Make as many meatballs, 1 inch in diameter, as you can. Set aside.

2. In a large casserole or skillet, melt the butter over medium-high heat. Brown the meatballs with the potatoes until light golden on all sides, about 4 minutes. Pour in the beef bouillon and season with salt and pepper and the paprika. Reduce the heat to low, cover, and cook for 30 minutes. Uncover, raise the heat to medium, and cook until the potatoes are tender, about 30 minutes.

3. Sprinkle with parsley 5 minutes before the stew is done, and serve immediately.

Makes 4 to 5 servings

SWEDISH SAILOR'S BEEF STEW

T HIS SWEDISH STEW CALLED *SJÖMANSBIFF-gryta* is one of the most typical family stews, which every Swede knows. This is one of those "lots of bang for the buck" types of stews. It's so simple, yet the taste it delivers is so satisfying. It is best to cook it in an enameled cast-iron casserole because it goes into a very hot oven for quite a while, and all the liquid gets absorbed and the casserole becomes a little crusty. I know it seems like an awfully long time to keep a stew in such a hot oven, but trust me, it works. You can deglaze the casserole a bit with water if you like and pour it over the stew, which should be transferred to a serving bowl.

2¹/₂ pounds boneless beef chuck, trimmed of any large pieces of fat and cut into 1¹/₂-inch cubes
6 tablespoons (³/₄ stick) unsalted butter
2¹/₂ pounds onions (about 5), quartered
2¹/₂ pounds boiling potatoes, peeled and cubed
Salt and freshly ground black pepper to taste
3 cups beer (lager)

---

1. Preheat the oven to 450°F. Toss all the ingredients except the beer into a large oven-proof casserole.

2. Pour the beer over the stew, cover, and cook until the meat is very tender, the potatoes are breaking apart, and the beer is absorbed, about 2 hours.

Makes 6 servings

BEEF AND MUSHROOM STEW FROM FINLAND

MY MOTHER'S MOTHER, KATRI, WAS A Finn who came from Turku to New York in the early part of the twentieth century. She met my grandfather, an Italian from southern Italy, got married, and had four children. My mom remembers that her father taught her mother how to cook the Italian food he loved. But when she had the chance, she would whip up some traditional Finnish dishes too. As my mom says, those Finnish stews will always have some kind of cream in them. In this recipe, called *palapaisti*, which is adapted from Beatrice A. Ojakangas's *The Finnish Cookbook*, you'll use sour cream, the richer the better.

---

¹/₄ cup (¹/₂ stick) unsalted butter
One 1¹/₂-pound beef brisket, cubed
1 large onion, sliced
¹/₂ pound button mushrooms, brushed clean and sliced
1 tablespoon unbleached all-purpose flour
1 teaspoon prepared hot mustard
1¹/₂ cups Beef Broth (page 3)
¹/₂ cup sour cream
Salt to taste
¹/₂ teaspoon freshly ground white pepper
1 tablespoon finely chopped fresh parsley leaves

---

1. In a stew pot or Dutch oven, melt the butter over medium-high heat. Brown the meat with the onion and mushrooms, turning and stirring, about 6 minutes. Stir in the flour, mustard, and beef broth. Cover, reduce the heat to low, and simmer for 1 hour.

2. Uncover and cook until the meat is tender, about 2 hours more.

3. Stir in the sour cream, salt, pepper, and parsley. Serve immediately or keep warm until serving, but do not let it boil, or the sour cream will curdle.

Makes 4 servings

CHOLENT

C*HOLENT* IS THE NAME GIVEN BY JEWS OF Eastern European origin, the Ashkenazim, to the festive meal eaten on Saturday, the Jewish Sabbath. Sephardic Jews, an appellation that today applies to all Jews of Mediterranean ancestry, were originally from Spain; they were expelled and emigrated to Turkey and Greece in the fifteenth and sixteenth centuries. They also make a Sabbath stew, but it is made quite differently and called *tafina* or *dafina* (page 78). This recipe is typical of how the Polish Jews would make *cholent*.

For religious Jews, the Sabbath (or *shabbat* in Hebrew) is a joyous day that is awaited throughout the week. On the Sabbath, a day of rest and spiritual enrichment, Jews set aside all their weekday concerns and devote themselves to higher pursuits. It is not like Sunday for Christians, who see the Sabbath more as a day of prayer. Jews pray on *shabbat* as well, but prayer is only one element. The Sabbath is the most important ritual observance in Judaism and the only ritual specified in the Ten Commandments. The feasting that occurs on the Sabbath day is elaborate and leisurely. Jews remember that in Exodus 20:11 after the Fourth Commandment is first instituted, God explains, "because for six days, the Lord made the heavens and the earth, the sea and all that is in them, and on the seventh day, he rested; therefore, the Lord blessed the Sabbath day and sanctified it."

The Sabbath, therefore, is a day of repose, and the preparations for the Sabbath begin on Friday afternoon, when Jews leave work, the house is cleaned, and the family dresses up. A festive table is set and a special meal prepared. The Sabbath begins at sunset, when men go to synagogue and women light candles at home. Then the family sits down for a special, leisurely dinner, but before it begins, the man of the house recites the Kiddush, a prayer over wine sanctifying the Sabbath. The usual prayer for eating bread is recited over two loaves of challah, a moderately sweet, eggy bread made of ropes of dough, braided together. The family then eats dinner, and the *cholent* for the next day is put on the stove to cook, unattended.

After morning services on Saturday, the family returns and the afternoon meal, the *cholent*, which has been stewing for nearly 18 hours, is eaten. The name *cholent* is said to come from the French words *chaud lent*, meaning "hot slow." The Jews were numerous and prominent in the communities of the Languedoc in southwestern France in the fourteenth century, before they fled persecution and ended up in Germany and Poland. It is thought that at this time *cholent* as it is known today, with its meat, potatoes, beans, and barley, had its start. Some people call this *cholent* a Jewish cassoulet, and it will certainly remind you of one with all the beans and flavor. But there are hundreds of versions of *cholent*, since every cook does it her own way. In America, *cholent* has gotten a bad reputation, reflected in a story told about a man who complains after eating his first *cholent*, "It wasn't very good," to which a guest at the table says, "It's not supposed to be." Try this recipe and you will see that it can be very good, for, after all, there are good cooks and bad cooks. Traditionally, a sausage filled with a flour-and-onion stuffing called *kishke* is served with *cholent*, along with chicken soup and *knaidlach*, or dumplings, and challah.

The use of honey in the *cholent* has a symbolic significance, recalling the "land of milk and honey." Once the *cholent* is cooking, it is left alone. The reason that it cooks unattended is because one must not work on the day of rest, on the Sabbath. But what constitutes "work" is a matter of rabbinical interpretation and debate.

4 pounds beef marrow bones
4 large onions (about 2 pounds), cut into chunks
4¹/₂ pounds beef brisket or flanken
1³/₄ pounds small Yukon Gold potatoes
   (12 to 15), peeled
4 teaspoons hot Hungarian paprika

Salt and freshly ground black pepper to taste
4 large garlic cloves, finely chopped
¹/₂ pound **schmaltz** *(rendered chicken fat),*
   chopped
1 cup dried red kidney beans, picked over, rinsed,
   soaked overnight in cold water to cover, and
   drained
1 cup dried white navy beans, picked over,
   rinsed, soaked overnight in cold water to cover,
   and drained
1 cup medium pearl barley, soaked overnight in
   cold water to cover and drained
2¹/₂ to 3 quarts water, as needed
¹/₄ cup honey

1. Preheat the oven to 200°F. Lay the beef marrow bones and onions on the bottom of a large, heavy ovenproof casserole with a tight-fitting lid. Then layer the beef and potatoes on top and season with half the paprika and some salt and pepper, and sprinkle the garlic around. Strew the chopped chicken fat over the meat and potatoes. Distribute the beans and barley over the top, season with salt and pepper and the remaining paprika, and add enough of the water to just barely cover the ingredients. Drizzle the honey over everything.

2. Place in the oven about 6 P.M. on a Friday night and leave until noon the next day. Serve immediately.

Makes 12 servings

HUNGARIAN GOULASH

T HIS RECIPE IS THE FAMOUS *GULYÁS* OF Hungary. It is not the goulash you may be expecting. If you are used to the American version of Hungarian goulash, which consists of not much more than carelessly dumping paprika and sour cream into a stew, you may be surprised. First, an authentic goulash *never* has sour cream in it. The dish with sour cream that we call goulash is what the Hungarians call *paprikás* (page 76). In Hungarian restaurants (in Hungary), goulash appears on menus under soups, because that is what it originally was. The word *gulyás* itself means something like "cowboy," so, this was cowboys' soup. In Hungarian, goulash is actually called *bogrács-gulyás*, which means "kettle goulash" because it was traditionally cooked by the drovers in a black kettle called a *bogrács*.

George Lang, the famous gastronome, restaurateur, and cookbook author, who wrote the best book on Hungarian cuisine, *The Cuisine of Hungary*, tells us that goulash was originally a soup with roots that are traced back to the ninth century when shepherds slowly cooked their meat in an iron kettle until the liquid evaporated. They dried the remnants in the sun and then put this pemmican in a bag made of sheep's stomach. When they needed to eat, they took a piece of dried meat out and reconstituted it either with a lot of water, in which case it was a soup (*gulyásleves*), or a little water, and it became a meat stew (*gulyáhús*). I have to quote George Lang here on the do's and don't's of goulash: "*Never* use any flour. *Never* use any other spice besides caraway [I guess he doesn't consider paprika a spice, because it's essential]. *Never* Frenchify it with wine. *Never* Germanize it with brown sauce. *Never* put in any other garniture besides diced potatoes or *galushka* [egg dumplings]."

───────●───────

2 tablespoons Freshly Rendered Lard (page 154) or rendered bacon fat (see page 348)
2 medium-size onions, very coarsely chopped
2 pounds beef chuck or rump, trimmed of any large pieces of fat and cut into ³/₄-inch cubes
¹/₂ pound beef heart, trimmed of valves and gristle and diced
1 large garlic clove, crushed
1 teaspoon caraway seeds
Salt to taste
2 tablespoons sweet Hungarian paprika
1 quart warm beer (lager)
1 quart warm water
1 large, ripe tomato, peeled, seeded, and chopped
2 green bell peppers, seeded and sliced into rings
1 pound boiling potatoes, peeled and cut into ³/₄-inch cubes
Hungarian Egg Dumplings (optional, recipe follows)

───────●───────

1. In a large casserole or stew pot, melt the lard over medium-low heat, then cook the onions until translucent, stirring, about 10 minutes. Add the beef and beef heart and cook until they turn a darker color, about 8 minutes. Add the garlic and caraway, season with salt, stir, and remove from the heat.

2. Add the paprika, beer, and water and stir to blend everything. Return to the burner, and bring to a gentle boil. Reduce the heat to low, cover, and simmer for 2 hours.

3. Add the tomato and peppers and taste the stew to see if it needs any more salt. Increase the heat to medium-low and cook until the peppers are soft, about 1 hour. Add the potatoes and cook until everything is tender, about 1 hour more, stirring occasionally. The goulash will be thicker; the soup will look more like a gravy, but you will still need to eat it with a spoon. Serve, if desired, with Hungarian Egg Dumplings.

Makes 6 servings

HUNGARIAN EGG DUMPLINGS

These dumplings are called *galushka* in Hungarian.

1 large egg
1 tablespoon Freshly Rendered Lard (page 154)
1/3 cup water
1 teaspoon salt
1 1/2 cups unbleached all-purpose flour
2 tablespoons rendered goose fat (see page 348)
  or additional lard

1. In a medium-size bowl, mix together the egg, rendered lard, water, and salt. Lightly mix in the flour without working the dough too much, just enough to make it a uniform texture. Let it rest for 10 minutes.

2. Meanwhile, bring some salted water to a boil in a large pot. Drop tablespoon-size pieces of the dough into the water. When the dumplings have risen to the surface, remove them with a slotted spoon and drain.

3. Heat the goose fat in a skillet, and fry the dumplings for a few minutes. Season with salt, and serve with goulash.

Makes 4 servings

BOILED BEEF WITH ROOT VEGETABLES
IN THE STYLE OF SLOVENIA

SLOVENIA IS A COUNTRY CARVED OUT OF a region of northwest Yugoslavia bordering Italy and Austria. Slovenia was controlled for years by the Austria-Hungarian Empire, a country that disappeared after World War I. The Austrian and Italian influences are palpable in this stew, which is called *kuhana govedina* in Slovenian. This appears to be the Slovenian version of *bollito misto* (page 354). A whole rump steak is boiled for many hours in a court bouillon and served with boiled root vegetables. I hate to use the word because it has a negative connotation, but this beef stew is pleasingly bland. Rather than be tempted to spice it up, eat it as it was intended, perhaps with some traditional condiment, such as mustard, horseradish sauce, or just salt and pepper.

———————●———————

2 quarts water
One 2¹/₂-pound beef rump steak, trimmed of any large pieces of fat and tied, if necessary, with kitchen twine to form a regular, compact shape
¹/₂ teaspoon black peppercorns
2 allspice berries
1 bay leaf
2 cloves
Salt to taste
1 celeriac (about 1 pound), peeled and quartered
3 carrots, halved crosswise
1 large parsnip, peeled and halved
6 ounces pearl onions, peeled

———————●———————

1. Bring the water to a boil in a large stew pot over high heat, reduce the heat to medium-high, and place the rump steak in the water. Cook until foam appears on the surface and skim it off, about 10 minutes. Add the peppercorns, allspice berries, bay leaf, cloves, and salt. Reduce the heat to low and simmer, covered. After 2¹/₂ to 3 hours of cooking, add the celeriac, carrots, parsnip, and onions. Cover and continue to cook until the vegetables are tender, and the meat is very tender, about 3¹/₂ to 4 hours total cooking time.

2. Remove the meat from the stew pot and let stand for 10 minutes. Meanwhile, strain the broth, saving the vegetables. Slice the meat, arrange on a serving platter surrounded with the vegetables, pour some broth over both, and serve.

———————●———————

Makes 6 servings

STIFADO

THIS RECIPE, CALLED *STIFATHO* OR *STIFADO* in Greek, is a braised beef with onions. It is one recipe among thousands, since every family makes it a little differently, and it is so typical of rustic Greek mountain cooking. The name comes from the Italian *stufato* (page 15), and the Greek version probably results from the influence of Venetian overlordship in the Middle Ages, when Venice played such a large role in Greek affairs, especially in the Ionian Sea. On the other hand, the spices—the clove and cinnamon—as well as the walnuts and currants point to some Turkish or other Levantine influence, too, which is logical when

---

PEELING PEARL ONIONS

———————●———————

There is no need to struggle with these tiny onions when a recipe calls for peeling them. Bring a saucepan of water to a rolling boil, then drop the pearl onions in for 3 to 5 minutes. Drain and slice off the tip of the root end. The onion will pop out of its skin with a little squeeze between your thumb and forefinger.

STEWING BEEF

In many cookbooks, including this one, you will see recipes calling for stew beef. What exactly is it, other than the beef you use for stewing? *Stew beef* is a general term that refers to all the cuts of beef that come from the tougher parts of the cow, the parts that are muscled with lots of connective tissue and that the cow uses to move around, such as the shoulders, legs, and butt. The best cuts for stewing are the chuck, which comes from the shoulder, and rump or round. Chuck consists of several kinds of cuts, including eye roast, chuck short ribs, blade steak, arm pot roast, and stew beef, which is cubed chuck. Another cut is foreshank, which consists of shank cross cuts and, when cubed without the bone, it can be called stew beef also. Brisket comes from the part of the body where the fore leg meets the underbelly. Most of the underbelly meat, such as tip steak and short plate, can be stewed, although sometimes they are cooked in other ways too. The middle part of the cow, where one finds the ribs, short loin, and sirloin, is usually not used for stewing since it is tender meat best for grilling, broiling, roasting, or pan-frying. At the rear end of the cow comes more good stewing beef. The round, consisting of round steak, top round, bottom round, eye of round, cube steak, and rump steak, is a good stewing meat. In my recipes, when I call for stew beef, I mean either the packaged supermarket cut labeled *stew beef* or any of the above-mentioned cuts of beef used for stewing.

we remember that the Turks controlled most of Greece for five hundred years.

These soul-satisfying tastes are perfect once the weather becomes cool. This is a recipe that you can change any way you want, just as a Greek cook would. Maybe you would like to add carrots or potatoes or remove the walnuts—well, go ahead, it's a free-form Greek stew.

———————————

5 tablespoons unsalted butter
2 pounds boneless stew beef, trimmed of any
　　large pieces of fat and cut into 1-inch cubes, or
　　4 pounds meaty beef short ribs
1 medium-size onion, chopped
10 garlic cloves, lightly crushed
1 cup canned or fresh tomato puree

1/2 cup dry red wine
2 tablespoons red wine vinegar
2 bay leaves
1 cinnamon stick
4 cloves
1 teaspoon sugar
Salt and freshly ground black pepper to taste
2 pounds small white onions
2 tablespoons dried currants
1 cup walnut halves
1 cup crumbled Greek or Bulgarian feta cheese

———————————

1. In a large skillet, heat 3 tablespoons of the butter over medium-high heat, then brown the meat on all sides, about 5 minutes. Transfer the meat to a casserole. Add the chopped onion and garlic cloves to the skillet with the remaining 2 tablespoons of butter and cook until the onion is translucent, stirring, about 4 minutes. Add the tomato puree, wine, and vinegar and deglaze the skillet, scraping up any browned bits from the bottom. Pour this mixture over the meat in the casserole. Add the bay leaves, cinnamon, cloves, and sugar and season with salt and pepper.

2. Cover the casserole and braise over low heat for 1 hour. Add the small onions and currants and cook until the meat falls off the bone (if using short ribs), about 1 hour more. Add the walnuts and cook for 20 minutes more. Add the feta cheese and cook for 5 minutes. Remove the whole spices and bay leaves, then serve.

Makes 4 servings

TURKISH BEAN STEW WITH PASTIRMA

P ASTIRMA IS A CURED FILET MIGNON THAT is very popular in Turkey. A beef fillet is rubbed with a spice mix and then sun-dried. It is eaten in very thin slices. In this country, it is usually sold in Middle Eastern or Greek markets, and through mail-order catalogues and the Internet. Ask for the Ohanyan's Bastirma and Soujouk Co. brand of Pastirma. In this stew, called *güveçte kurufasulye pastırma*, the *pastırma* is used in small quantity and provides a very nice flavor to the beans. This recipe is adapted from Chef Saban Özdemir of the Divan Hotel in Istanbul. Taste the *pastırma* first and, if it is salty (it shouldn't be, though), reduce the amount of salt called for in the ingredients list. There is no really good substitute for *pastırma*, although you could try some thinly sliced *bresaola*, available at Italian delis, and rub it with some paprika and fenugreek.

1¹/₂ cups dried white beans (about ³/₄ pound), picked over, rinsed, soaked overnight in water to cover, and drained
¹/₄ cup (¹/₂ stick) unsalted butter
1 large onion, chopped
4 large garlic cloves, finely chopped
1 pound ripe tomatoes, peeled, seeded, and chopped
2 green bell peppers, seeded and chopped
1 tablespoon tomato paste
3 cups water
5 ounces sliced **pastırma**
2 teaspoons salt
1 teaspoon red pepper flakes

1. Place the drained beans in a large saucepan and cover by several inches with salted cold water. Bring to a boil and cook at a boil until a bit tender but still resistant to the bite, replenishing the water if necessary, about 45 minutes. Drain.

2. In a large skillet or casserole, preferably an earthenware stove-top and oven-proof one, melt the butter over medium-high heat. Once the butter stops sizzling, cook the onion and garlic until soft, stirring so the garlic doesn't burn, about 5 minutes. Add the tomatoes, green peppers, and tomato paste and cook for another 5 minutes. Add the cooked beans and water. Stir, cover, reduce the heat to medium-low to low, and cook until the beans are nearly tender, about 30 minutes. Add the *pastırma*, salt, and red pepper flakes, stir, and cook until the beans are completely tender, about 20 minutes.

3. Meanwhile, preheat the oven to 400°F. Transfer the beans to an earthenware casserole if you have not used one up until now, cover, and bake for 10 minutes. Remove the lid and bake until the top looks crusty (but isn't), about another 5 minutes. Serve immediately.

Makes 4 to 6 servings

BEEF STROGANOFF

WHO HASN'T HEARD OF BEEF STROGA-noff? Surely it is one of the most famous stews, which means in America it is made improperly from coast to coast. I've had lots of really bad beef Stroganoff, so when I was researching this dish, I decided I would go straight to the heart of the matter and find an authentic Russian recipe. Darra Goldstein, a professor of Russian history and the author of

Taste of Russia, tells us that the dish was named in honor of someone in the Stroganov family, affluent merchants from Novgorod in northern Russia. Some people say it was named after Count Grigory Alexandrovich Stroganov, a prominent diplomat born in 1770, who in old age couldn't chew big bites of meat and had his chef invent this easily masticated dish. There are other suggestions too, but interestingly, it seems most likely that beef Stroganoff was invented by a French chef in the employ of the Stroganov family or a French-trained Russian chef during the nineteenth century (the different spelling came about during its transliteration from Russian). In a way, this is not a typical Russian dish, because most Russians traditionally preferred large pieces of meat that were braised or cooked in an oven and then sliced afterwards. This famous Stroganoff is exactly the opposite, since the recipe begins with strips of meat, reflecting a certain French touch to Russian cooking, a phenomenon of eighteenth- and nineteenth-century Russian francophilia.

Byefstroganov, as it is called in Russian, is a wonderful dish to serve guests. It is easy to make, and elegant, too, when made with filet mignon. It is traditional to serve it with French fries (see page 14) scattered on top of the finished dish. Darra Goldstein tells me that Russian sour cream is vastly different from our American sour cream. Although it tends to be thicker than Swedish *gräddfil*, it can still be poured, or at least spooned, without standing up in peaks. When you add Russian sour cream to soup, it swirls in beautifully instead of breaking up into little pieces and clumping like ours does. It also has a flavor that's less blatantly sour than American sour cream, something closer to crème fraîche, but with an earthier taste.

———●———

1 tablespoon dry mustard
1 teaspoon sugar
1/8 teaspoon salt
Freshly ground black pepper to taste
1 tablespoon hot water
2 tablespoons unsalted butter
3 tablespoons vegetable oil
1 pound button mushrooms, brushed clean and
   sliced
1 large onion, chopped
2 pounds filet mignon, cut into 3 x 1-inch
   strips, 1/8 inch thick
1 cup sour cream or crème fraîche

———●———

1. In a small bowl, mix together the mustard, sugar, salt, pepper, and hot water to form a paste.

2. In a large skillet, melt the butter with 1 tablespoon of the oil over medium-high heat, then cook the mushrooms and onion, still over medium-high heat, covered, stirring occasionally, until soft, about 20 minutes.

3. In another large skillet, heat the remaining 2 tablespoons of oil over high heat, then sear the meat on both sides in two batches. The meat should be completely raw in the middle and browned on the outside. Transfer the meat to the skillet with the mushrooms and onion.

4. Deglaze the skillet you cooked the meat in with a few tablespoons of water, scraping the bottom with a wooden spoon, and pour this mixture into the skillet with the mushrooms and onion. Season with salt and pepper, stir in the mustard paste, and cook over medium-high heat, covered, until the meat is rare or medium-rare, depending on your taste, 5 to 10 minutes. Stir in the sour cream, cook over medium heat only until the sour cream is heated, and serve immediately.

———●———

Makes 4 servings

KUYRDAK

KUYRDAK IS CONSIDERED THE NATIONAL dish of Kazakhstan when made in the traditional manner. Kazakhstan is a central Asian republic that was, for many decades, a part of the former Soviet Union. The traditional stew was made with a large part of a camel or horse, or else a whole goat or cow. The animal was boiled in a huge cauldron with vegetables and spices. Balls of dough were dropped into it when it was nearly finished, and a sauce of greens, cooked or raw, was poured over the entire animal, which was served over an enormous amount of rice, cooked in the same broth as the meat. Everyone sat around a *dashtarkan*, the traditional round table that is about a foot off the ground, and once the *bata* was complete, different parts of the animal were given to different people. The older people got the brain, for wisdom, the children were given the ears, so they would listen, and so forth. The guest of honor got the eyeballs. The *bata* was a ritual thanksgiving given before the meal was served. The guest of honor held his hands about one-and-a-half feet from his face, with his palms facing toward him, and said something like "May your cows be healthy, and may your table be forever filled with food." When finished, he placed his fingertips on his forehead and quickly ran them down his face. The other guests did the same. Then it was time to eat.

Since the Soviet era, *kuyrdak* is not served often in such an elaborate manner, and this recipe is more typical. It was given to me by Robert Wilson, who served in the Peace Corps in Kazakhstan in the 1990s. Before you start the sauce, get a pot of rice going to serve with the meat.

FOR THE MEAT:

¼ cup vegetable oil

1½ pounds boneless stew beef, trimmed of any large pieces of fat and cubed

3 medium-size onions, chopped

1½ cups Beef Broth (page 3)

1 teaspoon garam masala (see Note on page 34)

2 large, ripe tomatoes, peeled, seeded, and chopped

2 bay leaves

Salt and freshly ground black pepper to taste

FOR THE SAUCE:

½ cup vegetable oil

2 bunches scallions or spring onions, finely chopped

Leaves from 1 small bunch fresh parsley, finely chopped

Handful of fresh basil leaves, finely chopped

GOAT'S MILK YOGURT

Goat's milk yogurt is most likely to be found in a natural or whole-food store. If you can't find it, then you will have to use whole cow's milk yogurt, the creamier the better. When using cow's milk yogurt, be careful not to cook it; otherwise it will separate. Goat's milk yogurt will not.

Handful of fresh dill, finely chopped

1 large garlic clove, crushed

Salt and freshly ground black pepper to taste

½ cup full-fat plain goat's milk yogurt

1. To prepare the meat, in a large casserole, heat the oil over medium-high heat. Brown the meat on all sides with the onions, about 5 minutes. Add the broth, garam masala, tomatoes, and bay leaves. Season with salt and pepper. Bring to a boil, then reduce the heat to low, and simmer until the meat is very tender, about 3½ hours.

2. Meanwhile, to make the sauce, heat the oil in a medium-size skillet over medium heat. Add all the sauce ingredients, except the yogurt, and cook, stirring, until soft and mushy, about 6 minutes.

3. When ready to serve, stir the yogurt into the sauce and heat briefly. Remove the bay leaves from the meat. Ladle the meat over a bed of cooked rice and serve the sauce on the side.

Note: Kazakh and Uzbek garam masala is made with 1 part each ground cinnamon and cloves, 2 parts ground cumin, and ¹/₂ part each ground cardamom and freshly grated nutmeg.

———————•———————

Makes 4 to 5 servings

BEEF, ONION, AND CORIANDER STEW OF THE ALGERIAN JEWS

B OTH THE JEWS AND MUSLIMS OF NORTH Africa eat *ṭabīkha*, a word that means "stew" in this case, but can actually refer to any cooked dish. In Tunisia, it usually refers to a green vegetable stew, a *ṭabīkha khuḍrāt*. In Tataouine, in southern Tunisia, it is a specialty, a breakfast stew made with lentils and other vegetables. To the West, Algeria was home to a Jewish community that has emigrated to Israel. Algerian Jewish cooking is very similar to that of the Muslim population. What distinguishes Jewish food are the preparations made for special occasions. This dish is considered a prestigious one because it is often prepared for wedding ceremonies, usually for the bride following her wedding eve bath and also for bar mitzvahs. The only vegetable in the dish is the onion, to symbolize the sweetness and unctuousness of the marriage and the hope that it may not turn sour, to vinegar. The stew can be served with warmed Arabic flatbread.

¹/₄ cup extra virgin olive oil
2 large onions, grated
3 garlic cloves, chopped
*1 tablespoon **Harīsa** (recipe follows)*
Salt and freshly ground black pepper to taste
1 pound boneless stew beef, trimmed of any large
*   pieces of fat and cubed*
1 pound ripe tomatoes, peeled, seeded, and
*   chopped*
2 cups water
¹/₄ cup finely chopped fresh coriander (cilantro)
*   leaves*

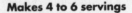

1. In a casserole, stew pot, or the bottom portion of a *couscoussier*, heat the olive oil over medium-high heat. Cook the onions until translucent, stirring occasionally, about 10 minutes.

2. Add the garlic and *harīsa*, season with salt and pepper, and stir to mix well. Add the beef and brown on all sides for 2 to 4 minutes, stirring. Add the tomatoes and water and stir. Reduce the heat to medium, cover, and cook for 45 minutes. Add the coriander leaves and cook until the meat is tender, about another 45 minutes. Serve immediately.

———————•———————

Makes 4 to 6 servings

HARĪSA

Harīsa is a spiced chile paste and the most important condiment used in Algerian and Tunisian cooking. This recipe must be made before you can make almost any Tunisian stew, in fact, and then you can store it in the refrigerator with a protective film of olive oil on top. *Harīsa* comes from the Arabic word for "to break into pieces," which is done by pounding chiles in a mortar, although today a food processor can be used. Be very careful when working with chiles, making sure that you do not put your fingers near your eyes, nose, or mouth. Wash your hands well with soap and water after handling chiles.

———◆———

2 ounces mildly hot dried guajillo chiles
2 ounces mild dried Anaheim chiles
5 garlic cloves, peeled
2 tablespoons water
2 tablespoons extra virgin olive oil, plus extra
   virgin olive oil for topping off the **harīsa**
1/2 teaspoon freshly ground caraway seeds
1/4 teaspoon freshly ground coriander seeds
1 1/2 teaspoons salt

———◆———

1. Soak the chiles in tepid water to cover until softened, 45 minutes to 1 hour. Drain and remove the stems and seeds. Place in a blender or food processor with the garlic, water, and 2 tablespoons of olive oil, and process for a few minutes until smooth, stopping occasionally to scrape down the sides.

2. Transfer the mixture to a small bowl and stir in the caraway, coriander, and salt. Store in a jar and top off, covering the surface of the paste with a layer of olive oil. Whenever the paste is used, you must always top off with olive oil, making sure no paste is exposed to air; other-

wise it will spoil. Stored properly, it will keep indefinitely.

Variations: To make a hotter *harīsa*, use 4 ounces dried guajillo chiles and 1/2 ounce dried de Arbol chiles.

To make *ṣālṣa al-harīsa*, that is, *harīsa* sauce usually used as an accompaniment to grilled meats, stir together 2 teaspoons *harīsa*, 3 tablespoons olive oil, 2 tablespoons water, and 1 tablespoon finely chopped fresh parsley leaves.

———◆———

Makes 1 cup

RAGOUT OF MEATBALLS STUFFED WITH CAULIFLOWER FROM TUNISIA

THIS RAGOUT IS CALLED *MUBAṬṬAN BRŪKLŪ* in Tunisian Arabic, meaning "hidden cauliflower." The word *mubaṭṭan* means "lined" or "filled," and is derived from the Arabic word for "to hide." And this is exactly what is done in this preparation. Ground meat is molded by hand around the florets of cauliflower to form stuffed meatballs, which are then cooked in sauce. Not all Tunisian cooks do this; sometimes they simply throw the two elements, the meat and the vegetable, into the sauce to cook together, while others mix the ground meat with the mashed vegetable and form a ball out of that mixture. This recipe can also be made with cooked artichoke hearts or pieces of cardoon or wild cardoon, called *simmāq* in Tunisian Arabic dialect, all stuffed inside meatballs.

FOR THE MEATBALLS:

One medium-size head cauliflower (about 1 pound)
1½ pounds ground beef, lamb, or veal
1 small onion, finely chopped
½ teaspoon ground cinnamon
Leaves from 1 small bunch fresh parsley, finely chopped
1½ teaspoons Tābil (recipe follows)
1 teaspoon salt
½ teaspoon freshly ground black pepper
2 large eggs, beaten
Unbleached all-purpose flour for dredging
1½ quarts olive oil or vegetable oil for frying

FOR THE SAUCE:

¼ cup extra virgin olive oil
2 tablespoons tomato paste dissolved in 1 cup water
1½ teaspoons Harīsa (page 34)
½ teaspoon ground red chile
Salt and freshly ground black pepper to taste

1. To begin the meatballs, bring a large saucepan of lightly salted water to a boil and cook the whole cauliflower until tender, about 10 minutes. Drain well and break into small florets.

2. Place the meat, onion, cinnamon, parsley, *tābil*, salt, and black pepper in a food processor,

in batches if necessary, and process until well blended. Remove to a large bowl.

3. Wet your hands, take a lemon-size piece of the meat mixture, and flatten it in your hand to make a thin patty. Place a cauliflower floret in the middle of the patty and surround it with the meat, molding the meat with your hands so the entire piece of cauliflower is enclosed. Form this into an oval shape, then dip it into the eggs and dredge in the flour, tapping off any excess flour. Place on a baking sheet while you continue to make the rest, keeping your hands wet so the meat doesn't stick to them.

4. Preheat the frying oil to 375°F in a deep fryer or an 8-inch saucepan fitted with a basket insert. Cook the meatballs in batches until golden, without crowding the fryer, about 4 minutes. Remove from the oil with a slotted spoon, drain on paper towels, and set aside.

5. To make the sauce, in a casserole, heat the extra virgin olive oil over medium-high heat with the dissolved tomato paste, *harīsa*, and chile and season with salt and black pepper. Once the sauce starts bubbling, reduce the heat to low, cover, and simmer for 10 minutes. Add the meatballs and cook, covered, until very little sauce remains, about 25 minutes. Add a few tablespoons of water if the sauce begins to dry out before the end of the cooking time. Serve the meatballs covered with the remaining sauce.

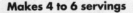

Makes 4 to 6 servings

TĀBIL

Tābil (pronounced "table"), which means "seasoning" in Tunisian Arabic, in earlier times was a word used for coriander. Today it is a spice mix associated with the cooking of Tunisia, featuring coriander seeds pounded in a mortar, then dried in the sun. It is often used in cooking beef or veal. My recipe uses all dried spices except the garlic, which you should air-dry a bit; otherwise replace it with garlic powder.

2 large garlic cloves, chopped and dried in the open air for 2 days, or 2 teaspoons garlic powder
¼ cup coriander seeds
1 tablespoon caraway seeds
2 teaspoons cayenne pepper

In a mortar, pound the garlic with the coriander, caraway, and cayenne until homogeneous. Store in the refrigerator or freezer. *Tābil* will keep in the refrigerator for up to 2 months if made with fresh garlic and indefinitely if made with powdered garlic, although the pungency will decline as time goes by.

Makes about ¼ cup

FRYING

Americans appear to be intimidated by the thought of deep-frying at home. But deep-frying is just one more method of cooking food in the cook's repertoire, and it does not have to be associated with greasy food. Greasy food comes about by improperly frying.

There's deep-frying and shallow-frying. In deep-frying, the entire food is submerged in hot oil or rendered fat to cook. In shallow-frying, only one side of the food touches the frying oil or fat. To deep-fry properly, you are best off getting a deep fryer for home use with a regulated heating element and thermometer. Alternatively, a saucepan with a basket insert can be used, but then you must pay closer attention to the temperature of the oil. The oil for frying should be clean, about 2½ to 3 inches deep, and at a temperature of between 365 and 375°F, which is achieved after about 10 minutes of preheating over medium-high heat. The last point to make about deep-frying is that you should never crowd the frying oil with too many pieces of food because that will lower the temperature of the oil too much and the food will absorb the oil instead of quickly developing a crunchy coating. When that happens, you end up with greasy food. Fry in batches.

BEEF AND GREEN OLIVE STEW WITH TUNISIAN SPICES

MORE THAN TWENTY YEARS AGO I studied Arabic, and my first Arabic teacher was a Tunisian fellow and a gourmet. I learned how to cook Tunisian food not only from hanging out with Tunisians in this country but by visiting Tunisia, where I was introduced to what is probably the best of an undiscovered Mediterranean cuisine. The use of chile pepper in Tunisian cooking appealed to me, and I realized from many visits that, in general, the food was pretty hot. But it took even more experience to realize that it is not universally so. Take, for instance, this simple home-cooked family stew of beef and olives called *maraqa al-zaytūn* or "olive ragout." Although it includes spices, it is not that hot, and the flavors become all the more balanced when the dish is served with pasta, rice, or couscous, as is standard in Tunisian homes. The Tunisians eat quite a bit of pasta, more than they do rice, I think. This dish would be very nice with a thick pasta such as *perciatelli*.

1/4 cup plus 2 tablespoons extra virgin olive oil
1 pound boneless stew beef, trimmed of any large pieces of fat and cut into bite-size pieces
Salt to taste
1/2 teaspoon freshly ground black pepper
1/2 teaspoon Tābil *(page 37)*
1 small onion, chopped
2 tablespoons tomato paste

1 1/4 cups water
1/2 teaspoon ground red chile
1 1/2 cups imported green olives (about 1/2 pound), pitted

---

1. In an earthenware casserole set on a heat diffuser, heat the olive oil over medium-high heat. (If you are not cooking with earthenware and a diffuser, cook over medium heat and check for doneness sooner.) Season the beef with the salt, black pepper, and *tābil*. Brown the beef on all sides with the onion, stirring, about 6 minutes.

2. In a 2-cup measuring cup, mix the tomato paste, water, and chile together. Pour into the casserole, stirring to mix well. Bring to a boil, reduce the heat to low, and cook for 1 1/2 hours.

3. Add the olives, stir to mix, and continue to cook, covered, until very tender, about another 1 1/2 hours. Correct the seasonings and serve with rice, pasta, or couscous.

Makes 4 servings

MADFŪNA

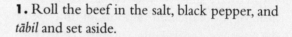

MADFŪNA IS A NORTH AFRICAN DISH whose name seems to have a variety of meanings. *Madfūna* can be a dish of eggplant stuffed with finely minced meat previously cooked in coriander and cinnamon with chickpeas, and then simmered in a sauce of onions, broth, and saffron sprinkled with rose water. Or it may be a stew of meat, cabbage, and spices, just like the famous Jewish Sabbath dish of North Africa called *tafīna* or *dafīna* (page 78). In Tunisia, *madfūna* means the meat and cabbage dish, but also a dish made of rice and legumes, and a third dish, meat such as veal feet or *andouillette* sausage cooked with Swiss chard and white beans. Yet another stew in the family is *mūrāliyya*, a quite similar Tunisian stew made with meatballs or beef or veal feet, Swiss chard, white beans, garlic, and spices. *Madfūna* is ideally made in an earthenware Tunisian-style tagine with its conical lid. If you do not have one, try any earthenware casserole, or a Dutch oven or heavy casserole as a last resort. Don't pass on the beef feet; they add a lot of flavor and body, and you don't eat them.

---

1 pound boneless beef round or chuck, trimmed
    of any large pieces of fat and cut into bite-size
    pieces
2 teaspoons salt
1¹/₂ teaspoons freshly ground black pepper
1¹/₂ teaspoons Tābil (page 37)
2 pounds Swiss chard with their white stalks,
    cut into strips
1 tablespoon Harīsa (page 34)
1¹/₂ teaspoons cayenne or other ground red chile
¹/₄ cup water
³/₄ cup extra virgin olive oil
2 pounds beef feet
¹/₂ cup dried white beans, picked over, rinsed,
    soaked in water to cover overnight, and
    drained

---

1. Roll the beef in the salt, black pepper, and *tābil* and set aside.

2. Bring a large saucepan of lightly salted water to a boil. Plunge the Swiss chard in the water and cook, covered, until it has wilted, 3 to 4 minutes. Drain well.

FLAVORING STEWS WITH FEET

I cook with feet and you should too. Many recipes in my book call for feet in the ingredients list. Beef feet, pork feet, lamb feet, veal feet, chicken feet—the more feet the better. If you want the real flavor of the stew to come through, don't pass on the feet. Generally, you don't eat the feet; they are only used for flavoring the stew. But, oh boy, what a flavor. Because of the gelatinous matter in the feet, the flavors they impart to the food cannot be replicated in any other way. To leave out the feet in some of these stews is like leaving out the onion in a French onion soup. I regularly find fresh beef and pig's feet in local supermarkets, but veal and lamb feet usually need to be ordered from a butcher.

3. Mix the *harīsa*, cayenne, and water together in a small bowl.

4. Put the Swiss chard in an earthenware casserole or terrine set on a heat diffuser. Pour the olive oil over it, and cook over high heat, uncovered, until the leaves take on a dull greenish color and any excess water has evaporated, about 25 minutes. (If you are not cooking with earthenware and a diffuser, cook over medium heat for about the same amount of time.) Add the beef, beef feet, *harīsa* mixture, and white beans. Push the beans down into the chard. Raise the heat to high and, once it starts sizzling, reduce the heat to low (with a heat diffuser) or very low (without a heat diffuser) and cook until the feet are falling apart, 2¹/₂ to 3 hours. Discard the feet, taste and adjust the salt, and serve.

Makes 4 servings

BEEF AND
ROOT VEGETABLE STEW
WITH PEANUT BUTTER
FROM SENEGAL

THIS DISH FROM THE WEST AFRICAN nation of Senegal is called *maffe*. Peanuts are used in much West African cooking because they grow well in that hot climate, and they are rich in oil, 43 to 55 percent, and protein, 25 to 28 percent. The peanut, a New World plant, was brought to Africa from Brazil by Portuguese traders after Columbus's voyages. This stew is a thick, rib-sticking preparation that is both nutritious and filling. The recipe is adapted from a number of different recipes I found on the Internet, but I have a feeling all the various recipes I looked at derive from the one found in Bea Sandler's *The African Cookbook*. One traditionally serves this stew over steamed rice.

¹/₄ cup peanut oil
1 medium-size onion, chopped
1 pound boneless stew beef, trimmed of any large
    pieces of fat and cut into 1-inch cubes
3 ounces tomato paste (half a 6-ounce can)
1 cup water
¹/₂ teaspoon cayenne pepper
Salt and freshly ground black pepper to taste
¹/₂ teaspoon dried thyme
1 small head green cabbage (about 1 pound),
    damaged outer leaves discarded, cored, and cut
    into 8 wedges
1 large boiling potato, peeled and quartered
3 small turnips, peeled
1 large sweet potato, peeled and quartered
¹/₂ cup smooth peanut butter

1. In a large casserole or Dutch oven, heat the peanut oil over medium-high heat. Cook the onions until translucent, stirring, about 5 minutes. Add the beef and, once it turns color, add the tomato paste, water, cayenne, salt and black pepper, and thyme. Reduce the heat to low, cover, and cook for 1 hour.

2. Add the cabbage, potato, turnips, and sweet potato. Cover and cook until tender, 2 to 2¹/₂ hours. Remove about ¹/₂ cup of the liquid from the casserole and stir into the peanut butter in a small bowl. Pour this sauce over the meat and cook for 5 minutes. Serve over plain rice.

Makes 4 to 6 servings

BEEF, PEANUT, AND YAM STEW WITH WEST AFRICAN SPICES

THIS RECIPE, WHICH I FOUND ON THE Internet, comes from an unknown source without any ancillary information about it. I wonder if it might be related to the Senegalese *maffe* (page 40). Many African stews typically have peanuts in them, either in the form of peanut butter, whole peanuts, or peanut oil. But this stew is so good that I suspect it might be a recipe from some upper class West African family, especially given that it calls for sirloin, a tender and expensive cut that doesn't really need to be stewed. The original recipe does not call for stewing but rather for quickly boiling all the ingredients until tender. I've transformed it into a stew, which I think is more appropriate to allow the variety of spices and vegetables to do their work. It is a delicious, full-bodied stew that is both fragrant and perfect served with steamed rice.

1 cup peeled and diced eggplant (about ¹/₂ pound)
1¹/₂ teaspoons salt, plus extra for sprinkling
1 medium-size red onion, diced
2 tablespoons peanut oil
1¹/₂ pounds sirloin, trimmed of any large pieces of fat and cut into ¹/₂-inch cubes
1 yam, peeled and diced
1 red bell pepper, seeded and chopped
2 large garlic cloves, finely chopped
2 teaspoons freshly ground cumin seeds
2 teaspoons freshly ground cardamom seeds
¹/₂ teaspoon cayenne pepper
¹/₂ teaspoon ground cloves
¹/₂ teaspoon ground fenugreek
1 cup water
3 cups Beef Broth (page 3)
1 cup sliced okra
¹/₂ cup smooth peanut butter
1 cup chopped roasted unsalted peanuts
1¹/₂ teaspoon freshly ground black pepper
1 cup ripped spinach leaves
1¹/₂ tablespoons finely chopped fresh mint leaves

1. Spread the eggplant on some paper towels, sprinkle with salt, and set aside to leach it of its bitter juices for 30 minutes. Pat dry with paper towels.

2. Place the onion in a large, heavy stew pot over high heat and cook until it starts to turn color, stirring almost constantly so it doesn't stick, about 4 minutes. Add the peanut oil, beef, and yam and brown the meat on all sides, 3 to 4 minutes. Stir in the bell pepper, garlic, cumin, cardamom, cayenne, cloves, and fenugreek. Add the water and beef broth, bring to a boil, and stir. Add the okra and eggplant and reduce the heat to low.

3. Remove 2 cups of the hot broth to a mixing bowl or 1-quart measuring cup. Blend the broth with the peanut butter and peanuts using a fork. Add the peanut butter mixture to the broth in the stew pot and stir to blend. Stir in the 1 1/2 teaspoons of salt and the pepper, partially cover the pot, and simmer until the yam is tender, about 1 1/2 hours.

4. Add the spinach and mint, bring to a boil, and cook for 1 minute. Serve immediately.

———●———

Makes 4 servings

BEEF SHANK AND ONION STEW WITH SPICES FROM YEMEN

———❧———

THIS YEMENI STEW IS CALLED *HUR'IY*, AN Arabic word that means "stewed very well until the meat shreds." And this is exactly what you do. Typically the dish is made with beef foreshank, although oxtail could be used too. At the end of the cooking, there should be just a little syrupy liquid left.

Yemen is a poor country, and this accounts for the generous use of spices, which is true of this stew. An otherwise bland cut of tough meat is simmered with a delectable blend of spices, and the resulting stew is complex, interesting, and savory. Serve it with rice and flatbread.

———●———

3 pounds beef shank, thickly sliced
2 large onions, quartered
12 large garlic cloves, crushed
3 large, ripe tomatoes, peeled and quartered
2 teaspoons freshly ground black pepper
4 dried chiles
1 teaspoon freshly ground caraway seeds
1/4 teaspoon ground saffron
1/4 teaspoon freshly ground cardamom seeds
1 teaspoon turmeric
2 teaspoons salt

———●———

1. Put the shanks in a large casserole with just enough water to cover. Bring slowly to a boil, skimming the surface of any foam.

2. Once the water is boiling, add the onions, garlic, tomatoes, black pepper, chiles, spices, and salt. Cover, reduce the heat to low, and barely simmer until the meat is so tender it would shred with the gentle tug of a fork, 4 to 5 hours. There should be very little liquid left. Serve immediately.

Makes 6 servings

SPICY YEMENI-STYLE OXTAIL STEW

THIS VERY LONG SIMMERING STEW IS called ʿakwa in Arabic. It is a spicy stew popular in Yemen, an Arab country in the southwest corner of the Arabian Peninsula. ʿAkwa means "the thickest part of the tail," which is the part that goes into this eponymous stew. The spice blend is what makes the fin-

TOASTING AND GRINDING SAFFRON

The best way to buy saffron is in threads, which are actually whole pistils of a crocus. In recipes that call for grinding the saffron, take a pinch, which is about 50 threads, place it in a toaster oven, and toast the saffron for about 1 minute. Remove and grind it in a mortar with a pestle.

ished dish so delectable because the stew cooks for a very, very long time. Serve with rice pilaf, Arabic flatbread, and a green salad.

4¹/₂ pounds oxtail, cut into pieces
1 tablespoon plus 1 teaspoon black peppercorns
2 teaspoons caraway seeds
¹/₂ teaspoon cardamom seeds
¹/₂ teaspoon saffron threads
1 teaspoon ground fenugreek
1¹/₂ teaspoons turmeric
Salt to taste
2 large, ripe tomatoes, peeled and chopped
1³/₄ pounds small white onions
10 garlic cloves, lightly crushed
Rice Pilaf (page 125)

1. Rinse the oxtails, then place them in a large casserole and cover with water. Bring to a gently bubbling boil over medium heat. Reduce the heat to low and skim the surface of any foam until there is very little left.

2. Crush the peppercorns, caraway seeds, cardamom seeds, and saffron together in a spice mill or in a mortar with a pestle. Stir in the fenugreek, turmeric, and salt.

3. Add the tomatoes, onions, garlic, and spice mix to the oxtail. Bring to a boil, then reduce the heat to very low, using a diffuser if necessary. Cover and barely simmer for 3 hours.

4. Uncover and continue to cook until the meat is falling off the bone, another 5 to 6 hours. The stew is done when the meat is falling off the bone and the sauce is much reduced. Serve over the rice pilaf.

───────●───────

Makes 6 servings

BOWSHAW STEW WITH DUMPLINGS

IN COLLECTING STEW RECIPES I FOUND A surprising treasure trove among my Saab mechanics, one Swedish and one English. This recipe comes by way of Tim Kitt, who now has a shop in Santa Barbara, California. He had this stew as a child growing up in England and got it from his mother, Eileen Rogerson Kitt. This is the way the Rogerson family originally made it at Bowshaw House, an old working farm in Dronfield, in Derbyshire, which has been in Tim's family for generations. Tim's mom tells us that this stew was made in large quantities to feed the family and people who worked in the house and that the dumplings made the meat go farther. In a letter to Tim she says that she likes to add herbs to the dumplings, and if the lid is left off the casserole, it gives a crustier top to them, "however, this was not the way Granny did things!" Tim's Uncle Ken used to make a large quantity of the stew on Mondays and bring it to a boil each day for his dinner (that is, midday meal). He always said that Friday, it was at its best—really rich and thick! In this recipe,

there are onions, which Mrs. Kitt uses, but she tells Tim that Granny didn't always use onions because Grandad didn't like them.

───────●───────

About 1½ cups unbleached all-purpose flour
Salt and freshly ground black pepper to taste
2 pounds stew beef, cut into 1-inch cubes
¼ cup shredded beef suet or beef drippings from
* a roast*
1 pound onions, coarsely chopped
1½ quarts hot Beef Broth (page 3)
1 pound carrots, cut into 1-inch-thick rounds
4 large potatoes (about 2 pounds total), peeled
* and cut into ¾-inch cubes*
1 teaspoon Worcestershire sauce
FOR THE DUMPLINGS:
1 cup self-rising flour
Salt to taste
2 ounces beef suet, shredded
¼ cup water

───────●───────

1. In a shallow bowl, season the flour with salt and pepper and toss the meat with the flour, patting off any excess.

2. In a skillet, melt the beef suet over medium-high heat. Brown the meat on all sides, about 8 to 10 minutes. Transfer the beef to a stew pot or casserole. Cook the onions in the remaining fat in the skillet until soft and lightly browned, about 8 minutes. Transfer the onions to the stew pot with the beef. Add 1 cup of beef broth to the skillet and deglaze it, scraping up the crust from the bottom with a wooden spoon. Transfer the brown bits and juices to the stew pot and add the carrots and potatoes.

Cover with the remaining 5 cups of hot beef broth, add the Worcestershire sauce, season with salt and pepper, and stir. Bring the stew to a boil, cover, and reduce the heat to low. Simmer until the meat is tender, about 2 to 3 hours.

3. To make the dumplings, mix the flour, salt, and suet together in a bowl. Add enough of the water to make a fairly soft, but not sticky, paste. Divide into 8 balls with well-floured hands and set aside. Twenty minutes before the stew is done, drop the dumplings onto the top of the stew. They should sit on top without sinking. Replace the lid, and simmer until the dumplings are firm, about 20 minutes. Serve the stew, making sure that each diner gets 1 dumpling.

Makes 8 servings

AMELIA SIMMONS'S "BEEF ALAMODE" FROM 1796

THIS RECIPE APPEARED IN THE BOOK *American Cookery* written by Amelia Simmons and published by Hudson and Goodwin in Hartford, Connecticut, in 1796. It is called the first American cookbook because it was the first book published in America that was not based on some English cookbook. And this, I suppose, is the first American stew. The original recipe reads:

TO ALAMODE A ROUND

Take fat pork cut in slices or mince, season it with pepper, salt, sweet marjoram and thyme, cloves, mace, and nutmeg, make holes in the beef and stuff it in the night before cooked; put some bones across the bottom of a pot to keep from burning, put in one quart Claret wine, one quart-water and one onion; lay the round on the bones, cover close and stop it round the top with dough; hang on in the morning and stew gently for two hours; turn it, and stop again and stew two hours more; when done tender, grate a crust of bread on the top and brown it before the fire; scum the gravy and serve in a butter boat; serve it with the residue of the gravy in the dish.

So try this "first American stew" and I think you will not only be pleased, but you will experience one of those rare connections with our history. This stew includes mace, cloves, and nutmeg, spices from the Far East, which means merchants were already importing spices to New England and cooks were enthusiastically incorporating them into their cooking in the eighteenth century.

One 3-pound boneless beef round steak
¼ pound pork fatback or salt pork, finely chopped
2½ teaspoons freshly ground black pepper
1 tablespoon salt
2 teaspoons dried marjoram
2 teaspoons dried thyme

1 teaspoon freshly ground cloves
1 teaspoon ground mace
½ teaspoon freshly grated nutmeg
Eight 2-inch-thick pieces beef marrow bones
(about 3 pounds)
2 cups dry red wine
1 medium-size onion, sliced
Flour paste rope (see page 9)
1 cup fresh bread crumbs

---

1. Puncture the piece of beef all over with a knife or larding needle, and widen the holes with your forefinger. In a bowl, mix together the pork fat, pepper, salt, marjoram, thyme, cloves, mace, and nutmeg. Stuff the holes with the mixture.

2. Arrange the marrow bones on the bottom of a heavy, ovenproof stew pot, casserole, or Dutch oven with sides no higher than 6 inches. Place the beef round on top, then pour the wine over and scatter the onion over the top of the meat. Cover with the lid and let the meat rest in the refrigerator overnight and part of the next day.

3. Seal the lid to the stew pot with the flour paste rope. Place the stew pot over a burner and turn the heat to high. Once the liquid starts to boil (you'll have to listen), reduce the heat to low, and simmer for 4 hours.

4. Preheat the broiler or set the oven at its highest temperature. Crack the flour-and-water seal, remove the lid, and cover the top of the meat mixture with the bread crumbs. Place the stew pot under the broiler or in the oven

MARROW BONES

Many stews utilize marrow bones. Marrow is the soft, highly vascular, modified connective tissue that occupies the cavities and cancellous part of most bones. The taste of marrow is quite delicious, and the word *marrow* has also come to mean "the choicest of foods." Marrow bones are usually sold in supermarkets, sometimes as "soup bones." The most common marrow bones to be found are beef femur bones, but ask for veal bones, too: they are, in my mind, even more delicious. The marrow not only flavors the stews, but can be scooped out of the bones afterward and eaten.

until golden and crispy, with bits of the bread crust slightly blackened, 2 to 3 minutes. Transfer the meat to a serving platter and slice into serving portions. Serve with a marrow bone and a ladle full of the broth.

Makes 6 servings

BEEF STEW WITH BOURBON

COOKING WITH BOURBON COULD ONLY have had its start in America. Typically, one finds it used in home cooking in places like Kentucky and Tennessee and out West, too. It's also a very common ingredient in the cuisine of American male cooks who don't cook often—there's something he-manly about bourbon in food. Just so you know that it is not too wacko, this recipe is actually quite good and the bourbon does lend a very nice element to the stew. The recipe comes from a cookbook written in the 1960s by Carol Truax and S. Omar Barker called *The Cattleman's Steak Book*. It's unclear where the authors got the recipe, but since Mr. Barker, the dean of Western writers, was born and raised in the Southwest, and Ms. Truax spent many years in Colorado, I suspect that it was dreamed up by some ranch cook or a restaurateur from a steak house in Colorado or New Mexico. The stew should cook slowly until the meat can be cut with a fork, a process that could take as long as five hours, depending on the quality of meat and your heat. The meat glaze they call for in the original recipe enriches the stew. Meat glaze is made by boiling down unsalted beef broth until it is several tablespoons of syrupy glaze. It can also be store bought.

———

3 tablespoons finely chopped beef suet or
 unsalted butter
2¹/₂ pounds boneless beef round, trimmed of any
 large pieces of fat and cut into 1-inch cubes
1 large onion, chopped
1 fat carrot, chopped
¹/₂ cup Beef Broth (page 3)
¹/₄ cup dry white wine
2 tablespoons tomato paste
Salt and freshly ground black pepper to taste
2 tablespoons meat glaze (optional)

¹/₃ cup bourbon whiskey
2 tablespoons finely chopped fresh parsley leaves

———

1. In a large casserole, heat the beef suet over medium-high heat until the fat has melted and the little remaining bits are crispy. Brown the beef on all sides, about 10 minutes. If using butter, wait until the butter stops sizzling before browning the meat. Remove the beef from the casserole with a slotted spoon and set aside.

2. Add the onion and carrot to the casserole and cook until the onion is translucent and sticks to the bottom of the casserole, 7 to 8 minutes. Return the beef, with its accumulated juices, to the casserole and let the juices deglaze the casserole for a few minutes, scraping the bottom. Add the beef broth, wine, and tomato paste. Salt lightly and season with pepper. Bring to a boil and reduce the heat to very low, using a heat diffuser if necessary. Cover and simmer until the meat is very tender, about 4 hours.

3. Add the meat glaze, if using, and bourbon and cook, uncovered, for 30 minutes more. Check the seasoning, stir in the parsley, and serve.

———

Makes 6 servings

OLD-FASHIONED AMERICAN BEEF STEW

A RECIPE FOR AN OLD-FASHIONED American beef stew is a must for a stew bible. But what a difficult time I had creating a recipe because there are thousands of different versions. I did know that I would want a beef stew from New England because that's where some early American beef stews were to be found. This recipe is from Massachusetts. Not from any particular place, but generally the kind of beef stew that some old Yankee would have made 50 years ago, perhaps in a place like Arlington, Massachusetts, where my neighbor Al Thyne lived for 96 years, until he died a few years ago. His family was from Cambridge, Massachusetts, and an old, hardy Yankee family like that with a gaggle of hungry children would love a beef stew like this one. Their small house on Spy Pond would be steamy with flavors, the windows clouded while outside a raging nor'easter piled snow up to the porch, and the kids would come in from sledding and gobble up a piping hot beef stew. I have not "modernized" this stew at all by adding wine or chile pepper or oregano; it's just old-fashioned. Typically, American beef stew is served with dumplings (recipe follows).

1³/4 pounds boneless beef chuck, trimmed of any large pieces of fat and cut into large bite-size pieces
¼ cup unbleached all-purpose flour
Salt and freshly ground black pepper to taste

3 tablespoons unsalted butter or finely chopped beef suet
1 medium-size onion, chopped
2 cups cold water
1 pound red potatoes, peeled and cubed
1¹/2 carrots, diced
1 large parsnip, peeled and diced
1 medium-size turnip, peeled and diced
1 recipe Dumplings (optional; recipe follows)

1. Dredge the beef in the flour, salt, and pepper, tapping off any excess. In a large casserole, Dutch oven, or stew pot, melt the butter over medium-high heat. Brown the meat on all sides, about 8 minutes. Add the onion and cook until soft, stirring and scraping the bottom of the pot, about 4 minutes. Pour in the water to barely cover, bring to a boil, then reduce the heat to low. Stir a bit, then simmer until the meat is tender, about 2 hours.

2. Add the potatoes, carrots, parsnip, and turnip and continue to cook until everything is very tender, about 1 hour more, stirring every once in a while. Add the dumplings, if desired, cover, and cook for 20 minutes without removing the cover. Serve immediately.

Makes 4 servings

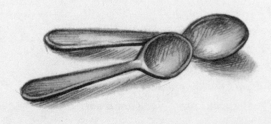

DUMPLINGS

This recipe is for very simple flour dumplings that typically get used in a variety of North American stews. You can add dumplings to any stew you would like, but they are particularly good with American beef or chicken stews. To keep the dumpling light and delicately flavored, do not use eggs and never take the cover off the pot while they cook.

---

1 cup unbleached all-purpose flour
Heaping ½ teaspoon baking powder
Heaping ¼ teaspoon salt
1 tablespoon unsalted butter
⅓ cup milk

---

1. In a medium-size bowl, sift the flour, baking powder, and salt together. Work the butter into the flour with a pastry knife or fork. Add the milk to make a soft dough.

2. Turn the dough out onto a floured surface and roll out into a square about ½ inch thick. Cut into 6 smaller squares.

3. When cooking dumplings, it is important that they be cooked under a tight-fitting lid, otherwise they will be leaden. Place them on top of the stew being cooked, cover tightly, and cook for 20 minutes without lifting the cover.

Makes about 6 dumplings

CHILI CON CARNE

CHILI CON CARNE IS NOT A MEXICAN dish. It is a classic dish of Texas cooking. Authentic chili is said to have been invented by cooks who served drovers and hands in the days of the trail drives in the Southwest. One writer claimed that the dish was invented by the first Spanish missionary to Texas and the Southwest, one Mary of Agreda, who taught it to the Indians. It may have been eaten by Mexicans in Texas in the early part of the nineteenth century. By 1857 S. Compton Smith published a book titled *Chile con Carne*.

For a Texan, a "bowl of red" is as epiphanic as "chowda" is for a Cape Codder. A true Texas chili con carne contains neither beans nor tomatoes, the purists say. However, I have had chilis with beans and chilis with beans and tomatoes and liked them very much. Chilis with red kidney beans are generally more common in the northern part of the United States and are sometimes called Cincinnati chilis. In a real chili, only finely diced beef chuck, not ground beef, is used. In New Mexico, I'm told, chili is sometimes made with lamb.

There are hundreds of different ways of cooking chili, and I looked at hundreds of recipes when researching the foundation to my recipe here. Rather than struggle to choose one, I made up this recipe, based on my experience of eating chili con carne and on four important basic recipes: First, there is the "Cin-Chili" Chili of Cindy Reed of Houston, Texas, back-to-back winner of the 1992 and 1993 Terlingua International Chili Championship.

SON OF A BITCH IN A SACK

In the old American West, there is a tradition that cowboys would swoon over a good "son of a bitch in a sack," the name of an old stew that cowboys once made. It lends itself to a ditty:

A bold buckarooster called Mac
Who wanted a wife in his shack
Said: "Never mind looks!
I want one who cooks
Good son of a bitch in a sack."

The making of a good son of a bitch in a sack utilized all those parts of the cow that we no longer eat, nor know much about. The stew contained beef liver, heart, tongue, sweetbreads, sirloin, neck meat, caul fat, intestines, brains, and marrowgut. The parts were browned in beef suet, then covered with water and stewed for six hours. The marrowgut is the first few feet of the small intestine after it leaves the stomach. It contains a viscous, milky looking fluid, a secretion of the pancreas that is the magic ingredient that gives the dish its flavor—so they say.

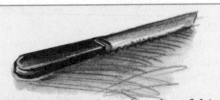

Another recipe that I found useful is called "Texas Red," and is from an unknown source. The third recipe I considered was the one given by President Lyndon B. Johnson, who said, "Chili concocted outside of Texas is usually a weak, apologetic imitation of the real thing. One of the first things I do when I get home to Texas is to have a bowl of red. There is simply nothing better." The fourth recipe I liked was from Bob Coats of Irving, Texas, whose "Out O Site Chili, Too" won the 1999 Terlingua International Chili Championship. Both Mr. Coats and Ms. Reed used tomatoes, which I have left out of mine in the interest of purity. Some other recipes I looked at use coffee and chocolate too. My recipe even complies with Texas law (which prohibits making chili with beans, so I'm told). For the record, I should state that I am not in favor of the many "championship" chili recipes that use some tomato paste or tomato sauce, as well as a variety of canned broths or prepackaged commercial seasonings—all additions that I believe emphatically do not make a spectacular chili. My recipe emphasizes fresh ingredients and freshly ground spices. It could be considered a three-alarm chili, in that it uses fresh serrano peppers, too. I believe a so-called four-alarm chili is too hot; the heat attacks your taste buds, and you find it difficult to discern the complexity of what you're eating. (Some of my friends might consider this a four-alarm chili, however.) Many cooks prepare chili in two or three stages, believing that it improves the taste. Another interesting chili-making phenomenon is the practice of soaking dried chiles and then blending them into a paste, which is identical to the method for making a Tunisian *harīsa* (page 34).

Serve chili con carne with cornbread, flour tortillas, or corn tortillas. In Texas, one would drink beer with chili con carne, but a light red wine would be very nice too, as would sangria.

2 tablespoons bacon drippings or rendered beef kidney suet (see page 348)

3 pounds boneless beef chuck, trimmed of any large pieces of fat and chopped in a food processor or by hand into 1/4-inch dice

1/4 cup dark chili powder

2 teaspoons dried, granulated garlic or garlic flakes

6 dried pasilla chiles (substitute ancho chiles, if necessary)

1 dried Anaheim chile (also called New Mexico, long green, or long red chiles)

2 dried guajillo chiles (also called mirasol)

2 cups cold water

3 cups Beef Broth (page 3)

2 tablespoons onion powder

2 large garlic cloves, crushed

1 1/2 tablespoons garlic powder

1 teaspoon ground red chile

2 teaspoons cayenne pepper

2 teaspoons freshly ground white pepper

1 tablespoon hot Hungarian paprika

1 teaspoon salt

1 tablespoon dried Mexican oregano

1 tablespoon gently crushed cumin seeds

2 cups beer (lager, such as Corona)

4 fresh serrano chiles, seeded and chopped

2 tablespoons red wine vinegar

2 tablespoons shaved bittersweet chocolate or unsweetened cocoa powder

1/2 teaspoon Tabasco sauce

1 tablespoon firmly packed brown sugar

1/4 cup masa harina (Mexican corn flour)

———— • ————

1. In a large casserole or Dutch oven, heat the bacon drippings or beef kidney suet over medium-high heat until melted. Brown the meat with 2 tablespoons of the chili powder and the granulated garlic, in batches if necessary, about 5 minutes. Turn the heat off and return all the cooked beef to the casserole if you cooked in batches.

2. Place the dried chiles in a small saucepan with the water, cover, and bring to a gentle boil. Reduce the heat to low, and simmer, covered, until soft, 20 minutes. Drain, reserving the cooking water. Place the chiles in a food processor with 2 to 4 tablespoons of the reserved cooking water and process into a smooth paste and until there is no evidence of any pieces of pepper skin.

3. Mix the chile puree into the beef, add 2 cups of the beef broth, and bring to a boil over high heat. Reduce the heat to low, cover, and slowly simmer for 30 minutes.

4. Stir the onion powder, garlic, garlic powder, red chile, cayenne pepper, white pepper, paprika, salt, oregano, cumin, the remaining 2 tablespoons of chili powder, the beer, and the remaining 1 cup of beef broth into the casserole. Bring to a boil, and reduce the heat to low. Add the serranos, vinegar, chocolate, Tabasco, and brown sugar, cover, and simmer for 45 minutes.

5. Stir a ladle full of broth with the masa harina in a small bowl until there are no lumps. Add this mixture to the casserole, and stir. Cook, uncovered, over the lowest possible heat, using a heat diffuser if necessary, until the meat is very tender and the gravy is thick, 1 1/2 to 2 hours. Stir occasionally so that the mixture doesn't stick to the bottom of the casserole. If the chili con carne is too thick, thin it with small amounts of boiling water. Serve immediately, or even better, refrigerate it overnight and serve it reheated the next day.

Makes 6 servings

ROPA VIEJA FROM PUERTO RICO

ROPA VIEJA MEANS "OLD CLOTHES," AND IT is also the name of a stew found throughout Spanish-speaking Latin America. It is popular in Mexico, where a recipe might be a little more elaborate than this Puerto Rican one, perhaps containing chiles as well. In Panama they make *ropa vieja* with flank steak, as they do in Cuba, where skirt steak is also popular. The reason flank steak, skirt steak, or a stewing meat is used in this dish is because the meat shreds easily after cooking and therefore resembles the tattered rags referred to in the name *ropa vieja*.

For this recipe you can use any of those, but if you choose beef chuck, you must precook it until you can shred it with two forks. To precook the beef chuck, brown it in some lard first and cook it for 3 hours in a court bouillon of water, onion, bay leaf, and parsley. Or use the skirt steak or flank steak, and avoid this step altogether. This stew is very nice with French fries or rice.

2 pounds cooked beef chuck or raw skirt steak or flank steak, trimmed of any large pieces of fat
1 teaspoon salt, or to taste
1 teaspoon freshly ground cumin seeds
3 large garlic cloves, finely chopped
2 tablespoons finely chopped beef suet or unsalted butter
2 large, ripe tomatoes, peeled, seeded, and chopped
2 green bell peppers, seeded and chopped
2 medium-size onions, chopped
1 tablespoon capers, drained
1/2 cup water or dry red wine

1. Season the cooked beef or raw steak with the salt, cumin, and garlic and set aside.

2. In a casserole, melt the suet over medium-high heat. Cook the tomatoes, peppers, and onions, stirring, until soft and beginning to stick to the pan, about 10 minutes. Add the meat, capers, and water, then reduce the heat to low and cook until the meat is very tender and can be shredded apart by pulling with two forks, about 1 1/2 hours.

Makes 4 servings

ROPA VIEJA FROM CUBA

THE MAIN INGREDIENT OF THIS DISH IS beef, usually flank steak or skirt steak, but some cooks use chuck too. The meat is stewed, then shredded along the grain and cooked in an aromatic tomato sauce. One might hear the expression *carne ripiada*, literally "shredded meat," to describe this dish. But that is only the name of the meat; the name of the finished dish is *ropa vieja*, "old clothes," as in tattered rags. In Cuba, they serve this with rice and black beans and fried plantains, while in Haiti it is served with *riz et pois*, rice and peas. *Ropa vieja* is also known throughout most of Central America in various other versions. In this recipe, homemade annatto oil is used to fry the *sofrito*, the mixture of finely chopped vegetables that is the foundation of the sauce. Annatto (*achiote* in Spanish) is a rusty red dried seed of a tropical American tree. It is available in Latin American and some Oriental markets, or try the sources listed at the back of the book. It may also be available in your local supermarket, tucked away with the "Mexican" or "International" foods.

One 1½- to 2-pound flank steak
2 large onions, 1 coarsely chopped and 1 finely chopped
1 bay leaf
1 tablespoon salt
Freshly ground black pepper to taste
2½ quarts water
¼ cup annatto oil (see recipe in Note on page 54)
2 garlic cloves, finely chopped
2 small green bell peppers, seeded and finely chopped
1 serrano chile, seeded and finely chopped
1 large carrot, finely chopped
6 medium-size, firm, ripe tomatoes (about 2 pounds), cut in half, seeds squeezed out, and grated against the largest holes of a grater down to the peel
⅛ teaspoon ground cinnamon
4 cloves, ground in a mortar
1 tablespoon capers, rinsed, drained, and chopped if large
1 whole canned pimiento, drained and finely chopped

---

1. Put the flank steak in a heavy 4- to 5-quart casserole, add the coarsely chopped onion, bay leaf, 2 teaspoons of the salt, and a pinch of pepper, and pour in the water. It should cover the steak by at least 2 inches; if necessary, add more water. Bring to a boil over high heat, reduce the heat to low. Partially cover the casserole, and simmer until the meat shows no resistance when pierced with the point of a sharp knife, about 1½ hours.

2. Transfer the steak to a place to cool. Strain the cooking liquid through a fine-mesh strainer set over a bowl, and discard the onion and bay leaf. When the steak is cool enough to handle, cut it along the grain into ¼-inch-thick strips and slice the strips crosswise into 2-inch-long pieces. Set the meat and cooking liquid aside. Clean the casserole and reuse for the next step.

3. Pour the annatto oil into the casserole and heat it over medium heat until a light haze forms. Add the finely chopped onion, garlic, bell peppers, serrano, and carrot and cook until the vegetables are soft, stirring frequently and making sure they don't burn or stick to the casserole, 5 to 6 minutes. Stir in the tomatoes, cinnamon, cloves, the remaining 1 teaspoon of salt, and a dash of pepper.

4. Return the meat to the casserole along with 1½ cups of the reserved cooking liquid and cook over medium heat, uncovered, until most of the liquid in the pan evaporates and the mixture is thick enough to hold its shape lightly on the spoon, stirring occasionally, about 1½ hours. Transfer to a heated platter or serving bowl, sprinkle the capers and pimiento on top, and serve.

Makes 4 servings

Note: To make annatto oil, heat ¼ cup of vegetable oil in a small skillet over medium heat until a light haze forms. Stir in ¼ cup annatto (achiote) seeds, reduce the heat a bit, and cover. Simmer for 1 minute. Remove the pan from the heat, uncover, and let the oil cool to room temperature. Strain the annatto oil through a fine-mesh strainer into a jar, cover tightly with plastic wrap, and refrigerate until ready to use. It will keep indefinitely. Discard the seeds before using. Makes about ½ cup.

BEEF, POTATO, AND CORN ON THE COB STEW FROM COLOMBIA

THIS COLOMBIAN STEW, CALLED *COCIDO bogotano*, is served in Bogotá. It is made with fresh corn on the cob, which is cut into 2-inch lengths. The potatoes, carrots, and celery are all cut up into sticks to cook in the stew. There is not much meat used, but feel free to double it if you like. The spicing, too, is light and not overpowering, just enough to give the simmering stew a delightful taste. Serve with steamed rice and corn tortillas. This recipe is adapted from one in the volume of the Time-Life *Cooking of the World* series on Latin America.

2 tablespoons extra virgin olive oil

1 small onion, coarsely chopped

1 medium-size, ripe tomato, peeled, seeded, and coarsely chopped

1 pound boneless stew beef, preferably chuck, trimmed of any large pieces of fat and cut into 1½-inch cubes

1 small bay leaf

1 teaspoon freshly ground cumin seeds

½ teaspoon dried oregano

¼ teaspoon turmeric

3 large garlic cloves, finely chopped

1 teaspoon salt

4 black peppercorns

1½ cups cold water

1 teaspoon cider vinegar

1/2 pound boiling potatoes, peeled, cut lengthwise into 1/4-inch-thick slices, then cut into 1/2-inch-wide strips

2 medium-size carrots, sliced lengthwise 1/4 inch thick, then cut crosswise into 1/2-inch-long strips

4 celery stalks, cut into 2-inch lengths

1/2 cup fresh or frozen peas

2 ears corn, cut into 2-inch pieces

1. In a large casserole, heat the oil over medium heat. Cook the onion until translucent, stirring frequently, about 5 minutes. Add the tomato and cook for 3 minutes, then add the beef, bay leaf, cumin, oregano, turmeric, garlic, salt, and peppercorns. Stir, then add the water and vinegar. Bring to a boil, then reduce the heat to very low, cover, and simmer for 1 1/2 hours.

2. Add the potatoes, carrots, and celery and stir. Cover and continue to cook for 1 hour. Add the peas and corn, cover, and cook until the beef is tender and the vegetables are soft, about 20 minutes. Check the seasoning and serve.

Makes 4 servings

STEWS WITH VEAL

Veal stews are made less frequently than beef stews, but there are some great ones. Take, for instance, the famous Ossobuco alla Milanese (page 66), a stew of veal shank that cooks in a rich tomato ragout until the meat falls from the bone. You eat it, marrow and all, with a powerful aromatic seasoning of finely chopped parsley, anchovies, garlic, and lemon zest called *gremolada*. Braised Veal Brisket with Pureed Potatoes (page 64) is nothing but French comfort food. The veal braises slowly with white wine and carrots. No stew book is complete without a Hungarian paprikash, and the one on page 76 will remind you of Budapest, I think. For a truly extraordinary stew, try the Catalan Fricandeau of Veal (page 59), a stew that cooks in a gravy made of onions, carrots, celery, chicken or veal broth, dried porcini mushrooms, tomatoes, and brandy and then is finished by stirring in a pesto made of garlic, almonds, saffron, Amaretti di Saronno cookies, and some white wine.

FRICANDEAU OF VEAL

A FRICANDEAU IS A LARDED VEAL ROAST braised in its own juices. The word derives from French cuisine, in which a *fricandeau* refers to sliced veal rump braised in white wine. It can also refer to fish cooked in this way. According to the Catalan gastronome Nèstor Luján, this preparation, called *fricandó de vedella* in Catalan, has a long history. The word *fricandó* was first used in 1767 to describe a dish made of chicken. But the word is obviously related to the French word that derives from fricassee. In Esteban de Terrerros y Pando's *Diccionario castellano con las voces de ciencias y artes y sus correspondondientas en las 3 lenguas francesa, latina, e italiana* the word is traced to a mention in 1552 of "a piece of larded veal cooked in its own juice and served on top of sorrel."

In this preparation, a Catalonian seasoning called a *picada* is used. A *picada* is an aromatic mixture of finely chopped or mashed ingredients, including nuts, which enhances and binds sauces. Also called for in the original recipe are *carquinyoli*, hard glazed cookies made of flour, eggs, sugar, and almonds. In its place I use Amaretti di Saronno cookies, which work very well. The *sofregit* mentioned in step 3 is the same thing as an Italian *soffritto* (see page 60). This recipe is adapted from the Restaurant Molí de la Barita in Catalonia.

1 cup dried morels or porcini mushrooms

1³/4 pounds boneless veal stew meat, trimmed of any large pieces of fat and cut into 1¹/2-inch cubes

Salt and freshly ground black pepper to taste

Unbleached all-purpose flour for dredging

¹/4 cup extra virgin olive oil

¹/2 pound onions, finely chopped

2 carrots, finely chopped

1 celery stalk, finely chopped

2 ripe tomatoes, cut in half, seeds squeezed out, and grated against the largest holes of a grater down to the peel

1 quart veal broth (see page 3) or Chicken Broth (page 181)

2 bay leaves

¹/2 cup brandy

1 lemon slice, peel and pith removed

FOR THE PICADA:

2 garlic cloves, peeled

10 blanched almonds, toasted lightly in a preheated 350°F oven and ground in a food processor

Pinch of saffron threads

2 Amaretti di Saronno cookies

2 tablespoons dry white wine

1. Soak the dried mushrooms in tepid water to cover for 15 minutes. Drain, saving ¹/4 cup of the soaking liquid, and set aside.

2. Season the veal with salt and pepper. Dredge the veal in the flour, tapping off any excess. In a large skillet, heat the olive oil over medium-high heat. Brown the veal until golden on all sides, 4 to 5 minutes. Transfer the veal to a casserole.

3. In the same skillet, make the *sofregit* by adding the onion, carrots, and celery and cooking until the vegetables look soft, stirring and scraping the bottom of the skillet to get up any browned bits, 5 to 6 minutes. Add the tomatoes and cook for 1 minute. Add 1½ cups of the broth and cook until bubbling and reduced by a quarter, about 5 minutes.

4. Transfer the *sofregit* to the casserole with the veal and add the remaining 2½ cups of broth, the bay leaves, brandy, and lemon slice. Turn the heat to medium and cook, uncovered, until the veal is tender, stirring frequently so the gravy doesn't stick to the bottom of the casserole, about 1 hour. Reduce the heat if the liquid is evaporating quickly. Cover the casserole and continue to cook for another 30 minutes, stirring frequently to avoid anything sticking to the bottom of the pan. Add the mushrooms and cook, uncovered, until the veal is very tender, another 30 minutes.

5. Meanwhile, make the *picada* by pounding the garlic, almonds, saffron, and cookies together in a mortar with a pestle until they form a paste. Slowly incorporate the wine into the *picada*, then add the *picada* to the veal stew. Cook for 1 minute, and serve immediately.

———●———

Makes 4 servings

WHAT'S A *SOFREGIT* OR *SOFFRITTO*?

———●———

Sofregit and *soffritto* are the same thing, the first being a Catalan word and the second an Italian word. Basically, both are the beginning point of a sauce or more involved dish. Both words derive from the word meaning to fry very gently (to underfry). The technique consists of sautéing very finely chopped onions and other ingredients in olive oil. These other ingredients may include celery, carrots, peppers, garlic, and herbs. Once the *soffritto* is ready, the remaining ingredients constituting the sauce go in, such as tomatoes.

VEAL, POTATO, AND MUSHROOM STEW FOR THE SPRINGTIME

I N THE SPRING, FRENCH HOUSEWIVES ARE likely to make their family a simple *sauté de veau printanier* with new carrots and new potatoes. In this *sauté de veau*, I also like to add mushrooms, which I think makes for an earthy stew. A cook could use the common button mushrooms and it would be just fine, but mixing mushrooms or using the more expensive chanterelles or porcini makes a fabulous stew. Pay attention also to the potatoes you use. New potatoes, whether the Yukon Gold called for here, or some other kind, like a fingerling potato, result in an improved stew. One could also enhance the stew by using a *fond brun de veau* or rich veal broth (see Variation on page 3) instead of water.

———•———

Unbleached all-purpose flour for dredging
Salt and freshly ground black pepper to taste
2 pounds boneless veal stew meat, trimmed of
    any large pieces of fat and cut into bite-size
    pieces
¹/4 cup (¹/2 stick) unsalted butter
2 medium-size white onions, chopped
¹/2 cup dry white wine
1 pound Yukon Gold potatoes, peeled and cut
    into chunks
2 carrots, cut into chunks
1 pound portobello mushrooms, stems discarded,
    caps brushed clean, halved, and thinly sliced
    crosswise
1 bouquet garni, consisting of 6 sprigs each fresh
    parsley, tarragon, and summer savory or
    thyme, 10 celery leaves, and 1 bay leaf, tied in
    cheesecloth
1¹/2 cups water
¹/2 pound green beans, ends trimmed and cut
    into 1-inch-long pieces

———•———

1. Season the flour with salt and pepper and dredge the veal in the flour, tapping off any excess. In a casserole, melt the butter over medium-high heat until light brown. Then brown the veal with the onions, seasoning with salt and pepper, 8 to 10 minutes. Add the wine and stir.

2. Add the potatoes, carrots, mushrooms, and bouquet garni and pour in the water. If the green beans are old, add them as well. If they are young, add them when there is only 1 hour of cooking time left. Bring the water to a boil, and season with salt and pepper. Reduce the heat to low and simmer until the veal is tender, about 2 hours. Remove and discard the bouquet garni. Check the seasonings and serve immediately.

———•———

Makes 4 servings

VEAL RUMP STEW
IN THE STYLE OF THE OLD PRESBYTERY

THIS NINETEENTH-CENTURY RECIPE IS from Anjou, whose capital, Angers, sits in the middle of fertile land and excellent vineyards in the Loire Valley. The traditional home cooking of Anjou was simple and not ostentatious. This recipe is adapted from the book *Recettes des provinces de France*, which was produced in honor of Curnonsky, the great nineteenth-century French epicure and food writer of the Belle Époque who was an Angevin native. Curnonsky commented that "Anjou is the paradise of dining in tranquility." I'm not sure he had this dish in mind, but it is very pleasing, velvety smooth, and perfect for a fall evening. The original recipe, *cul de veau à la mode du vieux presbytère*, is a wonderfully quirky nineteenth-century preparation that I can't imagine anyone making anymore in France.

But I think it's a recipe worth saving, so give it a try. The veal rump or butt—and shoulder roast can be used if your supermarket doesn't have rump—is rubbed with curry powder and wrapped in bacon, then slowly simmered for hours in Loire Valley white wine and beef broth. It's finished with mushrooms and tarragon, and I suspect you will think you died and went to heaven when you taste it. As an accompaniment you may want to try buttered egg noodles, plain rice, or parsleyed potatoes.

One 4-pound boneless veal rump (preferably) or
   veal shoulder
Salt and freshly ground black pepper to taste
1 tablespoon mild curry powder
6 ounces smoked bacon, 4 ounces thinly sliced
   and 2 ounces diced
$1/2$ cup (1 stick) unsalted butter
$1/4$ pound cooked ham, diced
1 medium-size onion, chopped
1 large carrot, chopped
$1/4$ cup unbleached all-purpose flour
1 cup dry white wine, preferably from the Loire,
   such as a Vouvray
1 cup Beef Broth (page 3)
$11/4$ pounds fresh morels or small button
   mushrooms
1 tablespoon finely chopped fresh tarragon leaves
3 large egg yolks
$1/2$ cup heavy cream

---

1. Rub the veal rump with salt, pepper, and half the curry powder. Wrap it up with the sliced bacon and tie off in 3 or 4 places with kitchen twine so the bacon doesn't fall off.

2. In a heavy casserole, melt the butter with the diced bacon and ham over medium heat until the bacon is crisp, stirring occasionally, about 15 minutes. Remove the bacon and ham and set aside, keeping them warm. Increase the heat to high and brown the veal on all sides, 8 to 10 minutes. Don't worry about the bottom of the casserole becoming encrusted, because the particles will all come up when you deglaze with the liquid. Add the onion and carrot and almost all of the remaining curry powder. Sprinkle with the flour and continue to cook until the onion is golden, 2 to 5 minutes. Add the wine and beef broth, and season with salt. Cover, reduce the heat to very low, using a heat diffuser if necessary, and simmer, turning the meat occasionally, until the veal is almost fork-tender but a knife is still needed to cut a small piece, $2 1/2$ to 3 hours.

3. Add the reserved bacon and ham and the morels. Season with salt, pepper, and the remaining curry powder. Add the tarragon, stir well, and cover again. Cook until tender, about another $1 1/2$ hours. During the last 45 minutes of cooking, uncover to let the liquid evaporate and the stew become saucier.

4. Remove the veal and discard the twine and larding bacon. Transfer to a serving platter, slice, and keep warm. Mix the egg yolks with the cream and stir into the casserole off the heat. Continue stirring to blend the ingredients, bring to a quick boil, and turn the heat off immediately. Ladle the mushrooms and sauce over the veal, and serve.

Makes 6 servings

BLANQUETTE OF VEAL IN THE OLD STYLE

THE LATE ELIZABETH DAVID, AUTHOR OF *French Provincial Cooking*, is universally admired. Her writing is enjoyable, but frankly I find her snobbishness annoying and much of what she says baffling. I've read what she has to say about paella, and I think she's off base. (She says that paella is the Spanish equivalent of risotto, its great characteristic being the diversity of ingredients and the combination of chicken and shellfish. Not true!) I disagree entirely with her take on making bouillabaisse (page 227) outside of the Mediterranean. And what does she say about blanquette of veal? "To my taste this dish with its creamy white sauce is rather insipid." I couldn't disagree more. You must make this famous old dish from the French countryside called *blanquette de veau à l'ancienne* and see for yourself. Remember that it's not a kick-in-your-pants spicy stew, but rather a tranquil, satisfying stew that delivers.

As we know by the name—*blanquette* is related to the word for "white," *blanc*—nothing in this stew browns. The explanation in Alan Davidson's *The Oxford Companion to Food* that the word is related to the English "blanket" is nonsense. *Blanquette* was first used by the famous French agriculturist Olivier de Serres in 1600 in relation to white wine, *vin blanc*, and the etymological root of the word derives from the Provençal *blanqueto*, a diminutive of *blanc*.

In the preparation of a blanquette of veal, some cooks use veal breast, others veal shoulder; some cooks don't use the bones and others do. Some cooks try to achieve a thicker sauce than I have here. This recipe is the result of my reading of several recipe sources, and my recollection of the numerous blanquettes I had when I lived in France as a child and when I traveled as an adult. I'm a big believer in using bones when stewing, and that is reflected in my recipe. Serve the stew with buttered wide egg noodles or with a timbale of rice.

***

One 4-pound veal breast
1 medium-size onion, peeled and studded with 2 cloves
1 leek (white and light green parts only), split lengthwise, leaving the leaves attached to the stem, and washed well
2 carrots, cut into thirds
1 garlic clove, crushed
1 bouquet garni, consisting of 3 or 4 sprigs each fresh parsley, thyme, and tarragon and 1 bay leaf, tied in cheesecloth
Salt and freshly ground white pepper to taste
2 quarts water
2 dozen pearl onions (about 1¼ pounds), peeled (see page 28)
½ pound small chanterelle or button mushrooms, brushed clean
¾ cup heavy cream
3 large egg yolks
1 tablespoon fresh lemon juice

***

1. Put the veal breast in a large casserole with the onion, leek, carrots, garlic, and bouquet garni. Season with salt and pepper and cover with the water. Bring to a gentle boil over medium heat, about 20 minutes. Reduce the heat so the water is only shimmering and cook mostly, but not completely, covered, until the veal is almost tender, about 2 1/2 hours.

2. Remove the veal from the casserole, cut the meat from the bone in chunks, discard the bone, and set the meat aside. Pour the broth through a strainer (a chinois, or conical strainer, would be ideal), and discard the vegetables. Line the strainer with cheesecloth and strain again. Return the broth to the casserole, check the seasonings, and add the veal. Bring to a boil, and add the pearl onions and mushrooms. Reduce the heat to low, cover, and simmer until everything is tender, about 30 minutes.

3. Transfer the veal, onions, and mushrooms to a bowl and keep warm. Increase the heat to high and reduce the broth by a little more than half.

4. In a medium-size bowl, beat together the cream, egg yolks, lemon juice, and a little broth, whisking all the time. Reduce the heat under the casserole to medium and pour in the sauce, whisking constantly and making sure that it never comes to a boil (otherwise the eggs will congeal) by regulating the heat as necessary. Continue whisking until the sauce is close to a custard, but still liquidy, about 10 minutes. Take the casserole off the heat, continue to whisk a little, and season with salt and pepper, if necessary. Return the veal, onions, and mushrooms to the casserole. Cover and let sit for 5 to 10 minutes to mingle the flavors, then serve.

Makes 4 servings

BRAISED VEAL BRISKET WITH PUREED POTATOES

VEAL BRISKET IS NOT ALL THAT COMMON, but whenever my supermarket carries it, I like to make this dish. The brisket is a cut of meat that is very tough and it needs long hours of simmering to break it down and make it tender. By then it will be very flavorful and appetizing. Browning the veal in onions, olive oil, and marrow provides a more intense flavor than usual. This recipe is typical of many stews and braises to be found in the Dauphine region north of Provence.

2 tablespoons unsalted butter or extra virgin olive oil
2 tablespoons veal or beef bone marrow
One 1 1/4-pound veal brisket
1 red onion, sliced and separated into rings
1 medium-size, ripe tomato, peeled, seeded, and chopped
2 cups dry white wine
1 sprig fresh mint
Salt and freshly ground black pepper to taste
3 ounces baby carrots
3 cups Mashed Potatoes with Garlic (recipe follows)
1 cup freshly grated Parmigiano-Reggiano cheese
Milk or heavy cream, as needed
2 tablespoons finely chopped fresh mint leaves

1. In a casserole, heat 1 tablespoon of the butter with the bone marrow over medium-high heat. Add the veal and onion and sauté until the veal is browned on all sides and the onion is soft, about 10 minutes. Add the tomato, wine, and mint sprig and season with salt and pepper. Reduce the heat to low and cook for 1¼ hours, covered. Add the carrots and cook, uncovered, for 1 hour more.

2. Meanwhile, prepare the potatoes (see below). Mix the remaining 1 tablespoon of butter into the mashed potatoes and warm them in a saucepan over medium heat or in a microwave for 1 minute on high. Stir in the cheese and enough milk so the potatoes have the consistency of Cream of Wheat cereal, soft and smooth. Serve alongside the veal, ladling some sauce from the veal onto the potatoes. Sprinkle with the chopped mint.

Makes 2 to 3 servings

MASHED POTATOES WITH GARLIC

One would think mashed potatoes would be the easiest thing in the world to make, but I've had enough goopy, heavy, unappetizing mashed potatoes to believe that it is not universally known how to make them.

1¼ pounds boiling potatoes, peeled and cut into 2-inch pieces

¼ cup (½ stick) unsalted butter
Salt to taste
6 to 8 tablespoons warm milk, as needed
1 or 2 cloves garlic, to your taste, finely chopped

1. Place the potatoes in a medium-size saucepan and cover with cold water. Turn the heat to medium and bring to a boil, about 20 minutes. Cook for about another 20 minutes, until a skewer can glide easily into the center of a potato. Immediately drain the potatoes and pass them through a food mill or mash them thoroughly with a potato masher. Don't mash them in a food processor or they will become gummy.

2. Return the potatoes to the saucepan and over very low heat, beat in the butter, a small slice at a time. Season with salt, then begin to stir in the warm milk, a tablespoon at a time. Add the garlic, taste, and correct the seasonings and alter the consistency by adding more milk if desired. Mashed or pureed potatoes must be eaten immediately; they do not "hold" well.

Makes 3 servings; 3 to 4 cups

RAGOUT OF "CINNAMONY" VEAL WITH TOMATO AND CREAM

I'VE COMBINED TWO SEPARATE CONCEPTS in this ragout. The first is seasoning the veal with cinnamon, a technique not that unusual in the Middle Eastern cooking of the Levant. But then the veal simmers in a rich tomato-and-cream sauce, which has the hallmarks of housewife cookery of Haute-Provence. This is quite a luscious preparation and is best served with a simple salad or green vegetable.

Unbleached all-purpose flour for dredging
Salt to taste
2 pounds boneless veal stew meat, trimmed of
  any large pieces of fat and cubed
3 tablespoons unsalted butter
1 tablespoon extra virgin olive oil
2 medium-size onions, finely chopped
2 celery stalks, finely chopped
1¹/4 cups dry white wine
1 cup water, or more, as needed
3 tablespoons finely chopped fresh parsley leaves
2 cups Quick Tomato Sauce (page 351)
2 cinnamon sticks
1¹/4 pounds small Yukon Gold potatoes
¹/4 cup heavy cream
Freshly ground black pepper to taste

1. Season the flour with salt and dredge the veal in the flour, patting off any excess. In a large casserole, melt the butter with the olive oil over high heat. Once the butter stops sizzling, brown the veal on all sides, about 5 minutes. Add the onions and celery and cook, stirring, until soft, about 4 minutes. Add the wine and scrape up the brown bits on the bottom of the casserole. Bring to a boil and reduce the wine by about half, stirring occasionally, about 3 minutes, Add the water, parsley, tomato sauce, and cinnamon sticks. Bring to a boil, then reduce the heat to very low, using a heat diffuser if necessary. Cook until the veal is tender, 1¹/2 to 2 hours.

2. Add the potatoes and cream, and taste and adjust the salt and pepper. Cover and cook until the potatoes are very tender, stirring often and thinning the stew if necessary with more water, about 1 hour. Discard the cinnamon sticks and serve.

Makes 4 servings

OSSOBUCO ALLA MILANESE

OSSOBUCO IS ONE OF THE BEST KNOWN Italian dishes. It is usually associated with the city of Milan, in Lombardy, and probably was born in one of the many *osterie*, neighborhood bar-restaurants that cater mostly to locals in big cities. Ossobuco refers to veal shank, a succulent piece of meat surrounding a wide, marrow-filled bone. The shank is cross-cut and then braised in a rich tomato ragout for hours, until the meat is falling off the bone. Once the shank has stewed for a long time, an aromatic mixture called a *gremolada*, made of finely chopped lemon zest, garlic, parsley, and anchovies, is stirred into the ragout. This seasoning is what elevates ossobuco to its glories. Then, for the final treat, one digs out the marrow in the center bone with a long-handled little spoon made just for this task. Ossobuco is traditionally served with *risotto alla milanese*, saffron risotto.

———————●———————

7 tablespoons unsalted butter
6 slices veal shank, each about ¹/₂ pound,
   4 inches in diameter, and 2 inches thick
Unbleached all-purpose flour for dredging
¹/₂ cup dry white wine
1 pound ripe tomatoes, peeled, seeded, and
   chopped
Salt and freshly ground black pepper to taste
FOR THE GREMOLADA:
1 garlic clove, finely chopped
Grated zest of ¹/₂ lemon
¹/₄ cup finely chopped fresh parsley leaves
2 salted anchovy fillets, rinsed

Risotto alla Milanese (optional; recipe follows)

———————●———————

1. In a large skillet, melt the butter over medium-high heat. Meanwhile, dredge the veal in the flour, patting off any excess. Once the butter has stopped sizzling, brown the veal

shanks on both sides, about 10 minutes. Pour in the wine and continue to cook until the wine is nearly evaporated, scraping the bottom of the skillet to pick up any browned bits, about another 10 minutes. Add the tomatoes, season with salt and pepper, and turn the veal a few times to mix. Cover, reduce the heat to very low, and cook until the meat is nearly falling off the bone, 2¹/₂ to 3 hours.

2. About 30 minutes before the veal is done, start the risotto, if desired. Meanwhile, in a small bowl, mix together the garlic, lemon zest, parsley, and anchovies. Add the seasoning mixture to the skillet, turn the veal, and stir the ragout several times to distribute the flavors. Serve immediately, accompanied by the risotto, if you wish.

———————●———————

Makes 4 servings

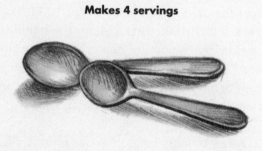

RISOTTO ALLA MILANESE

Saffron risotto is the traditional accompaniment to *ossobuco* (page 66). Although *risotto alla milanese* is named for the industrial city of Milan, in northern Italy, as early as the sixteenth century, the Renaissance chef Cristoforo da Messisburgo said he thought the dish was born in Sicily.

6 tablespoons (³/₄ stick) unsalted butter

1 small onion, finely chopped

2 tablespoons veal bone marrow

¹/₄ cup plus 2 tablespoons dry white wine

2 cups Arborio rice

5 cups veal broth or Beef Broth (page 3), at a
very gentle boil

1¹/₂ teaspoons salt

¹/₄ teaspoon ground saffron steeped in 3
tablespoons warm water

³/₄ cup freshly grated Parmigiano-Reggiano,
plus extra for sprinkling

1. Melt half of the butter in a heavy saucepan over medium heat. When it stops sizzling, cook the onion and veal bone marrow until soft, stirring, 7 to 8 minutes. Pour in the wine and cook until it is nearly evaporated. Add the Arborio rice and cook for about 2 minutes to coat the grains. Add 1 cup of the broth and the salt and cook, stirring, until the liquid is absorbed. Add another cup of broth (but no more salt) and continue in this manner until 5 cups of broth have been absorbed or until the rice is between *al dente* and tender.

2. A few minutes before the rice is done, add the saffron and water and stir. Then stir in the remaining 3 tablespoons of butter and the Parmigiano. Turn off the heat, cover the saucepan, and let the risotto sit for 5 minutes before serving. Serve with more Parmigiano, if desired.

Serves 4

OSSOBUCO IN SAFFRON AND FENNEL RAGOUT
WITH CAVATELLI, PINE NUTS, AND ALMONDS

THE CLASSIC *OSSOBUCO ALLA MILANESE* (page 66) is veal shank braised in a rich tomato and wine ragout, served with a *conza*, or seasoning mixture, of finely chopped lemon zest, parsley, anchovies, and garlic. It is the best known of the ossobuco dishes. *Ossobuco* simply means "veal shank," a cut from the lower portion of the leg below the knee. This recipe is a complex twist on the classic *ossobuco* of Milan. It's very good and quite satisfying in the wintertime, when using canned tomatoes is the norm. If you would like to be a bit European about it all, then serve the dish in two courses, first the *cavatelli* (see page 69), followed by the *ossobuco*. This stew reminds me vaguely of what would happen in a stew if there were two cooks, one from the sophisticated northern city of Milan with its sense of *alta cucina* and another from the slightly baroque Sicilian city of Palermo. Serve the meat as a second course with the reserved nuts sprinkled on top and some crusty Italian or French bread.

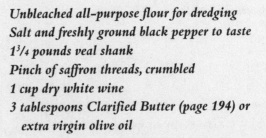

Unbleached all-purpose flour for dredging

Salt and freshly ground black pepper to taste

1³/₄ pounds veal shank

Pinch of saffron threads, crumbled

1 cup dry white wine

3 tablespoons Clarified Butter (page 194) or
extra virgin olive oil

2 tablespoons slivered blanched almonds
2 tablespoons pine nuts
1 tablespoon veal bone marrow
1 fennel stalk, with its leaves, finely chopped
2 shallots, finely chopped
1 celery stalk, finely chopped
3 garlic cloves, finely chopped
One 28-ounce can crushed tomatoes
1/2 teaspoon grated lemon zest
1 teaspoon fennel seeds
3/4 pound **cavatelli**
Freshly grated Parmigiano-Reggiano for
sprinkling

---

1. Season the flour with salt and pepper and dredge the veal shanks in the flour, patting off any excess.

2. In a small bowl, steep the saffron in the wine.

3. In a small skillet, melt 1 tablespoon of the clarified butter over high heat until nearly smoking. Brown the almonds, about 1 minute, and add the pine nuts, stirring until golden, about 1 more minute. Remove the nuts with a slotted spoon and set aside. To whatever remains in the skillet, add the bone marrow and leave to melt off the heat.

4. In a large skillet or casserole, melt the remaining 2 tablespoons of clarified butter over medium heat until it begins to turn brown. Then brown the veal shanks on both sides along with the fennel, shallots, celery, and garlic, stirring the vegetables often, 8 to 10 minutes. Pour in the wine and saffron and

reduce for 5 minutes. Add the tomatoes, lemon zest, and fennel seeds and season with salt and pepper. Stir well, reduce the heat to medium-low, cover, and cook for 1 hour. Reduce the heat to low and cook, covered, until the veal is nearly falling off the bone, about 1 more hour.

5. When the *ossobuco* is almost done, bring a large pot of abundantly salted water to a boil and cook the *cavatelli* until *al dente*. Drain and toss with several ladles full of sauce from the *ossobuco* and the marrow melted in the small skillet. Sprinkle with the Parmigiano and the reserved nuts and serve.

Makes 4 servings

CAVATELLI

Cavatelli, coin-shaped, flat pasta that is rolled up, is popular in southern Italy and Sicily. It derives its name from the verb *cavare,* "to pull away." The pasta dough is traditionally made only with hard wheat flour and water and is rolled out into long ropes that are cut off in segments to form small morsels. These are flattened into disks with the thumb, forming a pasta called *orecchiette* ("little ears"). These disks are rolled away in a quick movement with the thumb or a knife called a *rasaul,* doubling up on themselves to become *cavatelli.* If you can't quite picture how *cavatelli* are made, try renting the Francis Ford Coppola film *The Godfather, Part III,* where, in one erotic scene, the Corleone cousins make *cavatelli.*

VEAL SHANKS IN TOMATO SAUCE

THIS SOUTHERN ITALIAN *SPEZZATINO DI ossobuco al pomodoro* is as delicious as it is simple. (*Spezzatino* is a catch-all word for "stew.") The red wine, of course, enriches the stew, but I also like to add leftover cooked meats to the sauce. Once I added some leftover sliced meatballs and leftover roasted and sliced rabbit to the ragout, and it was even better. That is a typical way one uses leftovers in much Italian home cooking. Serve with some spaghetti.

3 1/2 pounds veal shanks
Unbleached all-purpose flour for dredging
5 tablespoons unsalted butter
1 large onion, finely chopped
1 celery stalk, finely chopped
10 large fresh basil leaves
1 cup dry red wine
2 pounds ripe tomatoes, peeled, seeded, and
   chopped
2 cups mixed cut-up leftover meat (optional; see
   headnote)
1/2 cup leftover tomato sauce, or tomato paste
   mixed with enough water to achieve the
   consistency of sauce
Salt and freshly ground black pepper to taste

1. Dredge the veal in the flour, tapping off any excess. In a large casserole, melt the butter over medium-high heat. When it stops sizzling, brown the veal on all sides with the onion, celery, and basil.

2. Add the wine and reduce by half. Add the tomatoes, any leftover meats, and tomato sauce. Season with salt and pepper, and reduce the heat to very low, using a diffuser if necessary. Cook until the veal is completely tender and falling off the bone, about 6 hours.

Makes 4 to 6 servings with spaghetti

SPEZZATINI

Spezzatini are Italian stews, and there are many more than are in this book. *Spezzatino alla napoletana* is a veal stew made with red bell pepper, mushrooms, and tomatoes. *Spezzatino alla romana* is similar to the recipe on page 91 in that it too is made with beaten eggs and lemon juice. In a *spezzatino alla toscana*, pieces of veal are stewed in a tomato sauce with black olives and onions. *Spezzatino al prosciutto* is a veal stew cooked with tomatoes, wine, and cooked ham, while *spezzatino alla contadina* is an aromatic stew of veal chunks braised with olive oil, onions, tomatoes, herbs, olives, capers, anchovies, and cheese. *Spezzatino alla paesana* is a country-style veal stew made with tomatoes, olive oil, onions, mushrooms, herbs, and cheese.

LA GENOVESA

THE NAME OF THIS STEW IS "THE Genoese," leading one to think that it is a native of the great Italian port city of Genoa. In fact, this stew is unknown in Genoa; it is a Neapolitan stew. It's not clear how it got its name, but in the fifteenth century, Genoese merchants were found in Naples, then under Spanish Aragonese rule, engaged in thriving businesses. They traded in bullion, textiles, wheat, and other commodities, and had even established hospices and churches for their community. They had insinuated themselves into many aspects of the life of the city, including somehow giving their name to this famous Neapolitan stew and macaroni dish. The name is meant to convey the rich kinds of dishes favored by this wealthy and powerful foreign merchant and financier class of Genoese who controlled the purse strings of so many cities in the Mediterranean during the Middle Ages. *La Genovesa* is made with macaroni or *maccharoncelli* (a smaller ridged kind of macaroni), beef or veal, prosciutto or pancetta, lots of onions, celery, carrot, marjoram, lard, Parmigiano cheese, and wine.

One 2-pound boneless veal shoulder roast
2 ounces pancetta, cut into strips
Salt to taste
2 tablespoons lard
1/4 cup (1/2 stick) unsalted butter
1/4 cup extra virgin olive oil
1 medium-size, ripe tomato, peeled, seeded, and chopped
3/4 pound onions, chopped
1 carrot, chopped
1 celery stalk, chopped
1 handful fresh basil leaves, chopped
Freshly ground black pepper to taste
2 cups Beef Broth or veal broth (page 3) or water
1 cup dry white wine
1 pound macaroni or maccharoncelli
1/2 cup freshly grated Parmigiano-Reggiano cheese

1. Lard the veal roast with the strips of pancetta using a larding needle (see page 16) or making holes with a thick skewer and stuffing them in. Season with salt. Tie the veal roast into a regular shape with some kitchen twine.

2. In a casserole, melt the lard, butter, and olive oil over high heat, then brown the veal on all sides, 3 to 4 minutes. Add the tomato, onions, carrot, celery, and basil and season with salt and pepper. Cook until the liquid is reduced somewhat and the onions are soft, about 8 minutes. Pour in the broth, and reduce the heat to medium-low. Cover and cook until the veal is firm, about 1 hour. Pour in the wine and cook, covered, until very tender, about another 1 1/2 hours. Remove the veal to a platter and keep warm. Turn the heat to high, and reduce the sauce by a quarter, about 15 minutes.

3. Pass the sauce through a food mill and return to the casserole. Add the veal to the sauce to moisten and heat for 10 minutes. Remove the veal to a cutting board, cut off the twine, and slice into serving portions.

4. Meanwhile, bring a large pot of abundantly salted water to a vigorous boil and add the pasta. Cook until *al dente* and drain well. Transfer the pasta to the casserole with the sauce, add the Parmigiano, and mix well.

5. Serve the pasta as a first course with some of the sauce, and the veal as a second course.

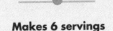

Makes 6 servings

BRAISED VEAL WITH WINE AND CAPERS FROM SARDINIA

THE USE OF VEAL IN SARDINIA IS RECENT, having become popular and more common after World War II. Traditionally, this preparation, which is sometimes called *vitello alla Sarda* or *vitello in casseruola*, was skewered in one piece and cooked very slowly for a long time over an open flame. In Sardinian, veal came to be called *mallòra*, meaning "heifer." Even younger calves, called *vitellini* in Italian, became known in Sardinia as *malloreddus*, the same name given to a special Sardinian form of tiny homemade gnocchi, which would make a good accompaniment for this dish. The recipe is quite nice because you hermetically seal the veal into the casserole with the wine, capers, and vegetables, and it becomes permeated with flavors as it braises.

2 tablespoons extra virgin olive oil
One 2¹/₂-pound boneless veal rump roast
Unbleached all-purpose flour for dredging
1 cup dry white wine
1 to 2 tablespoon capers, to your taste, drained, rinsed, and chopped if large
1 lemon slice, peel and pith removed
1 medium-size onion, coarsely chopped
¹/₂ cup loosely packed chopped fresh parsley leaves
2 large garlic cloves, finely chopped
Salt to taste
Flour paste rope (see page 9)

1. In a casserole that will fit the veal neatly, heat the olive oil over medium-high heat. Dredge the veal in the flour and pat off any excess. Brown the veal in the oil, about 5 minutes a side. Deglaze the casserole with the wine, scraping up any crusty brown bits from the bottom. Add the capers, lemon slice, onion, parsley, and garlic and season with salt. Reduce the heat to low.

2. Cover the top of the casserole with a sheet of aluminum foil, place the lid on top, and seal the lid to the casserole with the flour paste rope. Cook the veal, shaking the casserole now and then, until tender, 1¹/₂ to 2 hours. Do not remove the lid for at least 1¹/₂ hours.

3. When the veal is very tender, remove to a serving platter and keep warm by loosely covering with a sheet of aluminum foil. Turn the heat to high under the casserole and reduce the sauce a bit. Pass the sauce through a food mill or strainer. Slice the veal thinly and arrange on a serving platter. Pour the sauce over the veal and serve immediately.

Makes 6 servings

SARDINIAN VEAL STEW IN RED WINE

VEAL IS A RELATIVE NEWCOMER TO Sardinian cuisine, but the recipes for it are superlative examples of Sardinian taste. In this preparation called *vitello al vino*, "veal with wine," the veal is browned in lots of butter, which seems to indicate a return to an almost medieval style of cooking, and then it is slowly stewed in red wine and veal broth until very tender. If you have the time, you can make a broth from the veal bones after cutting off the meat, in which case see the Note below. Otherwise, use boneless veal and previously prepared veal broth.

½ cup (1 stick) unsalted butter
3 pounds veal shoulder on the bone or 2 pounds boneless veal shoulder, trimmed of any large pieces of fat and cut into small pieces
1 small onion, finely chopped
3 garlic cloves, finely chopped
¼ cup plus 1 tablespoon finely chopped fresh parsley leaves

Salt and freshly ground black pepper to taste
1 cup dry red wine
1 cup veal broth (see page 3 or Note below)
2 bay leaves
1 tablespoon unbleached all-purpose flour

1. In a casserole, melt 7 tablespoons of the butter over high heat. When it stops sizzling, brown the veal with the onion, garlic, and parsley, about 10 minutes. Lightly season with salt and pepper and pour in the wine. Let the wine evaporate over high heat until there is about ¼ cup in the casserole. Pour in the broth and add the bay leaves. Reduce the heat to low and simmer, partially covered, until the veal is very tender, 1½ to 2 hours.

2. Blend the flour with the remaining 1 tablespoon of butter, add to the sauce, and cook until the sauce is syrupy, about 10 more minutes. Serve immediately.

Makes 4 servings

Note: If you bought veal shoulder on the bone and want to make your own simple veal broth, put the veal bones, ¼ cup chopped leeks, 1 chopped small carrot, ½ cup chopped onions, 5 black peppercorns, and a bouquet garni of sprigs of fresh parsley, basil, and tarragon, plus 1 bay leaf in a large saucepan. Cover with 3 to 4 cups of water. Bring to a boil, and skim off the foam that forms on the surface until there is very little left. Reduce the heat to low and simmer for 4 hours. Strain through cheesecloth and use.

STRACOTTO
IN THE TUSCAN STYLE

PROPERLY CALLED *STRACOTTO DI VITELLO alla toscana*, this is the most famous of Tuscan stews. It is veal shoulder braised in the Tuscan style with fresh herbs such as rosemary, basil, and sage and aromatics such as carrots, garlic, celery, and prosciutto. There are different versions of *stracotto* and some cooks use the leftovers to stuff ravioli. Make a *stracotto*, and you will have a memorably delicious dinner. Because the veal shoulder is cut in two like a sandwich, you will want to ask the butcher to do this unless you find two like-sized pieces of veal shoulder.

3 pounds veal shoulder on the bone, in 2 equal pieces
2 garlic cloves, finely chopped
Leaves from 1 sprig fresh rosemary or tarragon, chopped
Salt
5 tablespoons extra virgin olive oil
1 medium-large onion, very finely chopped
2 ounces prosciutto, in one piece, very finely diced
1 celery stalk, very finely chopped
2 carrots, very finely chopped
10 large fresh basil leaves, very finely chopped
3 tablespoons finely chopped fresh parsley leaves
8 fresh sage leaves
1 cup dry red wine
3 cloves

1 pound ripe tomatoes, peeled, seeded, and pureed in a food processor or blender
Freshly ground black pepper to taste
Beef Broth (page 3) or water for moistening (optional)
¾ pound penne or macaroni
Freshly grated Parmigiano-Reggiano cheese for serving

1. Lay one piece of veal shoulder on a work surface and coat it with the chopped garlic and rosemary. Salt lightly and cover with the other piece of veal. Tie off the two pieces of veal with kitchen twine.

2. In a casserole, heat 3 tablespoons of the olive oil over medium-high heat. Brown the veal on both sides, 8 to 10 minutes in all. Reduce the heat to low and continue to cook for another 20 minutes.

3. Meanwhile, in a large skillet, heat the remaining 2 tablespoons of olive oil over medium heat. Cook the onion, prosciutto, celery, carrots, basil, parsley, and sage for 20 minutes, stirring occasionally. Add the wine and cook until it has nearly evaporated, about 12 minutes. Add the cloves and tomatoes and cook for 5 minutes.

4. Pass the sauce through a food mill or strainer into the casserole with the veal. Season with salt and pepper and stir. Reduce the heat under the casserole to low and cook, partially covered, until the meat is falling off the bone, about 2 hours. Moisten the sauce with beef broth or water if the liquid is getting too thick or drying out.

5. Remove the veal from the casserole and set aside, keeping it warm. Turn the heat to high and reduce the sauce by a quarter, about 5 minutes. Pour a ladle full or two of sauce over the piece of veal.

6. Meanwhile, bring a large pot of water to a rolling boil, salt abundantly, and add the pasta. Drain when *al dente*. Transfer the pasta to the sauce, toss, and serve immediately with Parmigiano. Serve the pasta, followed by the veal, cut into serving slices.

Makes 4 servings

STRACOTTO
IN THE STYLE OF FLORENCE

THERE ARE MANY VARIETIES OF *STRA-cotto*, which means "overcooked," such as this *stracotto di vitello alla fiorentina*, which comes from Florence, in Tuscany. Every family makes it a bit differently, although wine is always used and rump roast is the chosen meat in Florence. Serve with pasta or ravioli as a first course, using the sauce from the stew.

3 tablespoons extra virgin olive oil
3 tablespoons unsalted butter

One 3-pound veal rump roast, tied with kitchen twine if necessary to make it a uniform shape
¼ pound salt pork, finely chopped
1 medium-size onion, finely chopped
1 carrot, finely chopped
1 large parsnip, central core near stem end removed, if desired, peeled, and finely chopped
1 celery stalk, finely chopped
¾ cup dry white wine
2 tablespoons tomato paste dissolved in 1½ cups veal broth (see page 3) or Chicken Broth (page 181)
Salt and freshly ground black pepper

1. In a large casserole, heat the olive oil and butter together over medium-high heat and, once the butter stops sizzling, brown the meat on all sides, 6 to 7 minutes. Add the *soffritto* of salt pork, onion, carrot, parsnip, and celery and cook until soft, stirring, 4 to 5 minutes.

2. Add the wine, reduce the heat to low, and let the wine evaporate for 10 minutes, until it is nearly gone. Pour in the diluted tomato paste, season with salt and pepper, and stir a bit. Cover, reduce the heat to low, and simmer until the meat is very tender, turning and stirring occasionally, and scraping the sides and bottom, about 2 hours.

Makes 6 servings

A SHORT LESSON ON HUNGARIAN STEWS

Americans know goulash, but in Hungary things are a bit more intricate. As the Hungarian gastronome George Lang has pointed out, there are four pillars to Hungarian stews; *gulyás*, *pörkölt*, *paprikás*, and *tokány*. The *gulyás* (goulash) of the Hungarians is quite different than what we Americans know. The Hungarian version has roots in the ninth century as a shepherd's soup cooked in a heavy iron stew pot called a *bogrács*. In a Hungarian *gulyás*, the more meats and innards, the better. The stew always has lard, bacon, and onion, but never flour or any spice besides caraway and, of course, paprika.

The next stew is called a *pörkölt*, which literally means "roasted" but is actually closer to the French *etuvé*, a kind of dry stew. The meat is always diced and cooked with onions, lard or bacon, and paprika. This dish is actually closer to the American concept of goulash.

A *paprikás* is similar to a *pörkölt*, except that it is finished with sour cream. Sour cream or cream is never used to make the other stews.

A *tokány* derives from the Romanian *tocana*, meaning "ragout." The meat is stewed like a dry stew in its own juices with a little bit of onion, and rather than paprika, black pepper and marjoram are used. Sometimes paprika is used, but in lesser amounts than the other stews.

VEAL PAPRIKASH

THIS FAMOUS HUNGARIAN STEW IS CALLED *paprikás borjú*, or "veal paprika." A paprikash is considered one of the four pillars of Hungarian cuisine. It is different from the other three types of stews in its inclusion of sour cream as a finish. The stew cooks slowly with very little liquid, only that naturally exuding from the meat and vegetables. Near the end of the cooking, when the veal is tender and before you add the sour cream, the sauce will be a syrupy, rich, dark auburn gravy. This stew is best served with some dumplings and a salad.

2 tablespoons lard

1 small onion, finely chopped

2 pounds boneless veal stew meat, trimmed of any large pieces of fat and cut into 1-inch cubes

2 teaspoons sweet Hungarian paprika

Salt to taste

1 medium-size, ripe tomato, peeled, seeded, and chopped

1 green bell pepper, seeded and chopped

1 cup sour cream

1 tablespoon unbleached all-purpose flour

FOR THE OPTIONAL DUMPLINGS:

2 large eggs

1/2 cup unbleached all-purpose flour

2 tablespoons vegetable oil

Salt to taste

1. In a large casserole, melt the lard over medium-high heat. Cook the onion until it is light brown, stirring, about 6 minutes. Remove the casserole from the heat, stir in the veal and paprika, and season with salt. Return to the burner, cover, and continue to cook over very low heat, letting the meat stew in its own juices for about 15 minutes. Add the tomato and green pepper. Stir, cover, and cook until almost tender, about 1½ hours. If too much liquid has accumulated, you may need to uncover and reduce it during this time.

2. Uncover the casserole, stir in the sour cream and flour, and cook over very, very low heat, using a heat diffuser if possible, until the veal is very tender, about 40 minutes.

3. To make the optional dumplings, stir together the eggs, flour, vegetable oil, and salt. Drop them, ½ teaspoon at a time, into salted boiling water and cook for 3 minutes.

4. Serve the stew immediately, with the dumplings, if desired.

Makes 4 servings

VEAL TRIPE, CHICKPEA, AND PEPPER STEW FROM TURKEY

I N ANY STEW THAT USES TRIPE, IT IS important that the tripe be cooked a minimum of three hours before serving, and usually it takes more time than that. In this recipe the tripe gets cooked in a court bouillon. I love these kinds of stews, which in Turkey have a reputation for helping ease the effects of a hangover. This stew is called *işkembeli nohut yahni*, which means "tripe chickpea stew" and is adapted from Chef Zihni Yildiz of the Kuruçeşme Divan restaurant in Turkey. It can be ever so slightly sweet if you use fresh vegetables.

2 cups canned chickpeas, with their liquid
3 quarts plus ½ cup water
¼ cup white wine vinegar
Juice from ½ lemon, plus the rind
3 tablespoons sunflower seed oil
6 large garlic cloves, 1 whole, 5 finely chopped
1 leek (white and light green parts), halved lengthwise, then halved lengthwise again and washed well
1 small carrot, peeled
3 small onions, 1 whole, 2 finely chopped
1 pound veal or lamb tripe
6 tablespoons (¾ stick) unsalted butter
3 Italian long green peppers (peperoncini), seeded and finely chopped

1½ pounds ripe tomatoes, peeled, seeded, and
   finely chopped, or one 28-ounce can crushed
   tomatoes
1 teaspoon salt
½ teaspoon red pepper flakes

1. Put the chickpeas with their liquid in a large saucepan and add ½ cup of the water. Bring to a boil over medium heat and cook until quite soft, about 30 minutes. Drain and set aside, reserving the remaining liquid.

2. While the chickpeas are cooking, pour the remaining 3 quarts of water into a stew pot, add the vinegar, lemon juice, reserved rind of the lemon half, sunflower seed oil, whole garlic clove, leek, carrot, whole onion, and tripe. Bring the liquid to a boil and cook the tripe, uncovered, over medium heat until tender but chewy, 3 to 4 hours.

3. Remove the tripe and cut into 1½-inch squares. Save 1½ cups of the tripe court bouillon.

4. In an earthenware casserole set on a heat diffuser, melt the butter over medium-high heat. When the butter stops sizzling, cook the remaining onions and garlic and green peppers until soft, stirring, 6 to 7 minutes. (If you are not cooking with earthenware and a diffuser, cook over medium heat and check for doneness sooner.) Add the tripe and cook for a few minutes. Reduce the heat to low, then add the tomatoes and cook, uncovered, until most of their juice has evaporated, 45 to 50 minutes. Add the cooked chickpeas and their

remaining liquid and the reserved tripe court bouillon. Bring to a boil, reduce the heat to low, cover, and cook until the chickpeas are even more tender and the stew rather thick, about 1 hour. Season with the salt and red pepper flakes and serve.

Makes 4 to 6 servings

TAFĪNA

THIS SABBATH DISH OF THE TUNISIAN Jews, called *tafīna* or *dafīna*, is a veal, chickpea, and potato stew with turmeric. It is the North African version of the East European Jewish Sabbath dish known as *cholent* (page 24). *Tafīna* is obviously related to the now extinct dish known as *adafina* of the Spanish Jews, a kind of stew or hotpot that belongs to the same family of stews as *escudella* (page 145), *cocido* (page 54), *olla* (page 147), *cassoulet* (page 342), pot-au-feu (page 339), and *bollito misto* (page 354). For centuries, Spanish Jews made *adafina* on Friday nights to cook slowly and be eaten on the Sabbath. *Adafina* has died out among the Sephardim, the Spanish Jews who left for Turkey and Greece, but it is still popular among Algerian and Tunisian Jews (nearly all of whom have emigrated to Israel) as *tafīna*. It is a sumptuous meal reserved for festival days and, most often, for the Sabbath; Jewish housewives prepare the *tafīna* on Friday and keep it warm over the ashes of a *kannūna*, a brazier, to be served for Saturday lunch. It is sometimes accompanied by couscous.

———————●———————

1 pound veal bones
1 veal or beef foot, or 4 lamb feet
4 pounds veal breast, trimmed of fat
1 large onion, finely chopped
1 cup dried chickpeas (about ¹/₂ pound), picked
over, rinsed, soaked in water to cover over-
night, and drained
1 pound boiling potatoes, about the size of a
lime, peeled and left whole
1 head garlic
2 large eggs
1 tablespoon salt
1 teaspoon freshly ground black pepper
1 cinnamon stick
1 tablespoon turmeric
1 bay leaf
1 cup extra virgin olive oil
2¹/₂ quarts water

———————●———————

1. In a large casserole, stew pot, or the bottom portion of a *couscoussier*, place the veal bones and feet. Cover with the veal breast and the remaining ingredients, in the order in which they are listed.

2. Place the casserole over very low heat (or use a heat diffuser) at about 6 P.M., leaving it partially covered. Cook slowly until noon the next day. Check two or three times to see that the water level is fine, which it should be. Serve with rice or couscous.

———————●———————

Makes 4 servings

Note: If you feel uncomfortable with an unattended flame, preheat the oven to 175°F and leave the casserole in until noon the next day.

KEY WEST VEAL KIDNEY STEW

THE ORIGINAL RECIPE FOR THIS DISH calls for beef kidney, but I think veal kidney is a much better choice because it is milder tasting. This recipe appeared in an old spiral-bound cookbook put out in 1949 as the *Key West Women's Club Cookbook*. The cooking of the Keys is most obviously influenced by the Creole cooking of the Caribbean, but also feels the culinary effects of Cuba, Louisiana, and Italy, this last being the result of a significant immigrant population.

Kidneys need some special treatment when cooking. First, they should never be boiled. You can either simmer them gently, as in this recipe, or fry them quickly in a hot skillet. Some people cut off all the fat from kidneys, but I like to leave it on since I think it gives extra flavor to the stew.

1/4 cup chopped bacon fat

1 small onion, chopped

1 green bell pepper, seeded and chopped

1/4 cup plus 2 tablespoons unbleached
  all-purpose flour

Salt and freshly ground black pepper to taste

2 1/2 pounds veal kidneys, cut along their natural
  segments into walnut-size pieces

1 1/2 cups dry white wine

1/4 cup finely chopped fresh parsley leaves

1. In a large, heavy casserole, melt the bacon fat over medium heat. Cook the onion and green pepper until soft, stirring, about 12 minutes.

2. Meanwhile, mix together the flour, salt, and pepper in a medium-size bowl. Toss the kidney pieces with the flour mixture, tapping off any excess. Add the kidneys to the casserole and brown on all sides, stirring, 6 to 7 minutes. Add the wine, increase the heat to high, and, as the wine begins to bubble, reduce the heat to low. Add the parsley, and simmer until no blood runs from the kidneys and they are firm, about 15 minutes, stirring occasionally.

Makes 6 servings

STEWS WITH LAMB

Because lamb is my favorite stew meat, I've got nearly sixty lamb stew recipes in this chapter—everything from the first recorded lamb stew from Mesopotamia around 1700 B.C. (see page 136) to Squibnocket Lamb Stew (page 139) from Martha's Vineyard. There are a number of Italian lamb stews, including a very nice Abruzzi-style one that Italians call *agnello con salsina all'uovo e limone* (page 91), a stew cooked with onion and wine and finished with an egg-and-lemon custard.

Lamb is the number one meat in the Middle East and there are plenty of stews from that region of the world, such as Lamb, Cauliflower, and Coriander Stew from the Levant, made with lots of fresh coriander leaves (page 121). The Lamb Shank and Zucchini Stew from Lebanon (page 123) is stewed in tomatoes and tons of garlic and is spiced with a Middle Eastern spice mix that contains allspice and cinnamon. I also am fond of Arab-style stews that use nuts, for example, the pine nuts in the Lebanese-Style Lamb and Spinach Stew, which is seasoned with paprika and cinnamon (page 124). And there are more exotic stews from lands of the Thousand and One Nights, such as the Lamb and Fresh Coriander Stew with Pistachios and Almonds from Damascus (page 130), cooked for a long time and very slowly so that the lamb cuts like butter when done, and a thick, luscious gravy coats the delicate pieces of lamb. This stew includes almonds, pine nuts, and pistachios, and is seasoned with the famed Arab spice mix known as *bahārāt* (containing cinnamon, ground cardamom, nutmeg, cumin, and cloves) and garnished with beautiful slices of hard-boiled eggs. It's a stew fit for a sultan. Although the bulk of the lamb stews comes from the Mediterranean, I have not forgotten other famous lamb stews, such as an amazing Irish Stew (page 99), which one Irish friend declared "the best I've ever had."

THE CLASSIC LAMB STEW OF ANDALUSIA

A S THE SOUTHERN REGION OF SPAIN, Andalusia is the closest to Africa. Although very different, there are, in fact, some vague similarities in the cooking of Morocco and Andalusia, especially the use of spices such as saffron and cumin, fruit such as oranges and raisins, and nuts. This stew, called *caldereta de cordero*, is cooked in a small cauldron (hence the name) or kettle, and although it is eaten throughout Spain, it is thought to have originated as a dish prepared by the shepherds out of doors. On the other hand, this is only one among many very different recipes with the appellation *caldereta de cordero*, so it might simply be the local family stew prepared any which way. It can also be made with kid. Some cooks take this basic recipe and add chopped bell peppers, chopped ham, or bay leaves to the stew, and you can too, if you want. Add them at the same time you cook the onion. Dionisio Perez, author of *Guía del buen comer español* ("A Guide to Good Food in Spain"), suggests that this was a preparation of the drovers on market day and that it was found beyond the mountains of the shepherds. This recipe is said to be the classic and authentic one. Serve the lamb with roasted potatoes or rice.

---

3 pounds boneless leg of lamb, trimmed of any large pieces of fat and cut into 1¹/₂-inch cubes
1 cup white wine vinegar
3 cups water, or more as needed
3 tablespoons extra virgin olive oil
2 large garlic cloves
1 teaspoon salt
1 medium-size onion, finely chopped
1 tablespoon unbleached all-purpose flour
1 tablespoon hot Spanish paprika (pimentón)
¹/₂ teaspoon freshly ground black pepper
3 tablespoons finely chopped fresh parsley leaves

---

1. Soak the lamb in the vinegar and 1 cup of the water for 1 hour. Remove the lamb and drain, then pat dry with paper towels. It is important to pat the lamb pieces dry, otherwise they will not brown properly.

2. In a stew pot, heat the olive oil over high heat. Cook the garlic cloves until they begin to turn light brown, about 1 minute. Remove from the pot, set in a mortar, and pound them with the salt until mushy.

3. Brown the lamb in the hot oil on all sides, about 6 minutes. There will be a bit of liquid now. Add the onion and flour and cook over high heat until half of the remaining liquid has evaporated, about 8 minutes. Add the remaining 2 cups of water, stirring. Bring to a boil, then reduce the heat to low. Cover and cook until the lamb is tender, about 1¹/₂ hours.

4. Add the paprika, pepper, mashed garlic, and parsley and stir to blend well. Continue to cook, uncovered, until the lamb is very tender and most of the liquid has evaporated, about 1 hour. Serve immediately.

Makes 4 to 6 servings

LAMB, CHICKPEA, AND ALMOND STEW
IN THE STYLE OF CÓRDOBA

As I MENTIONED IN THE PREVIOUS recipe, there are many different *calderetas*. This Andalusian one is from the city of Córdoba, one of the greatest cities in the world in the thirteenth century. It's called *caldereta de cordero a la córdobesa* and, as its name implies, the succulent lamb is cooked in a small cauldron or kettle. Around Córdoba the cook will usually use saffron and almonds in the stew, clearly an Arab inheritance. This particular stew is quite different from the previous *caldereta* and has a palpable medieval feel and taste to it, which is, in this case, a good thing. The so-called "Spanish paprika" used in this recipe and the previous one is a bit hard to find, but worth the effort. I always buy mine from La Española (see the sources listed at the back of the book).

1/3 cup extra virgin olive oil
2 1/4 pounds boneless leg of lamb, trimmed of any large pieces of fat and cubed
2 tablespoons good-quality sherry wine vinegar
1 medium-size onion, finely chopped
4 large garlic cloves, finely chopped
1 green bell pepper, seeded and finely chopped
2 cups canned chickpeas, drained
1 cup dry white wine
1 dried red chile (optional)
2 bay leaves
*1 tablespoon hot Spanish paprika (**pimentón**)*

1 teaspoon dried thyme
1 teaspoon dried oregano
3 tablespoons finely chopped fresh parsley leaves
1/2 teaspoon crumbled saffron threads
2 ounces blanched whole almonds (1/2 cup), toasted in a preheated 350°F oven until golden

1. In an earthenware casserole set on a heat diffuser, heat the olive oil over medium-high heat. (If you are not cooking with earthenware and a diffuser, use a heavy stew pot, cook over medium heat, and check for doneness sooner.) Brown the lamb on all sides, about 8 minutes. Add the vinegar, onion, garlic, and bell pepper and continue to cook, stirring, until the mixture is bubbling, about 5 minutes. Add the chickpeas, wine, chile, if using, bay leaves, paprika, thyme, oregano, parsley, and saffron and bring to a boil. Reduce the heat to low, cover, and simmer, using a heat diffuser if necessary, until the lamb is tender, about 1 1/4 hours.

2. Add the almonds, cook another 15 minutes, and serve.

Makes 6 servings

LAMB, HEIRLOOM BEANS, AND FENNEL STEW
IN THE ANDALUSIAN STYLE

⬥

THIS ANDALUSIAN-STYLE STEW DISH MAY remind you vaguely of a *ropa vieja*, a Latin American type of stew in which the beef is shredded. I developed this recipe shortly after my friend Deborah Madison visited me bearing six different kinds of dried heirloom beans, which I could barely stand to cook because they looked so beautiful. But I went ahead and made this stew, and we loved it. The recipe includes *longaniza* sausage, sometimes found in Italian delicatessens and available from La Española (see the sources listed at the back of the book). Or you can try using hot Italian pork or turkey sausage.

3 cups mixed dried heirloom beans (at least 4 different kinds), picked over, rinsed, soaked in water to cover, and drained

Salt to taste

1/2 cup extra virgin olive oil

1 medium-size onion, finely chopped

4 fennel stalks with leaves, chopped

2 celery stalks, finely chopped

4 dried chiles

6 large garlic cloves, finely chopped

10 ounces lamb filet mignon, flank steak, or boned loin chops, cut into thin, short strips

2 quarts cold water

1 bouquet garni, consisting of 10 sprigs fresh thyme, 10 large fresh basil leaves, handful each of fennel and celery leaves, and 1 bay leaf, tied in cheesecloth

1 cup canned chickpeas, drained

1½ pounds **longaniza** sausage (see below)

Freshly ground black pepper to taste

LONGANIZA SAUSAGE

━━━⬤━━━

Longaniza sausage is a Spanish pork sausage seasoned with paprika, cinnamon, aniseed, garlic, and vinegar. *Longaniza* was the sausage that figured in the picaresque story of Lazarillo de Tormes, published in 1554. Lazarillo is important because it is the first ever picaresque novel, quite different from the novel of chivalry, the literary vogue of the time. Poor down-and-out Lazarillo was a servant at one point to a blind man who would not give any *longaniza* sausage to Lazarillo. So Lazarillo switched a rotten piece of turnip for the sausage and wolfed down the sausage. He put the turnip in a fried bread sandwich, but the blind man could tell the difference and thrust his nose down Lazarillo's gullet, which made him throw up the sausage.

To make *longaniza* sausage, follow the instructions on page 346 for *Saucisse de Toulouse*, adding 1/4 cup hot paprika, 2 teaspoons ground cinnamon, 3 tablespoons aniseed, 1/4 cup plus 2 tablespoons finely chopped garlic, and 1 cup red wine vinegar to the ground meat mixture.

1. Place the beans in a large saucepan and cover with 4 inches of cold water. Salt lightly and bring to a boil. Reduce the heat and simmer until the beans are *al dente*, about 1 hour. Drain.

2. In a stew pot, heat the olive oil over medium-high heat. Cook the onion, fennel, celery, chiles, garlic, and lamb, stirring frequently, until it is all soft. Add the beans, water, bouquet garni, chickpeas, and sausage. Stir, season with salt and pepper, and return the broth to a boil. Reduce the heat to low and simmer until the beans are very tender, about 1 1/2 hours. Serve immediately.

Makes 4 servings

A FOURTEENTH-CENTURY CATALAN STEW: "MEAT IN THE ARAB STYLE"

IN THE FOURTEENTH-CENTURY CATALAN cookery book known as the *Libre de sent soví*, this recipe is called *carn a la Sarreÿnesca*, "meat in the style of the Saracens." The original recipe is written in medieval Catalan:

QUI PARLA CON CUYNARETS CARN A LA SARREŸNESCA

Si vols cuynar carn a la sarreÿnesqua, ffé pesses de la carn, e leva-la bé ab aygua calenta. E puys mit la carn en la olla meyns d'aygua; e met-hi hom lart de cansalada bé grassa e un poc de vinagre, e seba manut tellada, e sal e salsa e jurvert e moradux tellat, e soffregits-ho ab la carn. E quant aurà bona pessa soffrit, mit aygua calenta ho brou que tengues ya aprés lo ffoc. E cogua tot entrò que la carn sia cuyta. Puys trau-ne hom la carn, e ffes del brou escudelles. E si y vols estovar les sopes, més ne valran.

I'm not providing a literal translation, but the recipe as I've written it below is pretty much true to the original, and if you know French or Spanish you might be able to figure out the medieval Catalan. For example, the first sentence begins "If you want to cook meat in the Saracen style ... wash it well in hot water." This recipe seems pretty straightforward, except for the lack of specified quantities. That is typical of medieval cookery manuscripts, so the quantities are provided by me, based on what I know about cooking. The only real problem concerns spices used in medieval texts. Rarely will it be specified which ones are used and how much. Usually the author instructs the reader to use *especias* or *salsa*, which is a mixed spice blend. Given what we know about the recipes for mixed spices and the spice markets of the time, my reading of *e met-hi ... e sal e salsa* is that it is a certain kind of spice mix. *Salsa* refers to "mixed spices," and I decided to use a spice mix that we know was common in the spice markets of Barcelona, Toulouse, and Montpellier in the fifteenth and sixteenth centuries, namely *pebre gingibre*. A statute from 1536 in the Municipal Archives of Toulouse gives a recipe for such a mix, which is reproduced here.

This recipe is modernized only slightly, in the initial browning of the meat. *Cansalada* would have been salted, dried preserved beef, but salt pork is a lot easier to find, even though pork would certainly not be "in the Arab style." Alternatively, you could use an unseasoned beef jerky—but that's hard to find too. Grains of paradise is a spice from West Africa popular in the Middle Ages as a replacement for black pepper when the peppercorn supply either dried up or became too expensive. Also called *melegueta* (*Aframomum melegueta*), grains of paradise can be found in some whole-food supermarkets as well as from the Frontier Natural Products Cooperative and the Kalustyan Company (see the sources listed at the back of the book).

———————●———————

¼ cup extra virgin olive oil
3 pounds boneless leg of lamb, trimmed
    of any large pieces of fat and cut into
    6 large pieces
½ cup sherry vinegar
1½ ounces salt beef or pork, diced
1 large onion, sliced and separated
    into rings
2 teaspoons salt
1 tablespoon ground ginger
1 teaspoon freshly ground black pepper
½ teaspoon ground cinnamon
½ teaspoon freshly ground cloves
½ teaspoon freshly grated nutmeg
½ teaspoon freshly ground grains of paradise
    (optional)
¼ teaspoon crumbled saffron threads
¼ cup finely chopped fresh parsley leaves
3 tablespoons finely chopped fresh marjoram
    leaves
1 quart Beef Broth (page 3)

1. In a large skillet, heat the olive oil over high heat. Brown the lamb on all sides until crispy brown, 8 to 10 minutes. Transfer to an earthenware casserole.

2. Pour the vinegar over the lamb and sprinkle the diced salt beef or pork, onion, salt, ginger, pepper, cinnamon, cloves, nutmeg, grains of paradise, saffron, parsley, and marjoram over the lamb, stirring just a bit to even things out.

3. Add the beef broth, cover, and bring to a gentle boil, using a heat diffuser, if necessary. Reduce the heat to low and cook until the lamb is very tender, 2½ to 3 hours. Serve immediately.

———————●———————

Makes 6 servings

A THIRTEENTH-CENTURY HISPANO-MUSLIM STEW: "THE SICILIAN DISH"

MOST OF SPAIN WAS UNDER ISLAMIC RULE for nearly seven centuries, and the vestiges of this golden age are still to be seen in architectural glories such as the Alhambra in Granada, in place names throughout Spain, and in many culinary delights. We have a record of the kinds of dishes prepared by the elite of Spain during the thirteenth century, and this dish is an interesting example. In the anonymous thirteenth-century Hispano-Muslim cookbook from the Almohad dynasty, the *Kitāb al-ṭabīkh* ("Book of Cooking"), a recipe is called "Sicilian dish." It is a lamb stew made with a huge amount of onions cooked in olive oil and flavored with olive oil, black pepper, cinnamon, "Chinese cinnamon" (*Cinnamomum aromaticum*, the ground dried bark of a tree in the laurel family), and lavender or spikenard (another aromatic herb), to which meatballs are added. After the stew was cooked, saffron dissolved in beaten eggs was whipped in and allowed to set. The fact that it was called "Sicilian" may mean that was how the royal court in Palermo cooked this dish, or it may simply mean that Sicilian cuisine, even in the thirteenth century, was recognized as exquisite and the Hispano-Muslim chefs wanted to emulate it. The Almohads ruled in parts of Spain from 1130 to 1269 and became a powerful kingdom, with their capital in Seville. The court of the Almohads was a splendid center of art and learning, and the renowned Islamic philosopher Averroës acted as the physician to the sultans. By the way, this preparation is not some culinary curiosity; it's actually quite magnificent.

FOR THE MEATBALLS:

2 pounds ground lamb
1 small onion, finely chopped
¼ cup finely chopped fresh parsley leaves
Salt and freshly ground black pepper to taste

FOR THE STEW:

1¾ pounds lamb breast riblets
1¾ pounds lamb shoulder on the bone, trimmed of any large pieces of fat and cut into bite-size pieces
1 pound lamb flank, cut into 2-inch squares

2 cups water
3 pounds onions, thinly sliced and separated into rings
Salt to taste
¼ cup extra virgin olive oil
Freshly ground black pepper to taste
1 teaspoon ground cinnamon
1 stick cassia or cinnamon
3 lavender sprigs
½ teaspoon saffron threads, crumbled
3 large eggs

---

1. To make the meatballs, in a large bowl, knead together the lamb, onion, parsley, salt, and pepper. Form into 20 meatballs and refrigerate for at least 30 minutes.

2. Put the lamb breast, shoulder, and flank meat; water, onions, and some salt in a large casserole, preferably an earthenware one set on a heat diffuser. Turn the heat to medium and cook, covered, until the onions are soft, about 25 minutes. Add the olive oil, pepper, cinnamon, cassia, lavender, and chilled meatballs. Bring the broth to a boil, then reduce the heat to low. Cook, using a heat diffuser if necessary, until the lamb is very tender, about 3 hours. There should be almost no liquid left. If there is too much fat and water in the casserole, remove up to 2 cups and discard.

3. Preheat the oven to 350°F. Beat the saffron into the eggs, and pour the eggs all around the casserole. Place in the oven until the eggs set, about 10 minutes. Serve immediately.

Makes 6 servings

ITALIAN CUTS OF LAMB

Italian butchers cut up lamb differently than American butchers. In Italy, both the head (*testa*) and the feet (*piedi*) are sold for stews. The neck (*collo*) is also a good stew meat, as is the shoulder (*spala*), which will often include the *ossobuco* (shank). The breast meat (*petto*) is usually used in braises and ragouts, while the loin and rib chops, called *quadrello* or *costolette*, are grilled, broiled, or baked. Whereas American butchers sell the whole leg, Italian butchers cut up the leg into the lower portion, called the *cosciotto*, and the *sella*, or saddle of lamb. Four types of lamb are sold by Italian butchers: *abbacchio*, or milk-fed lamb; *agnello*, mature lamb; *montone*, mutton; and *castrato*, castrated lamb. The milk-fed lamb is a milder tasting meat than the other cuts.

LAMB AND TOMATO STEW FROM AN ITALIAN FARMHOUSE

FAMILIES LOVE THIS EXCEEDINGLY SIMPLE stew, typical of farmhouse cooking in southern Italy, because of its intense flavors. The lamb and tomato seem to melt together. One of the reasons these kinds of southern Italian stews taste so good is because the marrow-rich shank bones are used, which enrich the gravy. Another is that they are cooked with wine, and wine in stew is so perfect that many Italian cooks associate one with the other. This is a wintertime stew, as you might guess from the fact that I call for canned tomatoes, fresh ones being out of season and generally not very good tasting at that time of year.

3 tablespoons extra virgin olive oil
1 medium-size onion, chopped
2 1/2 pounds lamb shank and shoulder on the bone, trimmed of any large pieces of fat and cut into chunks
5 garlic cloves, finely chopped
1 cup robust red wine
One 28-ounce can crushed tomatoes
Salt and freshly ground black pepper to taste

In a casserole, heat the olive oil over medium-high heat. Cook the onion until translucent, stirring, about 5 minutes. Brown the lamb on all sides, about 8 to 10 minutes. Add the garlic, wine, and tomatoes and season with salt and pepper. Reduce the heat to low and simmer, uncovered, until the meat is soft, about 4 hours.

Makes 4 servings

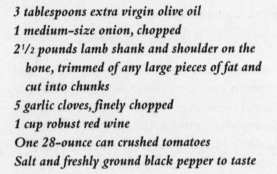

LAMB STEW FROM THE NEAPOLITAN COUNTRYSIDE

───●───

S PEZZATINO IS THE CATCHALL ITALIAN word for rough and rustic country stews, usually made from bite-size pieces of lamb. My grandfather was from the Neapolitan countryside, if you count his small village some 20 kilometers from Benevento as Neapolitan. Although my mother didn't make lamb stew much, this is a stew he would have enjoyed. There are many such dishes throughout Italy for *spezzatino d'agnello*, "lamb stew," from the Piedmont (where it is called *rustida*) to Sicily. This is a stew that I make quite often for my family because it's so easy, requires very little forethought, little preparation, and is gobbled up by all. Serve it with a simple salad and crusty Italian bread to soak up the gravy.

───●───

3 tablespoons extra virgin olive oil
2 garlic cloves, crushed
2 pounds boneless leg of lamb, trimmed of any
*   large pieces of fat and cubed*
Salt and freshly ground black pepper to taste
1 small bay leaf
2 tablespoons finely chopped fresh marjoram
*   leaves*
2 tablespoons finely chopped fresh basil leaves
1/2 cup dry white wine
1 pound ripe tomatoes, peeled, seeded, and
*   chopped*
1 cup water

1. In a large earthenware casserole set on a heat diffuser, heat the olive oil with the garlic cloves over medium-high heat until the garlic cloves begin to turn light brown. (Alternatively, use an enameled cast-iron casserole, and set it directly over medium heat.) Remove and discard the garlic.

2. Pat the lamb dry with paper towels, then salt and pepper it. Brown the lamb in the hot oil on all sides over medium-high heat, about 6 minutes. Add the bay leaf, marjoram, and basil, stir, and cook for 2 minutes. Pour in the wine and reduce the liquid until it is nearly evaporated, about 10 minutes. Reduce the heat to low and add the tomatoes and water, just enough to almost cover the lamb. Check the seasonings and cook, partially covered, until the lamb is tender and the sauce thick, about 1 1/2 hours. Remove the bay leaf and serve immediately.

───●───

Makes 4 servings

ABRUZZI LAMB STEW WITH EGG AND LEMON CUSTARD

───●───

T HIS TRADITIONAL AND PROTEIN-RICH dish from the Abruzzi region of Italy, called *agnello con salsina all'uovo e limone*, is typically served at Easter. It should be stewed in an earthenware stew pot or some kind of pot or casserole that can be brought to the table for serving. A variation of this stew is called *cacio e uovo*, made the same way but with the addition of pecorino and/or Parmigiano cheese. In this recipe, I've adapted it slightly so that the cheese is sprinkled on top rather than being incorporated into the sauce. The tricky part of the recipe is whisking the egg-and-lemon mixture to form a custard-like sauce. It is best to do this over low heat, whisking constantly and raising the heat only slightly if you feel it necessary. Keep a close watch for any sign of coagulation (which you don't want) and remove the sauce from the fire *and* pot immediately. The finished dish is rich tasting and perfect with a green leafy vegetable, such as spinach or Swiss chard.

---

¹/4 cup plus 2 tablespoons extra virgin olive oil
2 pounds boneless leg of lamb, trimmed of any
   large pieces of fat and cut into 1-inch cubes
1 large garlic clove, finely chopped
3 tablespoons finely chopped onion
¹/2 cup dry white wine
Salt and freshly ground black pepper to taste
2 large egg yolks
Juice from 1 lemon
Freshly grated pecorino cheese for sprinkling

---

1. In an earthenware casserole, heat the olive oil over medium-high heat, using a heat diffuser if necessary. Brown the lamb on all sides, about 10 minutes. Add the garlic and onion and cook until soft, about 4 minutes, stirring. Pour in the wine and reduce over high heat until the wine is somewhat evaporated, about 10 minutes if using a heat diffuser, otherwise, less. Reduce the heat to low, and season with salt and pepper. Cover, and simmer the lamb until fork-tender, moistening with small amounts of water occasionally if the sauce looks like it is drying out, 1 to 1¹/4 hours. Remove the lamb from the casserole and keep warm.

2. Remove the casserole from the heat. In a small bowl, beat the egg yolks and lemon juice together. Add a few tablespoons of the lamb broth from the casserole to the egg-and-lemon mixture and beat. Pour the egg-and-lemon mixture back into the casserole, return the casserole to low heat, using a heat diffuser if necessary, and whisk vigorously with the casserole juices, making sure the egg yolk does not get so hot that it coagulates. Remove the casserole from the heat occasionally as you whisk to play it safe. Continue whisking over low heat until the yolks increase in volume and look like a light and foamy custard. If you think this is taking too long—and it might take 10 minutes—you can raise the heat, but then you need to be more attentive.

3. Return the lamb to the casserole, mix to coat, sprinkle with pecorino cheese, and serve immediately.

Makes 4 servings

CALDARIELLO

W HY DOES THIS STEW FROM THE hinterland of Apulia, the region called the heel of the Italian boot, taste so incredible? Traditionally, the lamb is stewed very gently in wild fennel–flavored sheep's milk in a small, potbellied stew pot called a *caldariello*, which gives its name to the stew it-self. One can imagine the origin of this stew as the kind of soul-satisfying fare a shepherd's wife would cook. As sheep's milk is almost impossible to find in the United States, try using goat's milk, or lacking that, cow's milk. If you use whole cow's milk, add some cream to it to make it resemble raw milk. In America, only Californians have access to wild fennel, which grows by roadsides. Elsewhere use the leaves and bulb of a Florence fennel, the kind that is sold in supermarkets, along with 1 tea-spoon of ground fennel seeds. So why does this taste so good? Try it and let everyone tell you why. Serve with pieces of toasted or grilled Italian country bread.

2 large garlic cloves, finely chopped
Leaves from 1 small bunch fresh parsley, finely
    chopped
2 handfuls wild fennel leaves; or 1 small
    Florence fennel, bulb sliced thinly and leaves
    and stalk chopped, and 1 teaspoon freshly
    ground fennel seeds
1 medium-size onion, sliced
1/2 cup extra virgin olive oil
2 cups sheep's or goat's milk, or 1 1/2 cups whole
    cow's milk mixed with 1/2 cup heavy cream
1/2 cup heavy cream
1 3/4 pounds boneless leg of lamb, trimmed of any
    large pieces of fat and cubed
Salt and freshly ground black pepper to taste

Put the garlic, parsley, fennel, onion, and olive oil in an earthenware stew pot set on a heat diffuser and add the milk and cream. Turn the heat to high, but reduce it to low before the milk comes to a boil. (If you are not cooking with earthenware and a diffuser, begin on medium heat.) Once the milk is just quiver-ing on the surface, add the lamb and season with salt and pepper. Simmer over low heat, using a heat diffuser if necessary, until the lamb is fork-tender, stirring occasionally, about 2 1/2 hours. It is important that the milk never come to a boil. If it does, it won't affect the taste, but it will make the final dish a little less pleasing to look at. Serve immediately.

Makes 4 servings

LA PIGNETI

L UCANIA IS ANOTHER NAME FOR THE Basilicata region of Italy, what we could call the instep of the Italian boot. This stew takes its name from the earthenware container that is used for cooking the *pigneti*. The word comes from the Latin word *pinguia*, meaning "a jug used to store fat." In Basilicata, families hermetically seal the earthenware jug with clay and then place the *pigneti* in the embers of a fire to cook. This method locks in all the flavors. To approximate this method, you can form a paste rope made of flour and water and seal the lid to the stew pot—and if you have an earthenware casserole, all the better.

———•———

3 pounds boneless leg of mutton or lamb, trimmed of any large pieces of fat and cut into 2-inch cubes

2 pounds boiling potatoes, peeled, halved, and sliced ¼ inch thick

1 large onion, cut into 8 wedges and separated into layers

6 large, ripe tomatoes (about 3 pounds), peeled, seeded, and chopped

⅓ pound pecorino cheese, diced

1 dried chile, seeded and crumbled

¼ pound **soppressata della Basilicata** *or any hot, spicy salami or pepperoni, cut into small pieces*

1½ *cups water*

Salt to taste

Flour paste rope (see page 9)

———•———

1. Put all of the ingredients, except the flour and water for the rope, in a large enameled cast-iron or earthenware casserole, a potbellied stew pot or *marmite*, or the bottom portion of a *couscoussier*. Toss well and cover. Seal the pot and lid together with the flour paste rope.

2. Turn the heat to medium-low and cook for 1½ hours, shaking occasionally. Remove the rope and check to see if the lamb is tender and the potatoes cooked. If they aren't, reform another flour paste rope, reseal the pot and lid, and continue to cook until tender, up to 30 minutes more. Serve immediately.

———•———

Makes 6 servings

SOPPRESSATA

Soppressata is an Italian cold cut that should be easy to find in an Italian market. It is a salami made in southern Italy of coarsely chopped lean pork, pork fat, and bacon seasoned in one of two ways. A mild *soppressata* is seasoned with salt and pepper and wine, while the hot *soppressata* is seasoned with red pepper flakes, paprika, wine, salt, and pepper. The salami is lightly smoked and pressed to eliminate air pockets, giving the sausage its name, which means "pressed."

LAMB SHANK, ARTICHOKE, AND POTATO STEW

A SPRINGTIME STEW IS QUITE NICE WHEN the weather is still a bit cold but spring vegetables are in season. Today, artichokes can be found year-round in the supermarket, so they are rarely thought of as a spring vegetable. This southern and central Italian stew is heavily flavored with aromatic herbs such as parsley, mint, and marjoram, which gives a wonderful flavor to the potatoes and artichokes. And, of course, lamb shanks are luscious in a stew.

———————•———————

2 tablespoons extra virgin olive oil
2 tablespoon unsalted butter
1 medium-size onion, thinly sliced
4 lamb shanks (about 3¹/₄ pounds total)
Unbleached all-purpose flour for dredging
1 cup dry red wine
1 cup water
¹/₄ cup plus 2 tablespoons finely chopped fresh parsley leaves
2 tablespoons finely chopped fresh mint leaves
3 tablespoons finely chopped fresh marjoram leaves
4 large garlic cloves, finely chopped
1¹/₄ pounds White Rose or other all-purpose potatoes, peeled and halved
4 medium-size artichoke hearts (from about 1¹/₂ pounds artichokes, see page 307)
Salt and freshly ground black pepper to taste

———————•———————

1. In a casserole, heat the olive oil and butter together over medium-high heat. When the butter stops sizzling, cook the onion, stirring, until translucent, about 6 minutes. Dredge the lamb in the flour, tapping off any excess, and brown in the casserole on both sides, 6 to 7 minutes. Add the wine and water. Cover, reduce the heat to low, and simmer for 2 hours.

2. Add the herbs, garlic, potatoes, and artichokes, and season with salt and pepper. Cook

until the vegetables are tender and the meat is falling off the bones, about another 2 hours.

———————•———————

Makes 4 servings

LAMB STEW WITH TAGLIATELLE

THIS ITALIAN LAMB STEW, OR *SPEZZATINO*, is a very simple dish and an easy one to make. It's the kind of stew a housewife would make for an ordinary meal. For a fancier version, she might fry the onions first, then brown the shanks and add some wine. Traditionally, people eat this dish in two courses. First the *tagliatelle*, a pasta wider than fettuccine, is served with the ragout, then the lamb is eaten as a second course. Try not to use a substitute for the shanks called for in this recipe—that really is the meat you want here.

———————•———————

4 lamb shanks, about 3¹/₂ pounds
1 large onion, coarsely chopped
6 garlic cloves, chopped
10 black peppercorns
2 pounds ripe tomatoes, peeled, seeded, and chopped, with their juices
³/₄ cup water
³/₄ cup extra virgin olive oil
1 bay leaf
Salt to taste
*¹/₂ pound **tagliatelle** or fettuccine*
³/₄ cup freshly grated pecorino cheese

1. Put all the ingredients, except the pasta and pecorino cheese, in a casserole or Dutch oven. Turn the heat to medium-high, and cook for 8 to 10 minutes, covered. Reduce the heat to very low, cover, and simmer until the meat is falling off the bone, about 4 hours.

2. Bring a large pot of water to a rolling boil, salt abundantly, and add the pasta. Drain when *al dente*, toss with one or two ladles full of the lamb stew broth, and divide between 4 serving plates. Sprinkle with the pecorino cheese, place a shank on top of each, and serve.

Makes 4 servings

LAMB, CHICORY, BEANS, AND PASTA STEW

THIS DISH IS SO SATISFYING BECAUSE OF the interplay between the numerous beans, the pasta, and the flavorful lamb. It's perfect for a fall dinner. The recipe is a kind of farmhouse stew one could encounter in Calabria, Basilicata, or Sicily. You might raise your eyebrows at my using canned cooked beans, but they work quite well, are of high quality, and of course, make everything easier without harming the taste.

Chicory is a bitter-tasting wild herbaceous biennial or perennial found throughout the Mediterranean. There are a great many varieties, but for this stew, the large leafy green one is perfect, stems and all. You can find the fava beans sold in cans in Middle Eastern markets. They are labeled "foul medammes."

2 pounds boneless lamb shoulder or leg, trimmed of any large pieces of fat and cut into bite-size pieces
1 large onion, sliced ¼ inch thick and separated into rings
¾ cup coarsely chopped fresh parsley leaves
1 medium-size, ripe tomato, peeled, seeded, and chopped
½ cup dry white wine
Pinch of saffron threads, crumbled
¼ cup plus 1 tablespoon extra virgin olive oil
1 cup water
3½ pounds chicory, cut into chunks
One 12-ounce can fava beans, drained
One 12-ounce can chickpeas, drained
3 tablespoons finely chopped fresh mint leaves
Salt and freshly ground black pepper to taste
¼ cup cooked orzo or other cooked soup pasta

1. Put the lamb, onion, parsley, tomato, wine, saffron, and olive oil in an earthenware casserole with a cover or an enameled cast-iron casserole. Turn the heat to medium-low, and cook until the liquid has evaporated, about 1½ hours. Stir occasionally and check to see that the liquid is not evaporating too fast. If it is, add a few tablespoons water each time you stir.

2. Add the 1 cup of water and then the chicory, a handful at a time, stirring continuously. Let the chicory wilt so more handfuls can be added. Add the fava beans, chickpeas, and mint. Reduce the heat to low and season with salt and pepper. Cover and cook until the stew is unctuous, about 1 hour more, uncovering during the last half hour if the stew is very liquidy.

3. Stir in the orzo and let it get hot, then serve immediately.

Makes 4 servings

VENETIAN WETHER STEW

CASTRÀ IS THE VENETIAN DIALECT WORD for wether, a castrated lamb, which is a popular meat throughout all of Italy. The name of this preparation in Venice is *castrà in tecia,* meaning "wether in casserole." It may seem to you that my recipe has a lot of fat—in the form of olive oil and butter—and you're right, it is a lot, but this is how I received the recipe when I was living in Venice, and it is an authentic way of cooking it. When you serve the lamb (which you will have to use instead of wether because it is not sold in this country), use a slotted spoon and let the fat drip through. This dish is ideal accompanied by hot polenta (page 188).

¹/₂ cup extra virgin olive oil
6 tablespoons (³/₄ stick) unsalted butter

LAMB THOUGHTS

When you go into a supermarket to buy lamb stew meat, it will usually be so labeled. Shoulder, neck, and leg are all used for lamb stews. But there are other sheep products that we all could be buying if only there were the demand, such as wether, a castrated lamb; hogget, a one-year-old lamb (the term is also applied to pigs); and mutton, a mature sheep. The main difference in taste is that, as the animal gets older, the flavor is more dramatic and pronounced. You will see lots of Australian and New Zealand lamb being sold, and because it's imported, you may be led to believe that it is better lamb. I don't think it is; the best lamb is American lamb, especially lamb from California, Wyoming, Pennsylvania, Colorado, and Vermont. Australian and New Zealand lambs are leaner and older, with less fat, and are therefore less tasty. See the sources listed in the back of the book for top quality lamb.

1 medium-size onion, chopped
1 celery heart, finely chopped
1 carrot, finely chopped
Salt and freshly ground black pepper to taste
2¹/₄ pounds boneless leg of lamb, trimmed of any
    large pieces of fat and cut into 1¹/₂-inch cubes
2 tablespoons tomato paste dissolved in 2
    tablespoons water
¹/₂ cup dry red wine

1. In a casserole, heat the olive oil, butter, onion, celery, and carrot together over medium heat, stirring frequently, until the onion is translucent, about 5 minutes. Season with salt and pepper.

2. Add the lamb to the casserole and cook until browned on all sides, about 8 minutes. Add the diluted tomato paste and wine and mix well. Once the mixture begins to simmer, reduce the heat to low. Cover and cook until the meat is very tender, stirring frequently, about 3 hours. The sauce should be somewhat syrupy at the end of the cooking time. If it is not, uncover and reduce the liquid for a few minutes.

Makes 6 servings

STEW OF LAMB AND CHICORY COOKED IN AN EARTHENWARE CAULDRON

THIS GREENERY-LADEN DISH CALLED *agnello al calderotto* is from the Taranto region of southern Italy in the province of Apulia. A *calderotto* is an earthenware cauldron or *marmite* used for cooking stews. The amount of chicory called for in the recipe seems excessive, but it's not. The finished dish is very tender: flavorful lamb surrounded by the almost melted texture of chicory, which loses a lot of its bitterness in the cooking. If you can't find chicory, substitute escarole.

2 pounds boneless lamb shoulder or leg, trimmed of any large pieces of fat and cut into bite-size pieces
1 large onion, sliced
³/4 cup coarsely chopped fresh parsley leaves
1 medium-size, ripe tomato, peeled, seeded, and chopped
¹/2 cup dry white wine
Pinch of saffron threads, crumbled
¹/4 cup plus 1 tablespoon extra virgin olive oil
1 cup water
3¹/2 pounds chicory, cut up
Salt and freshly ground black pepper to taste

1. Put the lamb, onion, parsley, tomato, wine, saffron, and olive oil in an earthenware casserole with a cover or in an enameled cast-iron casserole. Turn the heat to medium-low, and cook until the liquid has evaporated, about 1¹/2 hours. Stir occasionally and check to see that the liquid is not evaporating too fast. If it is, add a few tablespoons of water each time you stir.

2. Add the 1 cup of water and then the chicory, a handful at a time, stirring continuously. Let the chicory wilt so more handfuls can be added. Reduce the heat to low and season with salt and pepper. Cover and cook until the stew is unctuous, about 1 hour more. Uncover during the last half hour if the stew is very liquidy. Serve immediately.

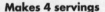

Makes 4 servings

IRISH STEW

SAMUEL BECKETT WROTE IN HIS NOVEL *Molloy*, "Irish Stew. A nourishing and economical dish, if a little indigestible. All honor to the land that has brought it before the world." All honor may go to Ireland, but what actually constitutes an authentic Irish stew is open to debate. That it originated in a big, black, three-legged pot over a fire is not in doubt. Some say the carrots and pearl barley one often finds in an Irish stew are not authentic and dilute the original taste. Mutton has always been the hallmark of a true Irish stew, although these days one is likely to find hogget (a one-year-old lamb) in Ireland. Some cooks add green vegetables to an Irish stew, but I think we can admit that that is a true abomination. This recipe is based vaguely on the one remembered by my friend Bill Grantham (an Irish lad), who does insist on mutton for authenticity and who says about the addition of carrots, "My God, no." It is also based on several other pirated recipes, one from the Ballymaloe Hotel in County Cork, and another from Biddy Whyte Lennon. There are other "Irish" stews that one finds in America and recipes abound, but this recipe is the one true one.

The amount of water or broth you need will depend on how good the seal is, that is, how heavy the lid to your casserole is, and whether you like a "wet" or "dry" stew. You may need as much as two cups or a little less than one cup. A good stew should have some gravy, but should not be flooded by it. I use a mixture of potatoes so that the floury ones dissolve a bit to thicken the stew, and the waxy ones retain their shape for a nice texture. Typical floury potatoes are Idaho or Russet Burbank, while typical waxy potatoes are White Rose, Yukon Gold, and Yellow Finn. The reason you will want the whole leg of mutton is in order to use the bone to make a mutton broth. One leg should give you about three pounds of meat. Keep in mind that this preparation takes two days: the first day to make the stock and the second day to make the stew. If you prefer to skip the mutton broth, see the Note on page 100.

Serve this with Irish soda bread.

FOR THE BROTH:

1 mutton leg (about 7 pounds, see Note on page 100)
1 leek, split lengthwise, washed well, and cut into chunks
1 large onion, quartered
1 large carrot, cut into chunks
1 bouquet garni, consisting of 1 small bunch fresh parsley, 10 sprigs fresh thyme, and 1 bay leaf, tied in cheesecloth
10 black peppercorns
3 to 4 quarts water

FOR THE STEW:

12 small white onions (about 1¼ pounds)
½ cup finely chopped fresh parsley leaves
2 tablespoons unsalted butter, at room temperature
1 tablespoon finely chopped fresh chives
Salt and freshly ground black pepper to taste
2 tablespoons dried thyme
4 medium-size floury potatoes (about 1 pound), peeled and quartered
4 medium-size waxy potatoes (about 1 pound), peeled and thinly sliced or quartered

1. To make the mutton broth, trim the fat off the mutton leg, then slice the meat off the leg (or ask the butcher to do this), reserving the fat and the bone separately. You should have 3 to 4 pounds of meat and a handful or so of fat. Cut the meat into 1½-inch chunks and set aside. Twist the mutton leg to break the joints and put it into a stockpot. Add the leek, onion, carrot, bouquet garni, and peppercorns. Cover with water and bring to a boil. Reduce the heat to low, partially cover, and simmer, skimming the surface of foam when necessary, for 4 to 6 hours. Strain the broth through a strainer (a chinois, or conical strainer, would be ideal), then line the strainer with cheesecloth and strain again. Discard all the bones, vegetables, and bouquet garni. Pour the stock into a container and refrigerate overnight. Remove the congealed fat from the top in the morning and reserve this fat. This step can be done well before you actually cook the Irish stew if you like. The stock will congeal like a jelly. Remove 2 cups of the stock for this recipe and freeze the rest for another use; it will keep in the refrigerator for up to a week and in the freezer for up to 6 months.

2. To make the stew, in a heavy casserole, render the reserved mutton or lamb fat that has been trimmed from the leg over medium-low heat. After about ¼ cup of fat has been rendered, remove and discard any solid bits that remain. If you do not have any fat to do this, then use the saved congealed fat from the top of the mutton broth, assuming you saved it, or use butter. Increase the heat to high and brown the mutton in the melted fat on all sides, 6 to 7 minutes. Remove the meat and set aside. Do this in two batches to avoid overcrowding in the casserole and to brown the meat evenly and properly.

3. Reduce the heat to medium-high, add the reserved mutton fat skimmed from the congealed broth or 1 tablespoon butter and cook the white onions until light golden all around, about 5 minutes. Add a ladle full of broth to deglaze the pan, scraping the bottom and sides with a wooden spoon to get up the browned bits.

4. Mix 1 tablespoon of the parsley with the softened butter and chives.

5. Reduce the heat under the casserole to low, season the onions with salt and pepper and a third each of the remaining parsley and the thyme. Lay the meat on top of the vegetables and season again with salt and pepper and another third of the parsley and thyme. Put the potatoes on top, season with salt and pepper and the remaining parsley and thyme. Pour in the remaining broth. Push the potatoes down a little into the broth. Bring to a boil, then reduce the heat to low. Cover and simmer until the meat and potatoes are tender, about 2½ hours.

6. Check the seasonings, then swirl in the herb butter, and serve.

Makes 6 servings

Note: If you do not wish to make the mutton broth, skip step 1 and substitute 2 cups of Beef

Broth (page 3). For the stew you will need 3 pounds of boneless leg of mutton (preferably) or lamb.

Broth (page 3).

adjust the cooking time downwards as needed. There is a natural affinity between the sweetness of parsnips and carrots and the bacon that makes this stew all the more appetizing.

---

1 large carrot, coarsely chopped
1 medium parsnip, peeled and coarsely chopped
1 celeriac (celery root), peeled and cubed
1 medium-size onion, coarsely chopped
1/2 cup chopped bacon or salt pork
2 pounds mutton, from the leg or shoulder, trimmed of any large pieces of fat and cut into 2-inch cubes
Salt to taste
2 1/2 cups water
1 garlic clove, crushed
1/8 teaspoon freshly ground black pepper
1/8 teaspoon paprika
1/4 teaspoon dried marjoram
1/4 teaspoon caraway seeds
1 cup firmly packed chopped kale leaves
1 cup green beans, ends trimmed and cut into 1-inch lengths
1 pound boiling potatoes, peeled and cubed

SLOVAK CUISINE

While the Czechs drink beer for the most part, Slovaks (also known as Moravians, geographically speaking) drink wine. While the Czechs prefer pork, the Slovaks prefer lamb and mutton. They also have a wider range of cheeses. A famous Slovak cheese is *bryndza*, a soft, sour, and often unpasteurized raw ewe's milk cheese that is allowed to ferment. It is an important ingredient in two traditional Slovak dishes: *haluški*, potato-and-milk dumplings cooked in the cheese, and *strapacky*, cabbage and onions served with the cheese as an accompaniment.

SLOVAK-STYLE MUTTON GOULASH

THE HEARTY SLOVAK STEW CALLED *skopový guláš* is adapted from a famous Czech cookbook by Joza Břízová called *Varíme zdrave chutne a hospodárne*, which was translated into English as *The Czechoslovak Cookbook* in 1965. Because mutton is an older sheep, it requires a lot more stewing than lamb. Figure on close to four hours. If you are unable to find mutton, which usually has to be ordered through a butcher, then use lamb and

1. In a large casserole or stew pot, cook the carrot, parsnip, celeriac, and onion with the bacon over medium-high heat until the onion is soft, stirring occasionally, about 8 minutes. Add the mutton, season with salt, and pour in 1 cup of the water. Bring to a boil and reduce the heat to low. Cover and simmer for 1 1/2 hours.

2. Add the garlic, pepper, paprika, marjoram, caraway seeds, kale, beans, potatoes, and the remaining 1¹/₂ cups water. Cover and simmer until the meat is very tender and the vegetables are soft, 3 to 3¹/₂ hours (less if using lamb).

———●———

Makes 4 servings

LAMB AND PARSLEY STEW FROM ALBANIA

IT SEEMS EVERYONE HAS CONQUERED Albania, the most underdeveloped country of Europe. The Ottoman Turks ruled Albania from 1501 to 1912 and the Turkish influence is evident not only in the cuisine, but in the fact that 60 percent of the population is Muslim. Albania is a mountainous country, where the ancient hill tribes have never really been conquered and where a fertile coastal strip has seen Macedonian, Roman, Byzantine, Turkish, and even Nazi armies rule.

Both Albania's geography and its history have determined its cuisine. This delightful, parsley-crazed recipe is adapted from one found in Maria Kaneva-Johnson's *The Melting Pot: Balkan Food and Cookery*, published in 1995. In Albanian it is called *mish shqeto*, which means "meat cooked without vegetables." The dish is eaten with a spoon and bread only. But I must insist on the bread, because otherwise some diners might find the stew bland, even though it contains so much parsley. Use a combination of French bread and pita bread,

both warmed in the oven. Use the bread as a utensil to eat pieces of lamb.

———●———

¹/₄ cup Clarified Butter (page 194)
3 pounds lamb shoulder on the bone, trimmed of any large pieces of fat and cut into 1¹/₂-inch pieces
1 cup water
Salt to taste
4 bunches fresh Italian parsley, thick stems discarded and finely chopped
Freshly ground black pepper to taste

———●———

1. In a casserole, melt or heat the clarified butter over medium-high heat. Brown the lamb on all sides, about 10 minutes. Add the water and bring to a boil slowly. Season with salt. Cover, reduce the heat to low, using a heat diffuser if necessary, and cook until the lamb is tender, about 2 hours.

2. Stir in the parsley and simmer until wilted but still bright green, 8 to 10 minutes. Season with pepper and serve immediately.

———●———

Makes 4 to 6 servings

LAMB, SCALLION, AND SPINACH STEW FROM BULGARIA

THE OTTOMAN EMPIRE CONQUERED Bulgaria in the late fourteenth century and controlled the country for centuries. This Turkish presence is still identifiable in some Bulgarian dishes, such as this lamb and spinach stew, whose Turkish-derived name is *gneshka yahniya sus spanak*. The paprika in this dish and the yogurt served as an accompaniment reflect a Turkish culinary mentality. This stew is popular in most of the formerly Turkish-controlled Balkans. Let the lamb stew a long time in the olive oil and scallions, which provide so much flavor, and then add the spinach at the last moment so it retains not only its nutrients but also its appetizing green color. Serve with a dollop of rich, high-quality, plain cow's milk yogurt. This recipe is adapted from Maria Kaneva-Johnson's *The Melting Pot: Balkan Food and Cookery*.

¼ cup extra virgin olive oil

¼ cup (½ stick) unsalted butter

2½ pounds lamb shoulder on the bone, trimmed of any large pieces of fat and cut into pieces

About 2 bunches (6 ounces total) scallions or spring onions (white and green parts), finely chopped

1 tablespoon tomato paste dissolved in ½ cup water

½ teaspoon paprika

Salt to taste

1 pound spinach, washed well, heavy stems removed, and chopped

1. In a casserole, heat the olive oil with the butter over medium-high heat. Once the butter stops sizzling, brown the lamb on all sides, about 5 minutes. Add the scallions and cook until wilted, about 4 minutes. Pour the diluted tomato paste over the lamb, stir in the paprika, and season with salt. Reduce the heat to low, cover, and simmer until the lamb is very tender, about 3 hours.

2. Add the spinach and cook until wilted, about 5 minutes. Check the seasonings and serve with yogurt on the side.

Makes 4 servings

ARNI YAHNI, THE CLASSIC GREEK LAMB STEW

THERE IS NO DOUBT THAT LAMB IS THE favorite meat for stewing in Greece. This recipe for *arni yahni* is derived from the many lamb stews I've had in Greece over the years, mostly eaten in small roadside tavernas. This lamb stew is served throughout the year, except when Greeks are observing a fast, which requires abstinence from meat. There are almost as many variations and recipes for this as there are families in Greece. Serve with pilaf or *manestra* (the Greek word for orzo-like pasta), browned first in butter.

———————

2 tablespoons extra virgin olive oil
1/4 cup (1/2 stick) unsalted butter
2 pounds boneless leg of lamb, trimmed of any
    large pieces of fat and cut into 1/2-inch cubes
1 large onion, chopped
1 cup canned tomato puree
2 garlic cloves, crushed
1/2 cup water
1/2 cup dry white wine
1 bay leaf
Juice from 1/2 lemon
Salt and freshly ground black pepper to taste

———————

1. In a large casserole, heat the olive oil with the butter over medium heat. Once the butter has melted and stopped sizzling, lightly brown the lamb on all sides, about 8 minutes. Remove the meat with a slotted spoon and set aside. Cook the onion in the casserole until lightly browned, 12 to 15 minutes, stirring occasionally.

2. Return the lamb to the casserole, and add the tomato puree, garlic, water, wine, bay leaf, and lemon juice, and season with salt and pepper. Reduce the heat to low, cover, and cook until the lamb is tender, about 2 hours.

Variation: *Arni yahni* is usually made with a vegetable. Chickpeas, winter squash, celery, okra, cauliflower, carrots, or cabbage cut into large chunks might be added at the same time as the lamb. Or vegetables that cook more quickly, such as thickly sliced zucchini, spinach leaves, or peas, might be added when there is only 45 minutes of cooking time left for the lamb.

———————

Makes 4 to 6 servings

LAMB STEW "KAPAMA" STYLE

I N GREECE, *KAPAMA* REFERS TO ANY KIND of meat cooked in a slightly sweetened and spicy tomato sauce with onions. Originally it was a Turkish dish, its name derived from the Turkish word *kapama*, a ragout of mutton simply cooked in butter, onions, water, salt, and pepper. *Kapama* is actually a genre of dishes cooked by a method that is between boiling and steaming. It is best made in cold weather, especially in the spring, and is usually prepared with lean lamb. Before serving, Greeks like to cover the stew with parsley and chopped raw onions. This dish is usually accompanied with fresh runner beans.

———————

2 1/2 pounds boneless lamb, cut from the shoulder
    or leg, trimmed of any large pieces of fat and
    cut into 1/2-inch cubes
Salt and freshly ground black pepper to taste
1 teaspoon ground cinnamon, or to taste

Juice from 1 lemon
¼ cup (½ stick) unsalted butter
2 tablespoons extra virgin olive oil
2 pounds crushed tomatoes, fresh (preferably) or
   canned
1 cup hot water, or as needed
½ cup finely chopped fresh parsley leaves
   (optional)
1 medium-size onion (optional), finely chopped

1. Season the lamb with the salt and pepper, and cinnamon. Place in a medium bowl, add the lemon juice, and stir. Set aside for 30 minutes.

2. In a large skillet, melt the butter with the olive oil over medium heat. When the butter stops sizzling, brown the lamb, about 8 minutes. Remove the meat from the pan with a slotted spoon and set aside. Add the tomatoes, bring to a boil, and cook for 5 minutes. Return the meat to the pan. Cook over low heat until tender, about 2 hours, adding the hot water if the pan dries out. Sprinkle the parsley and onion over the meat, if desired, and serve.

Makes 5 to 6 servings

PINK STEW
A TURKISH STEW OF LAMB WITH TOMATO AND YOGURT SAUCE

THIS TURKISH STEW IS A TYPICAL HOME-style stew: a boneless leg of lamb is braised for a long time in a sauce made of tomato puree and yogurt, hence the fact that the finished sauce is pink. As simple as everything looks here, rest assured that the final taste is explosively appealing to the taste buds.

One 3-pound boneless leg of lamb, tied with
   kitchen twine into one uniform piece
3 large garlic cloves, slivered
Salt and freshly ground black pepper to taste
2 tablespoons extra virgin olive oil
1 cup canned tomato puree
1 cup Stabilized Cow's Milk Yogurt (page 121)
1 teaspoon freshly ground allspice berries

1. Puncture the leg of lamb all over with a skewer or sharp tip of a knife and insert the slivers of garlic. Season the lamb with salt and pepper.

2. In a casserole, heat the olive oil over high heat, then brown the lamb on all sides, about 10 minutes. Reduce the heat to very low, using a heat diffuser if necessary. Stir the tomato puree, yogurt, and allspice together, then coat the lamb with this mixture. Season again with salt and pepper. Cover and cook until the meat is almost melting away, about 5 hours. Serve immediately.

———— ● ————

Makes 6 servings

GARLICKY LAMB SHANK AND WHITE BEAN STEW FROM TURKEY

T HIS TURKISH STEW CALLED *KUZU ETLI kuru fasülye güveçi*, literally, "dry claypot-cooked gobbets of lamb and bean stew," is a stew cooked with a little liquid for a very long time. Ideally you will use a large earthenware casserole with a lid, sitting on a heat diffuser if your burner can't go low enough. The lid is essential to keep all the moisture in the casserole, which will turn the tough shank into succulent pieces of lamb, melting off the bone. The beans will cook in the juices and fat of the lamb, and by the time it's ready, they too will be soft and melt in your mouth. Turkish red pepper is a kind of chile that is unusually dark colored, usually sun-dried and ground, and typically found in Middle Eastern markets. It sometimes goes by the name Aleppo pepper or else *maras biber*. You can get some from Kalustyan's (see the sources listed in the back of the book). Or substitute a blend of two parts sweet paprika and one part cayenne pepper.

¹/₂ cup (1 stick) unsalted butter
5 pounds lamb shanks
2 medium-size onions, chopped
8 large garlic cloves, finely chopped
1 quart water
2 tablespoons tomato paste
5 cups peeled, seeded, and chopped fresh tomatoes (about 3 pounds tomatoes)
4 cups dried white beans, picked over, rinsed, soaked overnight in cold water to cover, and drained
2 tablespoons Turkish red pepper
Salt and freshly ground black pepper to taste
6 Italian long green peppers (peperoncini), seeded and cut into rings
¹/₄ cup finely chopped fresh parsley leaves

———— ● ————

1. In a large earthenware casserole set on a heat diffuser, melt the butter over medium-high heat. (If you are not cooking with earthenware and a diffuser, place a Dutch oven over medium heat and check for doneness sooner.) When the butter stops sizzling, brown the lamb on all sides, about 8 minutes. Add the onions and garlic and cook for 4 minutes, stirring. Add the water, and bring to a boil. Reduce the heat to medium-low and simmer at a gentle boil for 1¹/₂ hours, skimming the surface of foam if necessary.

2. Add the tomato paste, tomatoes, beans, and red pepper. Season with salt and black pepper, cover, and bring to a boil. Reduce the heat to very low and simmer until the meat falls off the bone and the beans melt in your mouth, 4¹/₂ to 5 hours. The liquid in the casserole should bubble only slightly, if at all.

3. An hour before the stew is finished, add the green peppers, cover, and continue to cook. Serve with a sprinkling of parsley.

Makes 8 to 10 servings

LAMB, POTATO, AND PRESERVED LEMON STEW OF A TUNISIAN FAMILY

THIS TUNISIAN PREPARATION CALLED *al-kūsha bi'l-ᶜalūsh* is an old one. The Arabic word *al-kūsha* is used in North Africa to mean "bread oven," thought by some scholars to be a transformation from the Latin *coquere panem*, "to cook bread." In the Middle Ages, and until quite recently in certain parts of the Mediterranean, the people in towns like Bizerte, on the northern coast of Tunisia, would use public ovens to bake bread and foods. Throughout the Mediterranean families left their meals with the village baker, providing him with instructions on how they wanted them cooked. He would bake the food, and the family would pick up the meals later and bring them home.

These simple, family-style preparations prove the most surprising. Take this lamb, potato, and long green pepper (*peperoncino*) stew that is oven-baked in a very flavorful, thin broth of olive oil and lamb juice, with lots of parsley, red pepper, and preserved lemon. I first ate this at a lunchtime workingman's restaurant called Restaurant de Cuisine Tunisienne in Bizerte, after hours of strolling through this former Barbary corsair base with its beige-washed square dwellings. The lamb broth flavors the potatoes in such a way that you will admit that they are the best potatoes you've ever tasted—no matter what kind of waxy potato you use.

2 pounds lamb shoulder, on the bone, cut into 6 pieces and trimmed of fat
1 small onion, finely chopped
Salt and freshly ground black pepper to taste
1 tablespoon tomato paste
2 quarts water
¹/₃ teaspoon cayenne pepper
¹/₄ cup extra virgin olive oil
2 pounds new Russian Banana (fingerling) or new Yukon Gold potatoes, peeled and halved or quartered lengthwise
2 Italian long green peppers (peperoncini), seeded and quartered lengthwise
Leaves from 1 bunch fresh parsley, finely chopped
1 Preserved Lemon (page 108), sliced into thin wedges

1. Preheat the oven to 350°F. Toss the lamb and onion together with salt and pepper and arrange in a baking pan. Mix the tomato paste with 2 cups of the water, the cayenne, and olive oil, and pour it over the meat. Bake, covered, for 1 hour, spooning the pan juices over the meat occasionally as it bakes. Add another 3 cups of the water and bake another 1¹/₂ hours.

Moisten with the remaining 3 cups of water, as needed, to keep the stew from drying out.

2. Arrange the potatoes and green peppers in the baking pan with the meat. Spoon the pan juices over everything. Bake until a skewer glides easily into the potatoes without their falling apart, another 20 to 30 minutes. Check the seasonings.

3. Sprinkle the parsley over the meat and vegetables and toss well. Place the meat in the center of a deep serving platter or on individual plates and surround it with the vegetables and preserved lemon slices. Spoon pan juices over everything and serve.

Makes 4 servings

PRESERVED LEMONS

Preserved lemons are used in the everyday cooking of Morocco, Algeria, and Tunisia. In Morocco, they are known also as *ḥamaḍ muraqqaḍ* and, in Tunisia, *laymūn al—imallaḥ āqariṣ baldī imallaḥ, qāriṣ* being another word for lemon. Preserved lemons enhance a dish immensely and I find them quite beguiling and use them in non–North African preparations as well.

2 lemons, preferably thin-skinned ones, such as Meyer lemons

¹/₃ cup salt
¹/₂ cup fresh lemon juice
Extra virgin olive oil, as needed

Scrub the lemons, dry them, and cut each into 8 wedges. Toss the lemon wedges with the salt and place in a ¹/₂-pint jar with a glass or plastic lid. Cover the lemons with the lemon juice and screw on the lid. Leave the jar at room temperature for 7 days, shaking it occasionally. After 1 week, pour in the olive oil to cover and store in the refrigerator, where they will keep for up to 6 months.

Makes 1 cup preserved lemons

SIMPLE AND SPICY LAMB AND POTATO STEW FROM TUNISIA

THE ESSENTIAL IDEA BEHIND THIS STEW IS not so much the cayenne pepper, which makes it spicy—and that is a nice touch—but rather the broth that evolves from the stewing lamb and that flavors the potatoes in such a memorable way. Cook it slowly and let the lamb become very tender and the potatoes inundated with its flavor. Serve with plain rice pilaf (page 125) if you like, although the stew is probably better with a salad.

2 tablespoons extra virgin olive oil
2½ pounds lamb neck and shoulder on the bone
1 medium-size onion, chopped
1 quart water
4 garlic cloves, finely chopped
¼ teaspoon cayenne pepper
2 tablespoons tomato paste
Salt and freshly ground black pepper to taste
4 White Rose or red potatoes (about 1 pound),
   halved lengthwise

———————●———————

1. In a casserole, heat the olive oil over medium-high heat. Brown the lamb with the onion, stirring and turning occasionally, about 5 minutes. Add the water, garlic, cayenne, and tomato paste. Season with salt and pepper, cover, and reduce the heat to low. Simmer until the lamb is very tender, but not quite falling off the bone, about 4 hours.

2. Add the potatoes and continue to cook until the potatoes are tender and a skewer can glide easily into the center, about 1 more hour.

———————●———————

Makes 4 servings

SWEET LAMB AND QUINCE RAGOUT
IN THE TUNISIAN WAY

THIS TUNISIAN STEW, CALLED *MARAQA al-safarjal* or "quince ragout," is a kind of slowly cooked ragout that is sweet, rather than fiery hot as is typical of many Tunisian stews. A *maraqa* is actually what the French call an *etuvée*, a long-simmering, covered stew containing very little fat or liquid. (I call it a ragout since that's the word I believe readers are most familiar with.) In Morocco, they call this kind of stew a tagine. The amount of sugar in this stew may look excessive. It is not, but the stew is sweet.

This style of cookery, as well as the name *maraqa*, appears in Provence too, likely an introduction by the Pieds-Noirs, the former French settlers of North Africa, as evidenced by J.-B. Reboul's recipe for *la marga* in his nineteenth-century cookbook *La Cuisinière Provençale*. There Reboul has completely changed the concept, but the combination of ingredients is purely North African—lamb and chicken cooked with fava beans, chickpeas, cardoons, zucchini, artichokes, and onions, seasoned with cayenne pepper, cumin, and other spices.

Although I call for quince in this recipe, it can also be made with prunes or dried apricots. Dried rose petals are traditionally used as a flavoring, and they can usually be found in whole-food markets. Do not use rose petals from flowers purchased at a florist or garden center, only from organic roses. The provenance of this particular combination of lamb and fruit appears to be Persian, via the Ottoman Turks, although the Greeks know a similar dish called *arni me kithounia* or *kidonia*, which they make with veal or pork as well as the cinnamon. It too is probably derived from the Persians through the Turks. Instead of boneless leg of lamb, you can also use a beautiful lamb shank for a rather impressive-looking presentation.

1¼ pounds boneless leg of lamb, trimmed of all
fat and cubed, or 4 lamb shanks (about 3½
pounds)
½ teaspoon ground cinnamon
1 teaspoon dried and ground organic rose petals
or ¼ teaspoon rose water
Salt to taste
½ cup extra virgin olive oil
1½ pounds quince, cut into eighths and cored
(see Note)
3 to 4 cups water, as needed
1⅓ cups sugar

———————●———————

1. In a medium-size bowl, toss the lamb to-gether with the cinnamon, ground rose petals, and salt.

2. In a medium-size casserole, heat the olive oil over medium-high heat and brown the lamb, stirring, about 2 minutes. Add the quince, cover with the water, and bring to a boil. Reduce the heat to medium-low and cook for 1 hour, uncovered. Add the sugar and stir. Cover and cook until the lamb is very tender and the quince soft, about 1 more hour.

3. Remove to a serving platter with a slotted spoon and serve.

———————●———————

Makes 4 servings

Note: Quince are like very hard apples. Use a sharp knife, and don't cut them up until you need them because they discolor.

LAMB AND LENTIL RAGOUT WITH CAYENNE FROM TUNISIA

———~———

I N THIS *MARAQA BI'L-ʿADAS*, OR "LENTIL ragout," the lamb is used as a flavoring con-diment for the lentils. The taste is soothing and lusty, although my recipe actually has about twice as much lamb as a typical Tunisian family would use. So reduce the amount by half if you are a stickler for authenticity.

———————●———————

⅔ cup extra virgin olive oil
1½ pounds boneless lamb neck and shoulder,
trimmed of all fat and cubed
Salt to taste
1 teaspoon freshly ground pepper, plus extra for
seasoning the lamb
1 medium-size onion, chopped
2 tablespoons tomato paste
2 cups water
1¼ cups dried brown or green lentils, picked
over and rinsed
1 teaspoon cayenne pepper
1 teaspoon garlic powder

———————●———————

1. In a medium-size, nonreactive casserole, heat the olive oil over medium heat. Season the lamb with salt and pepper. Brown the lamb and onion together until the onion is soft and golden, stirring occasionally, 8 to 10 minutes.

2. Mix the tomato paste with the water. Add the tomato mixture, lentils, 1 teaspoon of black pepper, cayenne, and garlic powder to the lamb. Stir, cover, and reduce the heat to very low. Simmer until the lamb is very tender, stirring occasionally, about 2 hours. Serve.

Makes 4 servings

PIQUANT MUTTON AND ZUCCHINI STEWED IN VINEGAR FROM TUNISIA

IN TUNISIA AND ALGERIA THERE IS A CLASS of stews known as *madarbal*, which generally means that they are meat stewed with vinegar. This stew is called *madarbal qarᶜ*, and it is traditionally cooked in a stew pot called a *ṭanjara*, a cylindrical tin-lined *marmite*. *Qarᶜ* is an old word used by the twelfth-century Muslim agronomist Ibn al-ᶜAwwām to refer to a kind of small white gourd that he called "the best," perhaps a kind of colocynth (*Citrullis colocynthis*) or calabash gourd (*Lagenaria siceria*). Today the word refers to zucchini or any summer squash. If you are unable to find mutton, use lamb, of course, although it will need about an hour less cooking. This is a rather hot dish and, for that reason, it is best accompanied by something bland or cool, perhaps a cucumber salad.

3 pounds mutton leg on the bone, trimmed of any large pieces of fat and cut into chunks
Salt and freshly ground black pepper to taste
¾ cup extra virgin olive oil
1 medium-size onion, coarsely chopped
1½ tablespoons Harīsa (page 34)
¾ pound ripe tomatoes, cut in half, seeds squeezed out, and grated against the largest holes of a grater down to the peel
2 fresh red or green chiles or jalapeños
1½ teaspoons ground red chile
One 15-ounce can chickpeas, drained
2 cups water
1½ pounds yellow summer squash or zucchini, ends trimmed and thinly sliced
2 tablespoons white wine vinegar

1. Toss the meat with salt and black pepper. In a large casserole, heat 6 tablespoons of the olive oil over medium-high heat. Brown the meat with the onion, 6 to 7 minutes. Add the *harīsa*, tomatoes, fresh chiles, ground chile, chickpeas, and water. Bring to a boil, reduce the heat to low, and simmer, covered, until very tender, about 4 hours.

2. Meanwhile, in a large skillet, heat the remaining 6 tablespoons of olive oil over medium-high heat. Cook the squash until soft and golden, 5 to 6 minutes. Transfer to the mutton casserole, add the vinegar, and cook until the stew is gooey and the vinegar evaporated, about 15 minutes. Check the seasonings and serve.

Makes 6 servings

LEAFY GREEN VEGETABLE AND MUTTON RAGOUT FROM TUNIS

THIS TUNISIAN DISH CALLED *MARAQA al-khuḍra*, which means vegetable (*khuḍra*) ragout (*maraqa*), is typical of home cooking in Tunis. Some cooks might add leafy vegetables such as spinach, root vegetables such as turnips, legumes such as haricot beans, and even thistles such as artichokes, cardoons, or golden thistle (*Scolymus hispanicus* L.). There are almost as many different *maraqa*s as there are families. A *maraqa* is to a Tunisian family what *spezzatino* is to an Italian family (see page 70). This *maraqa* is typically cooked at midday by housewives and is often reheated for dinner.

1/2 cup extra virgin olive oil
1 pound boneless lamb or mutton shoulder, trimmed of any large pieces of fat and cut into 1-inch cubes
1 1/2 teaspoons Tābil (page 37)
1 1/2 teaspoons black pepper, plus extra for seasoning the lamb
2 medium-large onions, chopped
1 pound Swiss chard, washed well, trimmed of the lower, heavier part of their stems, and chopped, with rinse water left clinging to the leaves
Leaves from 1 bunch fresh parsley, chopped, with rinse water left clinging to the leaves
2/3 cup canned chickpeas, drained
2 tablespoons tomato paste

1 1/2 teaspoons Harīsa (page 34) mixed with 1/2 cup water
Juice from 1 lemon
1 1/2 teaspoons ground red chile

---

1. In a medium-size, nonreactive casserole, heat the olive oil over high heat. Toss the lamb or mutton with the *tābil* and some salt and pepper. Brown the meat and onions in the hot oil, stirring frequently, about 5 minutes.

2. Reduce the heat to low and add the Swiss chard and parsley. Cook until the liquid is mostly evaporated, about 10 minutes. Add the chickpeas, tomato paste, diluted *harīsa*, lemon juice, the 1 1/2 teaspoons black pepper, and the red chile. Mix well, cover, and simmer over very low heat, using a diffuser if necessary, until the meat is very tender, about 2 hours. Moisten the ragout with small amounts of water if it is drying out. Serve immediately.

Makes 4 servings

SWEET MUTTON, ALMOND, AND ROSE PETAL STEW FROM TUNISIA

IN TUNISIA, MOST STEWS ARE CALLED *maraqa* (singular), and sometimes tagine, whereas in Morocco a stew is known mostly as a tagine. But some specialized stews, for example, stews made for festivals or religious holidays, such as the ʿĪd al-Kabīr festival, the holiday that celebrates the sacrifice of Abraham, take on special names. This stew, made with mutton, chickpeas, sugar, raisins, and almonds, is called a *marūziya. Marūziya* is an old name, going back to a Hispano-Muslim preparation called *al-ʿāsima* that was made when the Spanish city of Granada in Andalusia was under Islamic rule in the fourteenth century. *Al-ʿāsima* was made with meat, salt, coriander, oil, a little honey, starch, almonds, and pears and exists today in Morocco, where it is called *marsiya*, a dish of boiled meat with honey, almonds, and raisins. It may be related to the Latin word *amorusia*, boiled meat. Some Tunisian cooks have their own variations on this stew. For example, chestnuts could replace the almonds and one could use plums, prunes, and fresh apricots too. As you can tell, the dish is sweet, but not overly so. In any case, you will definitely want to serve this stew with some kind of grain to subdue the very fragrant power of the mutton, such as steamed couscous or rice pilaf (page 125).

---

2 pounds boneless leg of mutton, trimmed of any
    large pieces of fat and cut into 1¹/₂-inch cubes
1 tablespoon Tābil (page 37)
1 teaspoon freshly ground black pepper
Salt to taste
³/₄ cup extra virgin olive oil
4 cups canned chickpeas, drained
1 cup blanched whole almonds (about 5 ounces)
2 cups water
²/₃ cup sugar
1¹/₂ cups raisins (about 6 ounces)
1 teaspoon dried and ground organic rose petals
    or ¹/₂ teaspoon rose water

---

1. Roll the mutton pieces in the *tābil*, pepper, and salt. In a casserole or stew pot, heat the olive oil over medium-high heat. Brown the mutton, stirring, 8 to 10 minutes. Add the chickpeas and almonds, cover with the water, and bring to a boil. Reduce the heat to low and simmer, uncovered, until the liquid has evaporated by about half, stirring occasionally, about 1¹/₂ hours.

2. Stir the sugar, raisins, and rose petals into the stew. Cook until the liquid has reduced by half again, stirring occasionally, about 1 hour. Serve immediately.

Makes 6 servings

FIERY WHITE HARICOT BEANS, ONION, AND LAMB STEW
OF THE HOUSEWIVES OF ALGIERS

THIS ALGERIAN STEW IS FAMILY FARE AND would typically be found at the table at lunch, the main meal in Algeria, for which the father returns home from work. The stew is made with lamb or often mutton and dried white haricot beans with lots of onions and tomatoes. It is seasoned until spicy hot with cayenne pepper, fresh chile, and the ubiquitous chile paste called *harīsa*. In Arabic, the name of this preparation doesn't even hint at the presence of the lamb, for it is simply called *lūbya baydā bi'l-basal wa'l-tūmātim*, "white beans with onions and tomatoes." In fact, the original recipe given to me that is the basis for this one called for nearly four pounds of dried beans to less than two pounds of lamb. Although it is not necessary to serve this stew with anything because the beans make it substantial enough, it would be delightful with a platter of fresh salad greens, seeded and sliced cucumbers, and ripe tomatoes, all chopped up and dressed with a drizzle of extra virgin olive oil, very finely chopped garlic, a dusting of cayenne, and fresh lemon juice.

1³/4 pounds boneless leg or shoulder of mutton or lamb, trimmed of any large pieces of fat and cut into ³/4-inch pieces

1 tablespoon salt, plus more to taste

2 teaspoons freshly ground black pepper, plus more to taste

1 teaspoon cayenne pepper

1/4 cup extra virgin olive oil

1 tablespoon Harīsa (page 34)

3 medium-large onions (1³/4 pounds), coarsely chopped

3 large, ripe tomatoes (about 1¹/2 pounds), peeled, seeded, and chopped

1 quart water

2 cups (1 pound) dried white haricot beans, picked over, rinsed, soaked in water to cover overnight, and drained

1/2 cup finely chopped fresh coriander (cilantro) leaves

---

1. Season the meat with the salt, pepper, and cayenne. In a large earthenware casserole set on a heat diffuser, heat the olive oil over high heat. (If you are not cooking with earthenware and a diffuser, cook over medium-high heat and check for doneness sooner.) Brown the meat for 5 to 10 minutes, stirring occasionally. Add the *harīsa*, stir, then add the onions and tomatoes. Reduce the heat to low, cover, and simmer for 15 minutes.

2. Add the water, beans, and coriander. Bring to a boil, reduce the heat to low, and let it simmer until the beans are tender, 2 to 2¹/2 hours, stirring occasionally. Correct the seasonings, then serve hot.

Makes 6 to 8 servings

QAMAMA: A LAMB AND SULTANA STEW

ANYONE FAMILIAR WITH MEDITERranean stews has probably heard of a tagine (pronounced tajEEN or TAJn), an Arabic word used in North Africa to denote a kind of earthenware casserole; in Morocco, to refer to a kind of stew; and in Tunisia, a frittata. The plural of tagine is *tawājin*, referring to a category of Moroccan-style dry stews similar to what the French call *étouffée* (which actually means "smothered") or *étuvée*, a slow braise with very little liquid. The best way to cook one of these stews is by very slowly simmering over low heat for hours and hours and never ever looking under the lid as it cooks. This stew is called *qamama*.

The tagines called *qamama* or *qamma*, an old Arabic word used in the *Thousand and One Nights*, connote a particular kind of lamb preparation. It seems to be a process of wrapping or, perhaps, smothering the lamb. The sweetness of this recipe, which uses sultanas, a type of golden raisin, is typical in Morocco.

———————•———————

3 pounds lamb shoulder on the bone, trimmed of
    any large pieces of fat and cubed
1/4 cup extra virgin olive oil
2 large onions, grated or finely chopped
3 garlic cloves, finely chopped
1 teaspoon ground ginger
1/2 teaspoon ground cinnamon
1/2 cup sugar
2 pinches of saffron threads, lightly toasted in a
    dry skillet and finely crumbled or powdered in
    a mortar with a little salt
Salt and freshly ground black pepper to taste
1 cup water
1 cup golden raisins

———————•———————

1. Place the lamb in a tagine or earthenware casserole with a cover, set on a heat diffuser. Add the olive oil, onions, garlic, ginger, 1/4 teaspoon of the cinnamon, 2 tablespoons of the sugar, the saffron, salt, pepper, and water. Toss so all the pieces of meat are coated. Bring to a boil over medium-high heat. (Or set an enameled cast-iron casserole or Dutch oven directly over medium heat and check for doneness sooner.) Reduce the heat to low, partially cover, and simmer until the meat is tender, about 2 hours. Remove the meat from the sauce and set aside.

2. Increase the heat to medium-low, add the raisins to the casserole, and continue to cook until the sauce is thick and unctuous, about 45 minutes. Tilt the casserole and spoon out any fat that has collected. Remove the sauce from the casserole to a measuring cup or a mixing bowl with a spout.

3. Preheat the oven to 325°F. Return the meat to the casserole and arrange on the bottom. Cover with the sauce, sprinkle with the remaining 1/4 cup plus 2 tablespoons of sugar and 1/4 teaspoon of cinnamon. Bake in the oven until the lamb is falling off the bone and very tender, about 1 hour. Serve hot.

———————•———————

Makes 4 to 6 servings

ḤARQMA

ḤARQMA IS A WELL-KNOWN NAME IN THE Maghrib, apparently introduced during Arab-Andalusian times of the Middle Ages, and a beloved dish during Ramadan. This spicy lamb trotters soup has an old history too. Ḥarqma was a word used by the lexicographer Pedro de Alcala in his *Vocabulista arávigo en lengua castellana*, published in 1505, to mean "ripe" or "intestines." The word was also used to refer to cow's hooves, to a kind of ratatouille, and to butcher's scraps made into a soup. In Morocco, ḥarqma is a tagine of sheep's trotters cooked with wheat and chickpeas, and is said to have been a breakfast favorite of the late king of Morocco Hassan II. Ḥarqma also exists farther east in Tunisia, where it is more of a stew soup, like this recipe, but can also refer to a ragout of tripe, feet, and heart. This recipe uses lamb shank. The preparation is so well loved in the Maghrib that North African friends of mine insisted it must be included in any book about stews. The lamb feet are essential in this recipe because of the flavor derived from their gelatin, but you will have to special order them from the butcher or find a ḥalāl (the Muslim equivalent of a kosher butcher market), where they almost always will be on hand (no pun intended).

1/4 cup extra virgin olive oil
2 pounds lamb feet
2 pounds lamb shanks
Salt and freshly ground black pepper to taste
2 tablespoons Harīsa (page 34)

2 quarts water
2 large eggs
2 tablespoons fresh lemon juice

---

1. In a large stew pot or casserole, heat the olive oil over medium-high heat. Season the lamb feet and shanks with salt and pepper. Brown the feet and shanks on all sides in the hot oil, 4 to 5 minutes. Stir the *harīsa* into the casserole. Once it has dissolved and blended with the oil, pour in the water. Bring to a boil, and reduce the heat to low. Cover and cook until the lamb is tender, about 2 1/2 hours.

2. Strain the stew and discard the feet and bones, removing and chopping any meat from the shank. Return the broth and chopped meat to the casserole.

3. Break the eggs into a bowl and whisk in the lemon juice. Whisk a ladle full of hot broth into the egg mixture. Once it is blended, whisk in another ladle full of broth. Now whisk the entire egg mixture back into the stew. Strain again and discard all bits of gristly meat and fat. Return the strained broth and nice bits of meat to the casserole, heat a bit, and serve.

Makes 6 servings

SWEETLY SAFFRONED LAMB, ONION, AND GOLDEN RAISIN STEW
OF THE JEWS OF MOROCCO

—•—

MOROCCAN JEWS TYPICALLY MADE THIS lamb stew they called *ṭājīn bi'l-laḥm* for the Passover feast by cooking it over a hardwood fire. The name is Arabic of course, the lingua franca of the Jews who lived in Morocco, and it simply means "lamb stew." The final dish is a sweet and unctuous preparation that is delightful. You can serve directly from the casserole and accompany the dish, if you like, with couscous.

—•—

2 pounds boneless leg of lamb, trimmed of any
    large pieces of fat and cut into large cubes
2 pounds small white or red onions, peeled and
    left whole or cut in half through the stem if
    larger than a lemon
¹/₄ cup extra virgin olive oil
Pinch of saffron threads, lightly toasted in a
    dry skillet and pounded in a mortar with
    2 teaspoons salt
¹/₂ cup confectioners' sugar
¹/₂ cup golden raisins
¹/₂ teaspoon ground cinnamon
3 tablespoons pine nuts

—•—

1. In an earthenware casserole, such as a tagine or *cazuela*, or an enameled cast-iron stew pot, put the lamb, onions, olive oil, and saffron and salt mixture. Toss with a ladle to mix the ingredients. If using earthenware, place on a heat diffuser and turn the heat to medium, otherwise, turn the heat to low. Cover and cook until the onions look soft, stirring occasionally, about 45 minutes.

2. Add the confectioners' sugar, raisins, and cinnamon, and stir to mix. Cover and cook until the meat is tender, about 30 minutes.

3. Meanwhile, preheat the oven to 400°F. Place the casserole in the oven and bake for 10 minutes. Sprinkle the top of the stew with the pine nuts and bake until they are lightly golden, about 5 minutes. Serve immediately.

—•—

Makes 4 servings

THE CLASSIC EGYPTIAN LAMB AND GREEN BEAN STEW

—•—

THE COOKING OF EGYPT IS KNOWN throughout the Arab world as a kind of second-class cookery. The Lebanese view Egyptian cookery in the same way the French look down upon British cooking: they're not very impressed. But, if you keep in mind that the country is poor, and that the Egyptians love life and are eternally optimistic, then you can begin to appreciate their stew cookery. Stew cookery in Egypt is usually very simple, always uses lamb (which is always cooked until the lamb falls apart), always contains a green vegetable, and always uses tomato sauce. This recipe is a typical Egyptian style of cooking lamb with beans called *yakhnat al-lūbya* ("green bean stew"). The spicing is very simple. Incidentally, tomato sauce is always used in the Egyptian style of cooking vegetables. The meat needs to cook a very long time, and for that reason, the lusciousness is quite powerful. Lamb shank is a really nice cut, which holds up well as it simmers.

1/4 cup (1/2 stick) unsalted butter
4 large lamb shanks (about 31/2 pounds)
2 large red onions, coarsely chopped
One 6-ounce can tomato paste
31/2 cups water
11/2 teaspoons freshly ground allspice berries
Salt and freshly ground black pepper to taste
1 pound green beans, ends trimmed and cut into
*   2-inch lengths*

---

1. In a large casserole, melt the butter over medium-high heat. Once it stops sizzling, brown the lamb on both sides with the onions, about 5 minutes. Dilute the tomato paste in 11/2 cups of the water. Stir the mixture into the casserole with the lamb and add the remaining 2 cups water and the allspice, and season with salt and pepper. Stir again, reduce the heat to very low, cover, and cook for 2 hours.

2. Add the green beans and continue to cook until the meat falls off the bone with a slight poke, another 2 to 3 hours.

Makes 4 servings

PALESTINIAN-STYLE GREEN BEAN AND LAMB STEW

I N 1560, A GREAT MEAT MARKET EXISTED in Jerusalem. The highest quality sheep— mutton and lamb being the two most popular meats—were called *turkumānī*, a reference to the Turcoman tribes who drove their sheep from northeastern Syria and Anatolia to the Palestinian markets. The other kind of sheep available was *balqāwī*, named for the area east of the Jordan River where Bedouin drove their sheep to the Jerusalem market. The most popular cuts of meat were the *majrūm*, or filet, and the *liyya*, the fat, tail-like, lower part of the sheep's back, which has no bones and is the fat equivalent to filet mignon.

This long-simmering stew, whose Arabic name *yakhnat al-lūbya* means simply "green bean stew," is flavored with a small amount of lamb and spices. It can be accompanied by rice pilaf (page 125) or it can be made with fava beans for a dish called *yakhnat al-fūl* (page 129).

---

2 pounds fresh green beans, ends trimmed and
*   cut into 2-inch lengths*
1/2 cup Clarified Butter (page 194) or unsalted
*   butter*
3/4 pound boneless leg of lamb or lamb shoulder,
*   trimmed of any large pieces of fat and cut into*
*   1/2-inch cubes*
2 medium-size onions, chopped

3 ripe plum tomatoes, peeled, seeded, and
   chopped, with their juices
1 cup water
1/2 teaspoon ground cinnamon
1/2 teaspoon **Bahārāt** (recipe follows)
1/2 teaspoon freshly ground allspice berries
1/4 teaspoon freshly grated nutmeg
Salt and freshly ground black pepper to taste
3 large garlic cloves, peeled
1 teaspoon salt

---

1. Bring a large pot of water to a furious boil and blanch the green beans for 3 to 4 minutes. Drain and place the green beans in ice cold water to stop their cooking. Drain and set aside.

2. In a large, nonreactive casserole or skillet, melt the clarified butter over medium-high heat. Brown the lamb on all sides, stirring, about 8 minutes. Add the onions and cook until they turn yellow, about 6 minutes, stirring a few times. Add the green beans and cook for 2 minutes, then add the tomatoes with their juices, water, cinnamon, *bahārāt*, allspice, and nutmeg. Season with salt and pepper and bring to a boil while stirring. Reduce the heat to low, cover, and simmer until the lamb and green beans are tender, 2 to 3 hours. Check occasionally for doneness.

3. In a mortar, mash the garlic together with the salt. Stir the garlic into the stew and serve.

Makes 6 servings

BAHĀRĀT: MIXED SPICES FOR ARAB STEWS

Bahārāt means "spice" in Arabic. It is derived from the word *bahār*, which means "pepper," so it is a mixed spice with black pepper. This particular all-purpose spice mix is used in Lebanon, Syria, Jordan, and Palestine, where it is found in many prepared savory dishes.

Bahārāt can be bought at Middle Eastern groceries and markets, but it is also quite easy to make a fresh batch for yourself and keep it stored in a spice jar. There are many different variations, all based on the basic ingredients of black pepper and allspice. Some mixes might include paprika, coriander seeds, cassia bark, sumac, nutmeg, cumin seeds, or cardamom seeds. This recipe is basic; if you like, you can fiddle with it by adding some of the other spices mentioned above.

1/4 cup black peppercorns
1/4 cup allspice berries
2 teaspoons ground cinnamon
1 teaspoon freshly grated nutmeg

Grind the peppercorns and allspice together, then blend with the cinnamon and nutmeg. Store in a jar in your spice rack, away from sunlight. It will lose pungency as time goes by, but properly stored, it will keep for many months.

Makes about 1/2 cup

LABAN UMMU

2 garlic cloves, finely chopped
2 teaspoons dried mint

LABAN UMMU MEANS "HIS MOTHER'S milk," the implication of the name being that the young lamb is cooked in its mother's milk. This Palestinian preparation is also popular in Lebanon, Jordan, and Syria. But this business of the mother's milk is just a method of cooking and does not have any religious or social connotation. This Levantine Arab stew finds the lamb meat slowly simmered in yogurt. The best cut to use for this recipe is lamb shank, which is a banana-shaped meat that runs the length of the shin bone and is very succulent and tender when stewed for a long time. Of course, you can use any lamb stew meat if you don't want to be bothered cutting the meat off the length of the shank. Also, remember that cow's milk yogurt will separate when cooked, so it must be stabilized by following the method described on page 121. Goat's milk yogurt, on the other hand, will not separate. Serve with rice pilaf (page 125).

1. Put the lamb in a casserole and cover with the water. Sprinkle with 1 teaspoon of the salt and add 2 of the white onions or a handful of the pearl onions. Bring to a boil and reduce the heat to low. Partially cover, and cook until the lamb is very tender, about 3 hours.

2. In the meantime, place the stabilized yogurt in a casserole or stew pot large enough to hold the lamb and onions. Boil the remaining onions separately in a large saucepan with water to cover until soft, about 20 minutes. Remove and stir into the yogurt.

3. Remove the lamb and onions from the casserole with a slotted spoon and transfer to the yogurt. Place over medium heat and keep warm, just below a boil, stirring a few times.

4. In a small skillet, melt the clarified butter over medium heat. Add the garlic, mint, and remaining teaspoon of salt and cook for 30 seconds to 1 minute, stirring. Add to the yogurt and lamb and cook until heated through, stirring occasionally, about 20 minutes. Serve immediately.

Makes 4 servings

1 pound boneless lamb stew meat, trimmed of any large pieces of fat and cut into 2-inch cubes
1 quart water
2 teaspoons salt
¹/₂ pound small white onions, halved or quartered, or red or white pearl onions, peeled
1 quart Stabilized Cow's Milk Yogurt (recipe follows)
2 tablespoons Clarified Butter (page 194) or unsalted butter

CAULIFLOWER IN THE MIDDLE EAST

Arab cooks are fond of cauliflower and have several names for it—*qunnabīṭ*, *qurnnabīṭ*, and *qarnabīṭ*. *Mufarraq* is a kind of cauliflower with a head that has many branches. In Lebanon, cauliflower is called *zahra*, flour, because it is white like flour. *Jummara* is the word used to refer to the white and tender part of a cauliflower. Cauliflower and broccoli are also both referred to by the word *brūklū*. In Egypt, *āsfīdhāj* is a word that refers to cauliflower; it is derived from the word for "makeup" because it resembles the ceruse, or pigment, used in makeup.

1. Beat the yogurt in a large, heavy saucepan with a fork until smooth. Beat in the egg white, cornstarch, and salt.

2. Place the saucepan over high heat and start to stir in one direction with a wooden spoon. As soon as the mixture starts to bubble, about 6 minutes, reduce the heat to medium and boil gently until it is thick, about 5 minutes more. Now the yogurt is ready to use in other dishes. It will keep for 1 week in the refrigerator.

Makes 1 quart

STABILIZED COW'S MILK YOGURT

Cow's milk yogurt will separate when heated beyond a certain point, so for cooking purposes it must be stabilized before heating. This process is necessary in all dishes requiring cooked yogurt.

1 quart good-quality full-fat plain cow's milk yogurt
1 large egg white, beaten
1 tablespoon cornstarch
1 teaspoon salt

LAMB, CAULIFLOWER, AND CORIANDER STEW FROM THE LEVANT

THIS FAMILY-STYLE STEW, COMMON IN Lebanon and Syria, is called *yakhnat al-qarnabīṭ*, "cauliflower stew," even though it has lamb in it. But you will notice that there isn't a great deal of meat, and that is typical of the kinds of stews made in Arab cuisines. The meat acts like a condiment. In this dish, a copious amount of fresh coriander (cilantro) is used, two bunches, and that is typical of how cooks in Damascus do it, while in the rest of Syria one is likely to find ground dried coriander leaves or seeds used instead. This stew is nearly always served with rice pilaf (page 125) or is eaten with pieces of Arabic flatbread, ripped up and used as a kind of utensil to eat from the plate or stew pot.

—————●—————

1 pound boneless leg or shoulder of lamb, trimmed of any large pieces of fat and cut into cubes the same size as the cauliflower florets
3 cups water
1 cup extra virgin olive oil
1 large head cauliflower (about 2 pounds), stem removed, and broken into florets
1/4 cup Clarified Butter (page 194)
8 large garlic cloves, pounded in a mortar with 1 tablespoon salt until mushy
2 cups finely chopped fresh coriander (cilantro) leaves (from about 2 bunches)
1/4 cup fresh lemon juice
Salt and freshly ground black pepper to taste

—————●—————

1. Put the meat in a medium-size saucepan and cover with the water. Bring to a boil and skim off the foam that forms on the surface. Reduce the heat to low and cook for 30 minutes. Remove the meat with a slotted spoon and set aside in a stew pot or casserole.

2. Meanwhile, heat the olive oil in a large skillet over medium-high heat. Cook the cauliflower florets until golden brown, in two batches if necessary to avoid crowding the skillet, 4 to 5 minutes. Remove with a slotted spoon and add to the meat.

3. To the same skillet, add the clarified butter and let it melt over low heat if it isn't liquid already. Then cook the garlic and coriander, stirring, until mushy looking and dark green,

about 2 minutes. Transfer the garlic-coriander mixture to the meat.

4. Add the lemon juice and season with salt and pepper. Cover and simmer over low heat until the cauliflower is falling apart and the lamb is tender, about 1 hour. Serve immediately.

—————●—————

Makes 4 servings

LAMB, TOMATO, AND CORIANDER STEW WITH YELLOW RICE PILAF
IN THE LEBANESE STYLE

I AM A GREAT LOVER OF ARAB-STYLE STEWS, which always means that the meat is lamb and the spicing is complex and evocative— and it is always served with rice. The *bahārāt* spice mix can be bought in Middle Eastern groceries, or you can make it rather easily yourself (see page 119). We know this is a winter dish because I ask you to use canned tomatoes, far better than some tasteless imported hothouse tomato in the middle of January. Remember to rinse the rice so that the pilaf will have tender and fluffy grains that do not stick together. Serve with a green salad and warm Arabic flatbread.

¹/₄ cup extra virgin olive oil

3¹/₂ pounds mixed lamb shank, neck, and other lamb stew meat

1 large onion, grated

6 large garlic cloves, very finely chopped

Leaves from 2 bunches fresh coriander (cilantro), finely chopped

1 tablespoon Bahārāt (page 119)

1 cinnamon stick

12 allspice berries

1 lemon

One 34–ounce can crushed tomatoes

Salt and freshly ground black pepper to taste

2 tablespoons unsalted butter

2 cups long-grain rice, soaked in tepid water for 30 minutes and drained or rinsed well in a strainer

2 teaspoons turmeric

Pinch of saffron threads, crumbled in a mortar

2 teaspoons salt

¹/₂ teaspoon freshly ground white pepper

1 quart hot water

———— ● ————

1. In a large casserole, heat the olive oil over medium-high heat. Brown the lamb on all sides with the onion, garlic, and coriander, about 10 minutes. Add the *bahārāt*, cinnamon stick, allspice berries, lemon, and tomatoes and season with salt and pepper. Bring to a boil, reduce the heat to low, and cook until the lamb falls off the bone, about 3 hours.

2. Meanwhile, melt the butter in a heavy 2-quart saucepan with a heavy lid over high heat. Once the butter stops sizzling, cook the drained rice for 2 minutes, stirring. Steep the turmeric, saffron, salt, and pepper in the water

for 5 minutes, then add to the rice. Bring to a boil, cover the saucepan with several sheets of paper towels, place the lid on top of the paper towels, and turn the heat off. Let sit until the lamb is done, about 1 hour. Serve immediately.

———— ● ————

Makes 5 servings

AN ARABIC PROVERB
——— ● ———

A woman first captures her husband with a pretty face, then with cheerfulness, and then by satisfying his stomach.

LAMB SHANK AND ZUCCHINI STEW FROM LEBANON

IN LEBANON, A STEW IS VERY MUCH A family kind of dish. Why would you order a stew in a restaurant when Mom can make it so much better? This *yakhnat al-kūsā*, which simply means "zucchini stew," uses medium-size zucchini cut into largish chunks. Lebanese cooks will cook the zucchini right along with the meat from the start and, as a result, the zucchini will be very soft. This is how Lebanese like it, but it you prefer zucchini with a bit more body, add them halfway through the cooking time. This stew can also be made with veal instead of lamb; if you do use veal, use boneless veal shoulder or leg meat cut into $1/2$-inch cubes and cook it for about 2 hours. For the lamb, ask the butcher to cut the lamb shanks for you, directly across the bone. This way the stew will have a lot more flavor. Serve with rice pilaf (page 125) and warm Arabic flatbread.

———————•———————

6 tablespoons ($3/4$ stick) unsalted butter or
   Clarified Butter (page 194)
1 medium-size onion, chopped
$2^{1}/2$ pounds lamb shank, cut into $1^{1}/2$-inch
   pieces, or 1 pound boneless lean stew veal, cut
   into $1/2$-inch cubes
2 teaspoons Bahārāt (page 119)
$1/2$ teaspoon freshly ground allspice berries
$1/8$ teaspoon ground cinnamon
3 pounds medium-size zucchini, ends trimmed
   and cut into 1-inch-thick rounds
$2^{1}/2$ pounds ripe tomatoes, cut in half, seeds
   squeezed out, and grated against the largest
   holes of a grater down to the peel
10 large garlic cloves, lightly crushed
Salt and freshly ground black pepper to taste

———————•———————

1. In a casserole, melt the butter over medium-high heat. Once it stops sizzling, cook the onion until light brown, stirring, about 8 minutes. Brown the meat with the *bahārāt*, allspice, and cinnamon, stirring, about 6 minutes.

2. Add the zucchini, tomatoes, and garlic, and season with salt and pepper. Bring to a boil, then reduce the heat to very low, using a heat diffuser if necessary. Cover and simmer until the lamb is falling off the bone, about 4 hours.

———————•———————

Makes 4 servings

LEBANESE-STYLE LAMB AND SPINACH STEW

L EBANESE FAMILIES EAT A GOOD MANY vegetable stews, such as green bean stew, zucchini stew, and artichoke stew—and the list goes on. They're easy to make and don't always have to cook for a long time. But they also always contain meat, even though they are called vegetable stews. The meat is never in abundance, just enough to provide flavor and a little substance. This spinach stew, called *yakhnat al-sabānikh*, is made with more spinach than lamb and it cooks for a short period of time. You could cook it longer, but it's not necessary because lamb leg meat does not need to be cooked very long to taste tender and succulent. These kinds of vegetable stews are usually accompanied by rice pilaf (recipe follows).

———————•———————

2 pounds spinach, washed well and heavy stems
   removed
$1/2$ cup Clarified Butter (page 194)
1 small onion, finely chopped

1 pound boneless leg of lamb, trimmed of any
  large pieces of fat and cut into bite-size pieces
½ cup pine nuts
Salt and freshly ground black pepper to taste
½ teaspoon ground cinnamon
½ teaspoon paprika
3 tablespoons water
Rice Pilaf (recipe follows)

1. Bring a large saucepan full of water to a boil and plunge the spinach in for 1 to 2 minutes. Drain well, pressing out any liquid with the back of a wooden spoon. Chop the spinach.

2. Melt ¼ cup of the clarified butter over medium heat in the same saucepan (after you dry it). Cook the spinach, stirring, for 3 minutes. Set aside.

3. In a large skillet or casserole, melt the remaining ¼ cup clarified butter over medium heat. Cook the onion, lamb, and pine nuts until the meat loses its color, about 5 minutes. Season with salt and pepper and stir in the cinnamon and paprika. Cover and cook until most of the liquid has evaporated, 10 to 15 minutes. Add the spinach and water, cover, and cook until the meat is tender and there isn't much liquid left, 5 to 10 minutes. Serve with rice pilaf.

Makes 4 servings with rice

RICE PILAF

Making fluffy rice pilaf is not hard to do.

1 cup long-grain rice, such as basmati
1 tablespoon unsalted butter
2 cups warm water
1 teaspoon salt

Soak the rice in water for 30 minutes, then drain it in a fine-mesh strainer. In a heavy, medium-size saucepan with a heavy lid, melt the unsalted butter over medium-high heat. Sauté the rice until it begins to stick to the bottom of the saucepan, stirring frequently, about 2 minutes. Add the warm water and salt and bring to a boil. Reduce the heat to low, cover, and simmer without removing the lid until all the liquid is absorbed, about 15 minutes. Never stir or uncover the rice until this time has passed. Remove the lid and let sit for 5 minutes before serving.

Makes 4 servings

CINNAMON-FLAVORED TOMATO AND LAMB STEW FROM LEBANON

THIS LEBANESE STEW IS CALLED *YAKHNAT al-banādūra*, tomato stew, because of the large amount of tomatoes used. There will be a lot of liquid from them, and it will have to evaporate over the many hours the stew simmers. The stew is ever so slightly sweet from the natural sweetness of the onions and the sweet spicing of cinnamon. Serve with rice pilaf (page 125), a green salad, and Arabic flatbread.

3/4 cup Clarified Butter (page 194)

1/4 cup pine nuts

1 1/4 pounds boneless leg or shoulder of lamb, trimmed of any large pieces of fat and chopped into small pieces

2 pounds onions, coarsely chopped

2 teaspoons salt

1 1/2 teaspoons freshly ground black pepper

1/2 teaspoon ground cinnamon

1 teaspoon Bahārāt (page 119)

4 pounds ripe tomatoes, cut in half, seeds squeezed out, and grated against the largest holes of a grater down to the peel

1. In a casserole, melt or heat the clarified butter over medium-high heat. Cook the pine nuts until light brown, stirring, about 2 minutes. Remove from the pan and set aside.

2. Add the lamb and onions to the casserole, season with salt, pepper, cinnamon, and *bahārāt*, and cook, stirring, until the onions are soft, about 8 minutes. Reduce the heat to very low, using a diffuser if necessary. Add the tomatoes, stir, and cover. Cook for 1 hour, then uncover and cook until the sauce is thicker and the meat very tender, about another 3 hours.

3. Serve with the pine nuts sprinkled on top.

Makes 4 to 6 servings

OKRA AND LAMB STEW FROM LEBANON

THIS LEBANESE DISH, CALLED *YAKHNAT al-bāmiya*, or "okra stew," is also very popular in Egypt. Okra (*Abelmoschus esculentus* [L.] Moench [syn. *Hibiscus esculentus*]) is a mucilaginous vegetable in the mallow family, as is cotton. Both Ethiopia and West Africa have been proposed as its place of origin, and its date of arrival in the Mediterranean is not known. The cytotaxonomy of okra is so confused that it is possible the plant has an Asian origin.

Lebanese and Palestinian cooks favor baby okra, small and tender, about the size of the last joint on your little finger. I have found them this size in some farmer's markets in California. Unfortunately, the okra sold in most American markets is mature, sometimes 3 1/2 inches long. You should cook them 10 minutes more than called for in this recipe. The meatless version of this stew, called *bāmyā*, is made with okra, tomatoes, onions, lots of garlic, and lemon juice. In Damascus, they would also add lots of fresh coriander, while in Homs and Aleppo, Syrian cities to the north of Damascus, the okra would be cooked with copious quantities of garlic, pomegranate molasses, and tomato juice. Serve this stew with rice pilaf (page 125) and Arabic flatbread.

———— • ————

4 garlic cloves, peeled
1 teaspoon salt
1 teaspoon freshly ground coriander seeds
1 pound fresh young okra
$^{1}/_{2}$ cup Clarified Butter (page 194), vegetable shortening, extra virgin olive oil, or corn oil
1 pound boneless lamb shoulder, trimmed of any large pieces of fat and cut into 1- to 2-inch pieces
1 medium-size onion, halved
$^{1}/_{2}$ teaspoon freshly ground black pepper
2 tablespoons tomato paste dissolved in 1 cup water
1 cup tomato liquid (squeezed from 2 large ripe tomatoes, not canned tomato juice)
$^{1}/_{4}$ cup fresh lemon juice

———— • ————

1. In a mortar, crush the garlic with the salt and coriander and pound until it is a paste.

2. Trim the stems from the okra, rinse with water, and pat dry with paper towels. In a large nonreactive casserole, heat the clarified butter over medium heat until very hot and slightly smoking. Cook the okra until light brown all

OKRA

———— • ————

Cultivated forms of okra (*Hibiscus esculentus* [syn. *Abelmoschus esculentus* (L.) Moench]) have a heavy woody central stem that branches into long stems with large and slightly spine-like leaves. The blossoms are yellow and grow from the leaf axils, and the ribbed and edible pods are attached to these. Okra has a mucilaginous texture that results from chemical compounds in the plant, namely, acetylated acidic polysaccharide and galacturonic acid. Botanists still do not know with certainty the place of origin of okra, although along the Nile River of Egypt or the Sudan has been suggested, and so have Ethiopia and tropical Africa. Okra has been cultivated in West Africa, Ethiopia, and the Sudan for a long time. It moved from West Africa to the southern United States with the slave trade.

around, about 6 minutes. Remove with a slotted spoon, drain well, and set aside.

3. In the same casserole, brown the lamb on all sides over medium heat, about 5 minutes, turning often. Add the onion halves, garlic mixture, pepper, and more salt if necessary. Cook, stirring, for 2 minutes. Add the diluted tomato paste and tomato liquid. Stir and cover. Reduce the heat to low and simmer for 1 hour.

4. Return the okra to the casserole and add the lemon juice. Stir once, and taste to see if you would like more lemon juice. Cover and cook until the lamb is tender and the okra heated through, about 10 more minutes. Serve immediately.

Makes 4 servings

TAS KEBABI

STEWS ARE POPULAR IN THE MUSLIM world for several reasons. Historically, fuel was scarce, and roasting was a profligate way to use up firewood. Second, stewing was a popular method of cooking meat because a wonderful sauce usually resulted from its being cooked with vegetables. A third reason is that long-stewed meat would not be bloody, avoiding the Islamic prohibition against eating blood. This stew is called *tas kebabı*, which means something like "stewed kebabs in a bowl." It begins with the cooking of the vegetables in butter in a method called *yağa vurmak* ("butter-infused"), before the meat itself is cooked in the same butter. The stew is made in a cooking bowl that is then inverted onto a plate. *Tas kebabı* is traditionally served surrounded by the eggplant cream known as sultan's delight, *hünkar beğendi* (page 316).

5 tablespoons unsalted butter
2½ pounds boneless lamb stew meat, trimmed of any large pieces of fat and cut into 1-inch cubes

2 medium-size onions, finely chopped
¼ cup plus 2 tablespoons seeded and finely chopped green bell pepper
¼ cup tomato paste dissolved in 1½ cups water
½ teaspoon freshly ground allspice berries
¼ teaspoon ground cinnamon
¼ cup finely chopped fresh parsley leaves
Salt and freshly ground black pepper to taste

1. In a large, heavy casserole, melt 2½ tablespoons of the butter over high heat. When it stops sizzling, brown the lamb on all sides, about 5 minutes. Remove the lamb pieces with a slotted spoon and set aside.

2. Reduce the heat to medium. Melt the remaining 2½ tablespoons of butter in the casserole, and cook the onions and green pepper, stirring, until the onions are soft, about 8 minutes. Add the diluted tomato paste. Stir well, scraping the browned bits from the bottom of the casserole. Add the allspice, cinnamon, and 2 tablespoons of the parsley, and season with salt and pepper.

3. Return the lamb to the casserole, and reduce the heat to low. Cover and simmer until the lamb is tender and the sauce thick, about 3 hours. Sprinkle the meat with the remaining 2 tablespoons of parsley and serve.

Makes 4 to 6 servings

YAKHNAT AL-FŪL

H ERE'S ONE OF THE MOST POPULAR AND common of Arab stews, and probably a stew with an old history. That's why I left the recipe title in the Arabic rather than translating it as "fava bean stew." This springtime Lebanese-style lamb and fava bean dish is a favorite among Lebanese families. The lamb is cut into small pieces, smaller than bite-size, and boiled separately before going into the stew with the peeled fava beans. The part of this stew that I like so much is the flavoring—lots of garlic pounded until mushy and stirred into the stew with a good amount of fresh coriander leaves. This taste is a familiar one in Lebanon and Syria, in stews and in vegetable dishes, and it is quite delightful here. Typically, one would serve this with a simple rice rilaf (page 125) and some Arabic flatbread, perhaps with a salad, too.

———— • ————

1³/₄ pounds boneless leg or shoulder of lamb, trimmed of any large pieces of fat and cut into small cubes
3 cups water
¹/₂ cup extra virgin olive oil
6 pounds fresh fava beans in the pod, shelled and skinned
1 large onion, finely chopped
8 large garlic cloves, pounded in a mortar with 1 tablespoon salt until mushy
¹/₂ cup finely chopped fresh coriander (cilantro) leaves
¹/₄ cup fresh lemon juice
¹/₄ teaspoon freshly ground allspice berries

PEELING FAVA BEANS

———— • ————

Six pounds of fava bean pods will yield about 2 pounds of beans with their skins on and 20 ounces with their skins off. To peel the skins, drop the beans in some boiling water for about 2 minutes, and drain. Find the black seam of the bean and, with your thumbnail, pinch it open and pop the bean out.

¹/₄ teaspoon ground cinnamon
1 teaspoon salt
Freshly ground black pepper to taste
Rice Pilaf (optional, page 125)

———— • ————

1. Put the meat in a medium-size saucepan and cover with the water. Bring to a boil and skim off the foam that appears on the surface. Reduce the heat to low and cook for 30 minutes, uncovered, without letting the water return to a boil. Drain, setting the meat aside and saving 1¹/₂ cups of the broth for the stew and the remaining broth for the rice pilaf should you decide to make it.

2. While the meat is cooking, heat the olive oil in a stew pot, casserole, or Dutch oven over medium–high heat. Cook the beans for 3 minutes, remove with a slotted spoon, and set aside.

3. In the stew pot or casserole in which you cooked the fava beans, cook the onion over medium–high heat until soft, stirring, about 3 minutes. Add the garlic and coriander and cook until fragrant, but not acrid smelling, stirring constantly, about 2 minutes. Add the meat, favas, lemon juice, and 1 1/2 cups of the reserved broth. Season with the allspice, cinnamon, salt, and pepper, and bring to a boil. Reduce the heat to low, cover, and simmer until the meat is tender, about 1 1/2 hours. Serve immediately, with rice pilaf, if desired.

Makes 4 to 5 servings

LAMB AND FRESH CORIANDER STEW WITH PISTACHIOS AND ALMONDS
FROM DAMASCUS

THIS *ṬĀJIN BI'L-LAḤM*, MEANING "LAMB stew," is popular cooked in a variety of ways throughout the Arab Levant, although this particular recipe is common in Syria. It is cooked a long time, and very slowly, so that the lamb cuts like butter when done. Very little liquid is used, and the final stew is a thick, luscious gravy coating the delicate pieces of lamb. The spicing I use is adaptable and different cooks will use different spice mixtures. This recipe is from Damascus, where they like to use lots of fresh coriander, while in other parts of Syria ground dried coriander leaves or seeds are preferred.

3 pounds boneless leg of lamb, trimmed of any large pieces of fat and cut into pieces the size of an egg
1/2 cup blanched whole almonds
1/4 cup pine nuts
1/4 cup shelled raw pistachios
2 teaspoons salt
1 1/2 teaspoons freshly ground black pepper
1 tablespoon Bahārāt (page 119)
1/4 teaspoon ground cinnamon
1/4 teaspoon freshly ground cardamom seeds
1/8 teaspoon freshly grated nutmeg
1 teaspoon freshly ground cumin seeds
1/4 teaspoon freshly ground cloves
1 large onion, chopped
1 cup finely chopped fresh coriander (cilantro) leaves (from about 1 bunch)
1/4 cup plus 2 tablespoons Clarified Butter (page 194)
1/2 cup water
1 teaspoon freshly ground coriander seeds
3 hard-boiled eggs, shelled and sliced

---

1. In a large bowl, mix together the lamb, 1/4 cup of the almonds, the pine nuts, pistachios, salt, pepper, *bahārāt*, cinnamon, cardamom, nutmeg, cumin, cloves, onion, and fresh coriander.

2. In a large, heavy casserole, melt or heat the clarified butter over medium-high heat. Add the lamb mixture and brown the lamb on all sides, 5 to 6 minutes. Add the water and reduce the heat to medium-low. Cover and cook for 45 minutes.

3. Add the ground coriander and reduce the heat to low. Cover and cook until the lamb is very tender, stirring occasionally, and adding small amounts of water if the stew is drying out, about 2 1/2 hours.

4. Transfer the stew to a deep serving platter, arrange the sliced eggs on top, and sprinkle with the remaining 1/4 cup almonds.

───●───

Makes 6 servings

SHAQRIYYA

THE SAFFRON IN THIS LAMB STEW FROM Syria colors it yellow, and the name of the dish, *shaqriyya*, means "the blond [dish]." In the medieval Muslim Mediterranean, as in the Christian Mediterranean, foods were imbued with magical properties. The influence of the alchemists was also felt in the gastronomic world. Alchemy was a quasi-scientific, spiritual endeavor whose goal, during medieval times, was the transmutation of the base metals into gold, the discovery of a cure for disease, and the discovery of an elixir of long life. The most important color in this search for the secret to the transmutation of base metals was the color of gold, namely yellow. Colors had symbolic connections, and yellow was thought to be beneficial or the source of gaiety. Endoring— coloring foods, and especially, coloring them yellow—was an important part of food preparation. For that reason saffron, safflower, and turmeric were important spices. Saffron was the rarest, as rare as gold, and the most powerful in its coloring potential.

The yogurt needs to be stabilized in this preparation, otherwise it will separate while cooking, so see the method described on page 121. Serve with rice and Arabic flatbread.

───●───

1/2 teaspoon saffron threads, lightly toasted in a
dry skillet
1/2 teaspoon salt
1 quart Stabilized Cow's Milk Yogurt (page 121)
3 tablespoons Clarified Butter (page 194) or
unsalted butter
1 1/4 pounds onions, coarsely chopped
1 1/4 pounds boneless leg of lamb, trimmed of any
large pieces of fat and cut into 1-inch cubes
1 1/2 tablespoons Bahārāt (page 119)
1 teaspoon dried mint
3 cups water

───●───

1. Gently pound the saffron in a mortar with the salt. Stir the mixture into the stabilized yogurt until blended. Leave to steep while you continue to make the stew, stirring every once in a while. The more finely you have ground the saffron, the yellower the yogurt will become.

2. In a large casserole, heat the clarified butter over medium-high heat. Cook the onions until softened, stirring frequently, about 5 minutes. Add the lamb and cook until it's no longer raw looking, 1 to 2 minutes. Add the *bahārāt* and mint, season with salt, and cook for 1 minute, stirring. Cover the meat with the water and bring to a boil. Reduce the heat to medium-low, and cook, partially covered, until the water is evaporated and the meat is coated with a thick sauce, stirring occasionally, about 1¼ hours.

3. Pour the yogurt over the meat and stir. Reduce the heat to low, cover, and simmer until the meat is tender, about 1 hour.

———●———

Makes 4 servings

PERSIAN GULF–STYLE BEDOUIN LAMB AND MUSHROOM STEW

THE COOKING OF THE ARABIAN GULF, better known as the Persian Gulf, was traditionally very simple and very poor. The residents were Bedouin tribes who roamed the borderless steppe desert until the creation of the modern states of Saudi Arabia, Kuwait, Iraq, Qatar, Bahrain, and the United Arab Emirates. The Bedouins still roam, but less so, and now with their cell phones. With the advent of the oil age, the population is overwhelmingly non-Bedouin in the Gulf.

Boiled lamb is a typical preparation among desert Arabs such as the Bedouin tribes, and they often enjoy using desert mushrooms, *fuṭr*, in their stews. Several items in the ingredients list can only be found in Middle Eastern or Greek markets. I would encourage you to find a local one. They're all over the place; just don't be intimidated about going in. The *lūmī* are not sold in supermarkets and can be found mostly in Middle Eastern markets in North America. They are dried limes used in stews in the Middle East, especially in Iraq, Iran, and the Arabian Peninsula. Some of these markets sell this product in ground form too. The *kashkaval* cheese used in the recipe is also only found in Middle Eastern and Greek markets. The same is true of mastic, a kind of gum resin used as an odor purgative in much Middle Eastern cooking, and red Aleppo pepper, which can be replaced by mixing 2 parts sweet paprika with one part cayenne pepper. In this preparation I use spaghetti to replace the more traditional rice. But this isn't too "made up" because today pasta is popular throughout the Middle East, where they like it cooked soft, and not *al dente*. The onion in the ingredient list is grated, which you can do by using one of the larger sized holes of a four- or six-sided grater.

———●———

3 tablespoons Clarified Butter (page 194) or extra virgin olive oil
1½ pounds lamb shank
1½ pounds lamb neck
Seeds from 12 cardamom pods, freshly ground
15 allspice berries, freshly ground
2 lūmī (whole dried limes), crushed and ground
6 cloves, freshly ground
1 tablespoon plus 1 teaspoon turmeric
1 cinnamon stick
2 teaspoons red Aleppo pepper
1 large onion, grated
4 large garlic cloves, very finely chopped
6 pieces mastic (about ½ teaspoon, optional)
1½ quarts water

KASHKAVAL CHEESE

In the Balkans, during the Middle Ages, cheese was made in wheels or balls like the famous mountain cheese called *cascaval*, from the region of the lower Danubian plain of Romania known as Wallachia. *Cascaval* is a ewe's milk cheese repeatedly boiled like *caciocavallo* in Sardinia and Italy. It is thought that the cheese was originally made in Kavalla, the port opposite the island of Thásos in Greek Macedonia, which once had numerous residents from Wallachia. The cheese was exported to Istanbul and Italy, where it is said to have become known as *caciocavallo*. But there is enough evidence to believe that *caciocavallo* does not derive from *cascaval*, today known as *kashkaval*, and that the Italian cheese was native to the region around Naples and southern Italy. In a register from Naples, at the time part of the medieval kingdom of Anjou, there is already mention in 1311 of *caciocavallo*, which seems to be related to the medieval Latin word used in Rome in 1071, *cavalcasi*, a kind of cheese.

Today's *kashkaval* is a semihard ewe's milk cheese made throughout the Balkans. It can be found in Middle Eastern and Greek markets. It is ivory colored inside and out, mild tasting, and is usually sold in two- to three-pound wheels. It is a good melting cheese and excellent with fruit. The closest equivalent is a mild provolone. In Romania, they make a similar cheese called *katschkawalj*, a plastic curd *caciocavallo* or mozzarella-like cheese made from ewe's milk, similar, too, to the cheese in Turkey called *zomma*.

---

2 pounds button mushrooms, brushed clean
1 pound spaghetti
2 cups high-quality, full-fat, plain cow's milk yogurt
1/2 cup freshly grated **kashkaval** or **Parmigiano-Reggiano** cheese
1/4 cup finely chopped fresh mint leaves

---

1. In a casserole, heat the clarified butter over high heat. Season the lamb with the cardamom, allspice, dried limes, cloves, turmeric, cinnamon stick, and Aleppo pepper. Cook the lamb with the onion and garlic until the meat is browned, stirring almost constantly to prevent burning, about 5 minutes. Add the mastic, water, and mushrooms. Return to a gentle boil, then reduce the heat to low, cover, and simmer for 1 1/2 hours.

2. Uncover and simmer until the meat is very tender, about another 1 1/2 hours.

3. Meanwhile, bring a large pot of abundantly salted water to a boil. Cook the pasta until soft and drain. Toss the spaghetti with the yogurt, cheese, and most of the mint and ladle the lamb and mushrooms on top. Garnish with some chopped mint and serve immediately.

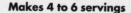

Makes 4 to 6 servings

LAMB AND EGGPLANT STEW FROM IRAN

THIS PERSIAN STEW, CALLED *KHORESHT-E badenjan* in Farsi, is adapted from a recipe by a Persian cook, N. Shaida. It is a typical family stew served with rice pilaf (page 125). Because you will have cooked the eggplant slices in oil, the stew will be heavier than expected and therefore will feed more people than you might think, given how little meat is in it. This is a stew that begs for an accompanying food that is more bland, such as rice or bread, to absorb all the delicious flavors. The sour grapes add an interesting tart effect to the stew. You can find sour grapes (as well as a great variety of flatbreads) in a Middle Eastern market, but you could also brine them yourself by putting small red grapes in a salt, vinegar, and water solution and leaving them for a week. Alternatively, you could replace the grapes with 2 tablespoons pomegranate molasses. And I'm sure someone will wisecrack during the meal, "There are no sour grapes at this table" (and no one will laugh).

4 pounds eggplant, peeled and cut into 1/4-inch-thick slices
Salt
1 quart olive oil for frying
2 tablespoons extra virgin olive oil
2 medium-size onions, sliced and separated into rings
2 teaspoons turmeric
Salt and freshly ground black pepper to taste
1 pound boneless leg of lamb, trimmed of any large pieces of fat and cut into 2-inch cubes
3 tablespoons tomato paste
1 pound ripe tomatoes, cut in half, seeds squeezed out, and grated against the largest holes of a grater down to the peel
1/3 cup sour grapes (about 2 ounces)
Juice of 1 lemon

1. Lay the eggplant slices on some paper towels and sprinkle with salt. Leave them to drain of their bitter juices for 30 minutes, then pat dry with paper towels.

2. Preheat the frying oil in a deep fryer or an 8-inch (3- or 4-quart) saucepan fitted with a basket insert to 375°F. Cook the eggplant, in batches to avoid crowding, until golden brown on both sides, about 4 minutes a side. Remove with a slotted spoon or tongs and drain on paper towels. Let the frying oil cool, strain, and save for a future use.

3. In a large skillet, heat the 2 tablespoons olive oil over high heat. Cook the onions until golden brown, stirring occasionally, 6 to 8 minutes. Reduce the heat to medium-high, add the turmeric, and season the onions with salt and pepper. Add the meat and cook until brown, about 5 minutes. Stir in the tomato paste, tomatoes, sour grapes, and lemon juice. Cover, reduce the heat to low, and simmer until bubbling well, about 30 minutes.

4. Add the eggplant, cover again, and simmer, stirring occasionally, until the meat is tender and the sauce well blended, about 30 minutes. Correct the seasonings and serve.

———— ● ————

Makes 6 servings

LAMB, SPINACH, AND PRUNE STEW FROM IRAN

T HIS STEW IS CALLED *KHURASH-Ī ISFANĀJ* (or *khoresht-e īsfanāj*) in Farsi, the Indo-European language of Iran, which is written in Arabic script. In this stew, the lamb cooks with the onions and spices for a long time alone, without the vegetables. Then, at the end of the cooking, the vegetables are added and cooked just until they are soft and well incorporated. Fenugreek leaves may be difficult to find—I have only found them at farmer's markets—but they provide an interesting and compatible taste. In their place you can use a teaspoon of freshly ground fenugreek seeds, added at the same time as the turmeric. The sour grape juice can be gotten by mashing sour grapes through a strainer. Sour grapes are usually sold brined in jars in Middle Eastern markets. I've made this stew with both sour grape juice and lemon juice and maybe it's my familiarity with lemons that led me to prefer them. This stew, like all stews in Iran, is served with or on top of plain steamed rice.

———— ● ————

1/4 cup Clarified Butter (page 194) or rendered lamb fat (see page 348)

2 large onions, sliced and separated into rings
1 1/2 pounds boneless lamb stew meat, trimmed of any large pieces of fat and cut into 1-inch cubes
2 teaspoons turmeric
1 teaspoon ground cinnamon
1 teaspoon salt
1/2 teaspoon freshly ground black pepper
2 1/2 cups water
1 pound spinach, heavy stems removed, washed well, and coarsely chopped
1/4 cup finely chopped fresh fenugreek leaves (optional)
2 cups chopped scallions (white and green parts)
1/4 cup sour grape juice or fresh lemon juice
12 pitted prunes

———— ● ————

1. In a casserole or Dutch oven, melt the butter or rendered lamb fat over medium-high heat. Cook the onions until golden, stirring, about 10 minutes. Add the lamb and brown on all sides, about 10 minutes. Add the turmeric, cinnamon, salt, and pepper. Stir and cook for a few seconds, then add the water. Bring to a boil, reduce the heat to low, partially cover, and simmer until tender, about 2 hours.

2. Add the spinach, fenugreek leaves, if using, scallions, sour grape juice, and prunes. Cover and continue to cook until the leafy vegetables are completely soft, but still maintain a little of their color, about 30 minutes. Check the seasonings, then serve.

———— ● ————

Makes 4 servings

THE FIRST RECORDED STEW

At some point in the antediluvian past, a pot was invented and once it was, the first stew was made over an open fire. But the first recorded stew comes from about 1700 B.C. in ancient Mesopotamia. It was called *me-e puhâdi* and was recorded in the extinct Akkadian language of Babylonia on cuneiform tablets and in a few other scattered records from the ancient city of Mari that reside in a collection at Yale University. The recipes were first published by Jean Bottéro, the emeritus director of Assyriology at the École Pratique des Hautes Études in Paris. The recipes give no quantities and were written for professional chefs. Because the meaning of many of the Sumerian words have not yet been agreed upon by philologists, we can't be sure what a number of the ingredients actually are. The raw materials for these stews, and all Mesopotamian cuisine, were very much like those of ancient Egypt during the same period. Bottéro has catalogued over a hundred different soups and stews that are distinguished by the number and variety of spices used.

In her book *Art, Culture, and Cuisine: Ancient and Medieval Gastronomy*, Professor Phyllis Pray Bober has attempted to recreate this lamb stew called *me-e puhâdi*. She admits that this endeavor is entirely speculative.

In a heavy pot, the fat from $1/4$ pound streaky salt pork is rendered, and 3 pounds of lamb shank and shoulder are browned. The meat is removed and some onions, garlic, leeks, and shallots are sautéed in the remaining fat. The lamb and salt pork are returned to the pot with salt, ground coriander, cumin, crushed juniper berries, and sumac. Boiling stock is added to cover the meats, and the stew is cooked for about 2 hours. Then fresh coriander leaves are sprinkled on for the last bit of cooking, and the broth is thickened with crumbled "oil cake" (probably some kind of wheat flour cake made with oil, rather than butter) and fresh, strained yogurt beaten with the white of an egg.

VEGETABLE AND HERB STEW FROM THE KHUZESTAN PROVINCE OF IRAN

I N FARSI, THE INDO-EUROPEAN LANGUAGE spoken in Iran, this vegetable stew is called *ghormeh-sabzi*. This particular recipe from the western province of Khuzestan, in Iran, is adapted from Soheila Amiri, who tells us that her version uses more vegetables than the version from Tehran. Khuzestan is notable for having a large Semitic population of Arabs, and the cooking of Iraq is felt there. If you like, you can chop all the vegetables and herbs in a food processor, but you need to be careful that you don't make it mushy. The dried limes (*lūmī*) can be found in Middle Eastern markets, where you can ask for "loomy."

1/2 cup extra virgin olive oil

1 large onion, very thinly sliced and separated
into rings

5 lamb shanks (about 4 1/4 pounds)

Salt and freshly ground black pepper to taste

1 teaspoon turmeric

1 dried chile, seeded and crushed

3 cups water

4 dried lemons or limes or 1 tablespoon dried
lemon powder

1 cup dried red kidney beans, picked over, rinsed,
soaked overnight in water to cover, and drained

2 pounds spinach, washed well, rinse water left
clinging to the leaves, heavy stems removed,
and finely chopped

Leaves from 1 small bunch fresh dill, rinse water
left clinging to the leaves, finely chopped

Leaves from 1 bunch fresh parsley, rinse water
left clinging to the leaves, finely chopped

Leaves from 1 large bunch fresh coriander
(cilantro), rinse water left clinging to the
leaves, finely chopped

4 leeks (green part only), split lengthwise,
washed well, and finely chopped

8 scallions (green part only) or 1 bunch fresh
chives, or both, finely chopped

Leaves from 1 bunch fresh fenugreek, rinse water
left clinging to the leaves, finely chopped
(about 1/2 cup); or 1/4 cup dried fenugreek
leaves; or 1 tablespoon freshly ground
fenugreek seeds

1 tablespoon fresh lemon juice

1. In a large casserole or Dutch oven, heat 1/4
cup of the olive oil over medium-high heat.
Cook the onions until golden, 7 to 8 minutes.
Add the lamb and brown on both sides, about

5 minutes. Add the salt, pepper, turmeric, and
chile. Stir and cook for 1 minute. Add the
water and dried or fresh limes with a hole
poked into each one so it doesn't sink. Bring
to a boil, then reduce the heat to low. Cover
and simmer for 2 hours, turning the shanks
occasionally.

2. Add the beans and cook for another hour.

3. Put the spinach, dill, parsley, coriander, leeks,
scallions, and fenugreek in a large saucepan and
cook over medium heat until the moisture has
almost evaporated, stirring frequently so the
mixture doesn't burn, about 25 minutes. Add
the remaining 1/4 cup of olive oil and cook
until the vegetables and herbs are dry, about 5
minutes. There should be no water left in the
saucepan.

4. Add the fried vegetables and herbs, now
looking mushy, to the lamb mixture and cook
until the meat nearly falls away from the bone,
about 1 hour. Stir in the lemon juice and serve.

Makes 4 to 6 servings

MASALA LAMB STEW

THIS INDIAN STEW IS MEANT TO BE "SPICY"
(hence the name, *masala*). It is indeed hot
and spicy, but not overly so. And the traditional way you would serve a spicy lamb stew

is with rice pilaf (page 125). The extra lemon juice added at the end makes for an ever so slight tang that is appetizing with the heat of the dish.

———————●———————

¼ cup vegetable oil
1¼ pounds lamb stew meat, trimmed of
    any large pieces of fat and cut into 1½-inch
    cubes
2 large onions, chopped
6 garlic cloves, crushed
1 tablespoon peeled and grated fresh ginger
1 cinnamon stick
½ teaspoon freshly ground black pepper
3 cloves
1½ teaspoons salt
½ teaspoon turmeric
2 fresh green chiles, seeded and chopped
2 tablespoons finely chopped fresh coriander
    (cilantro) leaves
3 tablespoons unsweetened grated coconut
2 cups water
1 pound green beans, ends trimmed and lightly
    steamed to remain crunchy
Juice of 1 lemon
Radishes, left whole, for garnish
Scallions, left whole, for garnish

———————●———————

1. In a casserole, heat the vegetable oil over medium-high heat. Brown the lamb and onions, stirring, 6 to 8 minutes. Add the garlic, ginger, cinnamon, pepper, cloves, salt, turmeric, chiles, coriander and coconut. Cook for a few minutes, then add the water. Cover, reduce the heat to low, and simmer until the meat is tender, 2 to 2½ hours.

2. Add the green beans, pushing them down under the sauce, and continue to cook, uncovered so that some of the liquid evaporates, until the beans are soft, about 1 hour.

3. Stir in the lemon juice and serve with raw radishes and scallions.

———————●———————

Makes 4 servings

ROGAN JOSH

T HIS IS A DISH WELL KNOWN TO ANYONE who has ever been to an Indian restaurant, although I think you will find this recipe from North India a little more unique and less "generic" than the ones found in Indian restaurants in North America. I developed this recipe from suggestions made by Indian friends. *Rogan josh* means "red stew." Serve it with rice pilaf (page 125) made with diced tiny carrots, sweet peas, and saffron.

———————●———————

8 large garlic cloves, peeled
3 tablespoons peeled and coarsely chopped fresh
    ginger
2¼ cups water
¼ cup plus 2 tablespoons vegetable oil
1 large onion, chopped
2 tablespoons freshly ground coriander seeds
1 tablespoon crushed poppy seeds
2 teaspoons freshly ground cumin seeds

1 teaspoon turmeric

1 tablespoon hot paprika

¹/₄ teaspoon freshly ground cardamom seeds

¹/₂ teaspoon cayenne pepper

¹/₈ teaspoon freshly ground cloves

¹/₈ teaspoon freshly grated nutmeg

¹/₄ teaspoon ground cinnamon

Pinch of saffron threads, freshly ground

1 bay leaf

2 pounds boneless leg or shoulder of lamb (or boneless stew beef, such as chuck), trimmed of any large pieces of fat and cut into 1¹/₂-inch cubes

³/₄ cup Stabilized Cow's Milk Yogurt (page 121)

1¹/₂ teaspoons salt

1 large, ripe tomato, cut in half, seeds squeezed out, and grated against the largest holes of a grater down to the peel

Freshly ground black pepper to taste

3 tablespoons finely chopped fresh coriander (cilantro) leaves

———————●———————

1. Put the garlic, ginger, and ¹/₄ cup of the water in a blender and process into a paste, scraping down the sides when necessary. Set aside.

2. In a casserole, heat the vegetable oil over medium-high heat. Cook the onion until golden brown, stirring, 8 to 10 minutes. Add the garlic-ginger paste, coriander seeds, poppy seeds, cumin, turmeric, paprika, cardamom, cayenne, cloves, nutmeg, cinnamon, saffron, and bay leaf and cook for 3 minutes, stirring. Add the lamb and cook for 5 minutes. Add ¹/₂ cup of the yogurt, stir, and add the salt, grated tomato, and the remaining 2 cups of water.

Cover, reduce the heat to low, and simmer the lamb until very tender, about 2¹/₂ hours.

3. Remove the lid and turn the heat to medium-high to evaporate some of the liquid. The sauce should be syrupy and reddish brown. Stir in the remaining ¹/₄ cup of yogurt and the pepper, garnish with the coriander leaves, and serve immediately.

———————●———————

Makes 6 servings

SQUIBNOCKET LAMB STEW

WHEN I WAS RESEARCHING THIS RECIPE, which I found in an old Time-Life series on New England, I was intrigued. As a child in the 1960s, my parents took me hosteling on Martha's Vineyard in the summer, and we visited Squibnocket, on the far southwestern peninsula of the island. Long before the phenomenal influx of summer renters and tourists, especially from New York and Boston, the island was home to a thriving whaling industry, and sheep roamed over the moors. One would think this is all gone now, but there is, in fact, still a sheep farmer there. Clarissa Allen, who runs a sheep farm on Martha's Vineyard, has never heard of a stew by this name and neither has the librarian at the *Vineyard Gazette*, so I'm not sure how true and legitimate it is. It is a very satisfying stew that's not as heavy as it sounds.

———————•———————

1/4 cup (1/2 stick) unsalted butter
2 pounds boneless lamb shoulder and/or leg of lamb, trimmed of any large pieces of fat and cut into 1 1/2-inch cubes
Salt and freshly ground black pepper to taste
2 cups finely chopped yellow onions (about 2 large onions)
2 large garlic cloves, finely chopped
2 tablespoons unbleached all-purpose flour
1 cup water
1 cup dry white wine
1 large, ripe tomato, peeled, seeded, and chopped
6 carrots (about 1 1/2 pounds), halved crosswise
6 small white onions (about 1 pound), peeled
1 cup frozen lima beans
2 tablespoons finely chopped fresh parsley leaves

———————•———————

1. In a large skillet, melt the butter over high heat. Season the lamb with salt and pepper, then brown the lamb on all sides, about 10 minutes. Transfer to a large casserole as the meat browns. Add the chopped onions and garlic to the skillet and cook, stirring, until translucent, about 5 minutes. Transfer to the casserole.

2. Add the flour to the skillet and cook for 1 minute, stirring. Don't worry if everything seems to be sticking to the bottom of the skillet; it will all come loose when you deglaze with the liquid. When the flour appears slightly golden, add the water, wine, and tomato and cook until the mixture begins to boil and becomes denser and smoother, stirring and scraping the browned bits from the bottom of the pan, about 5 minutes. Pour this sauce over the lamb and onions, and bring the contents of the casserole to a boil. Reduce the heat to low, partially cover, and simmer for 15 minutes, stirring occasionally. Check the seasonings.

3. Add the carrots, whole onions, and lima beans to the casserole, stir, and push the vegetables down into the stew to coat well. Simmer, covered, over very low heat, using a heat diffuser if necessary, until the lamb and vegetables are completely tender, about 2 hours.

4. Check the seasonings, sprinkle the top with the parsley, and serve from the casserole.

———————•———————

Makes 4 to 6 servings

MARTINIQUE-STYLE MUTTON CURRY

<small>◁▷</small>

MARTINIQUE IS ONE OF THE WINDWARD Islands in the French West Indies. It was discovered by Columbus in 1502 and colonized by the French in 1635. Sugar cane is a principal crop and rum a major export. Many tourists descend on the island not only for the usual fun in the sea, sand, and sun, but for a cuisine that is a delightful blend of French and Creole, an amalgam of African, French, Indian, and local Caribbean flavors. The curry that so often appears in Caribbean cuisine is a contribution of the Bengali workers who emigrated to the West Indies in the early part of the twentieth century. Originally called *carry de mouton*, this recipe was adapted from André Nègre's *Caribbean Cooking*, published in 1978. It is typically Creole and does not have to have curry powder in it to be called a curry. Serve with white rice.

¼ *cup (½ stick) unsalted butter*
1 *medium-size onion, finely chopped*
¼ *pound cooked ham, diced*
3 *large garlic cloves, crushed*
¼ *teaspoon dried thyme*
1 *bay leaf*
2 *cloves*
⅛ *teaspoon freshly grated nutmeg*
Pinch of ground cinnamon
3 *large, ripe tomatoes, peeled, seeded, and chopped*
2 *pounds lean boneless leg of mutton (preferably) or lamb, trimmed of any large pieces of fat and cut into large cubes*
1 *cup heavy cream*
1¾ *cups mutton broth (see page 99) or Chicken Broth (page 181)*
1 *cup unsweetened coconut milk (see Note on page 200)*
Juice from 2 small lemons
1 *teaspoon curry powder (optional)*

1. In a large casserole, melt the butter over medium-high heat. When it stops sizzling, cook the onion until soft, stirring, about 6 minutes. Add the ham, garlic, thyme, bay leaf, cloves, nutmeg, and cinnamon, and stir. Add the tomatoes, stir, and cook until the liquid from the tomatoes is evaporated, about 5 minutes. Add the mutton and cook for another 5 minutes. Stir in the heavy cream, broth, coconut milk, and lemon juice. Cover, reduce the heat to low, and simmer until the mutton is very tender, 3 to 4 hours.

2. Ten minutes before serving, add the curry powder, if desired.

Makes 4 servings

STEWS WITH PORK

Stews with pork are a group that we often forget about because we usually stew with other meats. Whether it's New Mexican Chile Verde (page 170), with its Anaheim chiles, pork shoulder, and fragrance of chipotle chiles, oregano, and cumin, or a rustic Quebec-Style Meatball Stew (page 171), flavored with cinnamon, nutmeg, and cloves, pork stews are a great comfort food. There's something about pork shoulder that makes it, in many ways, a perfect stewing meat. Personally, whenever I want a great stew, I always make Roast Pork Shoulder and Italian Sausage Stew (page 150) because the shoulder is so succulent and just melts away into the gravy.

CATALAN STEW OF PORK, BEANS, AND PUMPKIN

THIS IS A VERY SIMPLE, FAMILY-STYLE MEAL called *escudella de mongetes i carbassa*, which literally means "big bowl of beans and squash." It is quite representative of traditional Catalan home cooking in that it is actually rather bland, most of the flavor coming from the meat. It's an attractive dish, and looks very white. To spice it up for contemporary American tastes, all you need to do is add freshly ground black pepper, which I have left out of the ingredients list to maintain authen-

ticity. A tablespoon would be about right. Traditionally, a Catalan cook would throw a whole cooked or cured ham bone in the stew; you can replicate the same by using a pro-sciutto bone.

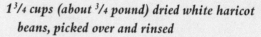

1³/₄ cups (about ³/₄ pound) dried white haricot beans, picked over and rinsed
2 quarts water
2 pounds various types of pork meat, such as shoulder, ribs, and sausage, trimmed of any large pieces of fat and cut into chunks
1 piece prosciutto or ham bone (about ¹/₄ pound) or one ¹/₈-inch-thick slice prosciutto
1 bay leaf
3 sprigs fresh thyme
2 large onions, cut up
1 pound peeled and seeded pumpkin, cut into chunks
¹/₂ cup medium-grain rice
1 tablespoon salt

1. Place the beans in a stew pot with the water, pork meat, prosciutto bone, bay leaf, and thyme. Bring to just below a boil, reduce the heat to very low, using a diffuser if necessary, and simmer for 30 minutes. Add the onions and pumpkin and continue cooking at a simmer until the beans are almost breaking apart and the meat is very tender, about ¹/₂ hour more.

2. When everything is tender, add the rice and salt and cook until the rice is tender, 15 to 18 minutes. Serve immediately.

Makes 6 servings

PROSCIUTTO BONES

In Italy, Spain, and Catalonia, cooks think it is quite essential to add a cooked or cured ham bone to many a stew. Stews utilize bones for flavor, whether it's a ham bone or some soup bones. The marrow, meat, and connective tissue that are found on these bones slowly break down over long simmering, add a deeper level of taste to the stew, and make it gelatinous in some cases. A prosciutto bone, because it is relatively easy to obtain, serves this function perfectly. Since it's unlikely that you buy whole prosciutto, you will have to visit an Italian market to get a bone (you don't need an entire one). If you can't find a pro-sciutto bone, use a thick slice cut from the fatty part. Insist to the slicer that he not take the skin off. He'll look at you strangely (unless he's Italian), but the skin of the prosciutto has lots of extractable flavor in it.

PORK, EGGPLANT, AND ALMOND STEW FROM CATALONIA

THIS TYPICAL FAMILY STEW OR *ESTAFADO* from Catalonia is traditionally cooked in an earthenware casserole. In this preparation, the saucy stew becomes syrupy as the pork and eggplant melt away. It's delicious and best accompanied by medium-grain rice cooked in a court bouillon of water, fresh coriander, orange zest, saffron, and black pepper.

---

2 medium-size eggplants (about 2 pounds), peeled and cut into 2-inch cubes
Salt to taste
½ cup extra virgin olive oil
2 large garlic cloves, sliced
1 slice French or Italian country bread, crust removed
12 blanched whole almonds, roasted in a preheated 350°F oven until golden brown and finely ground in a food processor
2½ pounds pork butt, trimmed of any large pieces of fat and cut into 2-inch pieces
Unbleached all-purpose flour for dredging
1 medium-size onion, finely chopped
1 large, ripe tomato, peeled and chopped
1 cup water

---

1. Lay the eggplant on some paper towels and sprinkle with salt. Leave them to release their bitter juices for 30 minutes, then pat dry with paper towels.

2. In a large skillet, heat the olive oil with the garlic over medium-high heat. Once the garlic starts to sizzle, remove from the pan and set aside in a bowl. Cook the bread slice in the hot oil until golden, 1 to 2 minutes, then quickly remove and set aside with the garlic. Leave the oil in the skillet. When they are cool, chop the bread and garlic together and mix with the almonds.

3. Dredge the pork pieces in the flour, tapping off any excess. Cook them in the skillet in which you cooked the garlic and bread until golden on all sides, about 5 minutes. Remove the meat with tongs or a slotted spoon to an earthenware casserole. Add the onion to the skillet and cook, stirring, until translucent, about 5 minutes. Transfer the onions to the casserole.

4. Place the casserole, if earthenware, on a heat diffuser. Add the tomato, season with salt, and increase the heat to high until the mixture begins to bubble. Reduce the heat to medium-low and cook until the sauce is denser, about 12 minutes. Reduce the heat to low if the sauce is bubbling too vigorously. Add the eggplants and the nut and bread mixture, and stir well to mix. Add the water, and cook, covered, for 30 minutes.

5. Uncover and continue to cook until the eggplant is soft and the liquid has nearly evaporated, another 30 to 45 minutes. Serve very hot.

Makes 4 to 6 servings

WHAT'S A COURT BOUILLON?

Court bouillon means, literally, "a short bouillon," a quickly made poaching liquid of water, white wine, vegetables, aromatics of various kinds, and other seasonings. Cooks use court bouillon to poach chicken or fish, but it is excellent to make rice in too. I love to use all kinds of courts bouillons to cook all sorts of things. They're fun to dream up and they add a wonderful flavor to simple or blander foods such as rice, potatoes, and even macaroni.

THE CÓRDOBAN FARMER'S WIFE'S STEW

THIS ONE-POT FARMHOUSE FARE OF cabbage and chickpeas with the distinctive smell and taste of cumin is an *olla* (stew) from the hilly farmlands around Córdoba, in Andalusia. It is called an *olla cortijera de Córdoba*, meaning "the way the farmer's wife makes it," and it is an example of the simplest of preparations from *cocina pobre*, the "cuisine of the poor." This stew can be frozen and will be excellent thawed and warmed later in the week.

5 *quarts cold water*
2 *cups dried chickpeas (about 1 pound), picked over, rinsed, soaked overnight in cold water to cover, and drained*

1 *large onion, chopped*
3 *large garlic cloves, peeled*
3 *tablespoons extra virgin olive oil*
Salt to taste
1 *teaspoon freshly ground cumin seeds*
½ *pound Irish or Canadian bacon, diced*
1 *small head green cabbage (about 1¾ pounds), cored and chopped*

1. Bring the water to a boil in a stew pot. Add the drained chickpeas, onion, garlic, olive oil, salt, and cumin. Reduce the heat to medium and cook for 2 hours.

2. Add the bacon. Cook until the chickpeas are soft, about 1 hour more.

3. Add the cabbage and cook for 1 hour. Taste and correct the seasonings, and serve.

Makes 8 servings

GARBURE

GARBURE IS THE CLASSIC PEASANT farmer's stew from the Béarn and Gascony in southwest France. It is the regional version of the stew known throughout the country as *potée*. The main difference between the two is that a *garbure* contains dried white haricot beans and a ham bone. A *garbure* also can contain cabbage, a little meat such as bacon, salt pork, sausage, ham hock, or *confit* of

CUISINE OF THE POOR

Throughout the world there is a kind of cooking that the Italians call *cucina povera* and the Spanish, *cocina pobre*, "poor people's food." Historically, it was a food marked by blandness, inferior grains, simple or rough ingredients, and very little meat. But that didn't mean it couldn't be tasty. These days, poor people's food has taken on a kind of cachet among some restaurant chefs and the culinarily sophisticated. Polenta, a famous poor people's food, is now being served with regularity in fancy restaurants—and at high prices too. Suddenly we have begun to see such quintessential poor people's grains as millet and barley also showing up on menus. The poor would undoubtedly find this odd, but taste is a strange thing, and a simple stew such as the Córdoban Farmer's Wife's Stew (page 147) can reach some rather exalted heights.

Atlantiques, which hosts an annual festival of the local cooks' best *garbures*.

The origin of *garbure* is controversial. The first mention of a *garbure* in French is apparently from Molière in 1655. The word *garbure* is of obscure origin, although in Gascon it is *garburo*, perhaps derived from the Spanish word *garbías*, meaning a ragout. This is how the sixteenth-century Spanish cookbook writer Ruperto de Nola used the word in 1525 to describe a preparation called *fruta llamada garbias a la catalana* made of borage, Swiss chard, fresh cheese, and fine spices. So it seems as if the *garbure* might have Catalan origins. Another idea, which I don't accept, is that the word derives from the Basque *garbe*, meaning "sheaf" or "bunch," the *garbure* being a bunch of vegetables.

Sometimes the soupy part of the stew is served first with toasted or dried bread and the meat and vegetables are served afterwards. Notice that I do not take the peels off the fava beans. That's because the stew cooks so long that you will not need to, and the beans will keep their textural integrity and taste. This *garbure* is so good, you may want to double it. If you do, double all the ingredients listed except the ham bone and the bouquet garni.

---

3 quarts water
1 pound smoked bacon in one piece, preferably on the bone with its skin
2 tablespoons rendered goose or duck fat (see page 348)
1¼ pounds fresh ham hock
½ pound leeks, washed well and sliced
6 garlic cloves, finely chopped

duck, and a variety of seasonal vegetables. And an authentic *garbure* requires that a piece of *confit* of duck, goose, or pork be thrown in half an hour before it's done. The smoked bacon piece, which in some ways is the most critical ingredient, is best found in a German, Hungarian, or Polish delicatessen. In the Béarn, the Basques make a *chalorot* by adding a bit of red wine into the broth. It is said that the most famous *garbure* comes from the town of Oloron-Sainte-Marie in the Pyrénées

1/2 celery stalk, chopped

1/2 pound carrots, cut into rounds

1 ham bone

2 fresh pork sausages (about 1/2 pound total),
cut into 1-inch-thick rounds

1/2 cup dried white haricot beans (about 1/4
pound), rinsed and picked over

1 cup shelled fresh fava beans with skins on
(about 1/4 pound)

1/2 pound turnips, peeled and cubed

4 medium-size boiling potatoes (about 1 pound
total), peeled and halved lengthwise

1 small head green cabbage (about 1 1/4 pounds),
damaged outer leaves discarded, cored, and
quartered

2 small onions, each studded with 1 clove

1 bouquet garni, consisting of 10 sprigs each
fresh parsley and thyme, handful of celery
leaves, and 1 bay leaf, tied in cheesecloth

Salt and freshly ground black pepper to taste

1 pound duck confit (see page 345)

6 large slices Italian or French bread, toasted
and rubbed with cut garlic

1. In a 2-quart saucepan, bring 1 quart of the water to a boil and blanch the bacon piece for 30 minutes. Drain, saving the water, and set the bacon aside.

2. In a large stew pot, melt the goose fat over medium-high heat. Brown the ham hock slightly with the leeks, garlic, celery, and carrots, stirring frequently so the garlic doesn't burn, about 5 minutes. Add the ham bone, sausages, haricot beans, fava beans, turnips, potatoes, cabbage, onions, bouquet garni, the remaining 2 quarts of water, reserved bacon cooking water, and the bacon piece. Season with salt and pepper. Bring to a boil, then reduce the heat to low and cook until the meats are tender, about 4 hours.

3. Remove the ham hock, ham bone, bacon, and bouquet garni. Take all the meat off the bones, and return to the stew. Discard the bones and the skin and fat off the ham hock, but keep the skin and fat of the bacon piece and return them to the stew. Add the *confit* of duck and continue to cook until the *garbure* is thick and a spoon could almost stand upright in it, about 30 minutes. If it is still soupy, remove extra liquid with a soup ladle.

4. Place a slice of bread at the bottom of each soup bowl, then ladle the broth and vegetables on top. Serve the meat in a bowl on the side.

Makes 4 to 6 servings

"QUICK" PORK, FENNEL, AND PUMPKIN STEW

THIS RECIPE IS TYPICAL OF SOUTHERN Italian home cooking. I've changed the traditional method by combining two incompatible concepts, namely "quick" and "stew," but I think you get the idea. Because this recipe cooks so quickly, it can't technically be called a stew. In order to get full flavor, given how few ingredients there are, the first step is to create a crusty aromatic film on the bottom of the saucepan that you will lift up by deglazing with water.

1/4 cup extra virgin olive oil, plus extra for drizzling
1 pound pork tenderloin, trimmed of fat and silverskin and cut into bite-size pieces
2 ounces salt pork, chopped
5 large garlic cloves, finely chopped
2 quarts water
2 1/2 pounds fennel bulbs, trimmed of all stalks except one and quartered lengthwise
1 1/2 pounds peeled and seeded pumpkin, diced or cubed
Salt and freshly ground black pepper to taste
1 1/2 cups ditali or other small macaroni

---

1. In a large saucepan or stockpot, heat 3 tablespoons of the olive oil over high heat. Brown the pork on all sides, stirring constantly and vigorously, about 2 minutes. Some of the pork will stick to the bottom of the pot, but that's all right; it will pull off when you deglaze later.

2. Remove the pork with a slotted spoon and set aside. Add the remaining 1 tablespoon olive oil and cook the salt pork and garlic until the salt pork begins to get a little crispy, stirring constantly and vigorously so the garlic doesn't burn, 1 to 2 minutes.

3. Remove the saucepan from the heat and deglaze with 1/4 cup of the water, scraping the bottom and sides of the pan. Return the

saucepan to the heat and let the water evaporate by half. Add the fennel and pumpkin, and with the heat still on high, cook until well coated, tossing frequently, about 6 minutes.

4. Add the remaining 7 3/4 cups of the water and cook over high heat until the vegetables are *al dente*, partially covering the pot once the broth begins to boil, about 20 minutes. Season with salt and pepper, and add the *ditali* and pork. Cook until the pasta is *al dente* and the vegetables soft, about 10 minutes.

5. Turn the heat off and let the stew sit for 3 to 5 minutes so everything settles down and the flavors blend. Serve in individual soup bowls with a drizzle of olive oil, if desired.

Makes 4 to 6 servings

ROAST PORK SHOULDER AND ITALIAN SAUSAGE STEW

SOMEONE ONCE ASKED ME WHAT MY favorite stew was. I pondered that question for a while and then rattled off cassoulet (page 342), bouillabaisse (page 227), and a few others. But he then said, "No, I mean what's your favorite plain-ole-stew that you could eat every day?" Without skipping a beat, I mentioned this stew, which is a typical stew made by Italian-Americans whose ancestry is found in the Neapolitan countryside. But I immediately began to apologize because it just seems so simple that it doesn't seem special. But then I remembered that it is a stew like this that evokes not only the feeling of something that tastes good, but that elemental gastronomic *je ne sais quoi*, or should I say *non lo so*, at the heart of good food. This stew is simple, good food. You'll go crazy over it; it's a stew you'll never find in a restaurant because it's pure home cooking.

Normally, this stew would be made with leftover roast pork shoulder, but I love this taste so much, I go ahead and roast the shoulder and then use it in the stew. To make it really special, go ahead and make your own Italian sausages: Follow the recipe on page 346, and add 6 tablespoons of fennel seeds, 1½ cups of freshly grated pecorino cheese, and 1 cup of red wine to the sausage mixture. I also throw into the stew several pieces of Parmigiano-Reggiano rinds that I have saved for just this purpose. After the stew is cooked, the tough rinds are softer and edible; they're a nice little surprise. Serve the stew on top of spaghetti or macaroni, with lots of freshly grated Parmigiano-Reggiano cheese and a nice fresh salad on the side or afterwards. And, of course, crusty bread. You've got to drink Chianti with this too. The leftover stew, if there is any, will probably taste even better the next day

---

One 4-pound pork shoulder roast on the bone with its skin
Salt and freshly ground pepper to taste

PARMIGIANO RIND

Don't throw away that rind from a chunk of Parmigiano-Reggiano once there is no longer any cheese to grate. Do as the Italians do, and save it in a zippered-top plastic bag in the refrigerator. Then, when you have a few, toss them into any Italian stew you're making; they not only add flavor, they're edible too, once they soften.

¼ cup finely chopped salt pork
2 tablespoons extra virgin olive oil
2 tablespoons unsalted butter
1 large onion, chopped
6 large garlic cloves, finely chopped
3 tablespoons finely chopped fresh basil leaves
3 tablespoons finely chopped fresh parsley leaves
2 pounds mild Italian sausage
One 35-ounce can Italian peeled plum tomatoes, with their juices
One 6-ounce can tomato paste
¾ cup water
1 piece Parmigiano-Reggiano rind (optional)
1 teaspoon sugar
1 tablespoon dried oregano

---

1. Preheat the oven to 300°F. Place the pork shoulder in a roasting pan with the skin side up. Season lightly with salt and pepper. Place in the oven and roast until almost tender, about 5 hours. Cut off the fat and skin. Cut the meat into large pieces and set aside. Discard all but 2 tablespoons of the accumulated fat in the pan.

2. In a large earthenware casserole set on a heat diffuser, cook the salt pork with the reserved pork shoulder fat, the olive oil, and butter over medium-high heat until the salt pork begins to turn crispy, stirring occasionally, about 6 minutes. (If you are not cooking with earthenware and a diffuser, cook over medium heat and check for doneness sooner.) Add the onion, garlic, basil, and parsley and cook until the onion is translucent, stirring frequently so the garlic doesn't burn, about 4 minutes. Add the sausages and brown for 5 minutes, turning occasionally. Reduce the heat to low, and add the pork shoulder, tomatoes, tomato paste, water, Parmigiano rind, sugar, and oregano. Stir to mix well and dissolve the tomato paste, then season with salt and pepper. Cover partially, and bring to a gentle boil. Reduce the heat to low again and simmer until the pork shoulder and sausages are very tender, about 2½ hours. Serve immediately, cutting up the sausages as desired.

Makes 6 servings

PORK, TOMATO, AND WINE STEW FROM NAPLES

ALTHOUGH THIS STEW IS CALLED *UMIDO di maiale*, literally "pork stew," cooks of the Campania region of Italy will more often than not serve this rich and delicious saucy stew with a dry pasta possessing some body, such as macaroni or *fusilli*, and that's what I recommend. The *soffritto* of lard, onion, celery, carrot, garlic, and marjoram is the beginning of a tomato ragout that is imbued with the richness that is typical when one stews pork shoulder.

¼ *cup extra virgin olive oil*
2 *tablespoons lard*
1 *large onion, very finely chopped*
1 *celery stalk, very finely chopped*
1 *carrot, very finely chopped*
8 *large garlic cloves, very finely chopped*
2 *tablespoons finely chopped fresh marjoram*
  leaves
3 *pounds pork shoulder bones with meat on*
  them
1 *cup dry red wine*
5 *pounds ripe tomatoes, peeled, seeded, and*
  chopped
1 *bay leaf*
2 *cups water*
2 *tablespoons tomato paste*
1¼ *pounds macaroni*

1. In a large casserole, heat the olive oil with the lard over high heat. Cook the onion, celery, carrot, garlic, and marjoram until the onion is soft and translucent, stirring so the garlic doesn't burn, about 4 minutes. Add the pork and brown, about 3 minutes. Add the wine and reduce by half, about 4 minutes. Add the tomatoes, bay leaf, water, and tomato paste. Reduce the heat to low, stir well to mix, and cook until the meat is falling off the bones and the bones are separating from each other, 2 to 3 hours.

2. Towards the end of the cooking time, bring a large pot of abundantly salted water to a rolling boil. Cook the macaroni until *al dente*. Drain the pasta without rinsing it, and serve with the ragout.

————●————

Serves 6

STEWED PORK SHOULDER WITH RAVIOLI AND SNAP PEAS

THIS IS A VERY SATISFYING DISH THAT needs to cook a very long time over low heat. It's ideally made on a weekend. The pork shoulder is cooked whole with the skin left on, giving the stew a delicious flavor. But you don't eat the skin, since it's fatty. The ravioli and snap peas are actually a suggestion. You could use another stuffed pasta such as tortellini or various kinds of macaroni and any number of vegetables.

————●————

2 tablespoons extra virgin olive oil
2 tablespoons Freshly Rendered Lard (page 154)
3¹/₂ pounds pork shoulder on the bone
1 medium-size onion, finely chopped
6 large garlic cloves, finely chopped

¹/₄ cup finely chopped fresh parsley leaves
1¹/₂ cups dry white wine
2 pounds ripe tomatoes, peeled, seeded, and chopped
Salt and freshly ground black pepper to taste
1¹/₂ pounds homemade or store-bought cheese ravioli
10 ounces sugar snap peas, tough strings removed
Freshly grated Parmigiano-Reggiano cheese for sprinkling

————●————

1. In a casserole, heat the olive oil and lard together over medium-high heat. Brown the pork with the onion, garlic, and parsley, 5 to 6 minutes. Add the wine and let it evaporate for 2 minutes. Add the tomatoes, and season with salt and pepper. Cover, reduce the heat to very low, using a heat diffuser if necessary, and cook until the meat is falling off the bone, about 6 hours.

2. Towards the end of the cooking time, bring a large pot of abundantly salted water to a vigorous boil and add the ravioli. Once the water returns to a boil, add the snap peas and cook for 7 minutes if the ravioli are not frozen, and 9 minutes if they are. Drain well and transfer to a serving platter or bowl.

3. Ladle some sauce from the pork over the ravioli and snap peas and place the pork shoulder in the center. Serve with Parmigiano cheese.

————●————

Makes 4 to 6 servings

FRESHLY RENDERED LARD

Cooks in southern Italy and Sicily use a kind of freshly rendered lard called *'nzugna, 'nzunza,* or *sugna,* depending on the dialect. This pig fat is vastly different and much more flavorful than the lard that one buys in the supermarket. The word *'nzugna* derives either from the Arabic word for impurity, *sankha,* or the Latin *axungia,* meaning "a wheel of fat."

One 2-pound chunk raw pig fat
2 bay leaves
2 teaspoons salt

1. Cut up the raw pig fat, and poach it in water to cover for 2 hours. Let cool and, when the fat has separated from the water, remove the fat. Put the fat in an earthenware casserole, pour in water to cover, and add the bay leaves and salt. Cook, covered, for 30 minutes over low heat. The cracklings are the pieces that haven't melted, and once they are floating in the water, the lard is ready.

2. Remove and dry the cracklings. Allow the fat to cool again, and drain off the water. Put the lard in a jar or earthenware vessel. Cover the cooled lard with parchment paper and secure it with kitchen twine. The *'nzugna* will keep for a long time in the refrigerator.

3. To test the lard, dip a wad of clean cotton into it and light it. According to tradition, if the flame is clear, the lard is perfect; if it's not clear, it's usable, but not perfect.

Makes about 2 pounds of lard

FAVATA

DURING SHROVETIDE, THE DAYS PRECEDing Ash Wednesday, this stew is prepared in Gocéano and Barbagia, on the island of Sardinia. Chunks of salt pork, a ham bone, homemade sausages, a handful of dried beans, some wild fennel, and other herbs are cooked in water until the meat is tender. Favata usually also contains fava beans or white beans, pork ribs, cabbage, onion, and tomato. Ask your butcher for the pork skin.

1 pound dried fava beans or white beans, picked over and rinsed
1/2 cup extra virgin olive oil
1 1/2 pounds luganega sausage or mild Italian sausage
1 pound pork loin back ribs or spareribs
One 1/2-pound piece slab bacon
One 2-inch square pork skin
1 large branch wild fennel, coarsely chopped, or 3 fennel bulbs, with leaves, chopped
2 medium-size onions, thinly sliced and separated into rings
2 garlic cloves, mashed into a paste in a mortar
1 small carrot, chopped
1 celery stalk, chopped
2 oil-packed sun-dried tomatoes, drained and chopped
Salt and freshly ground black pepper to taste
Freshly grated Parmigiano-Reggiano cheese for sprinkling
6 slices Italian bread, fried in olive oil until crispy

LUGANEGA SAUSAGE

Luganega sausage is a mild Italian sausage with a delicate flavor that is found mostly in Lombardy and the Veneto regions of northern Italy. It is also called *salsiccia a metro* because it is sold by the meter. The roots of this sausage can be traced to classical Rome: Varro, Cicero, and Apicius mention it. It is said that the best comes from Monza, in Lombardy. Lombardy might also be the birthplace of this sausage, since it has been argued that the Latin word for this sausage, *lucanicus*, derives from a Lombard word, not the name of a southern Italian people, the Lucanians, who lived in southern Italy at the time of its Greek settlement and the Roman Republic. In Basilicata, it is called *lucanica* or *lucania*, where it is a long, continuously coiled grilled pork sausage flavored with red pepper flakes. The name is also used in Spain, where *longaniza* or *llangonissa* is a pork sausage seasoned with paprika, cinnamon, aniseed, garlic, and vinegar. In Greece, *loukanika* sausage is traditionally made in the countryside after the *hirosfagi*, the hog slaughter between mid-November and New Year's Day.

1. If using fava beans, soak them in cold water to cover for 12 hours. Drain, then plunge them into boiling water for 5 minutes, drain again, and pinch off their skins. For white beans there is no advance preparation.

2. In a large casserole, heat the olive oil over medium–high heat. Brown the sausages and ribs, turning frequently, 4 to 5 minutes. Add the beans and water to cover (about 2 quarts). Add the piece of bacon, pork skin, fennel, onions, garlic, carrot, celery, and dried tomatoes. Bring to a gentle boil, then reduce the heat to low and simmer until the meat is very tender, almost falling off the bone for the ribs, about 2 hours. Add only very little water if necessary, as the stew should not be too liquidy. Check the seasonings, too, adding salt and pepper if necessary.

3. After 2 hours, remove the pork ribs and cut into separate ribs. Cut up the bacon into small cubes. Return the cut-up ribs and bacon to the casserole and continue to cook for about 1 hour more.

4. Serve the stew very hot with lots of Parmigiano cheese and 1 slice of toasted bread per person.

Makes 6 servings

RAGOUT OF PORK RIBS AND SAUSAGES

IN SOUTHERN ITALY COOKS LIKE TO KEEP pork and pork sausages on the fire for a long time to make wonderfully flavored stews. This is a succulent stew that simmers for several hours. It is flavored with anise, whose heavenly aroma perfumes the dish during its slow cooking. The kind of ribs you want are called country ribs, which have a lot more meat on the bone than back ribs. This stew is excellent served with baked ziti and broccoli.

2 tablespoons extra virgin olive oil
2 tablespoons Freshly Rendered Lard (page 154)
  or store-bought lard
2 1/2 pounds pork country ribs on the bone
1 medium-size onion, chopped
3 large garlic cloves, finely chopped
One 6-ounce can tomato paste
1 1/2 cups dry red wine
1 1/4 pounds hot Italian sausages
1 1/4 cups water
1 tablespoon aniseed
Salt and freshly ground black pepper to taste

1. In a casserole, preferably earthenware, heat the olive oil with the lard over medium-high heat. Brown the country ribs with the onion and garlic, 5 to 6 minutes.

2. Dissolve the tomato paste in 1 cup of the wine. Add the sausages, dissolved tomato paste, the remaining 1/2 cup of wine, the water, and aniseed and season with salt and pepper. Bring to a gentle boil. Reduce the heat to low and cook, uncovered, until tender, about 4 hours. Serve, saving any extra ragout for a future meal.

Makes 5 servings

CABBAGE AND SAUSAGE STEW FROM LOMBARDY

VERZE IS THE ITALIAN WORD FOR SAVOY cabbage, the crinkly leaved cabbage used in this stew called *verzada*. But the name of this stew may also refer to *de vêrs*, the small sausages, or *salsicciuoli*, that are used. They are a kind of *luganega* sausage (see page 155). This is a hearty dish that is best made with homemade sausages, but you can use a mild Italian sausage of any kind. Savoy cabbage is a delicate cabbage, more so than the familiar green head cabbage.

2 tablespoons unsalted butter
3 ounces pancetta, chopped
1 medium-size onion, thinly sliced and
  separated into rings
1 small head Savoy cabbage (about 1 3/4 pounds),
  damaged outer leaves discarded, cored, and cut
  into strips
2 1/2 tablespoons white wine vinegar
Salt to taste

3 fresh sage leaves, finely chopped
2 tablespoons finely chopped fresh parsley leaves
1½ pounds **luganega** *sausage or sweet Italian sausage*

---

1. In a large casserole, heat the butter and pancetta together over medium-high heat until the pancetta is soft, 4 to 5 minutes. Add the onion and cook until soft, stirring, about 5 minutes. Add the cabbage in handfuls and cook and turn them until the leaves are coated with fat. Reduce the heat to medium and cook, stirring, until portions of the cabbage begin to turn light brown, about 10 minutes.

2. Sprinkle on the vinegar, season with salt, and stir in the sage and parsley. Place the sausages on top of the cabbage, cover, and simmer over low heat for 1 hour. Serve.

Makes 6 servings

CREAMED SAUSAGE, YELLOW BELL PEPPER, AND MUSHROOM STEW

THIS RICH AND SATISFYING STEW INSPIRED by the stews of Val d'Aosta and Piedmont in northern Italy is best in winter. I usually serve it with rice. Although it is cooked separately, I've included the directions for the rice in this recipe for convenience. I don't know if all children will like this, but when my oldest son, Ali, was little, he loved it and had heaping seconds, a rather rare occurrence among children. Salt and pepper are not necessary in this stew, since plenty will be provided by the other ingredients. The combination of crème fraîche and mascarpone is not traditional, but it only enhances the richness of the stew.

---

2 tablespoons unsalted butter
2 tablespoons finely chopped salt pork
3 tablespoons extra virgin olive oil
1 medium-size onion, thinly sliced and separated into rings
2 scallions (white part only), chopped
1 yellow bell pepper, seeded and thinly sliced into rings
10 ounces button mushrooms, brushed clean and sliced
¾ pound mild Italian sausages, removed from their casings and crumbled
¾ pound Spanish- or Portuguese-style chorizo sausages or Polish kielbasa, chopped
½ pound cooked ham, chopped
1 cup crème fraîche
8 ounces mascarpone cheese
1 cup medium-grain rice, like Calarosa
2 cups water
1 teaspoon salt

---

1. In a casserole, melt the butter with the salt pork and 2 tablespoons of the olive oil over medium heat. Cook until the salt pork is a little crispy, stirring occasionally, about 5 minutes. Add the onion, scallions, bell pepper, and mushrooms and cook for 30 minutes, stirring occasionally and reducing the heat if it looks like it's bubbling too vigorously.

2. In a separate pan, brown the Italian sausage meat with a few tablespoons of water until it loses its color, about 8 minutes. Add the chorizo and ham and cook, stirring, until everything is browner and crispier looking, 15 to 20 minutes. Remove with a slotted spoon and add to the casserole, discarding the fat. Add the creme fraîche and mascarpone to the casserole and stir well to blend. Cover, reduce the heat to very low, and simmer for 2 hours.

3. About 20 minutes before the stew is done, prepare the rice. In a medium-size, heavy saucepan with a heavy lid, heat the remaining 1 tablespoon of olive oil over medium-high heat. Add the rice and cook for 1 minute, stirring to coat the grains with the oil. Add the water and salt, bring to a boil, then reduce to low and cover. Cook until tender, 10 to 15 minutes (check after 10 minutes). Transfer the rice to a serving platter, pour the stew on top, and serve.

Makes 4 to 6 servings

MINESTRA DI PASTA E FAGIOLI

THIS HEARTY AND DELICIOUS *MINESTRA*, or soup, of pasta and beans is so full-bodied that you only need a green salad to ac-company it. In Italy, *minestre* (plural) would be served as a first course and therefore are not technically stews in Italian culinary culture. But I make and serve *minestre* as stews because of how substantial they are. The prosciutto skin is used for flavoring and can easily be bought from the deli counter of an Italian market or supermarket. Often they will give it to you for free. If you decide to eat the prosciutto skin, cut it into strips, otherwise leave it in one or two pieces that can be discarded after the soup is cooked. I give you a range in the amount of broth to use so you can have a thicker or thinner stew.

3 tablespoons extra virgin olive oil
1 pound boneless pork shoulder or butt, trimmed of any large pieces of fat and diced
One 1/4-pound piece pancetta, cut into strips
One 1/4-pound piece prosciutto skin or skin from salt pork, left whole or cut into strips
1 large onion, chopped
6 garlic cloves, chopped
1 fennel bulb (about 3/4 pound), chopped
1 celery stalk, chopped
2 to 2 1/2 quarts Chicken Broth (page 181)
1 1/2 cups dried white beans (about 10 ounces), rinsed and picked over
1 cup canned chickpeas, drained
1 cinnamon stick
1 bay leaf
1 sprig fresh rosemary
1/4 pound Parmigiano-Reggiano cheese rinds (if you have any)
Salt and freshly ground black pepper to taste
1/4 pound tubetti, ditali, or other short macaroni

Extra virgin olive oil for drizzling
Freshly grated Parmigiano–Reggiano cheese for
sprinkling

---

1. In a large stew pot, heat the olive oil over medium-high heat. Cook the pork, pancetta, and prosciutto skin until they turn color, about 5 minutes. Add the onion, garlic, fennel, and celery and cook, stirring occasionally, until softened, 12 to 15 minutes. Add the chicken broth, white beans, chickpeas, cinnamon stick, bay leaf, rosemary, and Parmigiano rinds, if using. Season with salt and pepper. Bring to a boil, about 10 minutes, then reduce the heat to medium-low and cook until the white beans are soft, about 1½ hours.

2. Add the pasta and cook, stirring, until *al dente*, 12 to 15 minutes. Discard the cinnamon stick, bay leaf, and rosemary sprig. Both the prosciutto skin and Parmigiano crusts can be eaten, if desired. Serve with a drizzle of olive oil and sprinkling of Parmigano.

Makes 6 to 8 servings

PUMPKIN AND CABBAGE STEW

THERE'S PLENTY OF MEAT TO SATIATE ANY meat lover in this soul-satisfying northern Italian pumpkin and cabbage soup-stew called *minestra di zucca e cavolo*, and it's loaded with vegetables to provide a melody of flavors. The amount of herbs is quite copious, contributing to the fabulous flavor. This is a stew to make in October and November, when pumpkins are plentiful.

¼ *cup extra virgin olive oil*
1 *medium-size white onion, finely chopped*
4 *large garlic cloves, finely chopped*
1 *large carrot, finely chopped*
1 *celery stalk, finely chopped*
2 *ounces pancetta, chopped*
3 *tablespoons finely chopped fresh mint leaves*
Leaves from 2 sprigs fresh rosemary, chopped
¼ *cup finely chopped fresh parsley leaves*
3 *tablespoons finely chopped fresh coriander*
   (cilantro) leaves
¼ *cup finely chopped fresh basil leaves*
2 *tablespoons fresh thyme leaves*
1 *pound ground pork*
1¾ *pounds peeled and seeded pumpkin, cut into*
   small cubes
1 *small head green cabbage (about 1 pound),*
   damaged outer leaves discarded, cored, and
   shredded
1½ *quarts water*
One 2-inch-square piece Parmigiano–Reggiano
   cheese rind
¾ *pound veal marrow bones*
Salt and freshly ground black pepper to taste
¼ *pound small soup macaroni, such as* **tubet-**
   tini *or* **pennette**
Freshly grated pecorino cheese for sprinkling
Extra virgin olive oil for drizzling

---

1. In a large stew pot, heat the olive oil over medium-high heat, then add the *battuto* of onion, garlic, carrot, celery, pancetta, mint, rosemary, parsley, coriander, basil, and thyme and cook until the onion is soft, stirring occasionally so the garlic doesn't burn, about 6 minutes.

2. Add the pork and brown, breaking it up with a wooden spoon, about 3 minutes. Add the pumpkin and cabbage and toss a few times so all the ingredients are mixed well. Add the water and bring to a boil, then immediately reduce the heat to low. Add the Parmigiano rind and veal marrow bones, and cook until the pumpkin is tender, about 1 hour.

3. Season with salt and pepper and return the stew to a boil. Add the pasta and cook until *al dente*, about 10 minutes. Turn the heat off and let sit 10 minutes. Correct the seasonings and serve with a sprinkling of pecorino and a drizzle of olive oil.

Makes 6 servings

PASTA AND PEA STEW

THIS ITALIAN *MINESTRA DI PASTA E PISELLI* is a soup-stew of pasta and peas, perfect for the spring. As the pasta swells up during the cooking, the soup becomes denser, so you will want to eat it as soon as it's finished cooking. Left in the saucepan, the pasta will continue to

---

WHAT'S A BATTUTO?

In the Italian culinary vernacular, a *battuto* is often used in the same sense as a *soffritto* (see page 60), and is actually an uncooked *soffritto*. *Battuto* means "beaten" and is usually a very finely chopped mixture of aromatic ingredients and fat, such as salt pork, pork fat, or pancetta, and onions, carrot, celery, garlic, and herbs. Because it's all so very finely chopped, it looks beaten.

---

swell and absorb liquid until there is none left. This can be thought of as a yeoman recipe that serves well for a hungry family of four. The pasta I call for in this recipe, *semi di melone*, means "melon seeds," giving you an idea of their shape. They can be found readily in supermarkets with other so-called soup pastas, such as *acini di pepe* ("peppercorns"), any of which you could also use.

1/4 *cup lard*
1 1/2 *ounces prosciutto*
1 *medium-size onion*
1 *large garlic clove, peeled*
10 *large fresh basil leaves*
10 *ounces shelled fresh peas (from about 2 pounds fresh pea pods) or frozen peas*
1 *tablespoon tomato paste dissolved in 1 cup water*
2 *quarts boiling Beef Broth or vegetable broth (page 3)*
Salt and freshly ground black pepper to taste
1/2 *pound* semi di melone *or other soup pasta*

Freshly grated Parmigiano-Reggiano cheese for sprinkling

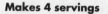

1. Make a *battuto* by finely chopping the lard, prosciutto, onion, garlic, and basil together, or better still, process them in the food processor until all the pieces are miniscule, scraping down the sides occasionally.

2. Put the *battuto* in a stove-top casserole or saucepan and cook over medium heat, stirring frequently, until the onion is soft and everything looks mushy, 8 to 10 minutes. Add the peas and the diluted tomato paste. Cook until the mixture begins to bubble vigorously, about 5 minutes. Then add the boiling broth, season with salt and pepper, and cook until the peas are *al dente*, 35 to 40 minutes for fresh peas, and according to the package instructions for frozen peas.

3. Add the pasta and cook until tender, about 11 minutes for *semi di melone*. Follow the package instructions for other soup pastas. Serve immediately with the cheese sprinkled on top.

Makes 4 servings

ITALIAN SAUSAGE AND PEPPER STEW

I'VE ALWAYS BEEN WILD ABOUT ITALIAN sausages and often make my own. The combination of sausages and bell peppers is typical of the kind of Italian-American home cooking one comes across in New York and on Long Island, where I went to high school. I'm not sure my mother ever made a stew like this, but this is the type of stew she could have made. Leftovers, as you can imagine, make for wonderful heroes. Take a soft Italian hero (also known as a submarine), roll and heat it in the oven until it begins to harden on the outside, then lay the hot leftover sausage and peppers in it with a sprinkle of Parmigiano cheese.

3 tablespoons extra virgin olive oil
4 green bell peppers (about 1¹/₂ pounds total), seeded and cut into strips
¹/₂ pound red onions, chopped
4 large garlic cloves, finely chopped
1¹/₄ pounds hot Italian sausages
1 pound ripe tomatoes, peeled, seeded, and chopped
1¹/₂ cups water
1 bouquet garni, consisting of 5 sprigs each fresh basil and mint, tied with kitchen twine
Salt and freshly ground black pepper to taste

1. In a stove-top casserole or Dutch oven, heat the olive oil over medium-high heat. Cook the peppers, onions, and garlic until the onions are translucent and the peppers slightly limp, stirring frequently so the garlic doesn't burn, about 5 minutes. Add the sausages, tomatoes, water, and bouquet garni and season with salt and pepper. Increase the heat to high until the mixture starts boiling, about 5 minutes. Then reduce the heat to medium and cook until the sausages are firm, stirring occasionally, 20 to 25 minutes.

2. Discard the bouquet garni. Slice the sausages or leave whole and serve.

Makes 4 servings

PORK AND BELL PEPPER STEW

T HIS ITALIAN-AMERICAN FAMILY STEW derives its inspiration from several southern Italian stews. It is colorful and appetizing. When all my children lived at home, they were always great fans of bell peppers, so anytime a stew contained them, I knew it would be well received. This stew is best made with lean boneless pork country ribs because you want to keep the amount of fat to a minimum, but cook the ribs for a long enough time to extract the flavor.

---

1 bunch broccoli
Salt
4 large green bell peppers
1 large red bell pepper
1 pound boneless pork country ribs
1/4 cup extra virgin olive oil, plus extra for coating the pork
Freshly ground black pepper to taste
1 small red onion, peeled
2 large garlic cloves, peeled
1/2 cup loosely packed fresh parsley leaves
1 pound ripe tomatoes, peeled, seeded, and chopped

---

1. Preheat the oven to 425°F.

2. Bring a pot of water to a boil, and blanch the broccoli for 3 minutes. Remove from the water with tongs, and plunge immediately in cold water. Break the head into small florets and cut the stalk into sticks; set aside. Bring the same pot of water to a boil, salt lightly, and boil the blanched broccoli for 5 minutes. Drain and set aside.

3. Roast the bell peppers on a baking sheet until their skins blacken and blister on all sides, about 35 minutes. Set aside until they cool, then remove the skins, stems, and seeds and cut into strips.

4. Preheat a cast-iron skillet or griddle over high heat for 10 minutes. Coat the pork with olive oil, season with salt and pepper, and place in the skillet or griddle, reduce the heat to medium, and cook until firm, about 10 minutes per side. Remove, slice, and set aside.

5. Finely chop the onion, garlic, and parsley together. In a casserole, heat the 1/4 cup of olive oil over medium-high heat. Cook the *soffritto* until translucent, stirring, about 4 minutes. Reduce the heat to medium, add the tomatoes and bell pepper strips, and season with salt and pepper. Cook, covered, for 20 minutes. Add the pork and broccoli and cook for another 20 minutes. Serve immediately.

Makes 4 to 6 servings

DUTCH BROWN BEAN STEW

DUTCH OF A CERTAIN AGE WILL TELL YOU many heart-rending stories about the terror of living under Nazi occupation during World War II, and they will tell you stories of near starvation and deprivation. There was very little meat, and beans were often the only food available. The Dutch developed many dishes using beans and this particular stew is one of them, although I don't know how old its roots are and its origin may predate the war. The name of this stew in Dutch is *vijfschaft*, which means "five kinds," because it is made with five different fruits and vegetables. After the war, of course, meat again became available and abundant. For the hunter's sausage, try a German or Hungarian deli.

1 cup dried red kidney beans (¹/₂ pound), picked over and rinsed

2 tablespoons finely chopped ham fat

¹/₂ pound smoked bacon, sliced

1 pound fresh or smoked Polish kielbasa or any German-style smoked hunter's sausage, cut into ¹/₂-inch pieces

1 pound carrots, cut into ¹/₄-inch-thick rounds

4 medium-size onions (about 1³/₄ pounds total), sliced ¹/₄ inch thick

2 Granny Smith apples, peeled, cored, and cut into wedges

2 pounds boiling potatoes, peeled and sliced ¹/₄ inch thick

1 teaspoon salt

1 tablespoon cornstarch dissolved in 2 tablespoons water

¹/₄ cup (¹/₂ stick) unsalted butter

1. Put the beans in a large casserole and cover with lightly salted water. Bring to a boil, and reduce the heat to low. Cover and cook until almost tender, 45 to 60 minutes. Drain, saving 3 cups of the cooking liquid. Return the beans to the casserole with the reserved liquid.

2. While the beans are cooking, in a large skillet, cook the ham fat over medium heat until it is sizzling vigorously. Brown the bacon and sausage together until the sausage is no longer pink, if using fresh sausage, or until the bacon edges are crisp, about 10 minutes.

3. Add the carrots, onions, and apples to the casserole with the beans and simmer over low heat for 15 minutes, covered, stirring occasionally. Add the potatoes and salt and continue to cook until the potatoes are tender, about 1¼ hours. Stir in the dissolved cornstarch to thicken the sauce, then stir in the butter.

4. Transfer the sausage and bacon and any accumulated fat to the casserole and push down into the stew. Heat for 5 minutes over low heat, covered. Then serve from the casserole.

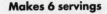

Makes 6 servings

SWEDISH SAUSAGE AND BRUSSELS SPROUT STEW

THIS STEW IS ONE SUGGESTED TO ME BY my Saab mechanic Håken Wiberg, who tells me that this stew, called *korv-och kål-gryta*, uses a kind of sausage called *falukorv* (or *falnkorv*), which comes from the town of Falun, northwest of Stockholm. It is a thick, bologna-like sausage popular throughout Sweden and made of beef, lean pork, and pork fatback. Sometimes dried milk is added to it. It is then smoked before finding its way into stews. The Swedes are nuts about *falukorv*, as you will see by visiting www.falukorv.net on the Internet. In this recipe it is cut into chunks to cook, after peeling the skin off. A good substitute would be a small, one-pound mortadella sausage, such as that made by Arzuman (ask your store manager). Arzuman uses dried milk.

If you prefer beef, try Hebrew National beef bologna. A Swedish housewife would typically use a beef bouillon cube, but if you do, make sure you don't use more salt than called for because the cubes are high in sodium.

1 pound small mortadella sausage or large cooked or smoked Polish kielbasa, skinned and cut into large dice
1 large onion, chopped
2 large carrots, cut into ¼-inch-thick rounds
1½ pounds small Brussels sprouts, sliced lengthwise into thirds
1 bay leaf
2 teaspoons salt
6 black peppercorns
2 cups Beef Broth (page 3)
1 cup water
Finely chopped fresh parsley leaves for garnish

1. Put all the ingredients, except the parsley, in a stew pot, and bring to a boil. Reduce the heat to medium, cover, and cook until everything is tender, about 12 minutes.

2. Sprinkle with parsley and serve.

Makes 4 to 6 servings

RHINELAND-STYLE SMOKED SAUSAGE AND LENTIL STEW

T HIS DISH, CALLED *LINSENEINTOPF* IN
German, is a rich, hearty, one-pot meal
that is perfect in cold weather. In the late
1960s I hitchhiked though the Rhineland, and
I seem to remember eating dishes like this in a
variety of youth hostels. If you like a soupier
stew, add more beef broth. Also, do try to get
smoked bacon, which I believe provides a
richer, earthier taste. That might mean a trip
to a German or East European delicatessen.
Lovage is an herb not very commonly seen or
used these days, but keep your eyes open for
it, especially at farmer's markets, because it
provides a delightfully musty touch to the stew.
In its place you can use four large leaves of fresh
sage. Be careful you do not overcook the
lentils, otherwise the dish will be mushy.

———————●———————

2¹/₂ *cups Beef Broth (page 3)*
1 *tablespoon tomato paste*
One ³/₄-*pound piece smoked slab bacon*
1 *pound dried black (beluga) lentils (preferably)*
   or green or brown lentils, picked over and
   rinsed
2 *carrots, diced*
2 *medium-size onions, coarsely chopped*
2 *leeks (white and light green parts only), split*
   lengthwise, washed well, and sliced
1 *celeriac (1¹/₂ to 2 pounds), peeled and diced*
³/₄ *pound boiling potatoes, peeled and diced*

Leaves from 1 bunch fresh parsley, finely
   chopped
2 *bushy sprigs fresh lovage, chopped*
1¹/₂ *pounds smoked Polish kielbasa, cut into*
   1-inch pieces
2 *tablespoons white wine vinegar*
Salt and freshly ground black pepper to taste

———————●———————

1. In a large casserole, bring the broth to a
gentle boil over medium-high heat, covered,
with the tomato paste and bacon, whisking a
bit to dissolve the paste. Reduce the heat to
low, and add the lentils, carrots, onions, leeks,
celeriac, and potatoes. Cover and cook until
almost tender, about 1¹/₄ hours.

2. Remove the piece of bacon and dice. Add
the parsley, lovage, and sausages and return the
bacon to the casserole. Cook until the sausages
are heated through, about 10 minutes. Sprinkle
with the vinegar, season with salt and pepper,
and serve.

———————●———————

Makes 6 to 8 servings

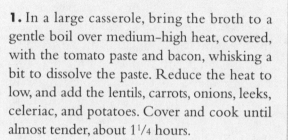

AUSTRIAN PORK AND CABBAGE STEW FROM VIENNA

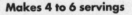

THE SNOWY WHITE AND COLD WINTER OF Salzburg, Austria, is charming. The air is crisp and smells like the forest, and as you gaze over the town, smoke glides lazily upwards from countless chimneys. When I lived in Salzburg through the winter of 1977, my hausfrau introduced me to many typical Austrian stews, which I still find so satisfying. I love these earthy central European stews and I think you will too. This *Wienereintopf,* "Viennese stew," is made with pork and cabbage and seasoned with ground caraway seeds.

———●———

6 tablespoons (³/4 stick) unsalted butter
1 large onion, cut into ¹/4-inch-thick slices and
   separated into rings
1¹/2 pounds boiling potatoes, peeled and cut into
   ¹/4-inch-thick slices
2 pounds boneless pork shoulder, trimmed of any
   large pieces of fat and cut into 1¹/2-inch cubes
2 large carrots, cut into ³/8-inch-thick rounds
¹/2 small head Savoy cabbage (about ³/4 pound),
   damaged outer leaves discarded, cored, and
   chopped
Salt and freshly ground black pepper to taste
2 to 3 teaspoons freshly ground caraway seeds,
   to your taste
2 cups Chicken Broth (page 181)

———●———

1. In a large casserole, melt the butter over medium-high heat. When it stops sizzling, cook the onion until yellow, stirring, about 10 minutes. Remove the onion with a slotted spoon and set aside. Pour off all the butter, leaving enough to coat the bottom of the casserole. Reserve the poured-off butter.

2. Preheat the oven to 350°F.

3. Layer the potatoes, pork, carrots, and cabbage, in that order, in the casserole, sprinkling each layer with salt, pepper, and some of the caraway. End with a layer of potatoes, and lay the reserved fried onions on top. Again sprinkle with salt, pepper, and caraway. Pour the reserved butter over the top. Pour the chicken broth over the potatoes. Cover the casserole tightly. Bake until the pork and potatoes are tender, about 2¹/2 hours.

4. Turn on the broiler and remove the top of the casserole. Broil until the top is browned, 3 to 4 minutes. Serve immediately.

———●———

Makes 4 to 6 servings

CROATIAN SAUSAGE AND SAUERKRAUT STEW

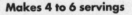

ONE FINDS STEWS LIKE THIS THROUGHOUT Eastern Europe and the Balkans, and even in the Trentino–Alto Adige province of northern Italy. This stew from Croatia, called *kobasice sa kiselim zeljem*, is a very simple rendition that is best made with a good smoked pork sausage, such as Polish-style kielbasa, Cracow sausage, or hunter's sausage, all found mostly in Polish-American, Hungarian-American, and German-American delicatessens.

———•———

2 tablespoons lard
One 2-ounce piece smoked slab bacon, sliced
1 small onion, chopped
2 large garlic cloves, finely chopped
4 juniper berries, crushed and ground in a
    mortar
1 teaspoon paprika
2 pounds sauerkraut, drained
1¼ pounds Polish sausage, cut into 1-inch
    pieces
Salt and freshly ground black pepper to taste

———•———

1. In a large casserole, melt 1 tablespoon of the lard over medium-high heat. Cook the bacon, onion, garlic, juniper, and paprika until golden, stirring frequently so the garlic doesn't burn, about 5 minutes. Add the sauerkraut, reduce the heat to medium, and cook, partially covered, until the sauerkraut is golden and soft, stirring occasionally and adding a few tablespoons of water to keep it from sticking, 25 to 30 minutes.

2. Meanwhile, in a skillet, melt the remaining 1 tablespoon of lard over medium-high heat. Brown the sausage, moving the pieces around with a wooden spoon, 8 to 10 minutes. Add the sausage to the sauerkraut. Taste, then season

with salt and pepper if necessary, and cook, covered, until the sausage becomes very tender, 15 to 20 minutes.

———•———

Makes 5 servings

CZECH CUISINE

———•———

When in 1993 Czechoslovakia broke into the two independent states of Slovakia and the Czech Republic, this was nothing but good news from a gastronomic perspective. Traditional foods had suffered under forty years of Communist rule, and with the privatization of farming, groceries, and restaurants, an impetus was given to the rediscovery of traditional foods. The Czech Republic is geographically what was called Bohemia. Bohemian food is heavy and robust with lots of pork. One of the most famous pork dishes is *Prazská šunka,* "Prague ham," a ham brined with its skin and bones in pepper, coriander, and bay leaves and smoked over a beech wood fire, giving it a salty, smoky taste. It is often cooked and served wrapped in bread dough.

CZECH-STYLE PORK AND SAUERKRAUT GOULASH

USED TO MAKE THIS RECIPE WHEN I LIVED in Salzburg, Austria, in 1977. I had just returned from Czechoslovakia and was quite enamored of Czech and Slovak food (which is more or less the same). It is a relatively simple dish, but rich with the sour cream, an ingredient very prominent in the cooking of the central Slavic countries. And the dish is just tart enough because of the sauerkraut. In Czech, it's called *Segedínsky guláš*. I believe that this dish is known originally in Transylvania as *Székely gulyás* and is also popular in Hungary.

———————————●———————————

¹/4 cup lard
1 medium-size onion, chopped
2¹/4 pounds boneless pork shoulder, trimmed of any large pieces of fat and cut into 1-inch cubes
¹/2 teaspoon hot Hungarian paprika
¹/2 teaspoon caraway seeds
Salt and freshly ground black pepper to taste
³/4 cup water
³/4 pound sauerkraut, drained
3 tablespoons unbleached all-purpose flour
1 cup sour cream

———————————●———————————

1. In a casserole, melt 2 tablespoons of the lard over medium-high heat. Cook the onion until translucent, stirring, about 5 minutes. Add the pork shoulder, paprika, and caraway. Season with salt and a little pepper, and brown on all sides, about 5 minutes. Add ¹/2 cup of the water, cover, and reduce the heat to low. Simmer until tender, but chewy, about 1 hour. Add half the sauerkraut and simmer for 30 minutes longer.

2. In a small skillet, melt the remaining 2 tablespoons of lard over medium-high heat. Brown the flour until light golden, stirring well. Add

to the meat with the remaining ¹/4 cup of water and simmer, uncovered, for 5 minutes. Add the sour cream and remaining sauerkraut, stir to mix well, and bring to a boil. Remove immediately from the heat, and serve.

———————————●———————————

Makes 6 servings

HUNGARIAN SMOKED SAUSAGE AND PRUNE STEW

THIS PREPARATION WILL CERTAINLY remind you of Hungary if you've ever been to that country. It's a rustic country-style stew that is very simple to cook. The sausage you use should not be spicy; a smoked Polish hunter's sausage or kielbasa would be perfect because it is mild enough to harmonize with the sweetness of the prunes. As there are a number of Hungarian and Polish communities in this country, it may not be so impossible to find these specific sausages at one of the delicatessens servings those populations. This dish is known as *aszalt szilva* in Hungarian and it is very delicious accompanied by Bavarian Vegetable Stew (page 310) if you'd like to stick to the stew theme.

———————————●———————————

1 pound pitted prunes
1 pound smoked Polish or Hungarian hunter's sausage or Polish kielbasa, sliced 1 inch thick

1 lemon slice, about ¼ inch thick
3 tablespoons water
¼ cup sour cream
1 teaspoon unbleached all-purpose flour

———————●———————

1. Place the prunes in a stew pot with the sausage, lemon slice, and water. Turn the heat to medium, and when the sausages begin to sizzle, reduce the heat to low. Cover and cook, stirring occasionally, until the prunes are falling apart and the sausage slices are browned on the edges, about 1 hour.

2. In a small bowl, mix together the sour cream and flour and dilute it with a little of the cooking liquid from the stew pot. Pour this mixture into the pot, stir, and cook until well blended, about 5 minutes. Serve immediately

———————●———————

Makes 4 servings

POT ETEN

MOST AMERICANS ASSOCIATE DUTCH immigration with Pennsylvania, and in fact, when they think of Dutch food it is often Pennsylvania Dutch cooking that comes to mind. But this recipe, adapted from a regional American cookbook published in the 1930s, is one from the Michigan Dutch. The Dutch arrived in west central Michigan in 1847, nearly two centuries after their brethren in New York and Pennsylvania. They settled around the towns of Holland, Kalamazoo, and Grand Rapids and played an important role in the introduction of mass celery production in this country. Their boiled dinner called *pot eten* is a throwback to an earlier time. It's nourishing, heavy, and mild, typical of Dutch cooking from a few centuries ago. Today, when so many cooks toss chiles into everything to spice it up, cooking such an old-fashioned stew as *pot eten* has a certain hearth 'n' home feel to it. It's heavy—clearly a dish invented for hard-working men—so I would serve it only with a crisp green salad as an accompaniment, perhaps after an incredibly vigorous day of cross-country skiing.

———————●———————

¼ cup pearl barley, soaked in water to cover
overnight and drained
Salt to taste
1 pound boneless pork shoulder, trimmed of any
large pieces of fat and cut into 2-inch cubes
2 Granny Smith apples, peeled, cored, and diced
1 pound boiling potatoes, peeled and sliced ½
inch thick

———————●———————

1. Place the barley in a stew pot and cover by 3 inches with cold water. Bring to a boil, then reduce the heat to low and simmer for 1 hour.

2. Lightly salt the barley, add the pork, and simmer, partially covered, for 1½ hours.

3. Add the apples and potatoes and continue to cook until the potatoes break apart and the meat is very tender, about 1 more hour, adding a little water if it is too thick. It should be ever so slightly soupy. When it's done, mash everything with a potato masher or fork and serve.

Makes 4 to 6 servings

CHILE VERDE

I F THERE IS A STATE DISH OF NEW MEXICO, *chile verde*, a pork and green chile pepper stew, might be it. This recipe comes from my friend Chris Hardy, a Los Angeleno whose grandmother is a native of New Mexico. But my excitement about making *chile verde* came from an unknown young man who was standing behind me on line at a supermarket in Santa Monica, California, when I was buying the pork and the Anaheim chiles needed for the stew. He was about twenty years old and asked me, as he looked lovingly at those two ingredients, if I was going to make *chile verde*. When I said yes, in surprise, he told me that he was from New Mexico and how much he missed *chile verde*. He went on about the stew and gave me a few pointers, which I've tried to incorporate into this recipe. Serve the stew with little side dishes of chopped onion, chopped fresh coriander leaves (cilantro), sour cream, and Mexican *crema*, *padilla*, or *cotija* cheese (available from Cacique, see the sources at the back of the book) or *queso fresco*, *ricotta salata*, or mild domestic cow's milk feta cheese

to crumble over the top. For accompaniments, steamed white rice, refried black beans cooked with epazote (see page 292), corn tortillas, and good Mexican beer are all traditional. Some cooks like to add chipotle chile paste too, which can simply be gotten from a can of chipotle chiles in adobo sauce.

10 fresh Anaheim (also called New Mexico)
    chiles
¼ cup extra virgin olive oil
1 large onion, coarsely chopped
4 large garlic cloves, passed through a garlic
    press or mashed in a mortar
2 pounds lean boneless pork shoulder or butt,
    trimmed of as much fat as possible and cut
    into 1-inch cubes
Masa harina (corn flour) for dredging
One 12-ounce bottle beer (lager)
1 teaspoon freshly ground cumin seeds
1 to 3 tablespoons chipotle chile paste, to your
    taste
1 bay leaf
1 tablespoon dried oregano
2 teaspoons salt
2 teaspoons freshly ground black pepper
½ cup coarsely chopped fresh coriander
    (cilantro) leaves

1. Preheat the oven to 450°F. Place the chiles on a baking sheet and roast until the skins blister and turn black, watching them carefully, 25 to 30 minutes. Remove and place in a paper bag to steam for 10 minutes. Remove and, when cool enough to handle, peel, stem, seed, and cut into strips.

2. In a casserole or Dutch oven, heat 2 tablespoons of the olive oil over medium heat, then cook the onion and garlic until translucent, stirring, about 8 minutes. Remove the onion with a slotted spoon and set aside. Add 1 tablespoon of the olive oil to the casserole and let it heat up. Dredge the pork in the masa harina, tapping off any excess. Brown the pork on all sides over medium heat, cooking in two batches if necessary so the pieces of meat don't touch each other, turning them with tongs, about 12 minutes for each batch. Use the remaining 1 tablespoon of olive oil for the second batch. Set the meat aside.

3. Deglaze the bottom of the casserole by pouring in about a quarter of the beer, scraping up the browned bits on the bottom with a wooden spoon. Once all the crust is picked up, add the remaining beer. Return the onion, garlic, and pork to the casserole. Add the cumin and leave to cook over medium-low heat for 10 minutes. Add the Anaheim chiles, chipotle chile paste (the lesser amount for a mild stew and the greater amount for a hot stew), bay leaf, oregano, salt, and pepper. Bring to a boil, and reduce the heat to low. Cover and cook until the pork is very tender, stirring occasionally, about 45 minutes.

4. Add the coriander leaves and cook for another 10 minutes, then turn off the heat and let it sit for 5 minutes. Remove the bay leaf and serve.

Makes 4 to 6 servings

QUEBEC-STYLE MEATBALL STEW

THIS STEW FROM QUEBEC IS CALLED *ragoût de boulettes*. It is a spicy meatball stew that is very popular and it is adapted from the book *Food—à la Canadienne*. It is heavy, a culinary phenomenon explained in part by the Canadian winters; therefore, it is most comforting to make when the weather is cold. I can't help but feel that this stew is somehow related to the *boles de picolat* that is found in Roussillon, that portion of Catalonia that is in France. The traditional Catalan *boles*, which means "meatball," is also flavored with cinnamon, a spice that seems unusual in meatballs. A unique part of this stew is the "brown flour" that is used to thicken it towards the end of its simmering. The flour is simply browned in a hot skillet, plain and unadulterated, until it turns a caramel color and emits a nutty aroma. It is a delightful addition and makes for a rich gravy. The gravy is made from pork broth, which I explain in the method, but for convenience you can use canned chicken broth or a concentrated chicken bouillon cube dissolved in water. I would serve this stew with French fries or some kind of crispy potato dish.

FOR THE PORK BROTH (OPTIONAL, SEE NOTE):
1/2 pound pork shoulder steaks
1 small carrot, cut into chunks
1 small onion, quartered with its peel
1/2 celery stalk, cut into chunks

6 black peppercorns
1 bouquet garni, consisting of 3 sprigs each fresh
    parsley and tarragon, 1 teaspoon dried thyme,
    1 sprig fresh basil, and 1 small bay leaf, tied in
    cheesecloth
3 quarts water
FOR THE STEW:
1 tablespoon unsalted butter
3/4 cup finely chopped onions
2 pounds ground pork
1/2 teaspoon ground cinnamon
1/2 teaspoon freshly grated nutmeg
1/8 teaspoon freshly ground cloves
1 teaspoon salt
1/4 teaspoon freshly ground black pepper
3/4 cup browned flour (see Note 2 on page 174)

1. Make the pork broth: Preheat the oven to 400°F. Place the pork shoulder steaks in a roasting pan and leave in the oven until they have released much fat and are well browned, 35 to 45 minutes. Remove from the oven, transfer the meat to a large saucepan, and add the carrot, onion, celery, peppercorns, and bouquet garni. Cover with the water and bring to a boil. Reduce the heat to low and simmer until the meat is falling apart, 4 to 5 hours. Strain and measure out 6 cups of broth. Set aside, and save the remaining broth for another use. Discard the solids.

2. In a casserole or stew pot, melt the butter over medium–high heat. When it stops sizzling, cook the onion, stirring, until translucent, 3 to 5 minutes. Transfer the onion to a large bowl. Add the pork, cinnamon, nutmeg, cloves, salt, and pepper. Mix and form into two dozen

meatballs about 1 1/2 inches in diameter. Refrigerate for 30 minutes, or longer if time allows.

3. In a stew pot, bring the pork or chicken broth to a boil, and reduce the heat to low. Add the meatballs and simmer until firm, about 1 1/2 hours. The broth should never boil, but only shimmer on top.

4. Sprinkle in the browned flour, stirring until smooth and thickened. If the gravy looks too liquidy, bring to a boil and evaporate some liquid for a few minutes. But it should be a little soupy. Serve immediately.

Makes 6 servings

Note: If you want to skip the pork broth, substitute 6 cups of canned chicken broth or chicken bouillon in step 3.

QUEBEC-STYLE PORK HOCK AND MEATBALL STEW

T HIS FLAVORFUL STEW FROM QUEBEC called *ragoût de pattes de cochon* is traditional for a Canadian Christmas. It is made entirely from pork and highly seasoned with sweet spices such as cinnamon and cloves. One of the reasons this stew tastes so good, besides the natural succulence of the pork and the spices, is due to the flours used. Oatmeal flour is incorporated into the meatballs and the gravy is formed with the nutty flavor of browned flour. Some would consider it a heavy stew, and one of the reasons that Quebecois food is so heavy is because of the rigors of the Canadian winters. When you're shoveling a foot of snow from the driveway every day, and putting on layers and layers of clothes, you build a big appetite. This recipe is adapted from one found in Mme. Jehane Benoit's 1963 edition of *L'Encyclopédie de la cuisine Canadienne*. Benoit was a well-known cook who appeared frequently on Canadian television and radio in the '50s and '60s. Serve with mashed yams or sweet potatoes, or mashed potatoes.

———— ● ————

FOR THE BROTH:

4 pork hocks (fresh ham hocks, about 3 pounds)
1 teaspoon salt
1/4 teaspoon ground cinnamon
1/4 teaspoon freshly ground cloves
1/8 teaspoon freshly grated nutmeg
2 tablespoons unsalted butter
1 large onion
1 bay leaf
1/2 teaspoon dried savory
1/2 teaspoon dried thyme
4 cloves
2 quarts water, or more to cover

FOR THE MEATBALLS:

2 pounds ground lean pork
1/4 cup oatmeal flour, or as needed (see Note 1 on page 174)
1 large onion, finely chopped
1 garlic clove, finely chopped

1/2 teaspoon ground cinnamon
1/2 teaspoon freshly ground cloves
Salt and freshly ground black pepper to taste
1 large egg, beaten
2 day-old slices French bread, crumbled
2 tablespoons unsalted butter

FOR THE ROUX:

2 tablespoons browned flour (see Note 2 on page 174)
2 tablespoons unsalted butter

———— ● ————

1. To make the broth, roll the pork hocks in the salt, cinnamon, ground cloves, and nutmeg. In a large casserole or Dutch oven, melt the butter over medium-high heat. When it stops sizzling, brown the pork hocks on all sides, about 4 minutes. Add the onion, bay leaf, savory, thyme, and whole cloves. Cover with the 2 quarts of cold water, or more if needed, bring to a boil, and skim off any foam from the surface. Reduce the heat to low and simmer very slowly until the pork hocks are tender and the meat is falling off the bone, 2 to 2 1/2 hours. Remove the pork hocks and cut the meat from the bones. Set aside, discarding the fat and bones. Strain the broth and skim off the fat or, alternatively, chill the broth, then remove all solid fat before continuing. You will need 3 cups of broth for the gravy.

2. While the broth simmers, make the meatballs: In a large bowl, mix together the ground pork, oatmeal flour, onion, garlic, cinnamon, cloves, salt, pepper, egg, and crumbled bread. Blend in more oatmeal flour if necessary in order to make the mixture firm. Form into meatballs about 1 inch in diameter.

3. In a large skillet, melt the butter over medium-high heat. Brown the meatballs on all sides, shaking the pan to prevent sticking. Or let them rest and stick and then scrape them up carefully with a metal spatula. Reduce the heat to low and cook until firm, about 15 minutes. Remove the meatballs and deglaze the skillet with a little broth, scraping up any browned bits from the bottom.

4. To make the roux, in the same casserole used to cook the pork hocks, melt the butter. When it stops sizzling, add the browned flour to form a roux, stirring. Cook for 1 or 2 minutes, then pour in the liquid that was used to deglaze the skillet. Slowly add the remainder of the reserved broth, stirring until blended. Cook over medium heat until thicker, like a velouté, about 20 minutes. Season with salt and pepper if necessary. Add the reserved meat from the pork hocks and the cooked meatballs and simmer gently until the gravy is a consistency you like and the meatballs are piping hot and firm, about 45 minutes.

———⚫———

Makes 4 servings

Note 1: To make oatmeal flour, put raw oatmeal in a food processor and pulverize.

Note 2: To make browned flour, spread the flour in a large, heavy skillet and heat over medium heat, stirring, until the flour turns medium brown, about 5 or 6 minutes.

MEXICAN PORK, CHORIZO, AND CHIPOTLE CHILE PEPPER STEW

———⚬———

THIS STEW FROM CENTRAL MEXICO, called *tinga poblana*, is typical of the cooking of Puebla, and can be made with a variety of ingredients, including chicken. There is a particularly alluring taste in this stew, which I believe comes from the roasted tomatoes, the chipotle chiles, and the chorizo. When buying chorizo sausage, make sure you buy the kind made from pork shoulder and pork fat and not the type made of lymph nodes and other parts, which is packaged in plastic skins and secured with metal staples. The latter type turns into mush and does not maintain the pleasing texture that should come from crumbled sausage meat. It doesn't taste bad—it's just a matter of texture. The Mexican *queso fresco* called for in the ingredients list is available in supermarkets or can be ordered from Cacique (see the sources listed at the back of the book). This stew should be served with a salad, tortillas, and beer. As with so many stews, I think this tastes best the next day.

———⚫———

3 tablespoons lard
1¹/2 pounds lean boneless pork butt or shoulder,
    cut into 2-inch cubes
1 medium-size onion, chopped
1 large garlic clove, finely chopped
1¹/2 pounds Mexican–style chorizo sausages,
    removed from their casings and crumbled

2 cups Chicken Broth (page 181)

1¹/₂ pounds ripe tomatoes, roasted (see Note), peeled, seeded, and chopped

¹/₂ pound green tomatoes, roasted (see Note), peeled, seeded, and chopped

3 canned chipotle chiles in adobo sauce, drained, seeded, and thinly sliced, plus 1 tablespoon adobo sauce

¹/₂ teaspoon dried thyme

¹/₂ teaspoon dried oregano

¹/₂ teaspoon dried marjoram

1 teaspoon salt

¹/₄ teaspoon freshly ground black pepper

¹/₂ teaspoon sugar

Wheat flour or corn tortillas, warmed

Mexican queso fresco or goat cheese, crumbled, for sprinkling

---

1. In a large, heavy skillet, melt 2 tablespoons of the lard over medium heat. Cook the pork with the onion until the pork has turned color and begins to brown slightly and the onion is soft, about 10 minutes. Stir in the garlic and cook for 2 minutes, stirring. Transfer the pork to a heavy casserole. Add the remaining 1 tablespoon of lard to the skillet, reduce the heat to medium-low, and heat the chorizo sausage until hot, stirring occasionally and breaking it up with a wooden spoon as you stir, about 10 minutes. Transfer the chorizo to the casserole.

2. Pour the chicken broth in the casserole and bring to a boil. Reduce the heat to low, cover, and simmer until the pork is almost tender, about 45 minutes. Add the ripe and green roasted tomatoes, the chipotles and sauce, the thyme, oregano, marjoram, salt, and pepper.

Cook until the pork is tender, 15 minutes. Stir in the sugar and serve with tortillas and Mexican queso fresco.

Makes 6 servings

Note: To roast the tomatoes, preheat the oven to broil and place the tomatoes on a baking sheet under the broiler until they get crinkly skinned and almost black on one side, then flip and do the other side, about 12 minutes in all, then remove them from the oven to cool.

POZOLE

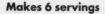

THIS FAMOUS MEXICAN STEW IS A STAPLE that is usually eaten at midday. It is not a rich man's stew. There are regional variations throughout Mexico, although some people claim it is native to Jalisco. Certainly, its origin is remote. In the Náhuatl language *pozolli* is the word for "foam" or "froth," meaning that the white corn flour foams up into hominy. Specifically, *pozole* refers to whole-kernel hominy, large kernels of dried corn that have been soaked in unslaked lime to remove their outer skins and puff them up, hence the idea of "foam." This form of cooking corn flour was spoken of in Bernardino de Sahagún's *Historia general de las cosas de la Nueva España*, published in 1590.

Because pozole is a stew, it is best to use cuts of pork that benefit from long, slow cooking, which breaks down their tough connective tissue and renders a meltingly soft and succulent meat—namely pork shoulder or butt or, as in this recipe, pig's head, snouts, feet, tails, or ears. The final stew should be somewhat soupy, so add water accordingly as it cooks, especially in the last hour. The *nixtamal* called for can be found in Hispanic markets and, in the Southwest, in the supermarket meat department, frozen food section, or specialty food section. Hispanic markets and supermarkets in the Southwest will also carry it. Typically pozole is garnished with crumbled fried corn tostadas and served with side dishes of sliced radishes, shredded lettuce, chopped cabbage, chopped coriander leaf, diced yellow onion, diced avocado, and lime wedges. This recipe is recorded from Aurora Jaramillo, a Mexican woman who lives in Los Angeles.

---

6 quarts water, plus more as needed

2 pounds (about 6 cups) Mexican-style whole-kernel hominy (nixtamal)

4 heads garlic, first layer of peel rubbed off

1 teaspoon salt, plus more as needed

1 pig's head or 4 pounds mixed pig's feet, tails, snout, and ears

8 dried guajillo chiles, seeded

2 dried de arbol chiles

1 tablespoon freshly ground cumin seeds

FOR THE GARNISH:

Sliced radishes

Finely shredded iceberg lettuce

Finely chopped green cabbage

Finely chopped fresh coriander (cilantro) leaves

Diced yellow onion

Peeled, pitted, and diced ripe avocado

10 lime wedges

Crumbled fried corn tortillas

NIXTAMAL

Nixtamal is a Mexican-style hominy. It is corn that has been processed by mixing water and unslaked lime with the whole dried corn kernels, which are cooked until the skins can be rubbed off. Then they are washed in water to remove all traces of the lime. Traditionally, the kernels are rubbed between the hands until they are free of hulls. **Nixtamal** is not cooked as long as canned hominy and needs further preparation to make it edible.

1. In a large stew pot, bring the water to a boil, then add the *nixtamal*, 1 head of the garlic, and ¹/₂ teaspoon of the salt and cook until the *nixtamal* is tender, about 3 hours. Keep the *nixtamal* covered with water, adding hot water whenever necessary.

2. Meanwhile, fill another stew pot with enough water to cover all the pork and bring to a boil. Add the pig's head or other parts. Add 2 heads of the garlic and the remaining ¹/₂ teaspoon salt and cook until the bones are falling apart, about 3 hours.

3. After the *nixtamal* and the broth have cooked for 2 hours, remove ³/₄ cup of liquid from each stew pot. In a medium-size bowl, soak the dried chiles until soft in the 1½ cups of the mixed broths, about 1 hour. Place the softened chiles in a blender with enough of their soaking liquid to allow the blender blade to twirl, about 1 cup, and blend until smooth.

4. Remove the pig head or parts from the stew pot and discard. (If using a pig head, you can save the brain and other meat, cut it up, and add it to the stew). Reserve the pig broth. Clean the stew pot unless you have a third large stew pot you can use. Pour 4 cups of the reserved pig broth into the clean stew pot along with the entire contents of the *nixtamal-*filled stew pot. Add the cumin, the remaining head of garlic, and the pureed chiles and their liquid, correct the seasonings, adding anywhere between 1 to 3 tablespoons of salt. Bring the mixture to a boil, then reduce the heat to low and simmer gently for 1 hour. Serve the pozole with the garnishes, as explained in the headnote.

Makes 10 servings

STEWS WITH FOWL, GOAT, AND RABBIT

There are some really rich and wonderful stews in this chapter, such as the *Olleta* (page 181) from the Valencia region of Spain. This is a stew that cooks all day. It's filled with various chicken parts and chorizo sausage and spiced with cumin, paprika, and saffron. The aroma of the stew as it simmers will beckon everyone to the table. Another great stew is Chicken and Sweet Potato Curry (page 202), a festive dish that is spicy-spicy, not spicy-hot, and is flavored with garlic, ginger, cumin, turmeric, paprika, and cinnamon. A stew you will surely make many times is the authentic *Waterzooi* (page 191), the most famous of Flemish stews. It is a rich chicken stew made with vegetables, cream, and egg yolks, cooked in wine, beer, or a chicken stock. Want to make a classic *Coq au Vin* from Burgundy? Well, it's here (page 183), and I instruct you on how to make it the old-fashioned way—with a rooster. If you're a duck fanatic like me, you'll go nuts over the Persian *Fesenjan* (page 201), a duck and pomegranate stew that is extraordinarily delicious and rich, made with ground walnuts, pomegranate juice, and molasses, and seasoned with cinnamon, nutmeg, sugar, and saffron.

CHICKEN BROTH

THIS IS A NICE HOMEMADE BROTH THAT can be used for recipes calling for chicken broth. For duck broth, replace the chicken bones and meat with a duck carcass and for rabbit broth, replace with rabbit bones. For recipes calling for a rich chicken broth, first roast the chicken bones in a 425°F oven until golden before proceeding with the recipe.

---

8 pounds chicken bones, with meat
2 carrots, sliced
3 celery stalks, with leaves, sliced
1 large onion, halved and separated into layers
1 leek, washed well and cut up
10 black peppercorns
1 bouquet garni, consisting of 6 sprigs each fresh parsley, thyme, and marjoram, 2 sprigs fresh sage, and 1 bay leaf, tied in cheesecloth
2 cups dry white wine
5 quarts cold water
Salt and freshly ground black pepper to taste

---

1. Put all the ingredients, except the salt and pepper, in a stockpot, and bring to a boil. Reduce the heat to a simmer and skim off the foam from the surface until no more appears. Partially cover the pot and simmer over very low heat for at least 6 hours.

2. Pour the broth through a strainer (a chinois, or conical strainer, would be ideal) and discard all the bones, vegetables, and bouquet garni. Now line the strainer with cheesecloth and pour the broth through again. Season to taste with salt and pepper. Place the broth in the refrigerator until the fat congeals and remove. The broth can kept, refrigerated, for up to 1 week, or frozen for up to 6 months.

Makes 3 to 4 quarts

STEWING CHICKEN

When stewing chicken, never let the liquid it is cooking in come to a boil, otherwise, the chicken will toughen. Keep the liquid simmering so that the liquid is only shimmering on top.

A so-called stewing chicken was a type of older chicken once sold and used for stews. Older chickens are tougher chickens, well suited to long simmering. Today a capon would be a good second choice, but capons—domesticated cocks that have been castrated in order to fatten them up—are big, too big usually. The chickens you will find in the supermarket are not the best for stewing, but if that's all you have, that's what you will use.

OLLETA

AN *OLLETA* IS A STYLE OF STEW THAT resembles the famous *olla*, an old stew with a history that is traced back to Cervantes's great novel *Don Quixote*. The *Diccionario de la*

real academia de la lengua defines an *olla* as a food prepared with meat, bacon, legumes, and vegetables, principally chickpeas and potatoes, along with seasonings and other ingredients. It is the principal family meal of Spain. This *olleta* comes from the Valencia region of Spain and uses two kinds of beans, along with chicken, chorizo sausage, and Swiss chard. This particular stew is richly flavored and spicy hot and is magnificent on a nasty cold winter's night, after you have allowed the stew to cook most of the day and let its aromas envelop you. Much of the flavor comes from a bundle of chicken feet and parts wrapped in cheesecloth, which percolates with the stew.

---

1 cup dried white beans, picked over and rinsed

1 cup dried Roman (red kidney) beans, picked over, rinsed, soaked overnight in water to cover, and drained

1/4 cup extra virgin olive oil

1 large onion, coarsely chopped

1 green bell pepper, seeded and coarsely chopped

2 fresh red chiles, seeded and chopped

2 celery stalks, sliced

2 pounds chicken feet, necks, bones, or carcasses

2 1/2 cups dry white wine

3 quarts cold water

10 garlic cloves, sliced

2 cloves

1 bay leaf

Pinch of saffron threads

1 tablespoon freshly ground cumin seeds

1 tablespoon paprika

Salt and freshly ground black pepper to taste

1 1/2 pounds turnip, peeled and quartered

1 pound Swiss chard, stems removed

1 1/4 pounds chicken thighs, trimmed of fat and skin

1 pound Spanish- or Portuguese-style chorizo sausage

---

1. In a large stew pot or casserole, heat the olive oil over medium-high heat. Cook the onion, bell pepper, chiles, and celery until soft, stirring frequently, about 8 minutes.

2. Meanwhile, spread out a large section of cheesecloth and place the chicken feet, necks, and other parts in the center. Lift the four sides of the cheesecloth bundle and twist, tying it off tightly with kitchen twine, and leaving a long piece of twine for pulling.

3. Pour the wine and water into the stew pot along with the chicken parts bundle, leaving the long piece of twine hanging over the edge of the pot for easy retrieval. Add the garlic, cloves, bay leaf, saffron, cumin, and paprika and season with salt and pepper. Bring to a boil, reduce the heat to low, and skim foam off the top. Simmer, partially covered, for 2 hours.

4. Pull the chicken parts bundle out of the broth by the exposed piece of twine and discard. Add the turnips, drained beans, Swiss chard, chicken thighs, and chorizo. Return to just below a boil over medium heat, about 45 minutes. Reduce the heat to low and simmer for 3 hours, partially covered. Cut the chorizo into portions and serve.

Makes 6 servings

COQ AU VIN

A VERY FAMOUS DISH FROM BURGUNDY, but claimed by other regions of France, such as the Auvergne, is *coq au vin*, a stew traditionally made with rooster. Today, even in France, it is quite common for the stew to be made with chicken, but I like to stick to the old-time way of cooking it because I just love to marinate that old rooster in wine for a day. A rooster can be ordered through a butcher, but you can also use the more widely available capon. If you do end up using chicken, remember that you will not need to marinate it. If you use capon, only marinate it for 6 hours. Many French cooks still thicken the stew in the traditional way by carefully stirring in the blood of the rooster at the end of the cooking time.

Cooking tough old birds in wine has a history in France going back to the earliest French cookbooks. In the *Ménagier de Paris*, an *aide-mémoire* written in 1393 by a Parisian bourgeois for his very young wife, a recipe for *brouet de chapon* calls for a capon to be cooked in wine and spices. The famous *Viandier*—written in the 1380s by Taillevent (Guillaume Tirel), who was the cook to King Philip VI in 1346—has a recipe for capon that is also cooked in wine with spices and bacon.

It is important that you pat dry the pieces of fowl when you remove them from the marinade, otherwise, they will not brown properly. You'll need two bottles of good, but inexpensive red Burgundy for this dish, such as Seguin, Leroy, or Potel.

FOR THE MARINADE:

One 7-pound rooster or capon

2 large onions, chopped

3 shallots, chopped

2 carrots, chopped

3 garlic cloves, chopped

1 bouquet garni, consisting of 4 sprigs fresh parsley, 3 sprigs fresh thyme, and 1 bay leaf, tied in cheesecloth

1 bottle red Burgundy wine

FOR THE CHICKEN BROTH:

1 medium-size onion, sliced

1 large carrot, sliced

1 celery stalk, sliced

1 bouquet garni, consisting of 4 sprigs fresh parsley, 3 sprigs fresh thyme, and 1 bay leaf, tied in cheesecloth

Salt to taste

FOR THE COQ AU VIN:

3/4 cup (1 1/2 sticks) unsalted butter

1/2 pound lean bacon, cut into thick matchstick lardons

14 to 16 small white onions (about 1 1/2 pounds), peeled

1/2 pound button mushrooms, brushed clean

1/2 pound chanterelle mushrooms, brushed clean

Freshly ground black pepper to taste

1/4 cup Cognac

2 tablespoons unbleached all-purpose flour

1 bottle red Burgundy wine

4 large garlic cloves, crushed

1 teaspoon dried savory

1/4 teaspoon freshly grated nutmeg

1 bouquet garni, consisting of 4 sprigs fresh parsley, 3 sprigs fresh thyme, and 1 bay leaf, tied in cheesecloth

16 slices French bread, crusts removed

1. To marinate the chicken, cut the bird into 10 pieces, saving the wings, neck, feet, and giblets for the broth, and place in a large ceramic baking dish or bowl. Add the chopped onions, shallots, carrots, garlic, and bouquet garni. Pour the wine over everything, cover with plastic wrap, and let marinate in the refrigerator for 24 hours for a rooster, 6 hours for a capon.

2. Drain the bird and pat the pieces dry with paper towels, leaving any tiny bits of the vegetables from the marinade on the chicken. Refrigerate while you make the broth.

FLAMBÉING

Adding alcohol to cooking food and then setting it alight is called flambéing, from the French word *flamber*, meaning "to flame." The easiest way to flambé is to make sure the alcohol is warm enough to ignite. Rather than pour the alcohol, tablespoon by tablespoon, into the skillet and try to ignite it with a match, simply pour a goodly amount, maybe more than is recommended in the recipe, directly from the liquor bottle right into the skillet. Shake the skillet vigorously back and forth so some of the alcohol jumps out onto the flame or heat from the burner and it will ignite. It will extinguish itself shortly, but you should be careful when you do this and make sure hair and clothing are not anywhere nearly where the flames will ignite. Be prepared for the possibility of the flame leaping as high as the exhaust fan, and you won't be surprised when it ignites.

3. To make the broth, put the wings, neck, feet, and giblets of the bird in a large saucepan and add the sliced onion, sliced carrot, celery, bouquet garni, and a little salt. Bring to a boil, then reduce the heat to low and simmer, partially covered, for 4 hours. Set aside 1 cup of the broth for the *coq au vin*, and store the rest for another use.

4. To begin the *coq au vin*, take the chicken out of the refrigerator. In a large earthenware casserole set on a heat diffuser, melt 4 tablespoons of the butter with the bacon over high heat. Cook until the bacon is not quite crispy, about 10 minutes. (If you are not cooking with earthenware and a diffuser, cook over medium heat and check for doneness sooner.) Remove the bacon to paper towels to drain and set aside. Add the onions to the casserole and cook until golden, adjusting the heat if blackening, about 10 minutes. Remove and set aside with the bacon. Add the mushrooms and cook until golden, 8 to 10 minutes. Remove and set aside.

5. Add 3 tablespoons of the butter to the casserole. Once it has melted, season the pieces of bird with salt and pepper and brown over medium-high heat, skin side down first, turning once, about 15 minutes total. Do this in batches if necessary so the casserole is not crowded and the pieces of bird don't overlap each other.

6. Pour the Cognac into the casserole and ignite, or heat the Cognac first in a butter warmer or small saucepan pan and light it, then pour over the bird (please see box, left, for directions on flambéing safely). Let the flames extinguish, then remove the pieces of bird with tongs and set aside. Add 1 tablespoon of the flour to the Cognac, stirring until it is incorporated. Pour in the bottle of wine and deglaze the casserole, scraping the browned bits off the sides and bottom.

7. Return the pieces of bird to the casserole, and add the reserved 1 cup of chicken broth, the garlic, savory, nutmeg, and bouquet garni, and bring to a boil. Reduce the heat to low and simmer, partially covered, until the chicken is tender, about 1³/₄ hours.

8. The liquid should be much reduced by now and almost syrupy. If it is not, remove the bird from the casserole, increase the heat to high, and boil until the liquid is reduced by a quarter to a half, or until there are about 3 cups of liquid in the casserole. Then return the pieces of bird to the casserole. (Traditionally, at this point, the blood would be added to thicken the sauce. An alternative method, which I use here, is to add a flour-and-butter mixture, called *beurre manié*, to thicken the sauce.) Mash together the remaining 1 tablespoon of flour with 1 tablespoon of the butter and whisk into the wine gravy (having removed the pieces of fowl). Return the pieces of fowl to the casserole and add the mushrooms, bacon, and onions. Cook until tender over low to medium-low heat, about 30 minutes.

9. Meanwhile, cut the bread into half-moons or hearts, if desired. In a large skillet, melt the remaining 4 tablespoons of butter over medium-high heat. Cook the bread on both sides until it is golden, about 5 minutes. Remove from the skillet and set aside.

10. Serve the *coq au vin* with slices of fried bread on top.

Makes 8 servings

DUCK WING STEW FROM THE LANGUEDOC

THIS FRENCH STEW FROM THE DUCK- AND goose-raising region of the Languedoc in southwestern France is called *alicuit*, from the words for "wing," *aile*, and "neck," *cou*. It is a very flavorful home-style dish from the countryside where duck-farming families usually make it after the duck slaughter. The stew traditionally contains only duck wings, but because duck and goose wings are not sold separately in American markets, you may need to collect them over a period of time and keep them frozen until needed. Although my recipe uses a variety of bird wings, you should try to have at least two pounds of goose or duck wings because that's where the special flavor comes from.

1 tablespoon rendered goose or duck fat (see page 348)

4 pounds duck, chicken, turkey, or goose wings and necks (or any combination of these, with the majority being duck and goose), trimmed of as much excess fat as possible

6 thick carrots, sliced into rounds

2 large onions, sliced and separated into rings

2 cups dry white wine

2 cups Chicken Broth (page 181)

1 bouquet garni, consisting of 4 sprigs fresh oregano, 2 sprigs fresh thyme, 1 sprig fresh sage, 1 celery stalk with its leaves, and 1 bay leaf, tied in cheesecloth

3 garlic cloves, crushed

Salt and freshly ground black pepper to taste

---

1. In a large casserole, heat the goose fat over medium heat. Brown the wings until golden on both sides and there is juice in the casserole, about 20 minutes. Remove the wings and set aside. Add the carrots and onions and continue to cook until the onions are yellow, stirring occasionally, about 20 minutes.

2. Deglaze the casserole with the wine and chicken broth, scraping the bottom and sides of the casserole to get up any crusty brown bits. Bring the wine and broth to a boil and return the wings to the casserole. Reduce the heat to low, add the bouquet garni and garlic, season with salt and pepper, and simmer until the wings are falling apart and easily pierced by a fork, about 2 hours.

Makes 4 servings

CHICKEN AND BUTTERNUT SQUASH MINESTRONE

D ON'T LET THE LONG LIST OF INGREDI-ents deter you from making this robust minestrone, perfect for a winter's day. Not only is it a beautiful looking preparation, with the golden colored pumpkin shining through and contrasting with the verdant green of the chard, it is also incredibly healthy, nutritionists will tell you. This *minestrone di pollo e zucca* is best when you make the chicken broth yourself by poaching the whole chicken. If this isn't possible, use about four quarts of the highest quality chicken broth, canned or concentrated cubes, but if you do, pay close attention to the sodium content. The *ditali* or *tubetti* called for are short macaroni. They should be relatively easy to find in a good supermarket, but you could use elbow macaroni instead. The *soffritto*, as the Italians call it, is a sauté of finely chopped onions and other vegetables in olive oil (see page 60).

FOR THE BROTH:

One 3-pound chicken, trimmed of any excess fat

1 bunch fresh coriander (cilantro), washed well

Salt and freshly ground black pepper to taste

1 bouquet garni, consisting of 6 sprigs each fresh tarragon and parsley and 1 bay leaf, tied in cheesecloth

1 large carrot, cut into chunks

1 medium-size onion, cut into chunks

1 celery stalk, cut into chunks

1 leek, trimmed, split lengthwise, washed well, and cut into chunks

10 black peppercorns

4 quarts water

FOR THE MINESTRONE:

1/4 cup extra virgin olive oil

1 small onion, very finely chopped

4 large garlic cloves, very finely chopped

1 celery stalk, very finely chopped

1 carrot, very finely chopped

2 dried chiles

1/4 cup very finely chopped fresh parsley leaves

1/2 cup dry white wine

2 1/2 pounds butternut squash, peeled, seeded, and diced

4 small carrots (about 6 ounces total), diced

3 small parsnips (about 1/4 pound total), peeled and diced

3 small turnips (about 10 ounces total), peeled and diced

1 cup ditali, tubetti, or elbow macaroni

4 large leaves Swiss chard (about 3/4 pound total), trimmed of the lowest, thickest part of the white stem

2 tablespoons salt

1 tablespoon freshly ground white pepper

Extra virgin olive oil for drizzling

Freshly grated Parmigiano-Reggiano cheese for sprinkling

6 thin slices Italian bread, fried in olive oil until crispy

———————●———————

1. To make the broth, stuff the chicken with the coriander, season with salt and pepper inside and out, and wrap in cheesecloth, tying it off. It's not absolutely necessary to use cheesecloth, but it does make retrieving the chicken later much easier. Place the chicken in a large stockpot with the bouquet garni, carrot, onion, celery, leek, peppercorns, and water. Turn the heat to high, and just as the water begins to shimmer on top, reduce the heat to low. At no time should the liquid boil because that will only toughen the chicken. Partially cover and cook until the meat would fall off the bone if you were not using cheesecloth, about 3 1/2 hours. Remove the chicken and unwrap from the cheesecloth. Once the chicken is cool enough to handle, remove all the meat and shred with a fork and knife into smaller pieces. Set the chicken aside until needed and discard the bones and skin. Strain the broth, discarding all the vegetables, and reserve the broth.

2. To make the minestrone, in a stockpot (you can clean the one you just used) heat the olive oil over medium-high heat. Then cook the *soffritto* of onion, garlic, celery, chopped carrot, chiles, and parsley until translucent and soft, stirring frequently, 4 to 5 minutes. Add the wine, and once it has almost evaporated, about 2 minutes, add the squash, diced carrots, parsnips, and turnips. Toss well with the *soffritto* and cook for 1 minute. Add the reserved broth, reduce the heat to low, and cook until the vegetables are *al dente*, about 30 minutes.

3. Add the pasta, Swiss chard, reserved chicken, salt, and pepper and cook until the pasta is *al dente*, about 20 minutes. Serve in individual bowls with a drizzle of olive oil, a sprinkling of Parmigiano cheese, and the fried bread.

———————●———————

Makes 6 servings

PIEDMONTESE TURKEY STEW

T HIS TURKEY STEW, CALLED *UMIDO DI tacchina*, is the kind of very easily prepared stew that could be found anywhere in the Piedmont, Val d'Aosta, the northern part of Lombardy, or the Swiss canton of Ticino. It's the stew of choice for a harried housewife feeding her family, and it's excellent served with polenta (my first choice) or mashed potatoes.

Polenta (optional; recipe follows)
1¹/₂ pounds turkey breast, boned, skinned, and cut into 2-inch cubes
¹/₄ cup (¹/₂ stick) unsalted butter, cut into 4 pieces
³/₄ pound ripe tomatoes, cut in half, seeds squeezed out, and grated against the largest holes of a grater down to the peel
1 medium-size onion, chopped
4 fresh sage leaves, chopped
2 tablespoons chopped fresh parsley leaves
2 tablespoons chopped fresh basil leaves
Salt and freshly ground black pepper to taste
1 cup dry, full-bodied red wine
2 tablespoons unbleached all-purpose flour

1. Start the polenta, if desired.

2. When the polenta is about half cooked, begin the stew. Put the turkey, butter, tomatoes, onion, sage, parsley, basil, and salt and pepper in a casserole or stew pot. Turn the heat to medium and cook until the liquid begins to bubble, 6 to 7 minutes. Add the wine, stir, add the flour, and stir again to blend. Reduce the heat to low and cook until the turkey is white and firm, stirring occasionally and making sure the broth doesn't boil, but only bubbles gently, 35 to 40 minutes. Serve immediately, with polenta, if desired.

Makes 4 servings

POLENTA

Polenta is a porridge made from specially milled cornmeal. It is very popular in northern Italy, but is eaten in southern Italy too, especially around Avellino and Benevento. I'm familiar with three ways to make polenta: the traditional, the semi-traditional, and the modern. The traditional way to make polenta is in a special copper saucepan, where you stir the cornmeal, water, and salt continuously for at least an hour. In the semi-traditional method, the polenta is cooked in a double boiler for an hour and a half, and is stirred once every half-hour. In the modern method, the polenta is stirred with water, salt, and butter, placed in a medium hot oven for an hour and a half, and stirred once, ten minutes before it's done. Personally, I feel the traditional method makes the best-tasting polenta, although few of us have the time and patience for all that stirring. The oven method is the easiest, but the final polenta is not as creamy and fluffy as it should be. So I end up using the semi-traditional method, outlined below.

1 quart water
1 cup medium-ground polenta cornmeal
1¹/₂ teaspoons salt

1. Get some water boiling in the bottom of a double boiler and then reduce to a simmer.

2. Bring the water to a boil in the top part of the double boiler and stir it to make a whirlpool. Slowly pour the cornmeal and salt into the center of the whirlpool, stirring all the time. Cook for 5 minutes. Lower the heat all the way, cover, and cook for 1¹/₂ hours, stirring every 30 minutes. You can then eat it soft or pour it into a greased baking dish and let it solidify to bake or grill later cut into squares.

Makes 4 servings

BRAISED DUCK
IN THE STYLE OF THE VENETO

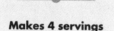

THIS *ANATRA IN UMIDO*, "STEWED DUCK," is a slow-cooked preparation from the Veneto region of Italy and is most appetizing when the weather gets cool in the fall. Duck appears on the tables of many homes and *trattorie* in the northern Italian provinces of the Veneto, Lombardy, and Piedmont. There are many lakes in this region and one will encounter many different dishes for a variety of waterfowl, such as teal or snipe. It is important

when cooking duck that you pay attention to the fat, otherwise your dish will be too greasy. Remove as much fat as you can before cooking; then the duck is roasted before being stewed to render even more fat. The finished dish is tender, flavorful, and satisfying, especially when served with soft, freshly made polenta (left) or boiled white beans.

One 4- or 5-pound duck
3 tablespoons extra virgin olive oil
¹/₄ cup (¹/₂ stick) unsalted butter
5 celery stalks, finely chopped
1 medium-size onion, finely chopped
1 carrot, finely chopped
2 tablespoons tomato paste dissolved in ¹/₂ cup water
¹/₄ cup plus 2 tablespoons finely chopped fresh parsley leaves
Salt and freshly ground black pepper to taste

1. Preheat the oven to 350°F. Cut the duck into 8 pieces with a cleaver or large, heavy chef's knife. Remove the skin and fat from each piece. Place the skin and fat on a wire rack in a baking dish and bake until crispy, about 1 hour. Save the fat for another use and save the skin to serve later, tossed with spaghetti, if desired.

2. In a stove-top casserole, heat the olive oil with the butter over medium-high heat. When the butter stops sizzling, lightly brown the duck pieces on all sides, about 10 minutes. Remove from the pan with tongs or a slotted spoon and set aside. Reduce the heat to medium-low and add the celery, onion, and carrot. Cook until the vegetables are soft and mushy looking, stirring and scraping the bottom as you do to get up the browned crispy bits, about 12 minutes. Add the diluted tomato paste and the parsley, season with salt and pepper, and stir.

3. Return the duck to the casserole and bring the sauce to a simmer. Cover, reduce the heat to very low, using a heat diffuser, if necessary, and cook the duck until tender, about 2 hours. Serve immediately.

Makes 4 servings

GERMAN CHICKEN STEW WITH CARAWAY DUMPLINGS

Every German hausfrau has her own favorite *Eintopfgericht*, or "meal made in one pot." Although the word means what we call casseroles, it also covers stews that are made in one pot. Many of these German stews are prepared days in advance and they are excellent reheated. This stew is called *Hühnereintopf mit Kummelklössen*. The stew also gives its name in Germany to a piece of music written for beginners playing solo on the flute.

In this stew there are two vegetables that you may be unfamiliar with: celeriac, also known as celery root, and parsley root. Both are cultivated for their starch-storing swollen corms or roots, rather than for their stalks or leaves. Both grow as big as a grapefruit and are ugly, gnarled balls with dangling rootlets. Celeriac has a zesty taste, and the dense consistency is a great, and lighter, alternative to root vegetables and tubers such as rutabagas or potatoes. Parsley root is also dense, and tastes vaguely like parsley. In Germany, celeriac and parsley root are very common ingredients in many stews. You need to slice off the outside of the celeriac and parsley root, which will reduce the weight quite a bit. For example, two full-grown parsley roots will weigh about 3 1/2 pounds and be reduced to about 2 1/2 pounds after peeling. The final stew will be tender, with the chicken falling off the bone, and if you make it with caraway dumplings, you'll have a substantial meal that can feed a group of people.

3 tablespoons unsalted butter
One 4-pound chicken, cut into serving pieces, plus gizzards, if any
1 small yellow onion, chopped
1/4 cup unbleached all-purpose flour
1/2 celeriac (about 3/4 pound), peeled and cubed
2 parsley roots (about 3 1/2 pounds total), peeled and cubed
4 carrots (about 1 pound), sliced
10 small white onions (about 1 1/2 pounds), peeled
10 black peppercorns
1 bay leaf
1 1/2 quarts boiling water
2 cups shelled peas, fresh or frozen
Salt and freshly ground black pepper to taste

3 tablespoons fresh lemon juice
1 recipe Dumplings, with 2 tablespoons caraway
added to the dough mixture (page 76)

---

1. In a large casserole or stew pot, melt the butter over medium-high heat. Once it has stopped sizzling, brown the chicken, gizzards (if they are included), and chopped onion until golden, turning occasionally, about 12 minutes.

CELERIAC AND PARSLEY ROOT

These are two vegetables used in a lot of stew cookery. You may be unfamiliar with them, but they are wonderful vegetables for a stew. Both, though, are big, bulbous, root-like vegetables with lots of ugly, hairy-looking rootlets coming off the central portion. The edible parts of celeriac, a hardy biennial grown as an annual, are the corm and leaves, which can be eaten cooked or raw. Celeriac is a form of celery that has been cultivated so that the lowest part of the stem, or corm, is enlarged. It is not the root of the plant. The best celeriac is that of medium size, without secondary corms, and with a modest clump of leaves. Peel celeriac before using.

Parsley root is grown specifically for large roots. The texture and density of the root are similar to those of celeriac. When planted densely, the roots will be small when harvested. Growers harvest parsley root in the fall or leave them in the ground through the winter because the cold makes for a sweeter-tasting root. They store well. Peel parsley root before using.

2. Sprinkle the flour over the chicken pieces and turn them to absorb the flour. Add the celeriac, parsley roots, carrots, whole white onions, peppercorns, and bay leaf. Cover with the boiling water, and bring to just below a boil. Reduce the heat to very low, using a diffuser if necessary, and simmer until the meat is nearly falling off the bone and the vegetables are tender, about 2 hours. At no time should the broth ever boil, otherwise the chicken will be tough. Add the peas and cook for 10 more minutes. Season with salt and pepper and add the lemon juice.

3. While the stew is simmering, prepare the dumplings. Drop the dough by the tablespoon on top of the stewing chicken, making sure the balls don't sink into the gravy. Cover and cook for 20 minutes without looking. Serve immediately.

Makes 6 servings

WATERZOOI

THE VERY PLEASANT CITY OF GHENT, AT the confluence of the Schedlt and Lys rivers, is the historic capital of Flanders in northern Belgium. It is also the home of the most famous of Flemish stews, *Gentse waterzooi* (or *waterzooi gantois* among the Francophones), a rich chicken stew made with vegetables and eggs and cooked in beer or a rich chicken stock. Many restaurants throughout Belgium advertise their expertise in preparing *waterzooi*, which can be made with chicken, rabbit, or fish. Traveling in Belgium will convince you that the population is completely loony about *waterzooi*. Try this stew and you will see why. The parsley root is an important part of *waterzooi*, so do make an effort to get it. Most good supermarkets carry it, but it's often buried next to some more popular vegetable, and you may not have noticed it before. Feel free to use a food processor to finely chop all the vegetables as required, but be careful you don't make them too mushy; pulse the machine. *Waterzooi* is very nice served with boiled potatoes or toasted French bread with some butter.

One 3½-pound chicken, cut into 8 pieces
Salt and freshly ground white pepper to taste
¼ cup (½ stick) unsalted butter, at room
    temperature
2 medium-size onions, finely chopped
2 shallots, finely chopped
3 leeks (white and light green part only), split
    lengthwise, washed well, and finely chopped
3 celery stalks, finely chopped
3 carrots, finely chopped
4 parsley roots (3 to 4 pounds total), peeled and
    cut into sixths
1 cup dry white wine
3 cups rich Chicken Broth (see headnote, page
    181)
4 large egg yolks
½ cup heavy cream
2 tablespoons finely chopped fresh parsley leaves
Juice from ½ lemon

1. Rub the chicken inside and out with salt and pepper. Butter the bottom of a large, heavy casserole with 2 tablespoons of the butter. Layer it with the onions, shallots, leeks, celery, carrots, and parsley roots. Lay the chicken pieces on top of the vegetables. Pour the wine and chicken broth over everything, season with salt and pepper, and bring to just below a boil over high heat. Reduce the heat to low, cover, and simmer very gently, without letting the broth come to a boil, until the meat on the chicken nearly falls off, about 2½ hours. Remove the chicken and set aside or bone it, if you desire. Continue to simmer the remaining ingredients until the parsley roots are soft, another 30 minutes.

2. In a medium-size bowl, beat together the egg yolks, heavy cream, the remaining 2 tablespoons of butter, and a few tablespoons of the broth from the casserole. Remove the parsley roots and pass them through a food mill or mash them. Stir them into the egg mixture. Slowly pour the egg mixture into the stew, whisking all the time so the eggs don't curdle. Add the parsley and lemon juice and stir. Ladle the broth over the chicken pieces and serve immediately.

Makes 6 to 8 servings

ROMANIAN CHICKEN STEW

ALTHOUGH THIS ROMANIAN CHICKEN stew is quite appetizing, you must pay some attention to it while cooking to ensure a perfect dish. Chicken flesh does not like to be boiled, which only serves to toughen it. A tender chicken, where each bite is pleasingly moist and flavor filled, can be achieved by never letting the broth reach a boil; it should only bubble very gently at most. For that reason, use a heat diffuser, unless your burner has a simmer setting. The unique flavor of this stew comes from the nutty and almost coffee-like taste of the roasted flour that is stirred into the stew at the end of the cooking time. In Romanian, this stew is called *tocană de pui*.

---

¹/₂ cup Clarified Butter (page 194)
1¹/₂ pounds boneless, skinless chicken breasts, cut into 1¹/₄–inch cubes and patted dry with paper towels
1¹/₂ pounds boneless, skinless chicken thighs, cut into 1¹/₄–inch cubes and patted dry with paper towels
1¹/₂ pounds onions, thinly sliced
¹/₄ cup tomato paste
2 teaspoons hot Hungarian paprika
1¹/₃ cups dry white wine
1¹/₂ teaspoons salt, or more as needed
2 small bay leaves
4 allspice berries
³/₄ cup unbleached all-purpose flour

Freshly ground black pepper to taste
³/₄ cup finely chopped fresh parsley leaves

---

1. In a large casserole, melt the clarified butter over medium heat. Cook the chicken until it turns color on all sides, stirring, 5 to 6 minutes. Remove with a slotted spoon and set aside.

2. Add the onions to the casserole, reduce the heat to medium-low, and cook, covered, until soft, about 20 minutes. Add the tomato paste and paprika and stir for 1 or 2 minutes to mix well. Return the chicken to the casserole, reduce the heat to low, add the wine, salt, bay leaves, and allspice berries. Simmer until the chicken is tender, never letting it come to a boil and stirring occasionally, about 1 hour.

3. Meanwhile, preheat the oven to 450°F. Spread the flour on a small baking tray and roast until it browns and develops a distinctive nutty or coffee-like aroma, about 15 minutes. Sift ¹/₂ cup of the roasted flour through a small strainer into the stew. Season with some black pepper and stir in the parsley. Save any remaining roasted flour for another time.

Makes 6 servings

CLARIFIED BUTTER

Clarified butter is butter that has had its milk solids removed. Cooks clarify butter because with the milk solids removed, the butter can be heated to a higher temperature without burning and it is also easier to preserve in regions where there traditionally isn't refrigeration. In the Arab world, clarified butter is called *samna* or *sman* and in India it is known as *ghee*.

———•———

Butter, as needed

———•———

1. Place the butter in a microwaveable dish and cover with plastic wrap. Microwave until the butter has melted and is bubbling slightly.

2. Remove the dish and spoon off the foam on top, then pour the clear part of the butter into a container for storage, being careful that the milk solids on the bottom don't fall in. Alternatively, pour the butter through a cheesecloth-lined strainer. One can also make clarified butter by melting the butter in a small saucepan over low heat and following the method above for removing the milk solids. This will keep, tightly covered, in the refrigerator for up to 6 months.

CHICKEN STEW FROM GREECE

IN THIS GREEK CHICKEN STEW, CALLED *kota stifado*, the gravy is a delicately perfumed one, achieved through the inclusion of a spice bouquet consisting of cumin, cinnamon, cloves, and allspice. When stewing this chicken, one should be careful that the sauce never comes to boil, otherwise the chicken will toughen. It's best to let it simmer gently, and if it doesn't appear to be done in the time recommended, continue simmering until it is. I like to serve this chicken with rice pilaf (page 125), but you could also serve it with a pasta such as orzo or even a long pasta with a hole in the middle, such as what the Italians call *perciatelli* and the Greeks call *makaronia tirpiti* ("macaroni with a hole").

In this stew, you will fry the cubes of cheese in a skillet until they are brown and crunchy, then turn them into the stew. The best cheese to use is either a *kefalotyri*, which is a hard, salty, light yellow cheese made of sheep's or goat's milk (you could use a young pecorino cheese in its place), or a *kashkaval*, a mild, creamy, sheep's milk cheese, provolone-like in texture, but saltier. Both cheeses are found in Greek and Middle Eastern markets.

———•———

6 tablespoons (³/₄ stick) unsalted butter
1 tablespoon extra virgin olive oil
One 4-pound chicken, cut into servings pieces
3 medium-size onions, grated on the largest holes of a grater

*1 tablespoon tomato paste dissolved in ¹/₂ cup
water*

*1 bouquet garni, consisting of 1 teaspoon cumin
seeds, 1 stick cinnamon, 3 allspice berries, 1
clove, and 2 bay leaves, tied in cheesecloth*

*12 to 14 small onions, a combination of red and
white (1 to 1¹/₄ pounds total), peeled*

*6 ounces kefalotyri or kashkaval cheese, cut
into ¹/₂-inch cubes*

---

1. In a large casserole, melt 4 tablespoons of
the butter over medium-high heat with the
olive oil. Once the butter stops sizzling and is
beginning to turn light brown, brown the
chicken pieces on all sides, 8 to 10 minutes.
Add the grated onion, cook for 1 or 2 minutes, then add the diluted tomato paste. Add
the bouquet garni, reduce the heat to low,
cover, and simmer for 45 minutes. Add the
whole onions and cook, covered, until the
chicken and onions are fork-tender, 45 to 60
minutes more.

2. Meanwhile, in a skillet, melt the remaining
2 tablespoons of butter over medium-high
heat. Once the butter stops sizzling, cook the
cheese cubes until crispy golden on one side,
about 1 minute. Scrape them up with a metal
spatula (make sure the crust doesn't stick to the
pan), and cook the other side until crispy.
Remove from the pan and add to the chicken
stew. Cook until they are beginning to melt,
about 5 minutes. Serve immediately, discarding the bouquet garni.

Makes 4 servings

SUMMER STEW, WINTER STEW IN TURKEY

The Turks are crazy about vegetables and they
prepare them in a variety of ways. In the summer,
vegetable stews usually contain tomatoes, eggplant, green beans, runner beans, bell peppers,
chiles, corn, potatoes, and onion. Many wild
greens are used too, collected by herders and
mountain village dwellers. Summer vegetables
are also pickled and dried. In the winter, stews
of spinach, Swiss chard, carrot, okra, celeriac, and
cauliflower become popular.

CHICKEN AND VEGETABLE STEW FROM TURKEY

IN TURKISH, THIS STEW IS CALLED *PILIÇ
güveçi sebzeli*, which means "chicken and
vegetable stew." As with so many *güveçi* (the
word refers both to the stew and the clay cooking pot in which it is made), the ingredients
are mixed and cooked slowly together for a
long time. I was initially suspicious of this stew
because it didn't contain any herbs or spices
and I thought it would be very bland. But
one forgets how flavorful a certain mix of
vegetables can be. This stew is cooked without
any liquid except that which will come from
the vegetables themselves. The key to this
summer stew is very fresh vegetables, preferably right from the garden.

½ cup (1 stick) unsalted butter

2 small onions, quartered

¾ pound green beans, ends trimmed and cut
into 2-inch lengths

2 medium-size zucchini, ends trimmed, peeled
lengthwise in strips like zebra stripes, then cut
crosswise into 1-inch-thick rounds

¼ pound fresh small okra, bottoms trimmed

4 green bell peppers, seeded and quartered

2 skinny, long eggplants, peeled lengthwise in
strips like zebra stripes, then cut crosswise
into 1-inch-thick rounds

Salt and freshly ground black pepper to taste

2 Cornish game hens (about 3 pounds total),
each cut into 4 pieces

2 large, ripe tomatoes, cut in half, seeds squeezed
out, and grated against the largest holes of a
grater down to the peel

—————●—————

1. In an earthenware casserole set on a heat
diffuser, melt the butter over medium-high
heat. (If you are not cooking with earthenware
and a diffuser, cook over medium heat.) Once
the butter stops bubbling, add the onions, green
beans, zucchini, okra, bell peppers, and eggplants. Season with salt and pepper, stir to mix
well, then lay the Cornish hen pieces on top.
Season again with salt and pepper, pour the
tomatoes on top, and reduce the heat to low.
Cover and simmer until the chicken is tender,
about 2 hours.

2. Uncover and cook another 30 minutes.
Serve immediately.

—————●—————

Makes 4 servings

TURKISH CHICKEN AND OKRA STEW

~

THIS PREPARATION IS ANOTHER *GÜVEÇI*,
an all-purpose Turkish word for stew,
one that always contains a vegetable and
tomatoes and is made with chicken, lamb, veal,
or beef. Serve this dish with chickpea pilaf,
yogurt, or plain bulgur pilaf. This stew is ideally
cooked in an earthenware casserole with a
cover. Turkish red pepper may also be called
Aleppo pepper in a Middle Eastern market.
You can make a vague rendition of your own
by mixing together three parts hot Hungarian
paprika with one part ground red chile.

—————●—————

1 pound fresh small okra, bottoms trimmed

3 tablespoons white wine vinegar

1 tablespoon salt

1 tablespoon unsalted butter

2 tablespoons extra virgin olive oil

4 to 5 chicken breast halves on the bone (about
3¼ pounds total)

2 medium-size onions, thinly sliced

2 teaspoons finely ground coriander seeds

1 teaspoon Turkish red pepper (see headnote)

5 large garlic cloves, pounded in a mortar with 1
teaspoon salt until mushy

½ teaspoon sugar

1 tablespoon dried oregano

1 tablespoon tomato paste

1½ pounds ripe tomatoes, peeled, seeded, and
chopped

Juice from 1 lemon

Freshly ground black pepper to taste

TURKISH STEWS

One kind of Turkish stew is called *güveç*, which consists, usually, of meat and vegetables stewed together in a clay pot with their own juices. The clay stewing pot, which looks like the kind of ovenproof earthenware bowl used for French onion soup, is called a *güveç*. Another class of stews is called *sahan*, in which the meat is cooked with *salça*, "sauce," usually tomato puree. A third type of stew is called *yahni*, in which vegetables and pulses are thrown into the stew pot.

1. Put the okra in a bowl and sprinkle with the vinegar and salt. Toss and let sit for 1 hour.

2. Meanwhile, in a large earthenware casserole set on a heat diffuser, melt the butter with the oil over high heat. Once the butter stops sizzling, brown the chicken pieces, about 12 or more minutes. (If you are not cooking with earthenware and a diffuser, cook over medium-high heat and check for doneness in about 8 minutes.) Remove the chicken and set aside.

3. Add the onions, coriander, and red pepper and cook until the onions soften, stirring and tossing, 6 to 8 minutes. Add the garlic, sugar, and oregano, stir, and add the tomato paste and tomatoes, stirring again to incorporate the paste. Bring to a boil, return the chicken to the pan, and reduce the heat to medium-low. Cover and cook until the meat is firm, turning it a few times, about 30 minutes.

4. Put the okra in a strainer and rinse under running water. Arrange them on top of the chicken, pushing them down a little into the broth, then pour the lemon juice over everything, and season with salt and pepper. Cover and cook until the okra is tender, shaking the casserole from time to time, about 40 minutes. Serve immediately.

Makes 4 to 5 servings

ALGERIAN CHICKEN, ALMOND, AND SAFFRON STEW

CHICKEN IS QUITE POPULAR IN ALGERIA, as are other fowl, especially pigeon. Many Algerian homes to this day have pigeon cotes in or attached to their houses for a ready supply of fresh birds. This Algerian chicken stew, called *maraqat al-dajāj bi'l-lawz* ("chicken ragout with almonds"), cooks slowly for some time, until the meat is about to fall off the bone. It is important to make sure the broth never comes to a boil, otherwise, the chicken will toughen. Just keep the broth percolating with tiny bubbles at the most. It's quite a luscious meal and it would be best to serve it with some blander food such as rice pilaf (page 125) or potatoes.

3 tablespoons Clarified Butter (page 194)
One 4-pound chicken, quartered
1 large onion, chopped
Salt and freshly ground black pepper to taste
¹/₈ teaspoon ground cinnamon
¹/₂ teaspoon saffron threads, crumbled
2 cups hot water
1 cup blanched whole almonds (about 5 ounces)
*³/₄ cup dried currants (about 3¹/₂ ounces), soaked
    in hot water to cover for 15 minutes and
    drained*

1. In a large earthenware casserole set on a heat diffuser, heat the clarified butter over high heat. Cook the chicken pieces and onion together, browning the chicken on all sides, 6 to 8 minutes. (If you are not cooking with earthenware and a diffuser, cook over medium heat and check for doneness sooner.)

2. Season the chicken with salt and pepper and add the cinnamon and saffron, stirring to mix evenly. Add the hot water, reduce the heat to low, and simmer until the chicken is no longer raw looking around the joint where the wing meets the body, 40 to 45 minutes.

3. Add the almonds and currants and continue to simmer until the chicken looks like it could fall apart, about 1 more hour. Correct the seasoning and serve with rice and butter.

Makes 4 servings

REMOVING THE SKIN FROM ALMONDS

Bring a saucepan of water to a rolling boil and plunge the almonds in the water. Boil for about 3 to 4 minutes, then drain. Once they are cool enough to handle, pinch the skin off by squeezing the almond between your thumb and forefinger.

GROUNDNUT STEW FROM GHANA

THE PEANUT IS A LEGUME USED EXTEN-sively in the cooking of West Africa. The English call the peanut "groundnut" and this groundnut stew comes from Ghana, a former British colony in West Africa. It is called *hkatenkwan* in the local language of the Kwa family of West Africa. You can make this stew as hot as you want with the addition of chiles. Typically, a Ghanian cook would make it very hot by pounding chiles in a mortar before turning them into the stew. You can also make the stew as thick or as liquidy as you would like. In Ghana, it is usually served with *fufu*: grated cassava is soaked in water and drained and the starchy sediment that remains is what makes *fufu*. The stew can also be served with dumplings (page 76).

One 3-pound chicken, cut into 8 pieces
One 1-inch piece fresh ginger, peeled
1 large onion, halved, 1 half left as is and 1 half
*   chopped*
2 cups water
2 tablespoons tomato paste
1 tablespoon peanut oil
1 cup peeled, seeded, and chopped tomatoes
²/₃ cup smooth peanut butter
2 teaspoons salt
1 to 2 fresh chiles, peeled, seeded, and crushed in
*   a mortar until mushy, or 1 to 2 teaspoons*
*   cayenne pepper, to your taste*
1 medium-size eggplant (about ³/₄ pound),
*   peeled and cubed*
¹/₂ pound fresh small okra, bottoms trimmed

1. Place the chicken in a medium-size stew pot or saucepan over medium heat with the ginger, onion half, and water. Bring to a gentle bubble, just below boiling. Reduce the heat to low and cook, partially covered, until the chicken is white, no more blood is coming out, and there are no longer any pink spots, 40 to 45 minutes.

2. Meanwhile, in another large stew pot, mix the tomato paste with the oil and cook over low heat for 5 minutes, stirring frequently. Increase the heat to medium and add the chopped onion and tomatoes. Cook, stirring occasionally, until the onion is soft, about 5 minutes.

3. Remove the partially cooked chicken pieces from the stew pot and put them, along with about half the broth, in the large pot with the tomato and onion. Add the peanut butter, salt, and chiles, stir to mix well, and cook for 5 minutes. Stir in the eggplant and okra. Reduce the heat to low and continue to cook, partially covered, until the chicken and vegetables are tender, 40 to 45 minutes. Add more broth as needed to maintain a thinner stew.

Makes 4 servings

CHICKEN AND COCONUT STEW FROM KENYA

I N THIS CHICKEN STEW FROM KENYA, called *ku ku paka*, the curry powder seems to reflect the influence of the Indian population that has been long established in this former British colony in East Africa. The broth used to stew is a coconut broth that is obtained by infusing boiling water with grated fresh coconut. The method for making this "coconut milk" is described in the Note on page 200. As with all chicken stews, the chicken should cook very slowly, so that the broth is under a boil and barely even bubbling. For this reason, you will want to use a heat diffuser if your stove doesn't have a very low simmer setting. In Kenya, many people like to add a fiery hot sauce made from chiles called *pillipilli* (see page 200). This recipe is adapted from Bea Sandler's *The African Cookbook*.

3 tablespoons peanut oil

2 medium-size onions, sliced 1/2 inch thick and
separated into rings

2 green bell peppers, seeded and cut into
1/2-inch-thick rings

1/2 teaspoon ground ginger

3/4 teaspoon curry powder

3/4 teaspoon salt

3/4 teaspoon sugar

2 garlic cloves, crushed into a paste

3 cloves

1 1/2 pounds ripe tomatoes, peeled, seeded, and
sliced

1 dried red chile, seeded and crumbled

1/4 cup vegetable oil

1 1/2 tablespoons grated lemon zest

One 4-pound chicken, cut into 8 or 10 pieces

2 cups coconut milk (see Note)

1 1/2 pounds sweet potatoes, peeled and cut into
1 1/2-inch pieces

1. In a large casserole or Dutch oven, heat the oil over medium-high heat, then cook the onions, peppers, ginger, curry powder, salt, sugar, garlic, and cloves until the onions are soft, stirring frequently, about 12 minutes. Add the tomatoes, chile, and lemon zest and cook for 2 minutes, stirring. Add the chicken and cook for 5 minutes. Then add the coconut milk and potatoes. Cover, reduce the heat to low, using a heat diffuser if necessary, and simmer until the chicken and potatoes are tender, about 2 1/2 hours.

2. Remove the chicken and stir the stew. Serve the stew in wide bowls with the chicken on top.

Makes 4 to 6 servings

Note: To make coconut milk, place 2 cups grated fresh coconut or packaged unsweetened coconut on a piece of cheesecloth and wrap it up. Place this in a sieve set over a deep bowl. Bring 1 cup of water to a rolling boil and pour it over the cheesecloth into the bowl. When cool enough to handle, squeeze any extra liquid out of the cheesecloth. Pour 1 more cup of boiling water over the cheesecloth and again squeeze it out. The resulting milky liquid is the coconut milk.

PILLI-PILLI SAUCE

Pilli-pilli sauce is a very hot pan-African chile sauce born in West Africa and used as an accompaniment or condiment to cooked foods, ranging from stews to grilled meats to sandwiches. It is typically made with the very hottest chile peppers, the habanero or cayenne pepper. There are a number of different recipes for pilli-pilli. It can be made by blending tomatoes, chiles, garlic, horseradish, and lemon juice together or by using only chile pepper, lemon juice, onion juice, and garlic. In any case, Africans use it with abandon.

FESENJAN

K*HOREST-E-FESENJAN* IS A FAMOUS PERSIAN duck and pomegranate stew (also transliterated as *khurash-i-fasanjan*). In Iran, a cook is often judged by the quality of the *fesenjan* she makes. This traditional stew, which sometimes contains eggplant, is made for the breaking of the Ramadan fast and comes from the province of Gilan on the Caspian Sea where wild ducks are to be found. One serves *fesenjan* with *chelou*, a buttered steamed rice. It is a rich preparation, so a plain rice is the best accompaniment. It is important when you are carving up the duck into pieces that you remove as much fat as possible. Remove the skin too, except from the breasts. The stew can also be made with chicken, lamb, or meatballs in place of the duck. The pomegranate juice and pomegranate molasses can be found in Middle Eastern markets and some supermarkets.

1¹/₂ *cups ground walnuts*
One 4- to 5-pound duck, skinned (except for the breast), trimmed of excess fat, and cut into serving pieces
2 large onions, grated
¹/₄ *cup extra virgin olive oil or unsalted butter*
¹/₂ *teaspoon ground cinnamon*
¹/₂ *teaspoon freshly grated nutmeg*
Salt and freshly ground black pepper to taste
2 cups pomegranate juice
3 tablespoons sugar
¹/₂ *teaspoon saffron threads, crumbled and steeped in 2 tablespoons water*

¹/₄ *cup plus 1 tablespoon pomegranate molasses*
2 tablespoons fresh lemon juice

---

1. In a large, dry skillet, cook the ground walnuts over medium heat until it looks a little browner and smells vaguely like popcorn, about 6 minutes. Transfer to a plate and set aside.

2. Put the duck in the skillet with half of the grated onions and turn the heat to medium-high. Once the duck is sizzling, reduce the heat to low and simmer, uncovered, until it turns color, about 15 minutes, turning occasionally. You will not need any fat or liquid to do this because the duck will provide the fat and there is enough liquid in the grated onion. Cover, reduce the heat to low, and simmer, continuing to turn the duck occasionally, until the meat is golden, firm, but tender, about 1¹/₄ hours. Remove the duck pieces and let them cool. Once you can handle them, remove the meat

POMEGRANATE MOLASSES

Pomegranate molasses is an essential ingredient in much Middle Eastern cooking. The molasses consists of pomegranate juice that has been boiled down with sugar and lemon juice until it is a thick, molasses-like syrup. It has a luscious, sweet-tart flavor. You can find pomegranate molasses in Middle Eastern markets; a good brand to look for is the Lebanese brand called Cortas.

from the bone. Discard the bones and skin and any unmelted fat, but save the liquid in the skillet; there should be about 1¹/₂ cups.

3. In a large casserole or Dutch oven, heat the olive oil over medium-high heat, then cook the remaining grated onion until light golden, stirring, about 8 minutes. Add the ground walnuts, cinnamon, and nutmeg and season with salt and pepper. Stir and add the pomegranate juice, the reserved duck liquid from the skillet, sugar, diluted saffron, pomegranate molasses, and lemon juice. Bring to a gentle boil, then reduce the heat to low. Cover and simmer until dense and gravy-like, about 20 minutes.

4. Add the duck meat to the casserole and continue to simmer over low heat until bubbling gently and thick, about 30 minutes. While the stew is simmering, make the rice. When the stew is done, adjust the taste by adding sugar if the sauce is too sour or more pomegranate molasses if it is too sweet. Check the seasonings and correct with salt and pepper if necessary. Serve with the rice.

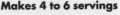

Makes 4 to 6 servings

CHICKEN AND SWEET POTATO CURRY

CHICKEN IS A POPULAR MEAT IN INDIA, probably second only to lamb. It is considered a festive delicacy, and this recipe of stewed chicken curry is quite a delight. It is spicy, but that does not mean it is spicy hot. In fact, the preparation has a vague sweetness that comes from the very small amount of brown sugar used. Serve the dish very hot with some plain rice pilaf (page 125).

2 medium-size onions, cut into several large pieces
2 large garlic cloves, peeled
One 1-inch cube fresh ginger, peeled
2 teaspoons freshly ground cumin seeds
1 teaspoon turmeric
1 teaspoon paprika
3 tablespoons white wine vinegar
¹/₄ cup vegetable oil
One 3-pound chicken, cut into serving pieces
4 cloves
One 2-inch cinnamon stick
2 teaspoons brown sugar
1¹/₂ teaspoons salt
1¹/₂ cups water
3 sweet potatoes (about 2 pounds total), peeled and quartered

1. Put the onions, garlic, ginger, cumin, turmeric, paprika, and vinegar in a food processor and process into a smooth paste.

2. In a large casserole, heat the vegetable oil over medium-high heat. Brown the chicken pieces on all sides, about 6 minutes. Remove from the pan and set aside.

3. Add the onion paste to the casserole and cook for 1 to 2 minutes, stirring. Add the cloves and cinnamon and cook for another minute.

4. Return the chicken to the casserole along with the brown sugar, salt, and water. Cover, reduce the heat to low, and simmer for 30 minutes. Add the sweet potatoes and continue to simmer over low heat, covered, until the sweet potatoes are tender and the chicken falls off the bone with a little tug from a fork, about 1 hour.

5. If there is a lot of liquid left in the casserole, remove the chicken and sweet potatoes and reduce over high heat for a few minutes. Return the chicken and sweet potatoes to the casserole, and heat for 1or 2 minutes before serving.

Makes 4 servings

BARBARA SHULGASSER-PARKER'S CHICKEN STEW WITH PRUNES

MY FRIEND BARBARA SHULGASSER–Parker called this stew she made up *poulet d'Inde aux pruneaux*. I must have said something to her about it when she first served it to me because sometime later she asked me about the stew, and I couldn't remember having eaten it. She responded, knowing I was writing a book on stews, "You ate it the first time you had dinner here and raved about it, admonishing me for not writing down the recipe. How about it? A succulent and tangy dish that can be adjusted to suit one's taste for heat and sweetness. Serve with baked yams or sweet potatoes, or over rice. Whaddaya think?" Well, I think it was quite good, and Barbara is a good cook, so here's her *poulet* stew.

3 tablespoons extra virgin olive oil

1¹/₂ large onions, sliced ¹/₄ inch thick

One 3¹/₂-pound chicken, quartered, skinned, rinsed, and patted dry with paper towels

Salt and freshly ground black pepper to taste

3 cups Chicken Broth (page 181)

2 teaspoons mild Indian curry

1 teaspoon ground sage

1 teaspoon chopped fresh rosemary leaves

3 tablespoons honey

¹/₂ pound large pitted prunes

Juice of 1 lemon or ¹/₄ cup white wine

1. In a large skillet, heat the olive oil over medium-high heat. Cook the onions until translucent, stirring, 6 to 7 minutes. Push the onions to one side of the skillet, season the chicken pieces with salt and pepper, and brown the chicken on both sides, meatier side down first. Once the chicken has been turned, move the onions on top of the chicken pieces to keep them from burning, about 8 minutes total. Season with more pepper.

2. Add enough of the chicken broth so there is about 1 inch of liquid in the skillet. Turn the chicken and onions together and bring to a gentle simmer over medium heat. Dust the curry over the chicken and with a wooden spoon, scrape the browned bits off the sides and bottom of the skillet into the simmering broth. Sprinkle with the sage and rosemary. As the mixture returns to a light simmer, drizzle in the honey and stir. Add the prunes, placing them between the chicken pieces in the sauce. Check the seasoning. Add more broth as needed to keep the liquid level at about 1 inch. Simmer, covered, for 30 minutes. Then uncover and cook, turning the chicken occasionally and spooning sauce over it, until the meat looks ready to fall off the bones, about 1 hour.

3. Stir in the lemon juice to achieve a sweet-and-sour flavor and serve.

Makes 4 to 5 servings

POULET PRUNE

RUMMAGING THROUGH MY FRIEND Kimba Hills's cookbook shelf, I wasn't surprised to find a cookbook from Tennessee, Kimba's home state. It was a Junior League of Nashville collection called *Nashville Seasons Cook Book*, published in 1964. In it I found this intriguing recipe that supposedly represents Tennessee cooking, offered by one Mrs. Joseph G. Erwin, Jr. What intrigued me was the fruit: prunes, apple brandy, and apple cider, and it all seemed vaguely Spanish in a way. I don't mean Latin American Spanish, but Iberian Spanish, given the combination of the bell peppers, paprika, olives, and whole onions. I've adapted the recipe only slightly and I have not tried to modernize it in any way. It is really quite enjoyable, and the only thing you need to pay attention to is to make sure you don't overcook the chicken or toughen it since breast meat is delicate. For this reason, don't let the broth boil. This stew is very nice with steamed rice.

6 chicken breast halves on the bone with the skin (about 4 1/2 pounds total)

2 teaspoons salt

3/4 teaspoon freshly ground black pepper

1/2 cup (1 stick) plus 1 tablespoon unsalted butter

1 teaspoon paprika

1 1/2 cups chopped yellow onions

2 garlic cloves, finely chopped

2 green bell peppers, seeded and cut into thin strips

1 cup apple brandy
1 cup apple cider
2 tablespoons white wine vinegar
12 pitted prunes, soaked in tepid water to cover
for 30 minutes and drained
12 large stuffed Spanish olives
12 small white onions, peeled
2 cups small cubes peeled boiling potatoes
2 tablespoons capers, drained and rinsed
2 links hot Italian sausage (about ½ pound
total), sliced

———————●———————

1. Season the chicken with salt and pepper. In a 12-inch skillet, melt the stick of butter over medium-high heat. Once it stops sizzling, add the paprika and brown the chicken on all sides,

about 5 minutes. Transfer the chicken to a large casserole.

2. Add the chopped onions to the skillet and cook until soft, stirring frequently, about 5 minutes. Add the garlic, peppers, brandy, cider, and vinegar to the skillet and deglaze it, scraping the bottom to get up any browned bits. Transfer the onion-and-pepper mixture to the casserole, cover, and bring to just below a boil. Reduce the heat to low and cook until the chicken is firm but tender, making sure the broth never comes to a boil but only bubbles very slightly, about 1 hour.

3. Remove the chicken from the casserole and let cool. Once it is cool enough to handle,

OLIVES, OLIVES, OLIVES

———————●———————

In the old days (in the United States, anyway), there were two kinds of olives, black ones and green ones, and they were sold in cans and they were tasteless. Green olives are olives that have been harvested through the ripening cycle after they have reached their full size but before their color change. Green olives are processed in two ways: with fermentation (called the Spanish type) or without fermentation (called the Picholine or American type). Today we blessedly, if bewilderingly, have an enormous variety of olives to choose from. The number of varieties of olives available to the American consumer changes constantly as we become better educated about them. Among black table olives (as opposed to olives used

for oil) the Italian Gaeta or Greek Kalamata have long been available. Now it is not uncommon to find big green Sicilian olives (Paterno) or the Cerignola olives from Italy being sold. There are the small French Niçoise, Louques, or Picholine olives, the Greek Amphissa olives, Spanish Manzanilla or Cacereña, Syrian al-Dawbly, and Turkish Gemlik. And there are oil-cured olives, dry salted olives, deliberately bruised olives, olives in a wide variety of different brines, and specialty olives stuffed with anchovies, garlic slivers, or pimento. Which ones should you buy? Well, all of them, of course—keep experimenting and you will introduce yourself to a new world.

remove all the meat from the bones and discard the skin and bones. Cut the chicken into bite-size pieces and set aside.

4. Meanwhile, add the prunes, olives, whole onions, potatoes, and capers to the casserole. Correct the seasonings, cover, and cook over medium heat until the potatoes are soft, 30 to 35 minutes. Meanwhile, in a small skillet, melt the remaining 1 tablespoon of butter over medium-high heat. Brown the sausage slices on both sides, 4 to 5 minutes. Add the reserved chicken and sausage to the casserole, cover, and cook until heated through over medium heat, about 10 minutes. Serve immediately.

Makes 8 servings

NEW MEXICO–STYLE CHICKEN STEW

I N THIS OLD-TIME STEW FROM THE SOUTH-western United States, the flavoring is more reminiscent of Spanish cooking than the so-called Southwest cuisine that became popular in the 1980s and early 1990s. The chicken should simmer gently, never coming to a boil, otherwise it will be tough. Stir in the olives just before serving.

1/4 cup vegetable oil
One 4-pound chicken, cut into 8 pieces and skin removed
1 large onion, sliced and separated into rings
2 large garlic cloves, finely chopped
2 green bell peppers, seeded and shredded in a food processor
1 1/2 tablespoons unbleached all-purpose flour
1/4 teaspoon freshly ground cloves
1/2 teaspoon ground red chile
Salt and freshly ground black pepper to taste
1 pound ripe tomatoes, cut in half, seeds squeezed out, and grated against the largest holes of a grater down to the peel
1/3 cup raisins, soaked in tepid water to cover for 20 minutes and drained
3/4 cup dry sherry
1/3 cup sliced stuffed olives

1. In a large skillet, heat the oil over medium-high heat. Brown the chicken on all sides, 6 to 8 minutes. Transfer the chicken to a large cast-iron casserole or Dutch oven.

2. Add the onion, garlic, and green peppers to the skillet and cook over medium heat until soft, scraping the bottom with a wooden spoon to loosen up all the bits from the chicken, about 8 minutes. Transfer to the casserole with the chicken, and stir in the flour. Once it is blended, add the cloves, ground chile, salt, black pepper, and tomatoes. Bring to just below a boil and cook for 5 minutes.

3. Add the raisins and sherry and cover tightly. Simmer until the chicken is tender, about 1 1/2 hours. Uncover and cook another 30 minutes, or until the liquid is thicker.

4. Add the olives, stir, and serve.

Makes 4 to 6 servings

CHICKEN STEW
IN THE STYLE OF VERACRUZ

THOSE FAMILIAR WITH BOTH MEXICAN and Spanish cooking will recognize that the cooking of Veracruz, in Mexico, reflects the influence of the Iberian peninsula. This chicken stew from Coatepec, *estofado de gallina*, is a recipe I've adapted from Juanita Rebolledo de Sosa, which appears in the cookbook *La cocina Veracruzana*. A number of elements point to an old Iberian and specifically Catalan influence: witness the combination of almonds, olives, capers, cinnamon, and raisins. Ideally, this stew should never come to a boil; the chicken would toughen that way and you want to achieve a delicately braised chicken that pulls apart easily and is moist and tender. Serve with rice.

2 pounds ripe tomatoes
1 large onion, quartered
2 large garlic cloves
2 1/2 cups Chicken Broth (page 181)
1/4 cup extra virgin olive oil
Salt to taste
1/4 cup chopped blanched almonds
15 imported green olives, pitted and chopped
1 tablespoon capers, drained, rinsed, and
   chopped if large
1/4 cup golden raisins
1/2 teaspoon dried thyme
1/4 teaspoon dried marjoram
1 teaspoon dried oregano
4 bay leaves
1 cinnamon stick

One 3 1/2-pound chicken, cut into 6 pieces
1/4 cup dry sherry

1. Preheat the oven to 425°F. Place the tomatoes, onion, and garlic in a baking dish, preferably earthenware, and moisten with 1/4 cup of the broth. Bake until the tomato skins are crinkly and the onion light brown, 30 to 35 minutes. When they are cool enough to handle, remove the peels and chop all three.

2. In a large casserole, heat the olive oil over medium heat. Cook the chopped tomatoes, onion, and garlic with a little salt until most of the liquid has evaporated, stirring occasionally, about 20 minutes. Add the almonds, olives, capers, raisins, thyme, marjoram, and oregano to the tomato sauce. Stir to mix, then add the bay leaves, cinnamon stick, and the remaining 2 1/2 cups of broth. Season with salt, add the chicken, and bring to just below a boil. Reduce the heat to low, cover, and cook until the chicken is very tender, turning the pieces occasionally, 1 to 1 1/4 hours. Stir in the sherry, cook for 5 minutes, and serve.

Makes 4 servings

COOKING GOAT

A kid is a young goat, and it is a very nice meat for stewing. Because goat is older and tougher, it is used in stews almost exclusively. The first time you cook goat, you will be quite surprised at how tough it remains even after three hours of cooking. In fact, you should plan on cooking goat at least five hours, and maybe more. Even with that amount of time, the meat will still cling pretty securely to the bone. Just remember the time factor when you are making a goat recipe.

Goat is a popular meat in the Mediterranean, where you can find it prominent in the cuisines of Corsica, southern Italy and Sicily, and North Africa. It is also popular in the Caribbean, especially Jamaica and Puerto Rico. So the best places to find goat are stores frequented by the people from those places mentioned.

GOAT STEW FROM THE HILLS OF USERES

WE KNOW FROM *DON QUIXOTE*, THE great novel by Cervantes (1547-1616), that goat stews were eaten regularly in sixteenth-century Spain. This stew from the Useres hill country of Castellón, in Valencia, is traditionally cooked in a copper kettle called a *perol* or *peroles*. Even though saffron was known in Roman Spain, many culinary historians recognize that the cultivation of saffron was resurrected by the Arabs in Spain, and they point to the use of saffron as a Muslim heritage. Goat can be quite tough and may need more time cooking than called for here, so allow some extra time just in case.

¹/₂ cup extra virgin olive oil
2 pounds goat leg or shoulder meat on the bone, trimmed of any large pieces of fat and cut into smaller pieces
Salt to taste
2 cups water
Pinch of saffron threads, crumbled
1 bay leaf
15 black peppercorns
10 garlic cloves, finely chopped, or 40 whole garlic cloves, peeled

1. In a large casserole, heat the olive oil over medium-high heat. Season the goat meat with some salt and brown on all sides, about 10 minutes. Cover with the water and add the saffron, bay leaf, and peppercorns. Bring to a boil, then reduce the heat to low. Cover and simmer until the meat is quite tender, shaking the casserole occasionally, at least 2¹/₂ hours.

2. Add the garlic to the casserole, reduce the heat to very low, or use a heat diffuser, and simmer for another 1 to 2 hours, until the meat almost falls off the bone. Serve by draining the meat with a slotted spoon and transferring it to a serving platter.

Makes 4 servings

CORSICAN-STYLE GOAT RAGOUT

CORSICA, A LARGE MEDITERRANEAN island that is today part of France, was centuries ago a domain of the Duchy of Savoy, and during another period of its history, it was under the control of the Genoese. Corsica is a mountainous island and historically was outside the main flow of trade. Shepherding and goat herding have always been a preoccupation of the population. This stew, called *cabri en ragoût*, calls for goat rather than kid, and because goat meat tends to be old and tough, it will require at least an hour

more of cooking than lamb, which is what I suggest you use if you can't find goat.

$^1/_4$ *cup extra virgin olive oil*
$3^1/_4$ *pounds goat or lamb meat on the bone, cut from the shoulder, leg, and shank, trimmed of any large pieces of fat and cut into pieces*
$2^1/_2$ *cups dry red wine*
Salt and freshly ground black pepper to taste
$^3/_4$ *pound ripe tomatoes, peeled, seeded, and chopped*
3 bay leaves
6 large garlic cloves, crushed
$^1/_2$ *cup hot water*
1 long strip orange zest

1. In a large earthenware casserole set on a heat diffuser, heat the oil over medium heat. Brown the goat or lamb on all sides, about 10 minutes. (If you are not cooking with earthenware and a diffuser, check for doneness sooner.) Add $^1/_2$ cup of the wine and let it nearly evaporate, about 10 minutes. Season with salt and pepper and reduce the heat to low. Add the tomatoes, bay leaves, and garlic and cook for 2 minutes, stirring to blend. Pour in the remaining 2 cups of wine, the hot water, and add the orange zest. Cover and cook until the meat is falling off the bone, about 3 hours for lamb and 4 hours for goat.

2. Discard the bay leaves and orange zest before serving, although it is attractive to leave them in the stew too.

Makes 4 to 6 servings

A CARIBBEAN GOAT STEW FROM ARUBA

❧

ARUBA, AN ISLAND OFF VENEZUELA AND a former Dutch colony, along with Cura-çao and Bonaire form part of the Lesser Antilles of the Caribbean. The island has an interesting blend of Afro-Spanish-Dutch culture, and its Caribbean climate draws many tourists. Goats are to be found on the island and goat stew, naturally enough, is quite popular in home cooking. This recipe has an obvious Creole feel to it. Goat, because it is an older animal, can be quite tough and you may have to cook it as much as six hours, so be prepared. There's no problem with cooking the goat meat the day before, too. Serve with rice, black beans, and fried plantains.

━━━━━●━━━━━

2¼ pounds goat leg on the bone, trimmed
    of any large pieces of fat and cut into large
    chunks
2 medium-size onions, 1 quartered with its peel
    and 1 peeled and chopped
1 bay leaf
Salt to taste
½ cup vegetable oil
2 green bell peppers, seeded and chopped
2 celery stalks, chopped
2 medium-size, ripe tomatoes, peeled, seeded,
    and chopped
2 teaspoons curry powder
¼ teaspoon freshly grated nutmeg
4 large garlic cloves, finely chopped
2 tablespoons finely chopped fresh basil leaves

1. Put the goat, quartered onion, bay leaf, and a little salt in a stew pot and cover with water by several inches. Bring to a boil and continue to boil until tender, replenishing the water when necessary to keep the goat covered with water, 4 to 6 hours. When the goat is tender, it will not fall away from the bone on its own, but with a little tug of a fork it will. Remove the meat from the broth with a slotted spoon and set aside.

2. In a casserole, heat the vegetable oil over medium-high heat. Cook the chopped onion, goat, bell peppers, celery, tomatoes, curry, nutmeg, garlic, and basil until everything is sizzling. Reduce the heat to low and cook until the vegetables are soft, about 30 minutes. Serve immediately.

━━━━━●━━━━━

Makes 4 servings

"POOR FOLK'S" PEPPERED RABBIT STEW FROM ANDALUSIA

❧

IN ANDALUSIA, AS ELSEWHERE IN THE Mediterranean, rabbit and hare find their way into many recipes, especially stews. Rabbits are born naked and blind, while hare are born furred and open-eyed; that's the main difference between the two. Traditionally, the husband would come home with a rabbit, hare, or game bird from his hunt and into the pot it would go, freshly butchered, with whatever local ingredients were available. This recipe from the cuisine of the city of Córdoba is called *conejo en pobre*, "poor folk's rabbit." But the name of this dish must be purposely ironic because any "poor folk's" stew would hardly be flavored with expensive cinnamon, pepper, and olive oil. There are many such culinary ironies in the *cocina córdobesa*; the name refers to the simplicity of the ingredients, not their relative cost.

Interestingly, much farther north in Provence, there is a similiar recipe called *lapin à la pebrado*, "peppered rabbit," which is served with *la sausso au paure ome*, "poor man's sauce." In Andalusia this same sauce is called *pebre*; it is made of garlic, black pepper, parsley, and vinegar and is used with various meats.

One 4-pound rabbit, cut into serving pieces
¹/₄ cup extra virgin olive oil
2 tablespoons finely chopped fresh parsley leaves
3 garlic cloves, finely chopped
1 to 3 teaspoons freshly crushed black peppercorns, to your taste
2 cups boiling water
¹/₂ teaspoon ground cinnamon
Salt to taste
1 lemon, thinly sliced

---

1. Brush a cast-iron griddle or skillet and the rabbit pieces with 1 tablespoon of the olive oil. You must have the griddle very hot, so turn the heat to medium-high and wait until the film of oil is smoking and the griddle or skillet is very hot, about 20 minutes of preheating. Grill the rabbit until golden on both sides, 6 to 7 minutes total.

2. Transfer the rabbit to a large nonreactive casserole. Sprinkle with the remaining 3 tablespoons of olive oil, the parsley, garlic, and black pepper. Toss well, turn the heat to low, and simmer until flavorful, about 30 minutes. Pour in the boiling water, sprinkle with the cinnamon and salt, and cover with the lemon slices. Bring to a boil, reduce the heat to medium-low, and cook until the rabbit is tender and most of the liquid has evaporated, 1¹/₄ to 1³/₄ hours.

Makes 4 to 6 servings

RABBIT OR BUNNY?

Bunnies are pets and rabbits you eat. Anyway, that's what I think. I have never figured out why Americans don't eat rabbit. It tastes so much better than the tasteless, waterlogged, industrial chickens that we scarf down endlessly. My children, who have eaten rabbit all their lives, regularly ask why we aren't eating rabbit when I happen to make chicken. Most rabbit is farm-raised and sold frozen already cut up and rarely fresh. Always look or ask for fresh rabbit first; then, if you don't find it, look for it in the frozen food section of the supermarket.

BRAISED RABBIT AND MUSHROOMS IN WINE SAUCE FROM BRITTANY

THIS FRENCH COUNTRY STEW FROM Brittany is the type of dish favored by housewives because it is easy, tasty, and appreciated. In the Nantes region the stew would be made with a dry white wine such as Muscadet, while farther to the north cider would replace the wine. The stew simmers for about two and a half hours, until the rabbit is very tender and flavorful. At the end of the cooking time, the sauce will be a rich, "mushroomy" gravy that will go very well with roasted turnips and beets. Although olive oil is not a typical ingredient in Brittany, I like it here for the flavor. For authenticity, increase the butter by an equal amount.

One 2¹/₂-pound rabbit, cut into 6 pieces
Unbleached all-purpose flour for dredging
Salt and freshly ground black pepper to taste
3 tablespoons extra virgin olive oil
3 tablespoons unsalted butter
1 cup chopped shallots
1 pound portobello mushrooms, brushed clean, stems discarded, and sliced
1 teaspoon dried summer savory, thyme, or oregano
2 cups dry white or red wine
2 tablespoons finely chopped fresh parsley leaves (optional)

1. Dredge the rabbit in the flour, patting off any excess. Season with salt and pepper. In a large casserole, heat the olive oil with the butter over medium-high heat. When the butter stops sizzling, brown the rabbit pieces with the shallots, stirring and turning the rabbit, about 12 minutes. Add the mushrooms and cook for 2 minutes, turning them over to coat. Add the summer savory and the wine. Cover, reduce the heat to low, and cook for 1¹/₂ hours.

2. Remove the cover and cook until the rabbit is fork-tender, about 1 more hour. Serve with a sprinkle of parsley.

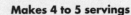

Makes 4 to 5 servings

BRAISED RABBIT
IN THE STYLE OF LICODIA EUBEA

THIS BRAISED RABBIT RECIPE, *CONIGLIO alla licodiana*, was collected many years ago in the village of Licodia Eubea, southeast of Caltigirone, Sicily, by the Sicilian food authority Pino Correnti. Licodia Eubea was a strategic location in the twelfth century. By the fifteenth century, a castle was built by the Santapau, a Catalan family, but it was destroyed in the earthquake of 1693.

Wild rabbits, hunted by local shepherds and farmers, are a popular food in this mountainous region, and this recipe is typical of the robustly flavored dishes the local people prepare. The preparation of the dish begins in the morning with a marinade.

———————⬤———————

One 3-pound rabbit, cut into serving pieces
6 cloves
1 cinnamon stick, broken into small bits in a
    mortar
1 cup robust red wine
2 tablespoons extra virgin olive oil
1 medium-size onion, thinly sliced and
    separated into rings
2 tablespoons tomato paste
3 garlic cloves, finely chopped
2 tablespoons finely chopped fresh mint leaves
2 tablespoons finely chopped fresh parsley leaves
Leaves from 2 sprigs fresh rosemary, finely
    chopped
Salt and freshly ground black pepper to taste

———————⬤———————

1. Place the rabbit pieces in a ceramic dish and sprinkle the cloves and cinnamon over them. Pour the wine over the rabbit, cover with plastic wrap, and let marinate in the refrigerator for 6 to 8 hours. Drain and save the marinade, then pat the rabbit dry with paper towels. Drying the rabbit is important in order for it to brown properly. Strain the marinade, reserve 1 cup, and discard the rest.

2. In a large casserole, heat the olive oil over medium-high heat. Brown the rabbit pieces on both sides with the onion, about 5 minutes. Add the reserved marinade, the tomato paste, garlic, mint, parsley, and rosemary, season with salt and pepper, and stir. Cook until blended,

4 to 5 minutes. Reduce the heat to low, cover, and simmer until the rabbit is fork-tender and the sauce syrupy, about 2 hours.

———————⬤———————

Makes 4 servings

BRAISED RABBIT WITH GREMOLADA

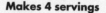

I N THIS NORTHERN ITALIAN RECIPE, A *gremolada* is turned into the sauce. *Gremolada* is a mixture that is usually stirred into the finished preparation of *ossobuco alla milanese* (page 66). Here I take that traditional condiment of lemon zest, parsley, anchovies, and garlic and partner it with a slowly cooked rabbit. This is really quite a nice dish, and not a dainty one, because you must pick up those pieces of rabbit with your fingers and enjoy yourself.

———————⬤———————

3 tablespoons unsalted butter
1 tablespoon lard
One 2³/4- to 3-pound rabbit, cut into 6 pieces
1 medium-size white onion, chopped
1¹/4 cups dry white wine
1¹/4 pounds ripe tomatoes, peeled, seeded, and
    chopped
1 cup Beef Broth (page 3)
2 large garlic cloves, finely chopped
Salt and freshly ground black pepper to taste

FOR THE *GREMOLADA*:

Grated zest of ½ lemon
2 salted anchovy fillets, rinsed and chopped
¼ cup finely chopped fresh parsley leaves
1 garlic clove, finely chopped

1. In a large earthenware casserole set on a heat diffuser, melt the butter and lard together over medium-high heat. When the butter stops sizzling, brown the rabbit pieces, about 5 minutes per side. Add the onion and cook, stirring, until translucent, about 5 minutes. (If you are not cooking with earthenware and a diffuser, cook over medium heat and check for doneness sooner.) Add the wine and let it evaporate by three-quarters, 5 to 8 minutes. Add the tomatoes, beef broth, and garlic. Bring to a boil, then reduce the heat to very low, and season with salt and pepper. Cook until the rabbit is very tender, about 3 hours.

2. To make the *gremolada*, combine the lemon zest, anchovies, parsley, and garlic in a small bowl. Stir into the braised rabbit and serve immediately.

Makes 4 servings

RABBIT AND LEMON RAGOUT FROM GREECE

IN THIS PREPARATION, KNOWN AS *KOUNELI me lemoni*, the preparation of the rabbit begins in the morning so it can marinate all day. Then, in the evening, it is braised in lemon juice and over the course of two slow hours of cooking becomes a delectable golden brown. There will be very little liquid left in the skillet or casserole, and what is left is a gravy that you can spoon over the rabbit pieces and serve with *manestra* (the Greek word for what is more commonly known by the Italian, "orzo") browned in butter. This preparation is more typically served as a main course, but sometimes it is served as a *meze* in Greek tavernas.

One 3-pound rabbit, cut into 6 pieces
2 cups red wine vinegar
3 cups water
1 garlic clove, halved lengthwise
Salt and freshly ground black pepper to taste
1 tablespoon dried oregano
3 tablespoons unsalted butter
3 tablespoons extra virgin olive oil
Juice from 2 lemons

1. In the morning, arrange the rabbit pieces in a ceramic bowl or casserole. Mix the vinegar with 1 cup of the water and pour over the rabbit to cover. Marinate, covered with plastic wrap, in the refrigerator for 8 to 10 hours.

2. Drain, discarding the marinade, wash well, and pat dry with paper towels. It is important to dry the rabbit, otherwise it will not brown properly. Rub the rabbit pieces with the garlic halves, then sprinkle with salt, pepper, and oregano. In a casserole or skillet, melt the butter with the olive oil over medium-high heat. When the butter stops sizzling, brown the rabbit well on all sides, 8 to 10 minutes. Pour in the lemon juice a little at a time, pouring in more as it evaporates, until none is left. Add the remaining 1 cup of water and reduce the heat to low. Cover and cook until the meat is tender, moistening with more water to keep it from drying out (it shouldn't need any though), about 2 hours. There should be very little liquid left except the butter and olive oil at the end of the cooking time. Serve immediately.

⎯⎯⎯ ● ⎯⎯⎯

Makes 4 to 6 servings

BRUNSWICK STEW

⎯ 🌿 ⎯

BRUNSWICK STEW WAS ORIGINALLY A squirrel stew claimed by three groups of Americans: by the citizens of Brunswick County, Virginia, by those in a county of the same name in North Carolina, and by the people of Brunswick, Georgia. Virginians of Brunswick County make the strongest claim for having invented Brunswick stew. They say it was officially served first at the home of Dr. Creed Haskins on the banks of the Nottoway River in the Old Dominion at a Democratic rally in 1828 for Andrew Jackson.

VENISON STEW

⎯⎯ ● ⎯⎯

A good venison stew is hard to come by, because good venison is hard to come by. If a hunter friend has bagged a deer and invited you to cook it, this is likely how he would prefer it: Have the venison shoulder and leg cut up into chunks, and then, if you like, marinate them in red wine for 24 hours. Drain the meat and pat it dry, then sear it in bacon fat. Stew it for a long time with potatoes and carrots, and a variety of spices and herbs, such as allspice and oregano and perhaps some other flavorings like Worcestershire sauce, garlic, celery, onions, or bay leaves. This method is typical of a stew from Wisconsin's north woods. Some cooks also like to add fruit to the stew, in the form of prunes, juniper berries, raspberry preserves, or lingonberries.

Dr. Haskins was a member of the Virginia legislature and wanted the gathering of his friends to be not only a political but also a social event. He asked his longtime cook, Jimmy Matthews, who had made this stew during their hunting trips, to whip up a giant batch of it, an original concoction of squirrel meat, onions, stale bread, and seasonings.

This story may be myth or legend. I suspect the stew goes back further, as a dish concocted by early American frontiersmen in the eighteenth century, and was probably originally made with only squirrel and onions. Perhaps it is much older and actually derives from Native American cooking. Today, Brunswick stew is more often than not made with chicken or rabbit, because an American way of life, which saw people catching and dressing their own squirrel up until the 1940s, at least in rural areas, has now disappeared. The whole point to the stew is to get the delicious game taste that one gets from squirrel. Modern farm-raised chicken and rabbit just don't cut it; they are too bland. My recipe doesn't have potatoes, but some do. Other recipes move even further away from the original concept and start mixing meats, such as the recipe provided in *The Time-Life American Regional Cookbook*.

4 slices thickly cut bacon
2 plump squirrels (about 3 pounds total),
    dressed and disjointed, or one 3-pound rabbit,
    disjointed, or one 3-pound broiler chicken, or
    1¹/₂ pounds rabbit and 1¹/₂ pounds chicken
Unbleached all-purpose flour for dredging
Salt and freshly ground black pepper to taste
3 medium-size onions, thinly sliced
1¹/₂ cups boiling water
3 ripe tomatoes (about 1¹/₄ pounds), peeled and
    sliced
2 red bell peppers, seeded and cut into thin strips
1 teaspoon dried thyme
2 cups fresh or frozen lima beans
3 ears of corn, husked and kernels scraped off
    (about 2 cups corn kernels)
¹/₂ pound fresh okra, bottoms trimmed
¹/₂ teaspoon cayenne pepper
1 tablespoon finely chopped fresh parsley leaves
1 tablespoon Worcestershire sauce

1. In a cast-iron casserole or stew pot or Dutch oven, render the fat from the bacon over medium heat until the bacon is crispy and you have 6 to 8 tablespoons of bacon fat in the pot, about 25 minutes.

2. Cut the meat into 8 portions. Dredge the pieces in the flour, salt, and pepper, tapping off any excess. Brown the meat with the onions until the onions are soft, the meat has turned color, and the bottom of the pot is crusty with residue, about 10 minutes. Add the boiling water and deglaze the pot, using a wooden spoon to scrape up the crusty parts. Then add the tomatoes, bell peppers, and thyme, and reduce the heat to low. Cover and simmer for 1 hour, stirring every once in a while.

3. Add the lima beans, corn, okra, cayenne, parsley, and Worcestershire, and mix well. Let simmer, covered, until the meat and vegetables are tender, about 1¹/₂ hours. The consistency should be that of a rich soup, but sometimes the broth is thickened slightly with roux or some fine bread crumbs.

Makes 6 servings

VENEZUELAN-STYLE RABBIT AND COCONUT STEW

THIS RECIPE, CALLED *CONEJO EN COCO*, is a Venezuelan classic and comes from a native-born woman, Teresa Gallardo. She uses chile pepper, which I leave out of this recipe. The preparation of the stew involves pureeing the coconut meat in a blender until smooth, then blending tomatoes, onion, and garlic until they too are smooth. The two are combined and cooked a bit before the rabbit is stewed in this sauce. Contrary to the sound of the dish, it actually is not too "coconutty." When buying a coconut, shake it to make sure it's full of milk. But if it is not, follow the instructions on page 200. The stew is delectable with steamed rice, some fried plantains, and lightly dressed salad greens.

1 coconut
6 tablespoons (³/4 stick) *unsalted butter*
1 pound ripe tomatoes, *peeled, seeded, and chopped*
6 garlic cloves, *peeled*
1 small onion, *chopped*
1 teaspoon salt
¹/2 teaspoon freshly ground white pepper
One 3-pound rabbit, *cut into 8 pieces*

1. Preheat the oven to 400°F. Find the "eye" of the coconut, the opposite end from the tapered one. Place a screwdriver over it and hammer it through to make a hole. Drain the milk from the coconut and set aside. You should have about ¹/2 cup, or a little less. Place the coconut in a roasting pan and bake for 15 minutes. Remove and tap the shell with a hammer. It should break easily and the flesh should separate from the shell. Scrape or peel off the brown skin with a vegetable peeler. Cut the coconut flesh into 1-inch pieces and place in a blender with the coconut milk and as much water as necessary to get the blender blade to twirl. Blend at high speed for 1 minute. Transfer the coconut to a food mill.

2. In an enameled cast-iron casserole, melt the butter over high heat. While it melts, pass the coconut through the food mill into the casserole. Bring the coconut puree to a boil over high heat. Reduce the heat to medium and simmer, uncovered, until a bit denser, 10 to 15 minutes. Put the tomatoes, garlic, and onion in the blender and blend for 1 minute. Stir into the coconut sauce, season with salt and pepper, and simmer over low heat for 15 minutes, stirring occasionally.

3. Add the rabbit pieces to the casserole and stew over low heat until the rabbit is tender, basting the rabbit with the sauce, about 2 hours. Serve from the casserole.

Makes 4 servings

A BEAR STEW

It's been years since I've heard of anyone cooking bear stew. I'm sure some hunters still do it, but I'm not a hunter. They tell me, though, that bear meat needs a long marination in wine or vinegar. In any case, here is a recipe that you can't actually make, unless you live in the region of Canada that this comes from, but it looks mighty intriguing. It's called Assiniboin bear stew.

The Assiniboin are North American Plains people who speak a Sioux-related language. Sometime before the seventeenth century, they split from the Yanktonai Dakota and lived in the area west of Lake Winnipeg, along the Assiniboin and Saskatchewan rivers in Canada. Their name is derived from the Ojibwa (Chippewa) language and means "One Who Cooks with Stones"; they are known as Stonies in Canada. The Assiniboin were great buffalo hunters known for trading pemmican (preserved buffalo meat) for firearms and other European goods brought in by traders on Hudson Bay and along the upper Missouri.

This recipe comes from an Inuit cookbook published in 1952, and as the unknown author wrote, "hope you are hungry." The recipe calls for several ingredients that may be unfamiliar. Coltsfoot salt could be *Tussilago farfara*, a member of the daisy family. Arrowhead tubers (*Sagittaria sagittifolia*), a perennial water or marsh plant whose starchy tuberous roots were an important part of the American Indian diet, also go into the stew. Indian women would find these plants underwater with their toes, pick them, and throw them in the canoe. The tubers were cooked in boiling water in kettles set over hot stones or roasted on sticks stuck into the ground near a fire.

The stew recipe calls for five pounds of bear meat to be washed and cut into 2-inch cubes. An open fire is built and the bear meat is skewered on sapling sticks and seared before the fire. Then 3 cups of maple or birch sap is poured into a pouch made from the bear skin, along with the seared bear meat, some water, "2 thumbnails of coltsfoot salt," 4 wild onions, 5 medium-size dandelion roots, 25 arrowhead tubers, 3 wild leeks, and some fresh mint. The pouch is dropped on hot stones and simmers for a long time, the stones constantly exchanged for other hot stones to keep the stew cooking.

STEWS WITH
FISH AND SHELLFISH

In this chapter, you will find that fish stews are favorites around the world, and they actually don't require long cooking. Their flavors can be as unusually exciting as Baja Seafood Stew (page 290), with its interesting blend of clams, crabs, and shrimp in a tomato broth flavored with garlic, wine, orange juice, coriander, and basil leaves, or as familiar and simple as a Maine Lobster Stew (page 274). There is also the classic and authentic Bouillabaisse (page 227) as it is made in Golf-Juan or Marseilles for the skilled home cook and what I call An Easier Bouillabaisse (page 231), which requires much less work. You'll find a wonderful recipe for that famous stew of South Carolina's Low Country, Pine Bark Stew (page 287) with catfish, bacon, tomatoes, and potatoes, as well as a gaggle of Italy's familiar *zuppe di pesce*. I think you will find a quite memorable stew in "Delicious" Swordfish Stew (page 239), which comes from Sicily and is a rich tomato and olive oil ragout. There are fish stews I think you probably have never heard of and certainly have never tasted, such as Monkfish Stew with "Burnt Garlic" and Clams (page 225), made in an earthenware casserole and the sauce bound by a preparation called a *picada*, a kind of pesto made of soaked bread seasoned with "burnt garlic" and a little saffron and parsley. The garlic is fried in olive oil until brown and then pounded in a mortar with fried parsley and fried bread. If that doesn't sound exotic enough, you'll swoon over Ragout of Saffron-Flavored Fish Dumplings from Morocco (page 270), which are saffron-flavored balls of mashed fish poached in an aromatic tomato ragout, seasoned with abundant onions and spices. You will also find in this chapter the one true clam chowder, a chowder to sing a hymn for (page 280).

FISH BROTH

THIS IS THE FISH BROTH THAT I USE FOR stews and soups and even for cooking certain risottos. Ask your fishmonger for some fish carcasses. He should give them to you for free, although some charge for it. Try to use a mix of fish—two or three kinds.

---

6 pounds mixed fish carcasses, any kind,
   including at least 1 or 2 fish heads
3 quarts cold water
2 cups dry white wine
2 carrots, cut into chunks
2 celery stalks, sliced
1 onion, quartered
10 black peppercorns
1 bouquet garni, consisting of 10 sprigs each
   fresh parsley and thyme, 6 sprigs fresh
   marjoram, and 1 sprig fresh sage, tied
   together in cheesecloth

Place all the ingredients in a stockpot. Bring to a boil, then reduce the heat to low and let simmer for 4 hours, skimming the foam that forms on the surface. Pour the broth through a strainer (a chinois, or conical strainer, would be ideal). Strain again through a cheesecloth-lined fine-mesh strainer. The broth will keep in the refrigerator up to 1 week and in the freezer for up to 6 months.

Makes 2 quarts

ZARZUELA

THE CATALAN SEAFOOD STEW CALLED *sarsuela de peix i mariscs* (in Catalan) or simply *zarsuela* (in Spanish) is said to have originated in the Catalonian city of Tarragona. The fish used depends on availability and the resources of the cook.

The word *zarsa* or *zarza*, from where the Spanish and Catalan words derive, originally referred to a bramble bush commonly found in central Spain, and which gave its name to the seventeenth-century hunting lodge outside Madrid frequented by the Spanish king Philip IV (1605–65) as *La Zarzuela*. This word might derive from the Arabic word *zariba*, which refers to a thorn-bush ringed enclosure of pasturelands in the Sudan. Or maybe it is a pre-Romanic word of unknown origin. The word *zarzuela* is also a musical term referring to satirical and witty Spanish light operettas that began in the fifteenth century and were immensely popular in the nineteenth century; they dealt with simple folk-oriented themes. Philip IV was fond of these light operettas, and they were christened *zarzuela* after being performed at his lodge. The connection between the operetta and the seafood dish is tenuous, but it is thought to be a reflection of a medley, just as an opera is a mixture of song, dance, and theater. By adding expensive ingredients like lobster, the dish becomes something heavier, like a full-fledged opera, in the words of Ignasi Domènech, a Catalan chef quoted by Colman Andrews, author of *Catalan Cuisine.*

In this preparation, a Catalonian cooking technique called a *picada* is used. A *picada* is an aromatic mixture of finely chopped ingredients that enhances and binds sauces and usually, but not necessarily, contains nuts. You will also make a *sofregit* of onion, garlic, and parsley. This culinary concept also exists in Italian cuisine where it is called *soffritto*, finely chopped vegetables that are sauteed in oil to become the foundation for a sauce or gravy.

Zarzuela is a complex affair, which includes flambéing. I would make it for a special occasion and for people who love seafood.

———————●———————

FOR THE *PICADA*:
¼ teaspoon saffron threads
½ teaspoon salt
¼ cup water
3 large garlic cloves, finely chopped
1 tablespoon finely chopped fresh parsley leaves
¼ cup blanched whole almonds, toasted in a preheated 350°F oven until golden, then ground
1 tablespoon extra virgin olive oil

FOR THE *ZARZUELA* (INCLUDES THE *SOFREGIT*):
16 mussels (about 1¼ pounds), scrubbed clean and debearded
1½ cups plus 2 tablespoons extra virgin olive oil
16 littleneck clams (about 1½ pounds), soaked in cold water to cover with 1 teaspoon baking soda for 1 hour and drained
1 medium-size onion, chopped
3 large garlic cloves, finely chopped
1 tablespoon finely chopped fresh parsley leaves
2 large, ripe tomatoes (about 1 pound total), peeled, seeded, and chopped
*1 teaspoon hot Spanish paprika (**pimentón**)*
Unbleached all-purpose flour for dredging

Salt and freshly ground black pepper to taste
1 pound whiting, hake, halibut, or cod fillets, cut into 4-ounce pieces
1 pound bass, monkfish, or grouper fillets, cut into 4-ounce pieces
1 pound John Dory, mahimahi, thickly cut firm red snapper, redfish, Pacific sculpin, or catfish fillets, cut into 4-ounce pieces
½ pound skinned and boned eel (or substitute yellowtail, bluefish, or mako shark steaks), cut into 2 pieces
½ pound squid, cleaned if necessary (see page 237) and body cut into rings with the tentacles
16 fresh jumbo shrimp (about ½ pound) with their heads, bodies shelled and shells added to the fish broth (listed below)
3 tablespoons Cognac
½ cup dry white wine
3 cups Fish Broth (page 221)
One 1¾-pound live lobster, claws cracked and separated, split in half lengthwise, each half of the tail cut into 3, and arms cracked
1 bay leaf

8 slices Fried Bread (page 224)

———————●———————

1. Make the *picada*. In a mortar, pound the saffron with the salt until the saffron is broken up. Stir in the water and transfer to a small bowl. Pound the garlic cloves, parsley, and almonds together in a mortar with a pestle until almost mushy. Incorporate the saffron and water and the olive oil and set aside.

2. To begin the *zarzuela*, place the mussels in a pot with 2 tablespoons of the olive oil, cover, and turn the heat to medium-high. Cook until

LIVE LOBSTERS

———————●———————

The lobsters most Americans are familiar with are the large-clawed ones called *Homarus americanus*. In the Mediterranean, and in Mexico, Florida, up the California coast, and in other parts of the world, the spiny lobster is common. These lobsters, *Palinurus vulgaris*, do not have claws.

You will always want to use live lobsters in your cooking. Lobsters are held alive in holding tanks of fresh oxygenated water before being bought by the consumer. When buying lobsters, make sure they come out of the water alive and kicking. If they look lethargic, pass them by.

Lobsters are covered with a hard shell, or exo-skeleton, and almost everything inside is edible, except for the soft, spongy gills and lung, and the stomach, all of which are located in the so-called head, which actually includes the tiny head as well as the larger body midsection of the lobster. The intestinal tract is not edible either, but all the other meat is. To get at the meat requires breaking and cracking through the hard shell. The pale green mushy stuff is the tomalley, or liver, and the harder red-orange stuff, called the coral, are the eggs. Both parts are not only edible, but considered by connoisseurs to be delicacies and are quite prized.

A number of recipes call for killing the live lobster and breaking it apart into smaller pieces to be cooked. To do this, hold the live lobster by its body with the belly side facing down. Hold firmly and be careful of any sharp, spiny protrusions from the shell. Dig the blade of a heavy 10-inch or larger chef's knife or cleaver into the crack between the two shell plates of the lobster about 1 inch or so behind the head. This will immediately kill the lobster, although muscle spasms will continue. Dig deep as you move the blade downward, splitting the lobster in half. Cut up the lobster and crack its various parts open as described by the recipe.

---

they open, 3 to 5 minutes. Remove the mussels, discarding any that remain very tightly shut. Now, in the same pot, steam the clams, 5 to 10 minutes in all, discarding any that remain tightly shut. Reserve the mussel and clam liquid remaining in the pot, and set the clams aside with the mussels in the refrigerator until needed.

3. Make the *sofregit* in a large, wide, earthen-ware casserole set on a heat diffuser. Heat ½ cup of the olive oil over medium-high heat.

Then cook the onion until translucent, stir-ring, about 5 minutes. (If you are not cooking with earthenware and a diffuser, cook over medium heat and check for doneness sooner.) Add the garlic and parsley, stirring for 1 minute. Add the tomatoes and paprika, reduce the heat to medium, and cook for 5 minutes. Set aside.

4. Season the flour with salt and pepper. In a large skillet, heat the remaining 1 cup of olive oil over medium-high heat. Dredge all the fish, eel, squid, and shrimp in the seasoned flour, tapping off any excess flour. Fry in batches until they turn color, but are not cooked through, about 2 minutes for the fish and squid and about 1 minute for the shrimp.

5. Transfer the seafood to a warm ceramic baking dish or platter, pour the Cognac over the seafood, and flambé (see page 184). Once the flames are extinguished, the fish can be refrigerated until needed.

6. Strain the fish broth, discarding the shrimp shells. Add to the *sofregit* in the earthenware casserole, along with the wine and the mussel and clam liquid. Bring to a boil over very high heat. Add the lobster and bay leaf and season with salt and pepper. Cook until the meat of the lobster is firm, 6 to 7 minutes. Add some more fish broth, if necessary, so the sauce is liquid but not soupy. Then bring the broth to a furious boil and add the squid immediately. Cook for 2 minutes. Add the remaining fish and cook until firm but not breaking apart, 3 to 5 minutes. Add the clams and mussels and cook for 1 minute to heat them. Carefully fold the sauce over the fish and shellfish so you don't break them apart, or try shaking the casserole.

7. Add the *picada* to the casserole, folding it into the sauce, and continue to cook until it is well blended, 3 to 5 minutes. Serve with the fried bread.

Makes 8 servings

FRIED BREAD

Crostini di pane is a basic preparation called for in many of the fish stews in this book. When pressed for time, I make it with toasted bread (see variation below).

*4 garlic cloves, 3 crushed and 1 halved
   lengthwise*
1 cup extra virgin olive oil
*1 round loaf Tuscan or Italian country bread
   (about 12 inches in diameter), quartered and
   sliced, or 1 loaf French bread, sliced*

1. Leave the crushed garlic cloves in the olive oil for 1 hour.

2. Brush the bread slices with the olive oil and fry on a griddle over medium heat until golden brown on both sides; then rub with the cut sides of the remaining garlic clove.

Grilled Bread: Preheat a gas grill for 20 minutes on high or prepare a hot charcoal fire. Brush each piece of bread with the garlic-oil mixture and place on the grill, oiled side down. Brush the top with more oil and grill until the bread is lightly brown, has developed sear marks, or its edges begin to burn. Remove the bread.

Toasted Bread: Toast each slice until golden, then rub both sides with the cut side of half a garlic clove.

Makes about 20 or more slices; 8 to 10 servings

MONKFISH STEW WITH "BURNT GARLIC" AND CLAMS

THIS STEW, CALLED *RAP ALL CREMAT AMB cloïsses* in Catalan, must be made in an earthenware *cazuela*, a flat-bottomed, round casserole with three-inch-high sides. The stew is very aromatic and flavorful, and the monkfish resembles the texture of lobster even more than usual. The binding element in this preparation is called a *picada*, and in this recipe it is a pesto made of *panada* (a bread-and-water paste), seasoned with "burnt garlic" and a little saffron and parsley. The garlic is fried in olive oil until brown, then pounded in a mortar with fried parsley and fried bread. This becomes the foundation to the ragout. The stew is best served in a pasta bowl with some rice cooked in a court bouillon and sautéed zucchini.

FOR THE *PICADA*:

³/₄ cup extra virgin olive oil
5 garlic cloves, thinly sliced
2 leafy sprigs fresh parsley, stems removed
¹/₂ pound French bread, sliced and crust removed
¹/₂ cup dry white wine
Pinch of saffron threads
1¹/₂ teaspoons salt
1 teaspoon freshly ground black pepper

FOR THE STEW:

2 medium-size, ripe tomatoes, cut in half, seeds squeezed out, and grated against the largest holes of a grater down to the peel

1 quart Fish Broth (page 221)
2 pounds monkfish fillet, cut into 2-inch chunks
3 garlic cloves, finely chopped
30 littleneck clams (about 3 pounds), soaked in water and 1 teaspoon baking soda for 1 hour and drained
1 teaspoon paprika

1. To make the *picada*, in an earthenware casserole set on a diffuser, heat the olive oil over high heat, then cook the sliced garlic until just light brown, stirring constantly, 3 to 4 minutes. (If you are not cooking with earthenware and a diffuser, cook over medium heat.) Add the parsley and cook for 15 seconds, then with a slotted spoon, transfer the parsley and garlic to a mortar.

2. In the same oil you fried the garlic, fry the slices of bread until golden, turning once, about 2 minutes. Transfer the bread to a bowl, squeeze out the excess oil, and soak the bread in the wine. Turn the heat under the casserole to low. Squeeze the wine out of the bread and put the bread in the mortar. Add the saffron, salt, and black pepper. Pound this mixture with a pestle until mushy, like a pesto. Moisten with a tablespoon or so of water. This is the *picada*.

3. To make the stew, turn the heat to high again under the casserole, and once the oil remaining in the casserole is hot, add the tomatoes and the *picada*. Be careful, because the oil will splatter at first. Stir and cook the tomatoes for a few minutes. Add the fish broth and bring it to a boil. Add the monkfish, chopped garlic, clams, and paprika. Correct the seasonings. Cook until the clams are open and the fish is cooked through and firm when poked, about 12 minutes. Turn the heat off and serve. If there are any clams that remain firmly shut, discard them.

———————◦———————

Makes 6 servings

FISH FOR FISH STEWS

———◦———

Although I call for particular fish in the fish stew recipes, you are best advised to get what's local and fresh. The most important thing to remember is to choose firm-fleshed fish that will hold up well to the boiling liquid. Ask the fishmonger for such fish if he or she doesn't have what I'm recommending. Flaky fleshed fish, such as certain kinds of sole, flounder, and fluke, don't do well in fish stews; they will disintegrate.

FISH STEW FROM HUELVA IN ANDALUSIA

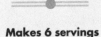

THIS FISH STEW, *CALDERADA DE PESCADO*, from La Palma del Condado, in the Huelva province of the Spanish region of Andalusia, is typical among the mariners operating out of a variety of small ports. It's a famous dish in those parts (it's made in Portugal too) and is somewhat unusual in that it contains lupine beans, which are normally eaten in the Mediterranean as a *meze*, tapas, or antipasto, and

hardly ever in a cooked dish. The fish stew simmers slowly even after the fish go in, a method quite different from many French fish stews, where you bring the broth to a boil before the fish are cooked. The lupine beans can come directly from a jar, but be sure to rinse them off—or, better yet, soak them in cold water to cover overnight if you have the time.

———————◦———————

1/2 pound lupine beans, rinsed
11/2 pounds boiling potatoes, peeled and cubed
1 large green bell pepper, seeded and chopped
1/2 pound ripe tomatoes, cut in half, seeds squeezed out, and grated against the largest holes of a grater down to the peel
1 small onion, chopped
2 large garlic cloves, finely chopped
1 bay leaf
1 cup dry white wine
1 cup water
2 teaspoons paprika
1/8 teaspoon freshly grated nutmeg
1 teaspoon salt
1/2 teaspoon freshly ground black pepper
1/2 cup extra virgin olive oil
1/2 pound red snapper fillets
1/2 pound hake, cod, pollack, haddock, or other mild-flavored firm white fish fillets
1/2 pound sea bass fillets
3 tablespoons unbleached all-purpose flour

———————◦———————

1. Put the lupine beans, potatoes, bell pepper, tomatoes, onion, garlic, bay leaf, wine, water, paprika, nutmeg, salt, and pepper in an earthenware casserole set on a heat diffuser. Pour the olive oil over everything. Turn the heat to high, and once tiny bubbles start to appear on the surface, in about 20 minutes, reduce the heat to low. Cover and simmer until the potatoes are three-quarters done, when they might break apart if cut with a fork, about 30 minutes.

2. Sprinkle the fish with the flour and arrange on top of the vegetables, pushing them down into the broth. Season the fish with a little salt and pepper, cover, and cook until the snapper fillet flakes with a tug of the fork, about 30 minutes. Do not let the broth come to a rapid boil; it should just bubble ever so slightly. Serve immediately.

Makes 4 servings

BOUILLABAISSE

THE MAXIM ONE OFTEN HEARS ABOUT bouillabaisse, the most famous fish stew of the Mediterranean, is that it cannot be made outside of its home on the French Riviera. The reason this is claimed is because of the special Mediterranean fish that go into the broth, fish such as scorpionfish (*rascasse* in French) or red gurnard (*grondin* in French). But I don't believe that the most distinguishing characteristic of a bouillabaisse is the fish, because all fish stews have fish. Rather, the uniqueness of the recipe comes from the flavoring, derived from saffron, fennel seeds, and orange zest. It is also often said that bouillabaisse is a fisherman's stew. This can't be right either because fish is very expensive in the Mediterranean, and the fisherman, whose life is and was economically precarious, would sell his best catch to the restaurants rather than keep it for himself. This was true five hundred years ago and it's true today; it's true in New England and it's true in France. As a result, I think bouillabaisse is probably a restaurant creation. It certainly has the hallmarks of restaurant cooking: it's sophisticated, expensive, and not particularly simple.

This recipe is one that I have patiently devised over the years to capture the taste of a true bouillabaisse as you would have it in Marseilles or Golfe-Juan. In fact, the best bouillabaisses I've had were at the Tètou restaurant in Golfe-Juan and at the Miramar in Marseilles, both making a wonderful bouillabaisse perfumed with leeks, fennel, and saffron and rich with fish like *rascasse*. There are tricks to making a good fish stew, and they include a variety of live or very fresh fish, an excellent extra virgin olive oil, saffron, and furiously boiling water (the most critical step). The reason this recipe is written in such an involved way is so that you can get it right.

My recipe calls for about 15 pounds of whole fish, half of which will be heads, tails, and carcasses. Traditionally bouillabaisse is eaten as two courses. First the broth is poured in bowls with some *sauce rouille* spread on *croûtes*. Afterwards, the fish platter is served, often with thinly sliced buttered potatoes.

½ teaspoon plus a pinch of saffron threads

¼ cup hot water

1¼ cups tepid white wine, such as Muscadet, Sancerre, or Cassis (the wine, not the blackberry liqueur)

8 pounds white-fleshed fish from 4 of the following fishes: redfish (ocean perch), red snapper, blue-mouth, rockfish, sea robin (gurnard), monkfish, cod, porgy (scup), grouper, halibut, haddock, dab, turbot, wreckfish, ocean pout (ling), cusk, wolffish (ocean catfish), tautog (blackfish), tilefish, sculpin

4 to 5 pounds oily, dark-fleshed fish from 2 of the following fishes: bluefish, moray eel, conger eel, mackerel, shark, dogfish, striped bass, sea bass, kingfish, Spanish mackerel, mahimahi (dolphinfish), yellowtail

5 tablespoons unsalted butter

2 medium-size onions, thinly sliced and separated into rings

2 quarts cold water

2 bouquets garnis, each consisting of 10 black peppercorns, 6 sprigs fresh thyme, 4 sprigs fresh parsley, and 1 bay leaf, tied in cheesecloth

1½ cups extra virgin olive oil

6 to 8 large garlic cloves, to your taste, finely chopped

2 large onions, finely chopped

3 leeks (white and light green parts only), split in half lengthwise, washed well, and thinly sliced

3 celery stalks, finely chopped

2 pounds ripe plum tomatoes, peeled, seeded, and chopped

1 long, thin strip orange zest

1 tablespoon fennel seeds

Salt and freshly ground black pepper to taste

2 tablespoons tomato paste

2 tablespoons anise liqueur, such as Pernod or ouzo

½ cup finely chopped fresh parsley leaves

Sauce Rouille (page 230)

Croûtes (page 230)

1. Crumble a pinch of the saffron threads, and steep in the hot water until needed. Steep the remaining ½ teaspoon of saffron in ¼ cup of the wine until needed.

2. Gut, scale, and clean the fish. If the fishmonger cleans and fillets your fish, have him save the heads, tails, and carcasses. Cut the fish into 4 x 2½-inch pieces.

3. Prepare the fish broth. Rinse the fish heads, tails, and carcasses in cold water. Break the carcasses into pieces. In a large stockpot, melt the butter over medium heat. When the butter stops sizzling, cook the sliced onions until soft, but not brown, stirring occasionally, about 6 minutes. Add the fish heads and bones and cover with the cold water. Add 1 of the bouquets garnis and the remaining 1 cup of wine. Bring to a boil, skimming the surface of any foam occasionally. Reduce the heat to low, partially cover, and simmer for 2 hours. Strain the fish broth through a strainer (a chinois, or conical strainer, would be ideal) and set aside to cool. Discard all the fish heads and carcasses. You will have 2½ quarts of fish broth when finished. Clean the stockpot because you will need it in step 5.

4. After you get the fish broth going, make a marinade for the fish with ¼ cup of the olive oil, half of the chopped garlic, and the saffron threads steeped in hot water. Marinate the fish pieces in a large ceramic or glass pan for 2 hours in the refrigerator. Keep the white fish and oily fish separate while they marinate.

5. In the large stockpot, heat the remaining 1¼ cups olive oil over medium heat. Then cook the chopped onions, leeks, and celery until soft, stirring often, about 15 minutes. Add the tomatoes, the remaining half of the garlic, the remaining bouquet garni, the orange zest, and fennel seeds. Stir in the reserved fish broth and the saffron steeped in wine and season with salt and pepper. Bring to a boil, then reduce the heat to medium-low and simmer for 40 minutes. The broth can be left like this, covered, for many hours, over very low heat, using a heat diffuser if necessary.

6. When you are ready to prepare the final stages of the bouillabaisse, bring the broth back to a furious boil. It should be boiling like mad. Keep the broth boiling furiously until the oil emulsifies. Add the oily fish and boil, uncovered, over very high heat for 8 minutes. Shake the pot to prevent the fish from sticking. Now put in the firm-fleshed white fish and boil hard for another 6 minutes. Add some boiling water if necessary to cover the fish. Shake the pot occasionally. If at any time the fish look as if they are going to break up, remove them immediately. Mix the tomato paste and anise liqueur together.

7. Carefully remove the fish from the broth with a slotted spoon and metal spatula or skimmer and transfer to a large bowl or deep serving platter. Arrange the fish on the platter more or less in the order in which you put them into the pot. Keep them warm by covering with a sheet of aluminum foil.

8. Strain the broth through a fine-mesh strainer into a soup tureen or large bowl, discarding what doesn't go through. Whisk in the tomato paste-and-anise mixture. Sprinkle the platter and soup tureen with the parsley and serve with the *croûtes* and *sauce rouille* on separate plates.

Variation: Some cooks, especially in restaurants, will add a cut-up live lobster when the oily fish go in.

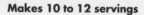

Makes 10 to 12 servings

SAUCE ROUILLE

Sauce rouille is the traditional saffron- and garlic-flavored mayonnaise accompaniment to bouillabaisse, containing abundant chile and garlic. Some cooks add tomato paste for coloring only, but I don't find this necessary because the saffron and cayenne contribute enough color.

———•———

1¹/₂ cups diced French bread, crusts removed
¹/₂ cup Fish Broth (page 221, or reserve some
  from the making of bouillabaisse, page 227)
3 to 5 garlic cloves, to your taste, pounded in a
  mortar with 1 teaspoon salt until mushy
¹/₂ teaspoon ground red chile
Pinch of saffron threads, crumbled
1 large egg yolk
Freshly ground black pepper to taste
1 cup extra virgin olive oil

———•———

1. Soak the diced bread in the fish broth in a medium-size bowl. Squeeze out the broth.

2. Place the bread, mashed garlic, red chile, saffron, egg yolk, and black pepper in a food processor and blend for 30 seconds. Pour the olive oil through the feed tube in a slow, thin, steady stream while the machine is running. If the rouille is separating, add 2 to 3 tablespoons of the fish broth and whisk until smooth and emulsified. Refrigerate for 1 hour before serving. Store whatever you don't use in the refrigerator for up to 1 week.

———•———

Makes 1¹/₄ cups

CROÛTES

Croûtes are the toasted pieces of bread used for bouillabaisse. Some people like to spread *sauce rouille* on the *croûtes* and then let them float in the bouillabaisse.

———•———

5 tablespoons unsalted butter
¹/₄ cup olive oil
1 clove garlic pounded in a mortar with
  ¹/₄ teaspoon salt
40 to 50 slices French bread (about 1 loaf)

———•———

1. In a large skillet, melt the butter with the olive oil over medium heat. Add the pounded garlic and cook until it begins to turn light brown. Remove and discard the garlic.

2. Lightly brush both sides of each bread slice with the melted butter and oil and set aside. When all the slices are brushed, place them back in the skillet and cook until very light brown on both sides. Set aside until needed.

———•———

Makes 10 servings of *croûtes*

Note: For a quicker method, see Toasted Bread, a variation of Fried Bread (page 224).

AN EASIER BOUILLABAISSE

THERE IS A GOOD DEAL OF MYSTERY AND excitement surrounding an authentic bouillabaisse. When I tell friends that I am making bouillabaisse, those who have been to the South of France will ask, "You mean, just like the one in Marseilles?" The bouillabaisse recipe on page 227 is the authentic one, the one that requires time, patience, and money, and the one that tastes like what you get in Marseilles. I developed this recipe to be easier. It's very good, but don't expect it to taste like the authentic version, although it captures much of the flavor. Please don't compare this recipe with that one, but do read the instructions in the introduction to that recipe so you can garner some basic ideas. This recipe approximates an authentic bouillabaisse but it involves at lot less effort and work.

$1/4$ teaspoon plus a pinch of saffron threads
$1/4$ cup hot water
$3/4$ cup tepid dry white wine
3 pounds white-fleshed fish fillets from 4 of the
 following fishes: redfish (ocean perch), red
 snapper, blue-mouth, rockfish, sea robin
 (gurnard), monkfish, cod, porgy (scup),
 grouper, halibut, haddock, dab, turbot,
 wreckfish, ocean pout (ling), cusk, wolffish
 (ocean catfish), tautog (blackfish), tilefish,
 sculpin, swordfish

$1^{1}/2$ pounds oily, dark-fleshed fish fillets from 2
 of the following fishes: bluefish, moray eel,
 conger eel, mackerel, shark, dogfish, striped
 bass, sea bass, kingfish, Spanish mackerel,
 mahimahi (dolphinfish), yellowtail
$3/4$ cup extra virgin olive oil
4 to 5 large garlic cloves, to your taste, finely
 chopped
3 tablespoons unsalted butter
1 medium-size onion, thinly sliced and
 separated into rings
2 to 3 pounds fish carcasses, fish heads, or any
 cut-up bits of fish sold as soup fish by the
 fishmonger
5 quarts cold water
2 bouquets garnis, each consisting of 10 black
 peppercorns, 6 sprigs fresh thyme, 4 sprigs
 fresh parsley, and 1 bay leaf, tied in cheesecloth
1 large onion, finely chopped
1 leek (white and light green parts only), split in
 half lengthwise, washed well, and thinly sliced
$1^{1}/2$ celery stalks, finely chopped
1 pound ripe plum tomatoes, peeled, seeded, and
 chopped
1 long, thin strip orange peel zest
2 teaspoons fennel seeds
Salt and freshly ground black pepper to taste
1 tablespoon tomato paste
1 tablespoon anise liqueur, such as Pernod or
 ouzo
$1/4$ cup finely chopped fresh parsley leaves
1 recipe Sauce Rouille (page 230)
24 Croûtes (page 230)

---

1. Crumble the pinch of the saffron threads, and steep in the hot water until needed. Steep the remaining ¼ teaspoon of saffron in ¼ cup of the wine until needed.

2. Cut the white-fleshed and oily fish fillets into 4 x 2½-inch pieces. Marinate the fish in a large ceramic or glass bowl or pan with ¼ cup of the olive oil, half of the chopped garlic, and the saffron threads steeped in water while you continue the preparation. Keep the white fish separate from the oily fish.

3. Prepare the fish broth. In a large stockpot or stew pot, melt the butter over medium heat. When it stops sizzling, cook the sliced onion until soft but not brown, stirring occasionally, 6 to 7 minutes. Add the fish carcasses, heads, or pieces along with the cold water. Add 1 of the bouquets garnis and the remaining ½ cup of wine. Bring to a boil, skimming the surface of foam occasionally. Reduce the heat to low, partially cover, and simmer for 30 minutes. Strain the fish broth through a strainer into another pot and set aside to cool. You should have about 5 quarts of fish broth. Discard the bouquet garni. Clean the stockpot because you will need it in step 4.

4. In the stockpot or stew pot, heat the remaining ½ cup of olive oil over medium heat, then cook the chopped onions, leek, and celery until soft, stirring often, about 15 minutes. Add the tomatoes, the remaining half of the garlic, the remaining bouquet garni, the orange peel, and fennel seeds. Stir in 4½ quarts of the reserved fish broth and the saffron steeped in wine and season with salt and pepper. Bring to a boil, then reduce the heat to medium-low and simmer for 40 minutes.

The broth can be left like this, covered, for many hours, over very low heat, using a heat diffuser, if necessary. Keep the remaining 2 cups of fish broth simmering in reserve in case too much broth evaporates.

5. When you are ready to prepare the final stages of the bouillabaisse, bring the broth back to a furious boil. It should be boiling like mad. Keep the broth boiling furiously so the oil emulsifies. Add the oily fish and boil, uncovered, over very high heat for 3 to 4 minutes, counting from the moment you put them in. Shake the pot to prevent the fish from sticking to the bottom. Now put in the firm-fleshed white fish and boil hard for 5 to 6 minutes, counting from the moment you put them in. Add more simmering broth if necessary to cover the fish. Shake the casserole or pot occasionally or push the fish around gently. If any of the fish looks like it is going to break up, remove immediately. Carefully remove the fish from the broth with a slotted spoon and metal spatula or skimmer when it is firm, but not flaking, and transfer to a large bowl or deep serving platter. Arrange the fish on the platter more or less in the order in which you put them into the pot. Keep them warm by covering with a sheet of aluminum foil.

6. Mix together the tomato paste and anise liqueur. Strain the fish broth through a fine mesh strainer into a soup tureen or large bowl, discarding what doesn't go through. Whisk in the tomato paste-and-anise mixture. Sprinkle the platter and soup tureen with the parsley and serve with the *sauce rouille* and *croûtes* on separate plates.

Variation: Some cooks, especially in restaurants, will add a cut-up live lobster to the fish broth when the oily fish go into the broth.

Makes 8 to 10 servings

ITALIAN "CREAMED" FISH STEW

MOST ITALIAN FISH STEWS ARE CALLED *zuppa di pesce*, but this preparation from the Adriatic coast of Italy, where the Marche, Abruzzi, and Romagna regions meet the sea, is called *crema di pesce in umido*, which means something like creamed fish in stew. Delicate, flaky white fish fillets are pureed with tomatoes in a food processor until creamy. This mixture is turned into the sauteed vegetables that make up the *soffritto* before becoming the basis of the stew. Because it is substantial, this dish is not eaten as a first course in Italy but is a main course. It is best accompanied by an Italian white wine, such as Trebbiano d'Abruzzi or Albana di Romagna.

---

¹/₄ plus 2 tablespoons extra virgin olive oil
³/₄ pound onions, finely chopped
1 carrot, finely chopped
1 celery stalk, finely chopped
3 tablespoons finely chopped fresh basil leaves
3 tablespoons finely chopped fresh parsley leaves
1³/₄ pounds fish fillets, such as sole, flounder, or fluke

1 pound ripe tomatoes, peeled and seeded
1 pound green bell peppers, peeled, seeded, and cut into strips
1¹/₂ cups dry white wine
Salt and freshly ground white pepper to taste
2 teaspoons paprika
8 slices fresh, crusty Italian bread, crusts removed
8 sprigs fresh parsley

---

1. In a large, ovenproof, stove-top casserole, heat ¹/₄ cup of the olive oil over medium heat. Add the onions, carrot, celery, basil, and parsley and cook until mushy and soft, stirring, about 10 minutes.

2. Meanwhile, put the fish and tomatoes in a food processor, in batches if necessary, and process into a smooth cream. Transfer the fish and tomatoes to the stew casserole, add the peppers and wine, and cook, covered, until creamy and quite thick, about 15 minutes. Season with salt, pepper, and paprika.

3. Preheat the oven to 400°F. In a large skillet, heat the remaining 2 tablespoons of olive oil and fry the slices of bread until golden on both sides.

4. Transfer the stew to individual ovenproof ramekins or leave it in the casserole, pushing the fried slices of bread into the stew. Place in the oven until piping hot, about 12 minutes. Serve, garnished with parsley sprigs.

Makes 6 to 8 servings

SALTED VERSUS OIL-PACKED ANCHOVIES

———————•———————

All my recipes that call for anchovies call for salted anchovies. Salted anchovies are whole anchovies that are packed in salt as soon as they are caught and are sold that way. Oil-packed anchovies are filleted, layered in small tin cans, and filled with oil. I prefer the salted anchovies because they taste so much better than oil-packed, which both look and taste anemic. Salted anchovies are sold in one-kilo cans by the Augustino Recca firm of Sicily. This product is imported into the United States and available almost exclusively at Italian markets and via the Internet from Esperya and Salumeria Italiana (see the sources listed in the back of the book).

To prepare salted anchovies for use, remove them from the can and wash them under running water. Then, using your thumb, separate the two fillets at the belly, pulling out and washing away the viscera.

BURRIDA

THE FAMOUS GENOESE FISH STEW KNOWN as burrida is related to the equally famous Provençal fish stew known as bourride. Colman Andrews, the author of Flavors of the Riviera: Discovering Real Mediterranean Cooking, suggests that the word may derive from the Spanish podrida, as in the stew made famous by Don Quixote, olla podrida, which means "rotten stew," referring to the quality and poverty of ingredients in a typical Spanish stew of the Middle Ages. This may be, but in Genoese dialect, the word simply means "fish in pieces" or "pieces of fish in stew."

The kind of fish used in this famous and traditional fish stew is varied. Some cooks use only salt cod or stockfish (air-dried cod that has not been salted), which seems to be the old, original way of making it, while others use only monkfish. I think it is best when three fish are used. Some other choices are hake, grouper, mackerel, squid, swordfish, bream, conger eel, whiting, sea bass, and John Dory. The stew is traditionally served from the casserole in which it is cooked, with toasted bread. Burrida was a famous restaurant dish in the early part of the twentieth century in the port osterie (taverns) of Genoa and is often claimed to be a dish imported from the east by mariners. To make the burrida more "stewy" than soupy, leave out the water. The initial pesto of pine nuts and anchovy is a typical Genovese sarsa des pescio sau', a condiment that starts off a sauce.

———————•———————

5 tablespoons pine nuts
6 salted anchovy fillets, rinsed
1/2 cup extra virgin olive oil
1 large onion, finely chopped
2 large garlic cloves, finely chopped
1 small carrot, finely chopped
1/2 celery stalk, finely chopped
2 tablespoons finely chopped fresh parsley leaves
2 tablespoons finely chopped fresh basil leaves
1 ounce dried porcini mushrooms, soaked in tepid water 15 minutes, drained, and chopped
1 1/2 cups dry white wine

1 pound salt cod or stockfish, soaked in cold
water for 3 days, changing the water 3 times a
day, or swordfish steaks, cut into 2-inch pieces
1 pound monkfish fillets
1 pound mackerel or mahimahi fillets
½ pound squid (optional; if not using squid,
increase the other fish by 2 ounces each),
cleaned if necessary (see page 237)
1 tablespoon unbleached all-purpose flour
2 pounds ripe tomatoes, peeled, seeded, and
sliced
Freshly ground black pepper to taste
1 cup water (optional)
Salt to taste

1. In a mortar, pound the pine nuts and anchovies together until transformed into a pesto.

2. In a large casserole, heat the olive oil over medium-high heat. Cook the onion, garlic, carrot, celery, parsley, and basil, stirring, until soft and mushy looking, about 8 minutes. Add the mushrooms and cook until blended, stirring, about 3 minutes. Add the pine nut-and-anchovy pesto. Stir and let simmer for 2 minutes. Pour in the wine and reduce by half, about 5 minutes. Reduce the heat to low, add the fish, squid, flour, and tomatoes, and season with black pepper. Cover and cook until the fish is cooked through and the squid is tender, adding some of the water if the sauce gets too thick, about 30 minutes. The broth should not be boiling, only bubbling gently. Season with salt and serve from the casserole.

Makes 6 servings

CACCIUCCO

CACCIUCCO IS THE NAME OF A FISH stew from the Tuscan port of Leghorn (Livorno), a stew also known in the town of Viareggio to the north, where traditionalist cooks add a stone taken from the sea to the stew so that it can reach its true height of earthly perfection. Tuscan culinary lore attributes the provenance of *cacciucco* to the Near East. This may be true, because the word *cacciucco* derives, in fact, from the Turkish word *kaçukli*, meaning "bits and pieces" or "odds and ends," which in turn is related to the word *küçük*, meaning "small" or "little." This is how the stew is put together, with odds and ends from the catch.

Leghorn had its beginning as a port in the late sixteenth century, when the Florentine Medici family wished to build a port to counter their reliance on the rival city-state of Pisa. Leghorn soon became an important maritime and cosmopolitan entrepôt for merchants, mariners, and slaves from the entire Mediterranean and there was a great intermingling of cultures.

This stew is composed of many odd fish and shellfish and is spiced in a way that many other Italian fish stews are not. This is not a glorified soup, but a main-course fish stew. One Tuscan tradition declares that there should be five fish in the stew, one for each *c* in *cacciucco*. There is a wide assortment of Mediterranean seafood from which the Livornese cook can choose, including red gurnard, armed gurnard (*Peristedion cataphractum* L.), a variety of squid, octopus, cuttlefish, scorpionfish, moray eel, conger eel, hake, dogfish, monkfish, swordfish, whiting, John Dory, red mullet, goby, shrimp, and mussels.

This recipe is based on the one that my friend Boyd Grove and I had with a bottle of Bosca Anniversary Spumante at the Ristorante Quattro Mori on the Via Enrico Bartelloni in Leghorn some years ago for 25,000 lira. The restaurant was suggested to me by my cousin Carlo De Ieso, who lived outside Florence and couldn't come with us that day because he had to work. Carlo told us that this was the best place to get *cacciucco*, and it was. This traditional dish of Leghorn served at Quattro Mori consisted of shrimp, prawns, mussels, baby octopus, larger octopus arms, cuttlefish, grouper, and one other little fish, a goby, and eels. The ragout was a rich tomato sauce with olive oil and it was spicy hot, seasoned with red chile, saffron, and a little thyme. (In a Tuscan cookbook from the earlier part of the twentieth century, a recipe for *cacciucco* calls for *zenzero*, which refers either to the Tuscan dialect word for chile pepper or it might even mean "ginger," so perhaps the dish originally contained ginger in the spicing.) There seems to be a lot of fish called for, but remember that only half of a whole fish is edible. Don't forget to shake the casserole, rather than stirring too much to keep the fish from disintegrating once the fish are cooking. I've made cuttlefish optional in the ingredients list because it is so hard to find. Cuttlefish are sometimes available in ethnic fish stores on the eastern coast of the United States in December, and they are sometimes sold frozen as "squid steaks."

1 small octopus (about 1¼ pounds), cleaned if necessary (see page 268)

½ cup white wine vinegar

¾ cup extra virgin olive oil

1 very large onion, very finely chopped

2 medium-size carrots, very finely chopped

1½ celery stalks, very finely chopped

2 or 3 fresh red chiles (about 4 inches in length), to your taste, seeded and very finely chopped

8 large garlic cloves, very finely chopped

6 large fresh sage leaves

1½ teaspoons dried thyme

¾ cup finely chopped fresh parsley leaves

1 large cuttlefish (about 1 pound; optional), cleaned (see page 237), skinned, and cut into strips with tentacles

10 to 18 small squid (about 2 to 2½ pounds), cleaned if necessary (see page 237), skinned, and body cut into rings with tentacles

1 cup dry red wine

2 pounds ripe tomatoes, cut in half, seeds squeezed out, and grated against the largest holes of a grater down to the peel

One 2-pound striped bass or red snapper or other fish with head, cleaned, gutted, scaled, head and tail removed and saved, and fish cut into steaks or fillets

6 to 15 small fish, depending on the size, such as porgies, butterfish, sardines, and smelts (about 2½ pounds total), cleaned, gutted, scaled, heads and tails removed and saved, or 1½ pounds fish fillets

Salt and freshly ground black pepper to taste

1½ quarts water

Pinch of saffron threads

1½ pounds yellowtail fillets, cut into 12 pieces

1½ pounds mahimahi (dolphinfish) fillets, cut into 12 pieces

CLEANING CUTTLEFISH AND SQUID

———•———

Cuttlefish are messy to work with, so when you begin to clean them, make sure your work area is uncluttered, clean, and easy to clean up. Cuttlefish differ from squid in being squatter and less stream-lined, with thicker flesh. They are slightly oval and contain a large internal calcified shell that is bone-hard and functions similarly to the plastic-like quill (technically called a chiton) inside a squid. Have this bone side closest to the table, with the "stomach" side facing up toward you. Lay the cuttlefish down with the tail pointing toward you. Grasp the body with one hand and, with the other hand, pull out the head, tentacles, and any viscera that attach to them. Cut the tentacles off below the eyes, wash, and set aside.

Slit the belly from top to bottom using a small, sharp paring knife, making sure you don't cut all the way through, which could damage the ink sack. The cuttlefish will be black with ink, but you will not yet have located the sack. Now push the bone through and remove. With your hands, begin to separate the skin from the body and discard all the skin. Rip the body down the middle where you have slit the cuttle-fish—carefully, because you don't want to have the ink sack burst on you (although it's not *that* fragile).

The ink sack can be pulled out with your hands. It is a very tiny, narrow white sack with a tube run-ning down. Carefully grab the tube, separating it from the body with your fingers, and pull the sack out, separating it from the surrounding tissue by using your fingers. The ink sack is covered with a white muscle-like tissue and will be surrounded on either side by eggs if you have a female. Remove the mouth, a kind of beak, in the center of the tentacles by popping it out with your fingers. Clean the cuttlefish under cold running water, pulling off all the skin and any other gelatinous-looking tissue. When the cuttle-fish is cleaned, it will be completely white.

Squid are cleaned in a similar manner, although their skin is easier to pull off. But their ink sacks are much harder to work with because they are much smaller animals.

---

36 mussels (about 2½ pounds), scrubbed clean and debearded
12 large fresh shrimp or prawns, with their heads on, shelled
12 slices Fried Bread (page 224)

———•———

1. Bring a large saucepan of water to a boil, add the octopus and vinegar, and let boil for 20 minutes. Drain, cut into 8 arms, and slice the head into 4 pieces.

2. In a large earthenware casserole set on a heat diffuser, heat the oil over medium–high heat until very hot. Add the onion, carrot, celery, chiles, garlic, sage, thyme, and parsley and cook, stirring, until soft and mushy look-ing, about 12 minutes. (If you are not cooking with earthenware and a diffuser, cook over medium heat and check for doneness sooner.) Add the octopus, cuttlefish, and squid and cook until their liquid has evaporated, stirring occasionally, about 25 minutes. Reduce the heat to low, add the wine, and cook for 10 minutes. Add the tomatoes, stir, and cook for 5 minutes. Remove the octopus and squid and set aside. Remove the casserole from the heat.

3. Add the heads and tail of the large fish to the casserole and also the heads and tails of the small fish, if you have them. Season with some salt and pepper and add the water. Bring to a boil, then reduce the heat to medium-low and cook for 20 minutes. Pour the broth through a fine-mesh strainer, pressing the vegetables against the strainer (the broth should be the consistency of a creamy soup). Return to the casserole, add the saffron, and heat for 10 minutes. Discard the heads and tails. The broth can rest at this point and you can cook the stew later if you like.

4. Bring the broth to a vigorous boil. Add all the fish (but not the shellfish) and cook for 8 minutes. Add the cephalopods (squid, cuttlefish, if using, and octopus) and push them down into the broth. Do not stir; shake the casserole, if you must. Add the mussels and shrimp and push them down into the broth, too. Cover and, over high heat, continue to cook until the shrimp turn orange and the mussels are opened, about 10 minutes. Add a few tablespoons of water if the stew is too thick, but remember that it should never become soupy. Turn the fish gently so they don't break apart or shake the casserole. Discard any mussels that remain tightly shut. Serve with a slice of bread for each diner and try to give everyone 1 piece of every seafood.

Makes 12 servings

FISHERMEN'S FISH STEW FROM THE PORT OF CAORLE IN THE VENETO

CAORLE IS A SMALL CITY ON AN ISLAND located between the Livenza and Lemene Rivers, between Venice and Trieste in the Veneto region of Italy. Fishermen operated out of Caorle and used fast boats, called *caorline*, that could quickly bring fish to market as well as transport fruits and vegetables along the intercoastal waterways to Venice. Speed was important to ensure freshness, and even today one can be surprised to find some of the fish one has bought at market wriggling a bit in the shopping bag. This stew, called *brodetto de pesse alla caorlotta* in the Venetian dialect, was traditionally made by the fishermen, who cooked it in a cast-iron pot on board ship. Wash all the seafood in clean seawater, if available.

1/2 cup extra virgin olive oil

3 large garlic cloves, finely chopped

1 1/2 pounds cuttlefish or squid, cleaned if necessary (see page 237)

1 quart plus 2 tablespoons water

1 pound dogfish, mako shark, yellowtail, mahimahi (dolphinfish), or kingfish steaks or fillets, cut into large chunks

1/2 pound firm-fleshed fish, such as grouper, ocean pout, cod, monkfish, or swordfish steaks or fillets, cut into large pieces

1/2 pound other white-fleshed fish fillets, such as redfish (ocean perch), red snapper, hake, or cusk, cut into large pieces

¼ *pound crabmeat, picked over for cartilage and*
    shells
1 *pound medium-size fresh shrimp, heads*
    removed, or ½ *pound previously frozen*
    headless shrimp, shelled
Salt and freshly ground black pepper to taste
¼ *cup white wine vinegar*
1 *bay leaf*
10 *sprigs fresh parsley tied together with kitchen*
    twine

———◆———

1. In a large casserole, heat the olive oil over medium-high heat. Cook the garlic and cuttlefish for 30 seconds, stirring constantly. Reduce the heat to low, add 2 tablespoons of the water, and cook until tender, stirring frequently so the garlic doesn't burn, about 30 minutes.

2. Add all the fish, crab, and shrimp, season with salt and pepper, and cook until firm, about 6 minutes. Cook in batches if necessary. Remove everything with a slotted spoon and set aside.

3. Increase the heat to medium, pour in the vinegar and the remaining 1 quart of water, add the bay leaf and parsley, and cook to reduce the broth by half, about 50 minutes.

4. Return all the fish, shellfish, and cuttlefish to the broth, increase the heat to high, and cook until thoroughly reheated, about 6 minutes. Discard the bay leaf and parsley and serve immediately.

———◆———

Makes 4 servings

"DELICIOUS" SWORDFISH STEW

———🌿———

THE "DELICIOUS" IN THE NAME OF THIS stew is not made up. It is a Sicilian stew in a rich tomato and olive oil ragout. A Sicilian cook would typically make this luscious stew, called *murina agghiotta*, with moray eel, an antediluvian sea creature that inhabits the creviced underwater rocks of this island in the sun, the largest and most important of the Mediterranean islands. The Sicilian word *agghiotta* derives from the word *ghiotta*, which literally means "delicious," as it did when it was used in the thirteenth century to refer to someone who loved tasty and savory food. One scholar believed the word derived from the Arabic *ghatta*, meaning dishes that are soaked or immersed in a sauce or liquid, but it more likely derives from the Latin word *gluttone*, "glutton," or *gutta*, "throat."

As perfect as moray eel is for this preparation, your chances of finding a fresh one are remote. The next best choice after eel are, in order of preference, swordfish, monkfish, and ocean pout (*Macrozoarces americanus* B. and S.). Mahimahi, yellowtail, kingfish, striped bass, and Spanish mackerel will also work. The moray eel was a popular seafood among the ancient Romans and Greeks. Archestratus, the fourth-century B.C. Greek Sicilian writer known as history's first cookbook writer, is said to have had a recipe for it, and the Greeks called the fish *muraena Helena*, the "daughter of Jupiter."

Now, if you can actually get hold of a fresh moray eel, have the fishmonger prepare it for you and be prepared for an extraordinary taste.

———●———

1/4 cup extra virgin olive oil
1 medium-size onion, thinly sliced and
   separated into rings
2 celery stalks, chopped
1/4 cup finely chopped fresh parsley leaves
1 1/2 pounds ripe tomatoes, peeled, seeded,
   and chopped
1 3/4 pounds moray eel (see below) or
   swordfish or shark steaks (or any other
   fish mentioned above), skinned (if eel)
   and cut into 8 pieces

WORKING WITH EEL

———●———

Eel are delicious-tasting seafood because of their high fat content (although still low when compared to that of land animals). If you don't catch them yourself, you will often find fresh eels around Christmastime in neighborhoods with Italian populations. The eel you are most likely to encounter in a fish store is the common eel. The moray eel and conger eel are rarer, but I actually prefer them. Eels are somewhat hard to prepare because you must take their skin off, and that is very slippery to do. In old times, whoever caught the eel would lay it on a wooden plank and drive a large nail through its head into the plank, then make an incision around the throat and start peeling the skin down by pulling it with pliers and scraping with a sharp filleting knife. I can assure you that this is difficult, so you will want to ask the fishmonger to do it.

1/2 cup pitted imported black olives
1/2 cup pitted imported green olives
Salt and freshly ground black pepper to taste
1 tablespoon finely chopped fresh basil leaves
   (optional)

———●———

1. In a large skillet, heat the olive oil over medium heat. Cook the onion, celery, and parsley until the onion is translucent, stirring frequently, 10 to 12 minutes. Reduce the heat to medium-low, add the tomatoes, and cook until a bit denser, about 20 minutes.

2. Add the fish and olives, season with salt and pepper, and cook until the fish is firm, about 12 minutes. Sprinkle with the basil, if using, and serve.

———●———

Makes 4 servings

THE HUMBLE TUNA STEW OF THE SICILIAN FISHERMAN

THE GREAT SICILIAN GASTRONOME Alberto Denti di Piraino commented on *tonno in umido* ("tuna in stew") by saying *questo piatto di umili pescatori è degno di figurare su mense regali!* ("This dish of the humble fishermen is worthy of being on a royal table!") This recipe is meant to taste a little vinegary, so it is important to use a very good quality vinegar. You could also marinate the tuna in wine, bay leaves, rosemary, and garlic for 2 hours, then pat dry, dredge the whole tuna in flour, and cook it in the strained marinade for 45 minutes. The portions are small, so I would serve this stew as an antipasto, but you can also double the recipe and eat it as a main course.

———— ● ————

1 pound fresh tuna, in one piece
1/4 cup plus 2 tablespoons white wine vinegar
3 tablespoons extra virgin olive oil
2 tablespoons unsalted butter
1 medium-size onion, finely chopped
1/4 cup finely chopped fresh parsley leaves
4 salted anchovy fillets, rinsed and chopped
1 tablespoon unbleached all-purpose flour
1 1/4 cups dry white wine
Salt and freshly ground black pepper to taste

———— ● ————

1. In a small glass baking dish, place the tuna in water to cover mixed with 3 tablespoons of the vinegar. Let soak for 1 hour, covered, in the refrigerator.

2. In a medium-size casserole, heat the olive oil and butter together over medium heat. When the butter stops sizzling, cook the onion and parsley until the onion is translucent, stirring occasionally, 7 to 8 minutes. Add the anchovy fillets and flour. Stir, and pour in the wine and the remaining 3 tablespoons of vinegar. Season with salt and pepper and cook for 1 minute, stirring.

3. Drain the tuna and pat dry with paper towels, then place in the casserole. Cover,

COOKING WITH WINE

———— ● ————

Always use good wine for cooking, preferably the same wine you are drinking, if it is not too expensive. Stay away from the so-called "cooking wine" sold in supermarkets, as it tastes really poor, even in a cooked dish.

reduce the heat to very low, using a diffuser if necessary, and cook until the tuna is firm, 40 to 50 minutes.

4. Transfer the piece of tuna to a serving platter and keep warm. Reduce the sauce in the casserole over high heat until it is a bit thicker, about 5 minutes, then cover the tuna with the sauce and serve.

———— ● ————

Makes 4 antipasto servings

TUNA RAGOUT FROM PALERMO

T HIS TUNA STEW IS KNOWN AS *TONNU A ragù* or *tunnu o' rau* in Sicilian. I have seen many recipes for this dish in Sicily and I'm not sure exactly which is the favorite method of doing it. In Palermo they seem to use mint leaves, while in eastern Sicily they use oregano. It's possible a cook would add a little cinnamon too. In any case, when buying the tuna, ask for a whole piece of tuna, preferably cut from the "shoulder." So some cooks advise, although other cooks say from the tail because that part is more tender. You will prepare the whole piece by making incisions with the sharp tip of a paring knife and stuffing the holes with mint, garlic, peppercorns, and salt. The tuna is lightly floured and cooked whole in a rich tomato ragout. It is excellent with a white Corvo wine and crusty Italian country bread with sesame seeds. Serve the sauce with spaghetti, *bucatini*, or *penne rigate* as a first course and the tuna as part of a second course.

———————

1³/₄ pounds fresh tuna, in one piece, preferably
   from the "shoulder"
20 fresh mint leaves
2 large garlic cloves, 1 slivered and 1 crushed
Salt to taste
8 black peppercorns, lightly crushed
Freshly ground black pepper
Unbleached all-purpose flour for dredging
³/₄ cup extra virgin olive oil
³/₄ cup dry white wine
2 medium-size onions, thinly sliced and
   separated into rings
1 pound ripe tomatoes, peeled, seeded, and
   chopped
¹/₂ cup boiling water

———————

1. With the tip of a paring knife, make several small incisions in the piece of tuna. Into each slit push 1 or 2 mint leaves, 1 small sliver of garlic, a little salt, and a chunk of peppercorn.

Sprinkle salt and freshly ground black pepper over the whole piece of tuna. Dredge the tuna in the flour, tapping off the excess.

2. In a casserole, heat the olive oil over medium-high heat. Cook the piece of tuna on all sides until it turns color, turning often with tongs, about 1 minute. Pour in the wine, reduce the heat to medium, and cook until the wine evaporates, about 3 minutes. Remove the tuna from the casserole and set aside.

3. In the remaining sauce, cook the onions and crushed garlic until soft and translucent, stirring frequently, about 10 minutes. Return the tuna to the casserole and cook for 6 minutes. Add the tomatoes and boiling water, and check the seasonings, adding more salt and pepper if necessary. Cover, reduce the heat to low, and cook for 10 minutes. Uncover and cook for another 10 minutes, or until the piece of tuna is firm and the liquid is denser.

4. Remove the tuna to a serving platter and flake apart or slice. Cover with the sauce and serve.

Variation: In step 3, add 1 cup fresh peas and 1 cinnamon stick for the final 20 minutes of cooking.

———————

Makes 6 servings

TUNA STEW WITH ROTINI

THIS SICILIAN *TONNO AL RAGÙ*, "TUNA IN ragout," requires one large, two-pound chunk of tuna, so you'll definitely have to go to a fish market for that. This stew recipe is typically made in the western part of Sicily, where the tuna fishing industry is based. Tuna fishing has an old history there, and cooks have innumerable ways of cooking it. Traditionally, the tuna would be eaten as a second course and the pasta as a first course with the ragout. I think this preparation is quite fun to make, and children seem to enjoy it with *rotini*, a corkscrew-shaped pasta.

¼ cup extra virgin olive oil
¼ cup very finely chopped onions
¼ cup very finely chopped fresh parsley leaves
6 garlic cloves, very finely chopped
1 cup dry white wine
3 cups fresh or canned tomato puree, or 1½
    pounds ripe tomatoes, cut in half, seeds
    squeezed out, grated against the largest holes
    of a grater down to the peel, and mixed with
    ½ cup water
Salt and freshly ground black pepper to taste
One 2-pound piece fresh tuna
¾ pound rotini

1. In a casserole, heat the olive oil over medium-high heat. Cook the onions, parsley, and garlic until the onions are soft, stirring almost constantly so the garlic doesn't burn, 2 to 3 minutes. Add the wine and tomato puree and season with salt and pepper. Reduce the heat to medium and cook until the sauce is denser, 30 minutes.

2. Add the tuna steak and cook until it is firm and the inside is medium-rare, 12 minutes.

3. Meanwhile, bring a large pot of water to a rolling boil, salt abundantly, and add the pasta. Cook until the pasta is *al dente* and drain. Transfer the pasta to a serving bowl or platter, toss with some of the sauce, lay the tuna on top, and nap with more sauce. Serve without cheese.

Makes 4 servings

PEELING GARLIC

Don't struggle with garlic cloves—arrange the garlic cloves to be peeled in a row and crush them lightly with the flat side of a 10-inch chef's knife. This will crack the peel, and then you will just pick it off the clove.

NEAPOLITAN-STYLE OCTOPUS STEW

WATCHING WIZENED OLD FISHERMEN beating the octopus they catch against the rocks in the Santa Lucia section of Naples, on a hot summer day, is part of the charm of an octopus stew. Why would you not want to eat it after all that tenderizing? Octopus is consumed mostly in the summertime in Naples because these creatures spend their winters in deep, cold water and approach the rocky shoreline in summer. Neapolitans insist on the "true" octopus, the octopus with two rows of suckers on its tentacles, rather than the octopus with one row of suckers that lives further out to sea. This octopus stew, called *polpo alla luciana*, is named after a section of Naples called Santa Lucia, where there is an old seafood market. Both octopus and squid are very popular in Naples, but in the United States octopus is regarded as exotic, and it is mostly sold frozen. That is actually a benefit, because the freezing and defrosting process helps tenderize the meat.

2¹/₂ pounds octopus, cleaned if necessary (see page 268)
2 tablespoons coarse sea salt
2 cups water
6 garlic cloves, finely chopped
2 dried chiles, seeded and crumbled, or ¹/₂ teaspoon red pepper flakes
¹/₂ cup finely chopped fresh parsley leaves
1 pound ripe plum tomatoes, peeled, seeded, and chopped
Freshly ground black pepper to taste
¹/₄ cup plus 3 tablespoons extra virgin olive oil
3 tablespoons fresh lemon juice
Salt to taste

---

1. Put the octopus in an enameled cast-iron casserole. Dissolve the sea salt in the water and cover the octopus with it. Add half the garlic, the chiles, 2 tablespoons of the parsley, and the tomatoes and season with black pepper. Add more water to cover if necessary. Cover the casserole with a sheet of aluminum foil, pinching down the edges so steam will not escape. Cover with a tight-fitting lid and cook over very low heat for 2 hours, using a diffuser if necessary. Do not lift the lid. Shake the casserole every once in a while to mingle the flavors and keep the octopus from sticking to the bottom of the pan.

2. Meanwhile, prepare the sauce by whisking the olive oil, the remaining half of the garlic, the remaining 6 tablespoons parsley, and the lemon juice together. Season with salt and pepper.

3. When it has finished cooking, remove the octopus, drain, and slice thinly. Pour the sauce over the octopus and serve.

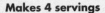

Makes 4 servings

ITALIAN EATING ESTABLISHMENTS

Italians eat in a variety of establishments and they are, from biggest to smallest,

• *HOTEL:* A restaurant in a hotel will match the size and elegance of the hotel in which it is located. The food in the grand deluxe hotel restaurants tend to be *alta cucina* ("haute cuisine") with heavy French overtones.

• *RISTORANTE:* A full-service establishment, it usually has tablecloths and a certain level of polish and a price to match, depending on the restaurant.

• *ALBERGO:* Usually what we call an inn. It is a small country hotel with its own restaurant. The food tends to be hearty and modest.

• *TRATTORIA:* This is a smaller, simpler restaurant usually found in alleys and side streets and is frequently a mom-and-pop establishment with a warm and friendly atmosphere. The food tends to be rustic and robust.

• *OSTERIA:* This is a tavern or inn serving lots of good home cooking to locals who live in the neighborhood, especially in big cities.

• *TAVERNA:* This is a small restaurant and drinking establishment with a traditional atmosphere serving traditional food.

• *ROSTICCERIA:* This is a barbecue snack bar where you usually eat standing up at a counter. The food is already prepared and served from large *bains marie,* as are sandwiches, hot dogs and other sausages, spit-roasted chicken, and salads.

• *PIZZERIA:* An establishment that serves nothing but pizza and drinks.

• *BAR:* Although it may serve aperitifs, beer, and brandy, an Italian bar, unlike its American counterpart, is mostly famous for its *caffe espresso* machine, which is in operation all day long.

GRAND SEAFOOD STEW
IN THE STYLE OF NAPLES

THIS FISH STEW, OR *ZUPPA DI FRUTTI DI mare,* is a special preparation typical of the grand seafood platters I've had in southern Italy and Naples. This preparation is meant to be impressive, so don't be shy or formal when serving this extravaganza. It is a rewarding feast for a large group of family and friends, ideally served outside during the summer in a very large and deep serving platter, from which guests serve themselves, or the host can act as expeditor. One time when I had made this festive meal in 1991, a large group of friends were being regaled by a young Iraqi man who had just escaped from Saddam Hussein's army and had riveting stories to tell about life in that most bizarre of fascist states as we picked through the seafood. The reason for the range in cooking time for the octopus is because one never knows how tenderized it may be.

Two 1½-pound live lobsters
6 crab claws or Alaskan King crab legs
One 3-pound octopus, cleaned if necessary (see
    page 268)
½ cup extra virgin olive oil
4 large garlic cloves, finely chopped
1 large onion, finely chopped
4 pounds ripe tomatoes, peeled, seeded, and
    finely chopped
1½ cups dry white wine
1½ cups Fish Broth (page 221)
6 large fresh basil leaves
Freshly ground black pepper to taste
1 dried chile
30 littleneck clams (about 3 pounds), soaked in
    water to cover mixed with 1 teaspoon baking
    soda for 30 minutes and drained
30 mussels (about 2½ pounds), scrubbed clean
    and debearded
2 pounds medium-size fresh shrimp with their
    heads on, or 1 pound previously frozen
    headless shrimp, shelled
12 slices Fried Bread (page 224)

—————●—————

1. In a large stockpot or lobster pot, bring 1 inch of water to a boil over high heat. Add the lobsters and crab, and partially cover. Reduce the heat to medium-high, and steam for 25 minutes. Drain, and when the lobsters are cool enough to handle, chop the claws in half so that all the meat can be extracted without the use of shell-crackers and forks, but leave the meat in the shell. Place the claws in a bowl and set aside. Remove the tail and any tomalley and coral from the lobster. If you wish, save the tomalley and coral in a bowl so you can later spread them on the fried bread.

Split the tail lengthwise, then chop into 2-inch segments, leaving the meat in the shell. Set aside in the same bowl. Break off the lobster legs, then break them in half and place in the bowl. Crack the crab claws so all the meat is exposed and set aside in the bowl with the lobster. Refrigerate until needed.

2. While the lobster is steaming, put the octopus in a pot and cover with lightly salted water. Bring to a boil over high heat, then reduce the heat to medium-high and boil the octopus for about 1¼ hours. After 45 minutes taste the octopus by cutting off a small piece: it should feel soft but slightly springy; if not, cook another 30 to 60 minutes. Drain the octopus and cool with cold water, rubbing off the purplish skin. Set aside in the refrigerator until needed.

3. In a pot or casserole that is large enough to hold all of the seafood, heat the olive oil over medium-high heat. Cook the garlic and onion until soft, stirring constantly, about 3 minutes. Add the tomatoes, wine, fish broth, basil, black pepper, and chile. Reduce the heat to low and simmer, partially covered, for 2 hours.

4. Thirty minutes before you want to serve, increase the heat to medium-high and add the clams. Cover and cook for 5 minutes. Add the mussels and the reserved lobster, crab, and octopus. Cook for 5 minutes more and add the shrimp. Continue to cook for another 15 minutes, moistening the sauce if necessary with more fish broth. With a long wooden spoon, stir the pot gently so the mollusks on the top will be mixed.

5. Remove all the seafood from the pot and transfer to a serving platter, discarding any clams or mussels that have not opened. Transfer the broth to a serving bowl or tureen. Serve immediately with the fried bread, spread with the reserved tomalley and coral, if desired. Save all leftover sauce for spaghetti the next day.

Makes 8 to 10 servings

ZUPPA DI PESCE AL DIAVOLO

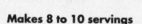

FISH STEWS ARE PREPARED ALL ALONG THE coastline of Italy, always using whatever local fish is available. In this country, we usually have access to nonlocal fish of varying degrees of freshness, so I believe it's always best to ask what's local and what's fresh. You can concoct a very nice fish stew with the simplest of local fishes. Whenever you come across the description *al diavolo* (of the devil) in Italian cooking, it means that the dish has chile pepper. This is indeed a spicy hot fish stew that can be made with either crayfish or shrimp. I particularly like to make it in the summer.

¼ cup extra virgin olive oil
1 medium-size onion, finely chopped

5 large garlic cloves, finely chopped
½ cup dry white wine
1 pound ripe tomatoes, peeled, seeded, and chopped
1 quart Fish Broth (page 221)
4 dried chiles
Salt and freshly ground black pepper to taste
1½ pounds live crayfish or fresh shrimp with their heads on or ¾ pound previously frozen headless shrimp, shelled
1½ pounds fish from 3 oily types, such as salmon, swordfish, and tuna
10 slices Fried Bread (page 224)

1. In a casserole, heat the olive oil over medium-high heat. Cook the onion and garlic until the onion is translucent, stirring frequently so the garlic doesn't burn, about 5 minutes. Pour in the wine and cook until nearly evaporated, about 4 minutes. Add the tomatoes and fish broth, reduce the heat to low, and simmer for 1 hour. Keep the broth on low heat or turn it off until you are ready to cook the fish.

2. Bring the broth to a boil, add the chiles, and season with salt and pepper. Add the crayfish, if using, and cook until they turn red, about 5 minutes. Add the remaining fish and shrimp, if using, and cook at a furious boil until the fish is firm, about 8 minutes.

3. Serve from the casserole, placing the fried bread in individual soup bowls.

Makes 4 servings

WHAT SIZE ARE YOUR SHRIMP?

Marketers of shrimp have categorized shrimp by size and count per pound.

Extra colossal are under 10 count per pound.

Colossal are under 15 count per pound.

Extra jumbo are 16 to 20 count per pound.

Jumbo are 21 to 25 count per pound.

Extra large are 26 to 30 count per pound.

Large are 31 to 40 count per pound.

Medium large are 36 to 40 count per pound.

Medium are 41 to 50 count per pound.

Small are 51 to 60 count per pound.

Extra small are 61 to 70 count per pound.

Tiny are over 70 count per pound.

ZUPPA DI PESCE WITH SAFFRON-FLAVORED SHRIMP BROTH

THE TWIST ON THIS SICILIAN RECIPE IS IN using a shrimp broth rather than water or fish broth. On top of which, it's flavored with saffron, making it all that more attractive. This is a terrific preparation, but remember that the seafood only cooks for about 3 minutes, so you need to be attentive and ready to serve immediately. The shrimp broth is best made with fresh shrimp that have their heads.

1/4 cup extra virgin olive oil

1 small onion, finely chopped

6 large garlic cloves, finely chopped

1/4 cup finely chopped fresh parsley leaves

10 ounces ripe tomatoes, peeled, seeded, and coarsely chopped

1 cup dry white wine

1 recipe Shrimp or Lobster Broth (recipe follows) with a good-size pinch of crumbled saffron mixed in

3 dried chiles

Salt and freshly ground black pepper to taste

8 extra colossal fresh shrimp with their heads on (about 1 pound), shelled and deveined if necessary, or 16 large previously frozen headless jumbo shrimp, shelled

16 small mussels (about 3/4 pound), scrubbed clean and debearded

10 ounces monkfish fillets, cut into 2-inch pieces

10 ounces mahimahi (dolphinfish), yellowtail, striped bass, or bluefish fillets, cut into 2-inch pieces

8 slices Fried Bread (page 224)

———— ● ————

1. In a large saucepan, *marmite*, or the bottom pot of a *couscoussier*, heat the olive oil over medium-high heat. Cook the onion, garlic, and parsley until the onion is soft and translucent, stirring frequently, 3 to 4 minutes. Add the tomatoes, cook for 1 minute, then pour in the wine and let it boil for a few minutes. Add the shrimp broth and chiles, season with salt and pepper, and simmer over low heat until you are ready to serve.

2. Bring the broth to a furious boil and put in all the seafood. Cook until the fish is firm, the shrimp are orange, and the mussels open, about 3 minutes. Serve immediately with the fried bread, discarding any mussels that remain firmly shut.

Variation: Add 1 cup of orzo to the boiling broth and cook until *al dente*, about 10 minutes. Add all the seafood and continue to cook until done, another 3 to 4 minutes.

Makes 4 servings

SHRIMP OR LOBSTER BROTH

I make shrimp broth and lobster broth whenever I've got leftover shells. It's so easy and you can extract so much more flavor from the shellfish, even when you think you're all done with that shrimp or lobster. Collect the heads and shells of the shrimp as well as any leftover lobsters shells if you are eating lobster.

Shells and heads of 2 pounds fresh shrimp, or shells from 1 pound previously frozen headless shrimp, or the shells and carcass of 1 or 2 cooked 1¹/₄-pound lobsters
1 medium-size onion, cut up
1 small carrot, sliced
¹/₂ celery stalk, sliced
1 bouquet garni, consisting of 2 sprigs each fresh parsley and thyme and 1 bay leaf, tied in cheesecloth

3 to 4 quarts water, depending on how much broth you want
Salt and freshly ground black pepper to taste

1. Put all the ingredients, except the salt and pepper, in a stockpot, and bring to a boil. Reduce the heat to a simmer and skim the foam off the surface until no more appears. Partially cover the pot and simmer over very low heat for at least 2 hours.

2. Pour the broth through a strainer (a chinois, or conical strainer, would be ideal). Discard all the shells, vegetables, and the bouquet garni. Line the strainer with cheesecloth and pour the broth through again. Season to taste with salt and pepper. Use immediately or store in the refrigerator for up to 1 week or in the freezer for up to 6 months.

Makes 2 quarts

FISH STEW WITH SHRIMP AND FENNEL

THIS NEAPOLITAN-STYLE FISH STEW, called *zuppa di pesce con gamberetti e finnochio*, is very fragrant, rich in taste, and heavenly, especially when made with this variety of fish seasoned in this way. If you are able to find some wild fennel, that would be great, but the fennel called for here will provide a nice touch.

FOR THE BROTH:

2 pounds fresh shrimp with their heads on or
   1 pound previously frozen headless shrimp
4 quarts water
1 medium-size onion, cut into chunks and
   separated into layers
1 celery stalk, cut up
10 black peppercorns
1 bay leaf

FOR THE ZUPPA:

1/4 cup plus 2 tablespoons extra virgin olive oil
1 small onion, finely chopped
1 fennel bulb with half its stalks (about 1 1/2
   pounds), coarsely chopped
5 large garlic cloves, finely chopped
1/4 cup finely chopped fresh parsley leaves
1 large, ripe tomato, peeled, seeded, and chopped
Salt and freshly ground black pepper to taste
1 pound small whole fish such as pompano, sea
   bass, red snapper, butterfish, or kingfish,
   scaled, gutted, and cleaned, with heads and
   tails left on
1/2 pound red snapper fillets, halved crosswise
8 slices Fried Bread (page 224)

1. To make the broth, shell the shrimp and, if using fresh shrimp, remove their heads. Refrigerate the shrimp until ready to use. Put all the heads and shells in a colander and rinse, then put them in a stockpot with the water, onion, celery, peppercorns, and bay leaf. Bring to a boil, and skim the surface of any foam that appears. Reduce the heat to low, partially cover, and simmer for 6 hours. Pour through a strainer (a chinois, or conical strainer, would be ideal). Then strain again through a cheesecloth-lined fine-mesh strainer and set aside. You should have between 2 and 3 quarts of broth.

2. To make the *zuppa*, in a stockpot, heat the olive oil over medium heat. Cook the onion, fennel, garlic, and parsley, stirring, until the onion is translucent, about 10 minutes. Add the tomato and cook for 5 minutes. Add 2 quarts of the shrimp broth. Then reduce the heat to low and cook, partially covered, for 45 minutes.

3. When you are ready to serve the *zuppa*, check the seasonings for salt and pepper, increase the heat to high, and return the broth to a furious boil. Add the whole fish and red snapper and cook for 2 minutes. Add the shrimp and cook until they turn pink, about 2 minutes.

4. Transfer the fish and shrimp to serving bowls, ladle some broth over them, and serve with the fried bread.

Makes 4 servings

ZUPPA DI PESCE WITH ESCAROLE

THIS FISH STEW, WHICH ONE MIGHT encounter in the home cooking of Apulia, Basilicata, or Calabria, is as good as any other, but it is a little more rustic, utilizing more vegetables than is usually common. The escarole, a slightly bitter salad green, cooks well and is found in a variety of stews and soups made throughout the Italian peninsula. The fish mentioned below are only suggestions. Choose at least three different fishes from whatever the daily catch offers.

1/4 cup plus 2 tablespoons extra virgin olive oil

4 large garlic cloves, finely chopped

2 shallots, finely chopped

1 celery stalk, finely chopped

1 teaspoon fennel seeds

3 tablespoons finely chopped fresh basil leaves

3 tablespoons finely chopped fresh parsley leaves

1/2 teaspoon dried thyme

2 dried chiles

10 ounces ripe tomatoes, peeled, seeded, and chopped

1 medium-size zucchini, ends trimmed, peeled, and cut into small dice

8 large escarole leaves

2 cups water

1 1/2 quarts Shrimp or Lobster Broth (page 249) or Fish Broth (page 221)

Salt to taste

2 1/2 pounds mixed fish fillets, such as red snapper, sand dab, and yellowtail, cut into chunks

1. In a large casserole, heat the olive oil over high heat. Cook the garlic, shallots, celery, fennel seeds, basil, parsley, thyme, and chiles until the shallots are translucent, stirring so the garlic doesn't burn, 4 to 5 minutes. Add the tomatoes, zucchini, and escarole and cook until the escarole wilts, about 3 minutes.

2. Add the water, broth, and salt, reduce the heat to low, and simmer for 40 minutes. When you are ready to cook the fish, bring to a furious boil, add the fish, and cook until they almost flake, 6 to 8 minutes. Discard the chile peppers and serve.

Makes 4 to 5 servings

ZUPPA DI PESCE WITH SPICY CHOPPED VEGETABLES

THIS IS A RICH STEW THAT GETS ITS HEAT from the chile peppers, which you will want to remove before serving. The toasted bread and *sauce rouille* are typical of how bouillabaisse is served in Provence, but work nicely here too. All the vegetables should be chopped

IS THIS FISH FRESH?

How do you tell when a fish is fresh? Today, if you are a consumer you can't tell very well because you will be hard pressed to find a whole fish to examine. There is a way to determine if a fish is fresh, but what's the point of me telling you if you'll never encounter a whole fish? No one, I mean no one, can look through a glass case at a filleted fish and tell whether it's fresh or not, although one can, if experienced, have a pretty good idea. For example, if the muscle fibers are separate, that would indicate the fish is probably not fresh. But there are too many tricks of the trade to make old fish look good, and everyone can be fooled. Even smelling isn't good enough if the fish has been doused in sodium benzoate. Almost all fish is now sold cut up into steaks and fillets, and the only way you can tell if it's fresh is by taste.

So forget about all the tricks of determining fresh fish. Learn instead how to pick a good fishmonger. The best will sell all their fish whole, but that usually is only the case in ethnic neighborhoods. So look for fishmongers, either independent fish stores or in supermarkets, that have vibrant-looking fish displayed on plenty of ice; there should be no discernable smell in the store, except that of the briny ocean. If the store smells fishy, that's not a good sign. The final arbiter will be when you taste the fish. If the fish tastes great, then that's where to buy your fish. Be discriminating. Generally, the fish in supermarket fish departments are not as top quality and fresh as those of independent fishmongers, whose livelihood and pride rest upon the best fish.

---

very finely so that none of them are too chunky. A nice mix of fish would include three or four of the following: swordfish, yellowtail, monkfish, tuna, salmon, mahimahi, and shark.

1/4 cup plus 2 tablespoons extra virgin olive oil

1 medium-size onion, finely chopped

6 large garlic cloves, finely chopped

1 celery stalk, finely chopped

1 leek (white and light green parts only), halved lengthwise, washed well, and finely chopped

1 small fennel bulb, stalks and leaves included, finely chopped

3 tablespoons finely chopped fresh basil leaves

3 tablespoons finely chopped fresh tarragon leaves

10 ounces ripe tomatoes, peeled, seeded, and finely chopped

3 cups dry white wine

3 cups Fish Broth (page 221)

Pinch of saffron threads, crumbled

3 dried chiles

Salt and freshly ground black pepper to taste

1 pound mixed fish steaks (see headnote)

4 slices Toasted Bread (see variation on page 224)

1/4 cup Sauce Rouille (page 230)

1. In a stew pot, heat the olive oil over high heat. Cook the onion, garlic, celery, leek, fennel, basil, and tarragon until they are soft and the onion is translucent, stirring frequently, about 10 minutes. Add the tomatoes, wine, broth, saffron, and chiles and season with salt and pepper. Bring to a boil, reduce the heat to low, and simmer for 45 minutes.

2. When its time to serve, bring the broth to a furious boil and add the fish. Cook until the fish is tender, but before it flakes, 3 to 5 minutes.

3. Serve immediately with the toasted bread spread with *sauce rouille* on top of the stew.

Makes 4 servings

ZUPPA DI PESCE SIRACUSANA

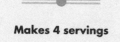

THE CITY OF SYRACUSE IS ONE OF THE most beautiful in Sicily, and it is the home to clear waters and delicious fish dishes such as this Syracuse-style fish stew. The gastronomy of Syracuse has been notable since the time it was a city-state of the ancient Greek territory Magna Graecia. In fact, the Greek philosopher Plato criticized the city-state's culinary excesses. It was also home to one of the earliest known writers on gastronomy, Archestratus, whose only known work was a gastronomic poem written about 348 B.C., called the *Hedypatheia*, which can be translated as "Life of Luxury." And in medieval times, in the twelfth century, the famed Arab geographer al-Idrīsī wrote about the richness of Syracuse's port and markets.

As with all fish stews, I think the more kinds of fish you use, the better, and you should choose what is locally available and fresh if the fish I call for are not. Some possibilities here are wolffish (ocean catfish), hake or cod, grouper or red snapper, redfish (ocean perch), monkfish, dogfish, shark, sea bass, halibut, yellowtail, striped bass, mahimahi (dolphinfish), pompano, bluefish, and ocean pout (ling).

2 pounds mixed fish fillets or steaks (see headnote), cut into large chunks
1 medium-size onion, thinly sliced and separated into rings
3 tablespoons finely chopped fresh parsley leaves
3 garlic cloves, crushed
1 1/2 celery stalks, finely chopped
1 bay leaf
1 large, ripe tomato (about 10 ounces), peeled, seeded, and chopped
1/4 cup plus 2 tablespoons extra virgin olive oil
1 cup dry white wine
3 cups water
Salt and freshly ground black pepper to taste
4 slices Toasted Bread or Grilled Bread (see variations on page 224)

1. Preheat the oven to 350°F.

2. Place the fish, onion, parsley, garlic, celery, bay leaf, tomato, olive oil, wine, and water in a large, deep casserole. Season with salt and pepper and stir well to mix everything. Bake until the fish is about to flake when tugged with a fork, about 45 minutes.

3. Serve with a slice of toasted bread in each serving bowl.

———————●———————

Makes 4 servings

ZUPPA DI PESCE ALLA CATANESE

OLIVES, SULTANAS (GOLDEN RAISINS), AND capers are an ingredient mix typical of the baroque style of cooking one finds in Catania, Sicily's second biggest city, on the eastern side of the island beneath the shadow of the active volcano of Mount Etna. This kind of cooking is mirrored in some of the architecture of the city as well, where one finds rather ornate buildings.

As is true of any fish stew, the more types of fish you can manage to put into it, the more delicious it will be. For the "mixed fish" below, try to use at least three of the following: bluefish, mackerel, Spanish mackerel, kingfish, mahimahi, yellowtail, or shark. If not, use some other types of dark-fleshed fish instead. Serve with slices of fried bread (page 224).

¹/₄ cup extra virgin olive oil
2 garlic cloves, lightly crushed
2 tablespoons tomato paste
¹/₄ cup golden raisins
¹/₄ cup capers, drained and rinsed
8 imported green Sicilian olives, pitted and cut in half
2 salted anchovy fillets, rinsed and chopped
¹/₄ cup finely chopped fresh basil leaves
¹/₄ cup finely chopped fresh parsley leaves
Salt and freshly ground black pepper to taste
4¹/₂ cups water
1 pound redfish (ocean perch), scorpionfish, sculpin, rockfish, or red snapper fillets, cut into pieces
1 pound mixed fish (see headnote)

———————●———————

1. In a large casserole, preferably an earthenware one set on a heat diffuser, heat the olive oil over medium-high heat. Cook the garlic until it begins to turn light brown, stirring. Discard the garlic and reduce the heat to medium. Add the tomato paste and stir it into the olive oil, then add the raisins, capers, olives, anchovies, basil, parsley, salt, pepper, and ¹/₂ cup of the water. Cook until the liquid is reduced by half or a little more, about 10 minutes.

2. Add the fish, cover with the remaining 4 cups of water, and increase the heat to high. Cover and cook until the more delicate fish begin to break up, about 12 minutes. Serve immediately.

———————●———————

Makes 4 servings

CLEANING MUSSELS, CLAMS, AND OYSTERS

Most mussels sold today are cultivated and don't need the vigorous cleaning and washing that wild ones do. But shellfish should be washed thoroughly in any case. Mussels have a little "beard" that hangs out of the hinge and once attached them to rocks or other objects. This needs to be pulled off. That's what the instruction "debearded" means. Clams and oysters should be rinsed well first, then soaked in cold water to cover mixed with 1 tablespoon of baking soda for 1 hour in the refrigerator to purge them of sand and grit. Then they should be rinsed again until the water runs clear.

MUSSEL STEW FROM TARANTO

THE CITY OF TARANTO IS NEAR THE middle of the coastline of the gulf of the same name, which forms the instep of the Italian boot. Mussels and oysters have been cultivated in the local beds since ancient times. The beds are located between the Mar Piccolo and the Mar Grande, in a lagoon fed by both freshwater and seawater, which flow through two channels on either side of the center of the city of Taranto, making it, in effect, an island. Local connoisseurs say the reason the mussels and oysters are so fine is because the tide is significant enough to bring the kind of food the bivalves require, as well as the right amount of salinity in the water to give them their particularly briny taste.

Years ago, as a kid, I collected the mussels in Laurel Hollow, on the North Shore of Long Island, and they were as excellent as anything I've ever tasted. But today most mussels are cultivated and they lack that briny taste. This stew, called *zuppa di cozze alla tarantina*, is simple to make and it allows the full flavor of the mussels to come forth.

2 garlic cloves, 1 crushed and 1 finely chopped
1 dried chile
¼ cup extra virgin olive oil
¼ cup tomato paste dissolved in ½ cup water
4 pounds mussels, scrubbed clean and debearded
1 cup dry white wine
6 slices Toasted Bread or Grilled Bread (see variations on page 224)

1. In a large casserole, preferably an earthenware one, cook the crushed garlic and chile in the olive oil over medium heat, stirring, and using a heat diffuser if necessary, until the garlic begins to turn light brown, about 3 minutes. Discard the garlic and chile. Add the diluted tomato paste and cook for 10 minutes, stirring occasionally.

2. Add the mussels, cover, and cook until the mussels open, shaking the casserole once in a while, about 5 minutes. Discard any mussels that remain tightly shut. Increase the heat to high, add the wine and chopped garlic, and cook, stirring, for 7 to 10 minutes.

3. Place 1 piece of toasted bread in each individual bowl; then, serving the soup from the casserole, pour a ladle full of mussel soup on top. Serve immediately.

———•———

Makes 4 servings

MEDITERRANEAN SEAFOOD RAGOUT

THE FISH SOUPS, RAGOUTS, AND STEWS found along the littoral of the wide arc that reaches from Sicily around the Tyhrrenian Sea, through Provence, and down the Spanish Costa Brava and Costa del Sol are vaguely similar and can be thought of as a progressive culinary rainbow. This seafood ragout is a family stew, which means that it is prepared with the minimum of fuss. The ragout is all the better with a nice mix of fish, say four different kinds. The fish listed are only recommendations; buy whatever is local and fresh. The stew is spiced with saffron and cayenne pepper and fragrant from fresh basil and wine. I would serve this stew with slices of fried bread (page 224) or perhaps some rice.

———•———

¼ cup plus 1 tablespoon extra virgin olive oil
1 medium-size onion, finely chopped
4 large garlic cloves, finely chopped
¼ cup finely chopped fresh basil leaves
1½ pounds ripe tomatoes, peeled, seeded, and chopped

Pinch of saffron threads, pounded in a mortar with 1 teaspoon salt
½ teaspoon cayenne pepper
Salt and freshly ground black pepper to taste
¾ cup Fish Broth (page 221) or water
2 pounds mixed fish fillets or steaks, such as yellowtail, mahimahi (dolphinfish), striped bass, and swordfish, cut into 2-inch cubes
½ cup dry white wine

———•———

1. In a large skillet or casserole, heat the olive oil over high heat. Cook the onion, garlic, and basil until the onion is translucent, stirring so the garlic doesn't burn, 5 to 6 minutes. Add the tomatoes, saffron, and cayenne and season with salt and pepper. Stir, add the fish broth, and cook over high heat until the sauce becomes dense, 8 to 10 minutes.

2. Add the fish and wine and cook until the wine has evaporated and the fish is cooked through, 10 to 12 minutes. Serve immediately.

———•———

Makes 4 to 6 servings

SWEDISH SALMON STEW FROM VÄXJÖ

THIS STEW, CALLED *LAXGRYTA* ("SALMON stew"), is apparently an old one in the family of Thyra Svensson, of Växjö. She got the recipe from her grandmother and believes it goes back to the nineteenth century. In Sweden, the use of corn oil is unusual, my

Stockholm-born Saab mechanic Håken Wiberg tells me. Håken also advises that the Swedish *gräddfil* called for in Mrs. Svensson's recipe, and which is usually translated as sour cream, is actually much more sour than our sour cream, and not as creamy. There are some Swedish delicatessens around the country that may carry *gräddfil*, but you can also stir some crème fraîche into your sour cream too. Växjö is in the middle of the lake region of southern Sweden and is world renowned for its glassworks, such as the Orrefors glassworks. The surrounding lakes and rivers are filled with fat salmon, and this delicious stew is a result.

———————•———————

1¹/2 *pounds boiling potatoes, peeled and sliced*
   ¹/4 *inch thick*
Salt to taste
2¹/2 *pounds salmon fillets, cut into a total of 12*
   pieces
1 *tablespoon finely chopped fresh dill*
¹/4 *cup corn oil, heated*
¹/2 *cup plus 2 tablespoons dry white wine*
¹/4 *cup plus 2 tablespoons dry sherry*
¹/2 *cup peeled and grated fresh horseradish*
1¹/2 *cups sour cream, at room temperature*

———————•———————

1. Preheat the oven to 350°F.

2. Place the potatoes in a large saucepan and cover with several inches with water. Turn the heat to medium and bring the water to a boil. Cook the potatoes until they are pierced easily with a skewer, 15 to 20 minutes, then drain.

3. Layer the potato slices in a lightly oiled, heavy casserole with a lid and salt lightly.

Layer the salmon on top of the potatoes and sprinkle with the dill. Pour the heated oil over everything and salt again. Put the lid on the casserole and place in the oven until the salmon has turned color but is raw in the middle, 20 to 25 minutes. You can check by pushing the fish with your finger to peek into the center. Remove the casserole from the oven and pour in the wine and sherry. Return to the oven and cook, uncovered, until the fish is firm but medium rare on the inside, 5 to 10 minutes. It's best to err on the side of undercooking.

4. Meanwhile, stir the horseradish and sour cream together. Remove the stew from the oven, cover with the horseradish cream sauce, and serve immediately.

———————•———————

Makes 6 servings

WHAT POTATOES TO USE?

———————•———————

Different potatoes have different uses. For boiling or steaming, the best kind of potatoes are low-starch, high-moisture potatoes called waxy potatoes. These potatoes remain firm when they are cut up after cooking. They're excellent to use in stews. Some examples are red potatoes, White Rose, and fingerlings. For baking or mashed potatoes, starchy ones that turn out fluffy are best. Some examples are Russet Burbanks (Idaho potatoes are mostly this cultivar) and Yellow Finns. Some potatoes, such as Yukon Golds, can be used for both purposes.

FINNISH SALMON STEW

THIS FINNISH SALMON STEW IS CALLED *keitetty lohi* or *kalakeitto*, which simply means fish soup, but it is much richer than that. Finnish cooks make this with or without milk. Ideally it is made with a whole, freshly caught salmon weighing about three pounds. Since finding a whole salmon in a fish store is less and less likely these days, I've adapted this recipe to accommodate two fillets. At the end of May and in early June, my fish store has beautiful salmon that were caught in the Copper River, in Alaska. These are truly delicious fish, rich and fatty, whose flesh is the most inviting orange color. If you can get the same, make this stew. Even if you can't, make this stew—it's incredible.

1 bunch fresh dill
2¹/₂ pound salmon fillets
2¹/₂ quarts water
3 tablespoon white wine vinegar
1 tablespoon sea salt
1 medium-size onion, thinly sliced and
    separated into rings
1 bay leaf
10 white peppercorns
20 allspice berries
2 pounds new potatoes, such as Yukon Gold
    or fingerlings, cut into 1-inch cubes or left
    whole
2 cups whole milk (optional)
1 cup heavy cream

1. Set aside 10 sprigs of the dill and chop enough of the remainder to get ¹/₂ cup. Save the rest for another use.

2. Put the salmon in a fish poacher, if you have one, or a large and longish casserole. Cover with the water, vinegar, salt, onion slices, bay leaf, peppercorns, allspice, and dill sprigs and bring the water to just below a boil over high heat. As soon as the water begins the first little bubble, in 10 to 15 minutes, turn the heat off and remove the salmon from the water. Strain the liquid and pour into a large saucepan or return to the casserole. Salt and refrigerate the salmon if you are not going to prepare it immediately.

3. Put the potatoes in the salmon-poaching broth and bring to a boil over medium heat, about 20 minutes. Cook until tender, about another 15 minutes. Add the milk, if using, the cream, and the chopped dill. Place the salmon in the broth and cook until it begins to flake, about 5 minutes. Check the seasonings and serve immediately.

Makes 6 servings

FINNISH TROUT STEW

MY GRANDMOTHER WAS FROM TURKU, on Finland's western Baltic coast. She died before I was born, so I don't know if she made this stew, but my mom thinks probably not, since they mostly ate saltwater fish, being on the sea, and trout came from Finland's many streams and lakes. But there is no doubt they would have enjoyed soul-satisfying fish stews like this one. The trout is first delicately poached in a court bouillon flavored with onion and dill, then the broth is enhanced with cream, potatoes, butter, and more dill. Serve this with hot whole wheat or rye rolls and butter, of course. In Finland this stew is called *kalakeitto*. This recipe is adapted from Beatrice Ojakangas's *The Finnish Cookbook*.

———————————●———————————

1¹/₂ pounds trout, gutted, cleaned, and cut into
    2-inch steaks, head and tail reserved
1 medium-size onion, sliced and separated into
    rings
1 clove
6 sprigs fresh dill
2 teaspoons salt
1 quart water
3 medium-size boiling potatoes (about 1¹/₄
    pounds), peeled and diced
2 cups light cream
3 tablespoons unsalted butter, broken into bits

———————————●———————————

1. Put the trout, including the head and tail, the onion, clove, 4 sprigs of the dill, the salt, and water in a large saucepan. Bring to just below a boil and simmer, without ever letting the water get to a boil, until the fish pieces remain whole but are nearly ready to flake when pushed with a fork, about 10 minutes. Strain, discarding the head and tail and return-

ing the broth to the same saucepan. Carefully slide the flesh of the fish off the bone, using a knife and fork. Reserve the fish and discard the bones and skin.

2. Put the potatoes in the saucepan with the fish broth and bring to a boil over medium heat. Once it has reached a light boil, cook the potatoes until soft when pierced in the center with a fork, 10 to 12 minutes. Add the light cream and simmer until almost bubbling gently, but do not let it come to a boil, about 20 minutes. Chop the remaining 2 sprigs of dill. Add the pieces of butter and the fish, and garnish with the chopped dill. Serve immediately.

———————————●———————————

Makes 4 to 6 servings

KAKAVIA

KAKAVIA IS *THE* FISH STEW OF GREECE. The word *kakavia* refers to a three-legged cooking pot that was traditionally used to cook soup and stews. The stew is said to be an ancient Greek fish soup, mentioned by Aristophanes, which traveled from the Aegean to Massalia, the Greek colony that became Marseilles, in about 600 B.C. Some writers claim, in fact, that bouillabaisse is derived from *kakavia* and that the two have three things in common: both are named for the pot in which they are cooked (*kakavia* for the Greek and *bouillet* for the French), both are made from a variety of fish, and both remain the expression of simple fishing villages, not the big cities. I believe all three of these reasons are nonsense. First, bouillabaisse is not named after a pot called *bouillet*, second, all fish stews are made from a variety of fish and that is not the *sine qua non* of fish stews, and third, bouillabaisse is identified with Marseilles, a big city for centuries, and not small fishing villages. Finally, *kakavia* bears no resemble to bouillabaisse in taste. All that said, *kakavia* is a terrific fish stew that stands on its own and doesn't need the support of comparison with bouillabaisse.

This recipe is based on my memory of a number of fish stews I've had around the Aegean, on the islands of Mykonos, Ios, and Rhodes, as well as in Athens and Monemvasia in the Peloponnesus. In restaurants one often finds the chef using lobster in this soup-stew, but I feel that it is not necessary. As far as the choice of fish goes, there are two ways to approach it. First, you could use whole small fish, as suggested in the ingredients list. This would be more authentic and more flavorful, but given Americans' inability to properly eat fish on the bone, you may want to consider the alternative of using fillets or steaks, also suggested below. If you use sardines, you'll want 6, which will weigh about ³/₄ pound in all.

———————

¹/₂ cup extra virgin olive oil
1 medium-size onion, thinly sliced and separated into rings
3 large garlic cloves, finely chopped
1 small fennel bulb, thinly sliced
Leaves from 3 sprigs fresh parsley, finely chopped

1 teaspoon dried thyme
1 bay leaf
2 pounds ripe plum tomatoes, peeled, seeded, and chopped
2 cups dry white wine
2 cups water
Salt and freshly ground black pepper
4 pounds mixed whole fish and steaks from 3 of the following fishes: whole sardines, whole porgy, whole butterfish, whole redfish (ocean perch), whole sculpin, whole red snapper and/or cod, halibut, hake, bass steaks, whole fish cleaned, gutted, and scaled, with heads and tail left on; or 2 pounds mixed fish fillets and steaks from 3 of the following fishes: red snapper, halibut, cod, bass, hake, and haddock
1 pound mussels, scrubbed clean and debearded
2 pounds fresh shrimp with their heads on or 1 pound previously frozen headless shrimp, shelled
10 slices Toasted Bread (see variation on page 224)

———————

1. In a stew pot or stockpot, heat the olive oil over medium heat. Cook the onion and garlic until soft, stirring so the garlic doesn't burn, 6 to 7 minutes. Add the fennel, parsley, thyme, and bay leaf, and cook for 1 minute, stirring. Add the tomatoes, wine, and water and bring to a boil. Season with salt and pepper and simmer for 45 minutes. Strain the broth through a fine-mesh sieve or strainer, return to the pot, and bring to a boil.

2. Add the fish and mussels to the boiling broth and add more water to cover only if there isn't enough broth. Reduce the heat to

HEAD-ON SHRIMP, HEAD-OFF SHRIMP

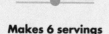

Nearly all shrimp sold in the United States is frozen shrimp. The shrimp you see in the market are defrosted shrimp of various sizes with their heads removed. Fresh shrimp are always sold with heads on, and they are always preferable to frozen shrimp. Shrimp deteriorate very quickly and that is one reason why they are so often sold frozen, but fresh shrimp are so vastly superior in taste that you will think you are eating something wonderful that has never been eaten before. Check with your local fishmonger and ask if and when they get in fresh shrimp. And when they do, count on eating lots of it. True shrimp connoisseurs buy only head-on fresh shrimp (that is, never frozen) and cook them whole. Then they separate the head from the tail and suck out all the juices in the head before eating the tail portion.

medium-low and simmer for 7 minutes. Add the shrimp and continue to simmer until the shrimp are orange and the mussels have opened, another 7 to 10 minutes. Discard any mussels that are tightly closed. Check the seasonings and serve with a toasted slice of bread in each bowl.

Makes 6 servings

GRAY MULLET AND CELERIAC STEW FROM TURKEY

GRAY MULLET (*MUGIL CEPHALUS* L.) IS A fish much appreciated by Turkish cooks, probably because it does not have a lot of annoying small bones. The fish is plentiful in the Black Sea and can actually be found in warm waters worldwide. If you are not able to get gray mullet, you can substitute striped bass, sea bass, or bluefish. This dish, called *kefal pilakisi* in Turkish, is best made in an earthenware casserole such as the Spanish *cazuela*, which is sold by Williams-Sonoma, among others (see the sources listed at the back of the book).

¹/₂ cup extra virgin olive oil

2 medium-size onions, thinly sliced

2 cups water

3 small Yukon Gold potatoes (about 10 ounces total), peeled and cubed

1 small celeriac (celery root, about ¹/₂ pound), peeled and cubed

2 carrots, split lengthwise, then cut crosswise into thirds

1 pound ripe tomatoes, peeled, seeded, and chopped

5 garlic cloves, finely chopped

2 pounds gray mullet, striped bass, bluefish, or sea bass fillets or steaks cut 2 inches thick

1¹/₂ teaspoons salt

Juice from 1 lemon

³/₄ cup finely chopped fresh parsley leaves

1. In a large earthenware casserole set on a heat diffuser, heat 2 tablespoons of the olive oil with the onions over medium-high. Cook the onions, stirring, until yellow, about 5 minutes. Add the water, cover, and cook until the onions look like they could melt, keeping them moistened with more water if necessary and stirring occasionally, about 30 minutes. (If you are not cooking with earthenware and a diffuser, cook over medium heat and check for doneness sooner.)

2. Add the potatoes, celeriac, carrots, tomatoes, and garlic. Cover, reduce the heat to medium, and cook until the root vegetables are *al dente*, about 1 hour.

3. Add the fish, the remaining 6 tablespoons of olive oil, and the salt. Increase the heat to high and cook until the fish is white and firm, 12 to 15 minutes. Gently stir in the lemon juice and parsley. Let the casserole rest for 5 minutes and serve.

Makes 4 servings

AL DENTE

The concept of *al dente* is usually applied to the cooking of pasta in Italy. It means "to the teeth," and that means the pasta should have an ever-so-slight bite to it. But *al dente* is a great concept that can be applied to any kind of cooked food that should have a little bite to it, such as the celeriac in the Gray Mullet and Celeriac Stew from Turkey (page 261).

TURKISH SEAFOOD STEW IN AN EARTHENWARE CASSEROLE

BECAUSE TURKEY IS SURROUNDED by four seas—the Black Sea, the Sea of Marmara, the Aegean, and the Mediterranean—its seafood cookery is refined and perfect. The Turks favor fish that is grilled or fried, but they also like poached fish and fish stews. Winter is a prime time for seafood because this is when many species of fish migrate from the Black Sea to the warmer waters of the Mediterranean and it is when most fish reach their mature sizes.

This Turkish preparation is called *güveçte deniz mahsülleri*, which means "mixed seafood stew." In restaurants it is typically served in individual earthenware crocks, such as the kind that are used for French onion soup. Although this recipe is adapted from one by Chef Özcan Ozan of the Sultan's Kitchen restaurant in Boston, Massachusetts, I remember fondly eating dishes like this in special fish restaurants and taverns that overlook many harbors up and down the Turkish coast. My favorites were always the small and modest ones, with their wooden tables and rickety wooden chairs, which offered extraordinarily fresh fish in an open-air dining section right by the sea. Waiters scurry about, running off to the kitchen, located you're not sure where—maybe across the street—while you examine the displayed fish, choosing the ones you want.

A problem that the cook will face in cooking a stew like this is being assured that all the seafood is cooked properly and finishes at the same time. The timing in this recipe is quite accurate, so it's best just to follow the recipe and not be too innovative. The Turkish red pepper called for in this recipe is usually found in Middle Eastern markets, where it may also be called Aleppo pepper. Alternatively, you can mix one part cayenne pepper with two parts Hungarian hot paprika to approximate the taste.

———◆———

18 mussels (about 1¹/₃ pounds), scrubbed clean and debearded

1 large shallot, finely chopped

2 large garlic cloves, finely chopped

2 bay leaves

¹/₄ cup plus 2 tablespoons finely chopped fresh parsley leaves

1 large green bell pepper, seeded and thinly sliced

2 pounds ripe tomatoes, peeled, seeded, and chopped

³/₄ cup dry white wine

¹/₂ cup extra virgin olive oil

1 pound swordfish steaks, cut into 1-inch cubes

1 pound red snapper fillets, cut into 2-inch squares

1 pound squid, cleaned if necessary (see page 237) and cut into 1-inch-thick rings with the tentacles

2 pounds fresh shrimp with their heads on or 1 pound previously frozen headless shrimp, shelled

Salt and freshly ground black pepper to taste

¹/₂ teaspoon Turkish red pepper

¹/₂ teaspoon dried oregano

3 ounces imported Greek or Bulgarian feta cheese, crumbled

1. Preheat the oven to 350°F. If you have two ovens, preheat the second one to broil.

2. Put the mussels in a large, nonreactive pot and add the shallots, garlic, bay leaves, parsley, green peppers, tomatoes, and wine. Cover, turn the heat to high, and cook until the mussels open, stirring to move the mussels on the bottom of the pot, about 6 minutes. Remove the mussels, and when cool enough to handle, remove them from their shells. Discard the bay leaves and save the broth. Discard any mussels that remain firmly shut.

3. In a large skillet, heat the olive oil over medium heat. Cook the swordfish, red snapper, squid, shrimp, and mussels until they turn color, carefully turning so the red snapper doesn't break apart, about 5 minutes. Season with salt, black pepper, red pepper, and oregano. Add the reserved mussel broth. Fold the broth and fish together gently, so the red snapper doesn't break apart, then remove from the heat immediately.

4. Divide the contents of the skillet evenly between 6 individual ovenproof earthenware bowls, making sure everyone gets at least 2 shrimp, or transfer everything to 1 large earthenware casserole or baking pan, and bake until the fish is cooked, about 15 minutes. Remove from the oven.

5. If you are using one oven, increase the heat to broil and let it reach that temperature, about 5 minutes, before placing anything in it. Sprinkle the feta cheese over the seafood and place under the broiler until the top begins to show some charred marks, 2 to 3 minutes. Serve immediately.

———●———

Makes 6 servings

EGGPLANT AND SEAFOOD STEW FROM GHANA

GHANA IS A FORMER BRITISH COLONY in West Africa and today English is widely spoken there. The food of Ghana shares many similarities with other West African countries, especially in the use of the cassava (taro), a variety of yams, corn, peanuts, melon seeds, eggplant, okra, and fish. This dish is called *froi* and is adapted from a recipe in *The African Cookbook* by Bea Sandler, who tells us that there are hundreds of varieties of *froi*, including ones made with beef, smoked fish, and okra. Serve with rice, mashed yams, or boiled plantains on the side.

———●———

2 pounds eggplant, peeled and diced
2 medium-size onions, chopped
9 ounces small okra, bottoms trimmed
1 green bell pepper, seeded and chopped
1 medium-size, ripe tomato, peeled, seeded, and chopped
1 cup water
2¹/₄ teaspoons salt

1 teaspoon freshly ground black pepper, or to taste
1 teaspoon cayenne pepper
¹/₄ cup peanut oil
2 pounds flat white fish fillets, such as sole, red snapper, or John Dory
1 pound fresh shrimp with their heads on or ¹/₂ pound previously frozen headless shrimp, shelled

———●———

1. In a large casserole or stew pot, put the eggplant, half of the onions, the okra, green pepper, tomato, water, salt, black pepper, and cayenne. Cover and turn the heat to high, stirring occasionally. Once the vegetables are boiling vigorously, about 10 minutes, reduce the heat to low and simmer until all the vegetables are tender, about 30 minutes. Pass the vegetables through a food mill and set aside.

2. Preheat the oven to 350°F.

3. In a large casserole or Dutch oven, heat the peanut oil over medium-high heat. Cook the remaining onion until translucent, stirring, about 5 minutes. Remove from the heat. Spread the pureed vegetables over the onion, then arrange the fish and shrimp on top. Bake until fish flakes and the shrimp are orange, about 30 minutes. Serve from the casserole.

———●———

Makes 4 to 6 servings

FIERY RAGOUT OF FISH BALLS FROM TUNISIA

TUNISIA HAS A VERY LONG MEDITER-ranean coastline running from Tabarka, near the Algerian border in the north, to Zarzis, near the Libyan border in the Sahel, in the south. As a result, there is quite a bit of good seafood cookery. This has been notable especially in Tunis, Sousse, Sfax, and on the islands of Kerkenna and Djerba since ancient and medieval times. The fact that this Tunisian fish stew is called a *ṭājin bi'l-ḥūt* ("fish casse-role") means only that it is cooked in the earthenware casserole of the same name and not that it is cooked with eggs, as nearly all tagines are in Tunisia. It is a spicy stew, typical of much of Tunisian cooking.

¼ pound stale Italian or French bread, crusts removed

1 large egg

2 pounds white-fleshed fish fillets, such as cod, hake, or halibut

¼ cup finely chopped fresh parsley leaves

6 large garlic cloves, finely chopped

1 large onion, finely chopped

2 tablespoons Harīsa (page 34)

1 tablespoon salt, or more as needed

2 teaspoons freshly ground black pepper

2 cups olive oil for frying

1¾ cups water

2 tablespoons tomato paste

1. Soak the bread in water and squeeze it out as if you were making a snowball. Place the egg in the food processor and run for 4 seconds. Add the bread, fish, parsley, 3 garlic cloves, the onion, 1 tablespoon of the *harīsa*, 2½ tea-spoons of the salt, and 1 teaspoon of the pepper and process until pasty, scrapping down the sides if necessary. If your food processor isn't big enough, you may have to do this in batches. Remove and make walnut-size balls from the mixture with wet hands (so they don't stick to the fish paste), then flatten the balls slightly so they look more like small hockey pucks.

2. In a large skillet, heat the olive oil over medium-high heat until smoking. Cook several fish balls until light golden brown, turn-ing once, 1 to 2 minutes on each side. Do not crowd the skillet as you cook them; cook in batches if you have to. The fish balls should be only half cooked.

3. In a casserole, preferably an earthenware one set on a heat diffuser, heat ¼ cup of the oil in which you cooked the fish with the water, the remaining 3 garlic cloves, the tomato paste, the remaining 1 tablespoon of *harīsa*, ½ teaspoon of salt, and 1 teaspoon of pepper until the water reaches a boil. Add all the fish balls, reduce the heat to low, and simmer until the sauce is reduced by half and the fish balls are springy to the touch, 18 to 22 minutes. Serve immediately.

Makes 6 servings

TUNISIAN FISH STEW
IN THE STYLE OF SFAX

☙

THE COASTAL TUNISIAN CITY OF SFAX is well known for its seafood. In fact, in the early twelfth century, when al-Idrīsī, the famed Arab geographer of the Norman court in Palermo during the reign of Roger II, traveled through North Africa, Sfax, he tells us, was well known for its fish, and it remained so throughout the Ḥafṣid era in Tunisia (1228–1574). This fish soup, called *maraqat al-ḥūt*, is traditional for the ʿĪd al-Ṣaghīr feast, the feast of the breaking of the Ramadan fast.

In Sfax, the most popular fish to use is grouper, although cooks also love other Mediterranean fish, such as scorpionfish, annular bream, hake, and red gurnard. Some Sfaxian cooks use raisins in this preparation, and I think you will find them a nice addition. When you pick the fish for this recipe, choose at least two, and look for the freshest fish. The best choices are grouper, porgy (scup), red snapper, redfish (ocean perch), ocean pout (ling), cod, haddock, wolffish (ocean catfish), hake, and mahimahi (dolphinfish, the closest in taste to grouper).

There are three ways you can eat this preparation: the broth can be eaten as a soup with some toasted, grilled, or fried bread (page 224) for the first course and the fish eaten as a second course, or you can eat the stew with macaroni on the side or in it, or you can eat the whole thing as a kind of North African *zuppa di pesce*.

2 teaspoons cumin seeds
6 large garlic cloves, peeled
1/2 teaspoon salt
1/2 cup extra virgin olive oil
1 medium-size onion, chopped
1 tablespoon tomato paste
2 quarts plus 1/2 cup water
1/2 teaspoon **Harīsa** (page 34)
1 tablespoon hot paprika
1 teaspoon cayenne pepper
1/2 teaspoon freshly ground black pepper
2 fresh green chiles, seeded
2 celery stalks, chopped
3 carrots, thinly sliced
Pinch of saffron threads, crumbled
10 sprigs fresh parsley, tied with kitchen twine
1 bay leaf
Salt to taste
2 1/2 pounds mixed fish, including 1 with its head on, if possible (see headnote for choices), scaled, gutted, and cleaned
1 lemon, quartered, or 1 Preserved Lemon (page 108)

━━━━━●━━━━━

1. In a mortar, grind the cumin into a powder with a pestle, then add the garlic and salt and pound until you have a paste. Set aside.

2. In a large, deep, stove-top casserole or stew pot, heat the olive oil over high heat. Cook the onion until softened, stirring, 1 to 2 minutes.

3. Meanwhile, dissolve the tomato paste in 1/2 cup of the water and add to the casserole along with the *harīsa*, paprika, cayenne, black pepper, and garlic paste. Add 1 quart of the water, bring to a boil over high heat, and cook for 10 minutes. Add the remaining 1 quart of water, the whole chiles, celery, carrots, saffron, parsley, and bay leaf and season with salt. Reduce the heat to medium-low and simmer for 30 minutes.

4. Strain the broth through a fine-mesh strainer, and discard the vegetables. Return the broth to the casserole or pot. Bring the broth to a furious boil and add the whole fish first, if using any. Cook the whole fish for 5 minutes, then add the remaining fish. Cook for 15 minutes, then remove the fish and bone the whole fish. Discard the chiles, bay leaf, and parsley.

5. Serve the broth as a first-course soup with quartered fresh lemons or preserved lemons. Keep the fish warm on an ovenproof serving platter in the oven, and serve as a second course.

Makes 4 servings

OCTOPUS STEW FROM THE ISLAND OF DJERBA

THE ISLAND OF DJERBA, OFF THE SAHEL, the desert region of southern Tunisia, was once thought to be the land of the lotus eaters made famous by Homer. Today Djerba is a tourist destination for northern Europeans and a delightful island with wonderful seafood. This octopus stew, *yakhna bi'l-ākhtabūṭ* in Arabic, is a specialty of the island. There the octopus men use special contraptions made of a series of chambers, from which the octopus cannot escape. This stew is traditionally cooked in an earthenware *marmite*, or what the Tunisians call a tagine, which sits atop an earthenware brazier filled with lump hardwood coals.

1 pound octopus, cleaned if necessary (see page 268)
¼ cup plus 2 tablespoons extra virgin olive oil
1 medium-size onion, chopped
3 large garlic cloves, sliced
2 tablespoons tomato paste
7 cups water
1 tablespoon Harīsa (page 34)
½ teaspoon freshly ground caraway seeds
½ teaspoon cayenne pepper
1 teaspoon freshly ground black pepper
3 cups fresh or canned crushed tomatoes
2 cups peeled, seeded, and diced pumpkin, butternut, turban, or acorn squash (about ½ pound)
Salt to taste
½ cup canned chickpeas, drained

1. Put the octopus in a medium-size pot filled with water to cover. Bring to a gentle boil, and cook for 40 minutes. Drain, and when cool enough to handle, rub off the skin, then dice.

2. In a *marmite*, the bottom portion of a *couscoussier*, or another deep, potbellied stew pot, heat the olive oil over medium-high heat. Cook the onion and garlic, stirring frequently

OCTOPUS

Nearly all the octopus you are likely to find in a fish store or supermarket will be sold frozen. These octopuses are mostly imported from the Philippines. Freezing an octopus helps tenderize it, so that's a good thing. And they will be already cleaned—another time-saving factor. But if you are using a freshly caught octopus, you've got your work cut out for you. First you must remove the "beak," where the mouth is. Then you must remove the viscera inside the head. It must be washed thoroughly and then it must be beaten. And beaten, and beaten, and beaten. Traditionally (and you can still see men in Greece, southern Italy, or Tunisia doing this) the octopuses are beaten against the rocks that dot the coastline where they are caught.

so the garlic doesn't burn, until the onion is translucent, about 6 minutes. Dissolve the tomato paste in 1 cup of the water, and add it to the pot along with the *harīsa*, caraway, cayenne, and black pepper. Stir and cook, covered, for 5 minutes, stirring or shaking the pot occasionally. Add the tomatoes, pumpkin, octopus, and the remaining 6 cups of water. Season with salt, bring to a boil, and continue boiling for 20 minutes. Add the chickpeas and continue to cook until the stew is thick and everything is tender, 45 minutes to 1 1/4 hours. Correct the seasonings and serve.

Makes 4 servings

MOROCCAN FISH STEW

THIS FISH STEW FROM CASABLANCA, called *ṭājin bi'l-ḥūt*, is traditionally made in an earthenware casserole with a cone-shaped lid, and the whole ensemble, as well as the dish, is called a *ṭājin* or *ṭājīn*, sometimes transliterated into English as tagine. The traditional Moroccan *ṭājin* (pronounced TAJn or TajEEN) is a round, handleless earthenware casserole. The tagine is set upon an earthenware brazier filled with red-hot lump hardwood coals and it cooks for some time. As the stew cooks, the conical cover traps the steam as it builds, allowing for some air circulation, which imparts an intense and aromatic flavor to the food. In place of an authentic Moroccan tagine, try to use any earthenware casserole with a lid, or lacking that, a Dutch oven or enameled cast-iron casserole or clay oven.

I learned how to make this recipe in Casablanca, where it would be made with grouper, amberjack, or liche, but I make it with swordfish, shark, and sea bass or slightly less firm fish such as grouper, pompano, jack, or red snapper.

Sharmūla *(recipe follows)*
4 firm-fleshed white fish steaks, such as swordfish or shark (about 1 1/2 pounds), cut about 1 1/4 inches thick
2 medium-size boiling potatoes, peeled and sliced 1/8 inch thick
Salt and freshly ground black pepper to taste
2 green bell peppers, seeded and cut into thin strips

2 large, ripe tomatoes, peeled, seeded, and thinly
   sliced
1/2 cup tomato puree, preferably fresh
2 tablespoons finely chopped fresh coriander
   (cilantro) leaves
2 tablespoons finely chopped fresh parsley leaves

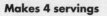

1. Prepare the *sharmūla*. Coat the fish steaks with half of the *sharmūla* and marinate for 2 hours in a ceramic or glass baking dish in the refrigerator.

2. Preheat the oven to 400°F. Lightly oil a tagine, Dutch oven, earthenware casserole, or enameled cast-iron casserole. Arrange the potatoes over the bottom, and lightly season with salt and pepper. Place the fish steaks on top of the potatoes. Cover the fish with the green peppers, then the tomato slices, arranging everything very neatly and decoratively. Lightly salt and pepper again. Spoon half of the remaining *sharmūla* over the tomato slices. Pour the tomato puree over everything and sprinkle with the coriander, parsley, and more salt and pepper. Spoon the remaining *sharmūla* over the top.

3. Bake the tagine, covered, until the potatoes are tender and the fish is cooked, about 1 hour. Do not check until at least 40 minutes have passed. Serve immediately.

Makes 4 servings

CANNED BEANS

Many professional cooks turn their noses up at canned foods. But there are several canned beans that are nearly as good as the dried ones. I often use canned chickpeas and fava beans. Their taste is almost identical to the taste of the dried chickpeas and fava beans that you would soak and boil yourself, and they are a great time saver. Some fava beans are sold under the name "foul medammes." These are the round beans known as "bath fava," not the more familiar kidney-shaped beans.

SHARMŪLA: A MOROCCAN FISH MARINADE

When cooking thicker cuts of fish, Moroccan cooks use a kind of relish-marinade of finely sliced or torn herbs and spices called *chermoulla*, *tchermila*, *chermoula*, or *charmoula*, which are various transliterations for *sharmūla*, derived from the Arabic word meaning "to tear lightly." Some cooks gently heat the *sharmūla* in a pan, others liquefy everything in a blender. The marinade can also be used for chicken. The amounts in parentheses are in case you decide to put everything in a food processor.

¹/₂ cup very finely chopped fresh coriander (cilantro) leaves (1¹/₂ cups lightly packed leaves)

¹/₂ cup very finely chopped fresh parsley leaves (1¹/₂ cups lightly packed leaves)

6 garlic cloves, very finely chopped

1 small onion, very finely chopped

Juice of ¹/₂ lemon

6 to 8 tablespoons extra virgin olive oil, as needed

1 teaspoon freshly ground black pepper

1 teaspoon hot paprika

¹/₄ teaspoon cayenne pepper

¹/₂ teaspoon freshly ground cumin seeds

¹/₄ teaspoon ground cinnamon

¹/₄ teaspoon ground saffron, or a pinch of saffron threads, lightly toasted in an oven and ground in a mortar

1¹/₄ teaspoons salt

———————●———————

Mix all the ingredients together, or if you like, process them in a food processor. Refrigerate for 1 hour before using.

———————●———————

Makes about 1 cup

RAGOUT OF SAFFRON-FLAVORED FISH DUMPLINGS FROM MOROCCO

MOROCCO WAS UNDER FRENCH RULE for a long time, and the French language is used throughout the country, especially since so many of the tourists are French too. In Casablanca they call this dish *boulettes de poisson* ("fish balls") in French, or in Arabic, *ṭājin bi'l-ḥūt* ("fish casserole" or fish stew"). The saffron-flavored balls of mashed fish are poached in an aromatic tomato ragout seasoned with abundant onions and spices. You don't necessarily need to use the fish called for here; you can use any white-fleshed fish that flakes readily. I'm sure you will find the taste of this ragout quite alluring and exotic.

———————●———————

1 large egg

2 pounds cod, scrod, hake, haddock, or any slightly bland white-fleshed fish fillets

¹/₄ teaspoon ground saffron

Salt to taste

¹/₂ teaspoon freshly ground black pepper

1 cup extra virgin olive oil

4 large, ripe tomatoes (about 2 pounds), peeled, seeded, and chopped

2 medium-size onions, chopped

3 large garlic cloves, finely chopped

2 teaspoons hot paprika

¹/₂ teaspoon cayenne pepper

¹/₂ teaspoon freshly ground cumin seeds
Romaine lettuce leaves as an accompaniment

---

1. Place the egg in a food processor and run for 4 seconds. Add the fish, saffron, salt, and black pepper. Run in short bursts until pasty. Form the fish mixture into walnut-size balls with wet hands (so the mixture doesn't stick) or use two soup spoons so you don't touch the fish at all.

2. Place the olive oil, tomatoes, onions, garlic, paprika, cayenne, and cumin in a casserole, season with salt and pepper, and bring to a boil over high heat. Reduce the heat to medium, add the fish balls, and cook at a simmer until they are all white and springy to the touch, about 15 minutes.

3. Serve the fish stew in individual bowls with raw romaine lettuce leaves on a separate platter for dipping into the sauce.

Makes 4 to 6 servings

LEBANESE-STYLE FISH STEW WITH RICE

THE ARABS ARE NOT FAMOUS FOR THEIR fish stews because the fishing grounds of the eastern Mediterranean are not abundant, except in some very localized areas. Nevertheless, the few fish recipes that do exist in Arab cuisine are, I believe, extraordinary. Whatever is lacking in the sea is more than compensated for by the creative ingenuity of Arab cooks. Take, for instance, this Lebanese fish stew, *yakhni samak*. It is finely spiced and delicate. Lebanese and Syrian cooks like to keep the fish on the bone while it cooks, which gives the oil it cooks in, as well as the fish, a better flavor. In Arab lands fish is almost always served with rice pilaf cooked with saffron. Read the recipe carefully a couple of times before beginning because it is a bit involved. You will need a large platter onto which you will invert the cooked fish and rice.

1³/₄ cups extra virgin olive oil
¹/₂ cup unbleached all-purpose flour
1 tablespoon plus ¹/₂ teaspoon salt, plus more to taste
1 teaspoon freshly ground black pepper
1 tablespoon plus 1 teaspoon freshly ground cumin seeds
1 pound sea bass steaks
5 medium-size onions (about 2 pounds), 4 coarsely chopped and 1 thinly sliced and separated into rings
2 cups long-grain rice, soaked in tepid water for 30 minutes and drained
1 quart water
Good-size pinch of saffron threads, crumbled
¹/₂ cup pine nuts
¹/₂ cup fresh lemon juice
¹/₂ cup tahini
1 large garlic clove, peeled

1. Preheat the olive oil in a large skillet over high heat until very hot and nearly smoking. Mix the flour with 1 teaspoon of the salt, the pepper, and 1 teaspoon of the cumin. Dredge the fish pieces in the seasoned flour, tapping off any excess. Cook the fish until golden, about 1 1/2 minutes per side, turning with tongs and a metal spatula. Remove from the pan and drain on paper towels. Separate the fish from its bones and arrange the flesh over the bottom of a large saucepan or round casserole. Reserve all the oil the fish was fried in.

2. Take 1/2 cup of the oil the fish was fried in and transfer it to a large casserole or skillet. Heat over medium-high heat and cook the chopped onions until golden, stirring almost constantly, about 15 minutes. Combine the rice and fried onions and spread over the fish pieces.

3. In a small saucepan, bring 3 cups of the water to a boil with 2 teaspoons of the salt, the saffron, and the remaining 1 tablespoon of cumin. Carefully pour the boiling water over the fish and rice, shake the pan to distribute, and simmer over low heat, covered, until all the water is absorbed and the rice is cooked, 20 to 50 minutes, so keep checking.

4. Meanwhile, in a small skillet, heat 3 tablespoons of the reserved fish oil over medium-high heat and cook the pine nuts until brown, tossing constantly, about 2 minutes. Remove from the pan with a slotted spoon and set aside.

5. To begin the fish sauce, put the sliced onion in a medium-size saucepan with the remaining 1 cup of water, season with salt, and turn the heat to medium. Once it begins to simmer, cook the onion for 15 minutes. Remove the onion from the water and let cool.

6. In a small bowl, stir the lemon juice into the tahini until smooth. Pound the garlic with the remaining 1/2 teaspoon of salt in a mortar until mushy. Stir the garlic, 1/4 cup plus 2 tablespoons of the remaining fish oil, and the sliced onion into the tahini and stir until smooth.

7. Place a large serving platter over the saucepan or casserole in which the fish and rice are cooking and invert the casserole carefully and quickly. Let it rest for 2 minutes without removing the pan. Remove the pan, garnish the platter with the toasted pine nuts, and serve with the tahini sauce on the side.

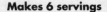

Makes 6 servings

TAHINI

Tahini is one of the most important ingredients in the Middle Eastern pantry. It is a paste made from sesame seeds with the consistency of peanut butter, and is usually sold in jars. There will be a layer of sesame seed oil on top of the paste, so mix the tahini before using. Tahini is always found in Middle Eastern markets and in many supermarkets too. It will keep, tightly covered and refrigerated, indefinitely.

FISH CURRY
IN THE BENGALI STYLE

M Y FRIEND CHITRITA BANERJI WROTE a wonderful book some years ago called *Bengali Cooking*. There she says that "if you ask a Bengali for the shortest description of Bengali food, the answer is likely to be fish and rice." Bengali food is nothing like the ubiquitous northern Indian food that defines virtually all Indian restaurants in America.

In this stew, the initial dusting of the fish with paprika and turmeric is not only for flavor but also helps the fish hold together during its first frying. Many Bengali Hindus cook classic fish and vegetable preparations in a yogurt sauce. Although I call this stew a fish curry, it is properly called *doi machh*, or "fish with yogurt."

FOR THE FISH:

1 teaspoon hot paprika
1/4 teaspoon turmeric
Salt to taste
1 1/4 pounds sea bass, cod, or halibut fillets, cut into a total of 6 to 8 pieces
2 tablespoons vegetable oil

FOR THE SAUCE:

2 tablespoons vegetable oil
3 large onions, finely chopped
2 garlic cloves, crushed
1/4 teaspoon cayenne pepper
1/4 teaspoon freshly ground cumin seeds
1/4 teaspoon freshly ground black (preferably) or yellow mustard seeds
1/8 teaspoon ground cinnamon
1/8 teaspoon freshly ground cloves
1/8 teaspoon freshly ground cardamom seeds
1/8 teaspoon turmeric
3 large, ripe tomatoes, peeled, seeded, and chopped
1 tablespoon finely chopped fresh coriander (cilantro) leaves
1/4 cup water
1 1/2 teaspoons salt
1/2 cup high-quality, full-fat, plain cow's milk yogurt

1. To prepare the fish, spread the paprika and turmeric and a little salt on a dinner plate or baking tray. Quickly dredge each piece of fish in the spice mixture and set aside. In a large skillet, heat the 2 tablespoons of oil over medium-high heat. Cook the fish until it turns color, turning once, about 1 minute per side. Remove from the pan and set aside.

2. To make the sauce, add the 2 tablespoons of oil to the skillet, and once it is hot, cook the onions and garlic until soft, stirring, about 10 minutes. Add the cayenne, cumin, mustard seeds, cinnamon, cloves, cardamom, and turmeric and cook, stirring, for 1 to 2 minutes. Add the tomatoes, fresh coriander, and water. Reduce the heat to low and simmer until the liquid from the tomatoes is mostly evaporated, about 40 minutes. Add the salt and yogurt and stir.

3. Return the fish to the skillet, cover, and simmer until the fish flakes, about 20 minutes. Serve immediately.

Makes 4 servings

MAINE LOBSTER STEW

THE STATE OF MAINE'S TWO GREAT CON-tributions to American cooking, I submit, are the lobster roll and lobster stew. Given how simple the two are to make, it's a mystery why it seems that they are properly done only in Maine. I believe the reason might lie in that very fact; that they are so simple. Non-Maine cooks just start adding all these superfluous things in the mistaken belief that the original is too bland. Well, nothing with lobster in it will ever be bland, so one secret to this dish is lots of lobster. This is the time to be extravagant. Some cooks add carrots and potatoes, or even onions and leeks. An abomination! Others garnish with parsley or paprika—but just remember that lobster stew has only three ingredients: lobster, butter, and milk. Now, it's true that the milk we have today is pasteurized and not as rich and creamy as it once was, so it's permissible to add some cream to bolster our thin milk. After you make the stew, you refrigerate it for six hours before serving, so allow enough time for this.

Two 2-pound live lobsters, steamed 20 to 25
   minutes
1/2 cup (1 stick) unsalted butter
1 quart unpasteurized, raw whole creamery
   milk, or 2 cups whole milk and 2 cups heavy
   cream
Salt and freshly ground black pepper to taste
   (optional)

1. Remove the meat from all parts of the lobster, including the legs and fantail, and cut into pieces just a wee bit smaller than bite size. Set aside the tomalley and coral.

2. In a large saucepan, melt the butter over medium heat with any tomalley and coral, stirring for about 8 minutes. Add the lobster and heat, then slowly add all the milk, stirring constantly. Add the cream, if using, and continue to stir until heated. Turn the heat off and refrigerate the stew for 6 hours.

3. When you want to serve the lobster stew, reheat it without ever letting it come to a boil. Serve in bowls and add salt and pepper at the table, if you desire.

Makes 4 servings

CAPE COD PORTUGUESE SEAFOOD STEW

I N THE NINETEENTH CENTURY, PORTU-
guése immigrants began populating fishing
towns on the Massachusetts coast, especially
New Bedford and Fall River. A community of
Portuguese fishermen and their families also
thrived in Provincetown on Cape Cod and a
few settled in Truro and Wellfleet. As a result,
a good number of traditional old Cape Cod
dishes are called Portuguese-style, such as this
luscious stew with fish, clams, linguiça sausage,
and kale. Many of the local clam shacks on
Cape Cod will offer a Portuguese kale soup
or a variation on this recipe. Every summer for
nearly fifteen years I would take my kids to our
little house on Drummer's Cove, in Wellfleet,
and we would make this stew, usually with
clams that the kids dug up at low tide near our
beach house. The Portuguese-style linguiça
sausage is rather easily found in supermarkets
in New England, but elsewhere you can use
Spanish-style (not Mexican-style) chorizo, hot
Italian sausage, Cajun andouille sausage, or
Polish kielbasa. The Russian kale I call for in
the recipe is a darker-looking kale, but go
ahead and use whatever is available.

½ cup diced salt pork
2 tablespoons extra virgin olive oil
1 large onion, chopped
2 garlic cloves, crushed
1 pound ripe tomatoes, cut in half, seeds
    squeezed out, and grated against the largest
    holes of a grater down to the peel
1 pound linguiça sausage, cut into 1-inch pieces
2 pounds fingerling potatoes, cut into 1-inch cubes
1 pound Russian kale, trimmed of heavier stems
    and sliced into thin strips
1½ quarts water
1 tablespoon dry white wine or sherry vinegar
1 teaspoon dried thyme
¼ teaspoon red pepper flakes
Pinch of saffron threads, crumbled
1 tablespoon plus 2 teaspoons salt
1 teaspoon freshly ground black pepper
2 pounds striped bass, sea bass, or other
    firm-fleshed fish fillets, cut into large chunks
2 dozen littleneck clams (about 2 pounds),
    soaked in cold water to cover mixed with
    1 tablespoon baking soda for 1 hour and
    drained

1. In a large casserole, brown the salt pork in
the olive oil until crispy over medium heat,
stirring occasionally, about 10 minutes. Add
the onion and garlic and cook, stirring,
until soft, about 5 minutes. Add the tomatoes,
linguiça, potatoes, kale, water, wine, thyme, red
pepper flakes, saffron, salt, and pepper. Bring to
a boil, then reduce the heat to low. Cover and
simmer until the potatoes are nearly cooked,
40 to 45 minutes.

2. Bring the broth to a furious boil, add the
fish and clams, and cook until the clams open,
8 to 10 minutes. Check the seasonings. Let
sit for 5 to 10 minutes, remove any clams that
remain tightly closed, and serve.

Makes 8 servings

WELLFLEET OYSTER STEW

AN OYSTER STEW IS A TYPICAL DISH ON Cape Cod, but to make something so simple properly (it is often abused—either too creamy, or too thick), you must pay attention to the ingredients and method. The oysters should be briny and freshly shucked. Wellfleet oysters are ideal, but those from Cotuit or Harwichport are fine too. Pacific oysters are not briny enough. Originally, people had access to raw fresh dairy milk, and the milk was richer. Today milk is quite watered down and processed, so this recipe tries to adjust for that fact. And don't skimp on the oysters. Oyster stew is traditionally served with oyster crackers in Wellfleet. You could, of course, buy them, but why not go for broke and make them yourself? (Recipe follows; they should be made a day or two ahead.) Once the stew is in the bowl, all it needs is salt and pepper. And remember, as one cook once wrote, the reason you use white pepper in this stew is to keep the kids from trying to pick out all the specks of black pepper.

6 tablespoons (³/4 stick) unsalted butter
1 quart freshly shucked oysters (from about 10
*   pounds oysters)*
1 quart unpasteurized (raw) whole creamery
*   milk or 3¹/4 cups half-and-half mixed with*
*   ³/4 cup heavy cream*
Salt and freshly ground white pepper to taste
Oyster Crackers (recipe follows)

1. In a 3-quart saucepan, melt the butter over medium heat. When it stops sizzling, add the oysters, and cook them until their edges begin to curl, about 4 minutes.

2. Pour in the half-and-half and cream or raw milk and cook until it begins to bubble on the edges and is well heated, another 4 to 5 minutes. Season with salt and pepper and serve immediately with homemade oyster crackers.

Makes 4 generous servings

OYSTER CRACKERS

Why not make your own oyster crackers? Sure it's more work, but not *that* much more, and everyone will appreciate it.

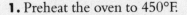

1 cup Bisquick
¹/3 cup plus 2 tablespoons milk

1. Preheat the oven to 450°F.

2. Mix together the Bisquick and milk in a bowl. Turn out the dough onto a floured work surface. Knead 10 times and flatten out until ¹/2 inch thick. With a small cooker cutter, cut out about 8 or 9 pieces and place on an ungreased cookie sheet.

3. Bake until the tops are golden, about 5 minutes. Remove from the oven and split the crackers in half. Lightly butter each half and set aside to become stale for 1 or 2 days before using.

Makes 8 or 9 crackers

NANTUCKET SCALLOP STEW

THE FIRST TIME I WENT TO NANTUCKET, the small Massachusetts island in the Atlantic, was as a teenager in the mid-1960s, when my mom and dad took my sister and me on a biking and hosteling vacation. In those days Nantucket was an idyllic and charming weather-beaten outpost in the Atlantic, and not the colony of frenetic New Yorkers it is today. After a twenty-year hiatus, my then wife and I decided to take our kids and some friends to Nantucket to give it a try again, since my memories had been so fond. We rented a house in desolate Madaket, on the southwestern end of the island, but, alas, we couldn't find any Nantucketers and soon realized the old days were gone. One could find blackened catfish on local menus in the 1980s, but no traditional scallop stew. Near Madaket is an expansive bay, the bottom of which is covered with scallops, seemingly by the millions. Bay scallops are a biennial crop, dragged mostly in shallow waters, and by Massachusetts law, only between October and April. Local scallopers—and I sometimes feel there are none left when I see hundreds of SUVs and no pickup trucks—once caught scallops by using a dip net and a window box made of a wooden frame and a piece of glass, which allowed the scalloper to look down to the bottom of the eel grass as he walked along. This scallop stew is traditional on Nantucket and it will make you feel like an old salt.

1 quart unpasteurized (raw) whole creamery milk, or 2 cups whole milk and 2 cups heavy cream

2 pints bay scallops (about 2 pounds), freshly shucked, if you are able to find them in the shell

4 walnut-size pieces unsalted butter

Salt and freshly ground black pepper to taste

1. In the top of a double boiler over simmering water, heat the raw milk or milk and cream, but don't let it come to a boil. Once it is hot, add the scallops and cook until they are firm, not more than 5 minutes, otherwise they will toughen and lose their delicate taste.

2. Place a piece of butter in each serving bowl and ladle in the scallop stew. Season with salt and pepper and serve immediately.

Makes 4 servings

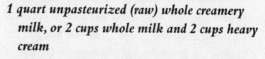

SHUCKING OYSTERS

It's hard enough actually showing someone how to shuck oysters, let alone giving a written description. But let me try. I will tell you my method, but there are many. First you must have a proper oyster knife. The Chesapeake stabber is a narrow, resilient blade with a bulbous, roundish handle preferred by professionals. The crack knife is one long piece of tempered steel that is used to "crack" clustered oysters. The Southern or Galveston knife is designed for Gulf of Mexico oysters and has a double, hollow grind for easier penetration. The New Haven knife is what I use, and it is the knife most commonly used in New England. It is a stubby knife with a wide blade, slightly rounded on one side, which fits nicely in the palm. I don't use any other equipment, but many would consider me foolish. But I have never cut myself and that's because of my method. Oysters can cut because of their sharp edges and rough shells. You can also put the knife right through your palm if you are not careful. So, novices should wear heavy rubber gloves or at least use a towel to hold the oyster in as you open it. Before oysters are shucked, they should be well washed of mud and grit. Run them under cold water, then let them soak in cold water to cover mixed with 1 tablespoon of baking soda for 1 hour. Drain and rinse again. Leave them in a bowl of water as you shuck them, and have another bowl of water ready to dip them into for a final rinsing after you have opened them and before the knife separates their shells.

There are four basic methods to shucking oysters. The stabbing method places the oyster on a wooden plank, or service, smack against a wooden cleat, which holds it in place. Then the knife gets wiggled in at the lip edge, not the hinge. The shucker stabs into the oyster with quick clockwise and counterclockwise twists of the knife. The cracker method places the oyster down on a service, the lip edge is cracked off with a hammer, and the knife is wedged into the oyster to open it. The side knife method is a difficult method, but you will find many experienced shuckers using this method because it is suited to raw bar service. The knife is held with the thumb extended on the blade almost to the point end, the curved side facing down, then the knife is wiggled sideways into the oyster.

A fourth method, the one I use, is the hinge method. It requires quite a bit of pressure and that's why raw bars don't use this method. But it is easy. Grasp the oyster in one hand with the deep shell half facing down, the flat shell half facing up, and the hinge towards your palm. Press the point of the knife against the hinge, where it is a bit blacker than the rest of the oyster and where the lower and upper shell halves meet. Wiggle the point in just enough to break the hinge ligament. Push the blade in a bit, and once the oyster is slightly opened, run the blade around the edge of the oyster to separate the two shell halves. The top, flat shell half should pop right open and the oyster itself will rest in the bottom, or deeper shell half. Cut the muscle holding the oyster in place and remove. When you are holding the oyster and about to apply pressure, make very sure that you are holding everything firmly and don't apply pressure until you are sure the knife tip is wedged well into the hinge and won't slip. Apply a little pressure at first, and then more pressure. As an added precaution, check your posture and hand angle so that if you do slip with the knife, it will fly off into thin air and not into your hand.

LOBSTER AND OYSTER RAGOUT

THE COMBINATION OF LOBSTER AND oysters is quintessentially New England. In 1630 the Reverend Francis Higginson, of Salem, Massachusetts, said of the local lobsters, so abundant people got sick of them, "I was soon cloyed with them, they were so great, and fat, and luscious. I have seene some my self that have weighed 16 pound, but others have divers time so great Lobsters as have weighed 25 pounds, as they assure mee." As late as 1880, lobsters were still so abundant they were used as bait for cod and striped bass fishing. (Today we use squid when we fish for striped bass off Martha's Vineyard.)

It is from this Victorian age in New England whence comes this classic ragout, made often in the nineteenth century. I've adapted the recipe from the original Fannie Farmer cookbook. I can easily imagine the cook of a Boston Brahmin family living on Beacon Hill preparing this dish for a luncheon in the fall of 1890.

When you buy the lobsters for this preparation, look for ones that come out of the holding tank kicking and squirming. If they look lethargic, pass them by. The best way to keep lobsters alive until you cook them is in a brown paper bag in the refrigerator with nothing else. Never put them in water, or they'll drown. Because lobsters deteriorate so quickly after they're dead, they are *always* steamed or boiled live for stews, ragouts, bisques, chowders, and boils. When you remove the meat from the cooked lobster, don't forget the small pieces of meat in the legs and fantail; it's a pain, I know, but a lobster is a precious thing that gave its life for you, so the least you can do is eat all of it.

———————

Two 1¼-pound live lobsters, steamed for 18 to 20 minutes and cooled, or 1½ to 2 cups coarsely chopped cooked lobster meat

40 oysters, very well washed and scrubbed of mud, soaked in cold water to cover mixed with 1 tablespoon baking soda for 1 hour, and drained

½ cup (1 stick) unsalted butter

½ cup unbleached all-purpose flour

2½ cups heavy cream

½ cup whole milk

2 teaspoons salt

½ teaspoon freshly ground white pepper

¼ teaspoon cayenne pepper

2 teaspoons onion juice (squeezed from a grated onion)

¼ cup Sauterne or other sweet dessert wine

2 tablespoons finely chopped fresh parsley leaves

———————

1. If you're starting with live lobsters, crack them open after they've cooled, and remove all their meat, coral, and tomalley, and coarsely chop.

2. Shuck the oysters (see page 278) and save all their liquor. You should have about 2 cups of oysters and oyster liquor all together. If you don't, add enough cold spring water to equal 2 cups. Strain the oysters through a cheesecloth-lined strainer, saving the liquor. Refrigerate the oysters until needed.

3. In a stew pot or large saucepan, melt the butter over medium heat, then stir in the flour to form a roux. Cook for about 2 minutes, stirring constantly as it foams. Remove the pot from the burner and whisk in the oyster liquor, heavy cream, milk, salt, white pepper, cayenne, and onion juice. Return the mixture to the burner and cook until it starts bubbling.

4. Add the oysters and cook just until the edges begin to curl up, never letting the broth get beyond a very gentle bubbling, 1 to 5 minutes, depending on the size of the oysters. Add the lobster, Sauterne, and parsley. Cook until the lobster is heated, about 3 minutes, and serve immediately.

Makes 6 servings

CAPE COD CLAM CHOWDER

TO PARAPHRASE ONE WRITER, A PROPERLY made New England clam chowder is a dish to preach about, a dish to sing hymns for, to fight for. I too feel very strongly about clam chowder. If one doesn't feel strongly, if one doesn't defend a particular way of cooking something, I believe one is not really interested in food and therefore can ignore my ranting and raving to come. Many fine cooks make many different fine chowders from coastal Maine down to Virginia, but a clam chowder wouldn't be worth writing about if I didn't dogmatically claim that this recipe, this recipe right here, is the only true one. Let those who disagree with me argue for their alternative, but in the meantime don't bother me—I'm eating chowda.

This recipe is a Cape Cod clam chowder, and I believe the best clam chowder is made on Cape Cod. Just as a proper chili con carne never has beans or tomatoes in it, for me a true clam chowder should never contain flour, nor cream, certainly never fish broth (might as well call it fish soup), nor, God forbid, a tomato. A true clam chowder is very simple, but rarely gotten right. Adding flour or cornstarch, popular with restaurant chefs, turns the elixir into an unappetizing and gummy "white mud." Cream is also a no-no, but can sometimes be beneficial (see below). Adding a tomato means you're from below the chowder Mason-Dixon line for New England chowderheads. A clam is a delicate creature and easily gets lost with too much starchy thickening, acidic vegetables, herbs, seasoning, or bacon as opposed to salt pork.

A clam chowder is made only one way (oh, pipe down, wait until you taste this), and you are more likely to find it well made on Cape Cod than in Boston, where chefs from other parts of the country work, and where they bulk up their chowders with flour. A true clam chowder is made with, and only with, live quahogs with their liquor (*Mercenaria mercenaria* Linn.), and never canned clams, and with diced lean salt pork (not bacon—too smoky; I don't buy Jasper White's speculation that the smokiness resembles the original), onion, potatoes, butter, salt, white pepper (not black pepper, so the kids won't try to pick the specks out), and, if you can manage it, raw fresh creamery milk. In the early twentieth century, Cape Codders could regularly get raw milk, which has a creamier taste than today's pasteurized and homogenized milk. Since that is hard to find, it's therefore permissible to mix whole milk with half-and-half or a little heavy cream to approximate that old-time taste. Clam chowder can also have a little celery and a little sprinkle of thyme, but that's it. It's always served hot, but not piping hot, and with common crackers. Clam chowder is always "aged." That is, it is best when it sits on a warm turned-off stove for some hours or if it is reheated.

Chowder has a history. "Chowder" appears to derive from the French word *chaudière*, a cauldron used by the fishermen of Brittany to cook up a fish chowder. Each fisherman would add a little to the cauldron, along with biscuits and some other condiments, and then he would be doled out his portion. It seems that these Breton fishermen were responsible for bringing their *chaudière* to Newfoundland, where it was made with fish or clams. From there, it spread to Nova Scotia and New England, probably via fishermen who fished the Grand Banks and would regularly put into local ports when severe storms arose. In John R. Bartlett's *Dictionary of Americanisms*, published in 1848, a chowder is described as a dish from New England made of fresh fish, especially cod, or clams, and stewed with slices of pork or bacon, onions, and biscuit, with the addition at times of cider or champagne.

The earliest chowders were fish chowders and they were always made in a clear broth. There is no record of clam, as opposed to fish,

CHOWDER IN MOBY-DICK

In "Chowder," the title of chapter fifteen of Herman Melville's *Moby-Dick or, The Whale,* we find Captain Ahab and Queequeg on Nantucket when they stop in at the Try Pots, an inn where Hosea Hussey is known for his famous chowders. Arriving tired and hungry, they express their desire for chowder and, when asked by Mrs. Hussey, "Clam or Cod?" they order clam. When they hear her yell to the kitchen "clam," they believe they will have to share a single clam for dinner, but are soon surprised, for "when that smoking chowder came in, the mystery was delightfully explained. Oh sweet friends! Hearken to me. It was made of small juicy clams, scarcely bigger than hazel nuts, mixed with pounded ship's biscuit, and salted pork cut up into little flakes; the whole enriched with butter, and plentifully seasoned with pepper and salt." Some commentators fail to mention that, as soon as they finished their clam chowder, they then ordered a fish chowder and ate that too. The Try Pots had great chowder, though as Captain Ahab said, "chowder for breakfast, and chowder for dinner, and chowder for supper, till you began to look for fish-bones coming through your clothes."

chowder before the mid–nineteenth century, although the first written mention of clams being used in chowder is from 1829 in Lydia Marie Child's *The Frugal Housewife*. But we know that the clam was thriving along the New England shore when the Pilgrims arrived in the early seventeenth century, and we know from their letters that clams and mussels were foods described as "at our doors." So it's possible they made clam chowder. The first mention of a chowder in print—and it was a fish chowder—was in 1732. In 1751, the Boston *Evening Post* published a recipe for chowder containing onions, salt pork, marjoram, savory, thyme, ship's biscuit (hardtack), and fish, to which was added a bottle of red wine. All of the chowders mentioned before the mid-nineteenth century were made with water and not with milk, although they did contain salt pork. By 1880, clam chowder had become a regional dish from Maine to Virginia. The dividing line between chowder made with milk and chowder made with tomatoes was also starting to form about this time and the division seems to be between southwestern Connecticut and south, where they use tomatoes, and Cape Cod and north, where they use milk. The no-man's land of this debate seems to be Rhode Island and southeastern Connecticut, where a clear broth is used.

There are other chowders. There are fish chowders, corn chowders, lobster chowders, parsnip chowders, and many others. But my favorite chowder is the one with quahogs I would either make every summer at my own stove in Wellfleet on Cape Cod or have at PJ's Dari-Burger in Wellfleet.

Now, let me talk a little about ingredients and techniques. Every ingredient is important in chowder. First, the quahogs (pronounced KO-hog) used are large clams that are also called hard clams, and, when they're smaller, littlenecks and cherrystones. They should be live. A quahog is too big and tough to be eaten raw; that's why they are used for chowder. Some cooks use littlenecks, razor shell, or soft-shell clams, but if you do, that's a different chowder. On Cape Ann, and on Cape Cod, soft-shell clams are used for fried clams, not chowder. In Maine, though, they'll use any kind of clam. Surf clams (*Spisula [Hemimactra] solidissima* Dillwyn) are large deep water clams that get washed up with the surf on the ocean side of Cape Cod. They can be used in chowders too, although my then 4-year-old son Seri believed they had another purpose: he would find a half-shell on the beach and yell out to my buddy, who still smoked cigarettes in those days, "Boyd, I found another ashtray," as we cringed in embarrassment.

Second, the milk is important. It should be rich fresh creamery milk, preferably raw. Since that's hard for most people to find, it's permissible to use whole pasteurized milk with the addition of half-and-half and/or heavy cream. Third, the potatoes should be waxy boiling potatoes such as Yukon Gold or Red Rose, which can handle boiling and still retain their shape. Don't use baking potatoes; they will disintegrate and make your chowder too potatoey. For the onion, I like to use any large yellow onion. I always use salt pork rather than bacon in chowders.

Many cooks have many secrets to a good clam chowder, and one of them is to cook the onions very gently so they caramelize a bit and disappear into the chowder. Cape Cod cooks like to "age" their chowders by cooking them the day before or letting them sit for some hours before serving. That's why you find many early recipes telling you to move the kettle to the back of the stove. Doctoring your chowder once it's finished with parsley or chives is a restaurant innovation to give the chowder "color." Just remember: chowda don't need no color, it's already got one—white. One last warning: Be very careful when heating the milk or it will curdle.

———————— ● ————————

20 pounds quahogs or large cherrystones
1 tablespoon baking soda
2 quarts water
2 pounds boiling potatoes (such as Yukon Gold), peeled and diced
¹/₂ pound lean salt pork, diced
1 large yellow onion (about 14 ounces), finely chopped
Salt, if necessary
Freshly ground white pepper to taste
¹/₂ teaspoon dried thyme
2 cups whole milk
3 cups half-and-half
1 cup heavy cream
6 tablespoons (³/₄ stick) unsalted butter
12 split common crackers (see Sources, page 377) or 2 recipes oyster crackers (page 276)

———————— ● ————————

1. Prepare the clams by letting them soak in cold, clean seawater (preferably) or tap water mixed with the baking soda for 1 hour. Remove the clams and rinse, then place them in a large stockpot filled with the water. Cover, turn the heat to high, and steam the quahogs until they all open, 25 to 30 minutes. Discard any clams that remain firmly shut. Remove the clams from their shells once they are cool enough to handle and discard the shells, but save all the liquid. Strain the liquid through a chinois, a conical strainer, into a smaller stew pot. Strain again through a cheesecloth-lined strainer if necessary. Chop the clams. You should have about 5 cups of chopped clams. You can do this in a food processor in pulses.

2. Add all the collected clam juice to the water you steamed the clams in. If you have less than 2 quarts of liquid in the stockpot, add enough water to make up the difference, although you will probably have more than 2 quarts (which is okay; just reserve the extra for another time).

3. Bring the reserved clam liquor to a boil, then cook the potatoes until three-quarters cooked and nearly tender, 8 to 10 minutes. Add the reserved chopped clams and cook at a boil for 5 minutes, then turn the heat off and let the chowder sit. If scum forms, skim it off at once.

4. Meanwhile, in a skillet, cook the salt pork over medium-low heat until nearly crispy, about 15 minutes, stirring. Remove the salt pork with a slotted spoon and set aside. Reduce the heat to low, add the onion, and cook until golden and very soft, about 30 minutes, stirring occasionally to deglaze the skillet. Add the salt pork and onion mixture to the potatoes and stir. Check the seasoning and add salt if necessary (it shouldn't be necessary if you've used quahogs from Wellfleet) and the pepper and thyme. Let the chowder age in the refrigerator, covered with plastic wrap, for 24 hours.

5. Remove the chowder from the refrigerator and reheat over low heat. Once it is hot, add the milk, half-and-half, and cream. Cover and heat the chowder until it is about 140°F. The broth should never even come close to a boil, though, or the milk will curdle. Stir in the butter and remove the stew pot from the burner, but leave it on the stove, covered, to stay warm for 1 hour or more. Serve with common or oyster crackers.

Makes 10 servings

NEW YORK'S GRAND CENTRAL OYSTER BAR RESTAURANT'S OYSTER STEW

T HE GRAND CENTRAL OYSTER BAR IS located in Grand Central Station in Manhattan, a famous and elegant Beaux-Arts edifice built in 1913. I have seen a number of different recipes for this stew and I have eaten

> Oysters are terrific bivalves,
> They have young ones by the score,
> How they diddle is a riddle,
> They just keep on having more
> —ANONYMOUS

the stew at the Oyster Bar itself. The most important thing to remember when making it is that the half-and-half will curdle if you let it boil or even come close to boiling; just let it get heated in the double boiler and pay close attention.

32 freshly shucked oysters with their liquor (see page 278)
4 cups half-and-half
1 tablespoon plus 1 teaspoon Worcestershire sauce
1/2 cup (1 stick) unsalted butter
1 1/2 teaspoons salt, or more to taste
1/4 teaspoon celery salt
2 teaspoons paprika, plus more for sprinkling
1/4 teaspoon ground red chile
Oyster Crackers (page 276), heated in a toaster oven

1. In the top of a double boiler set over simmering water, heat the oyster liquor, half-and-half, and Worcestershire without letting the mixture come even close to a boil and without letting the pan touch the water below. Turn the heat off if you think it's getting too hot.

2. In a skillet, melt the butter over medium heat with the salt, celery salt, paprika, and red chile. Once the butter has melted and is hot, add the shucked oysters and cook just until the edges curl, 1 to 5 minutes, depending on the size of the oysters. Be very careful you don't cook them too long, otherwise the oysters will toughen. Turn the oysters into the broth and heat for 1 minute (turn on the heat if you previously turned it off).

3. Serve hot, sprinkled with paprika, and accompany with the hot oyster crackers.

———•———

Makes 4 servings

TIDEWATER STEW

———🍃———

OYSTERING IS A HARD AND BACK-breaking occupation, and in the Chesapeake Bay men have been oystering since the first days of the English settlements. In the Chesapeake, oystermen are called "watermen." In St. Mary's County, Maryland, on the Chesapeake Bay, an oyster cook-off contest is held every October. It has grown large and is now called the National Oyster Cook-Off. This Maryland oyster stew recipe is adapted from that of Anita M. Meredith of Mechanicsville, who won second prize in the National Oyster Cook-Off sometime in the 1970s or early 1980s. This is a wonderful stew, but you will need to open a good amount of oysters to make up a pint. Be assured it's worth it. Serve with cornbread.

———•———

$^{1}/_{2}$ cup (1 stick) unsalted butter
$^{1}/_{2}$ cup finely chopped onion
$^{1}/_{2}$ cup finely chopped celery

$^{1}/_{4}$ cup seeded and finely chopped green bell pepper
$^{1}/_{2}$ cup slivered button mushrooms
1 pint freshly shucked oysters with their liquor (30 to 80 oysters, depending on their size; see page 278)
$1^{1}/_{2}$ cups whole milk
$^{1}/_{2}$ cup heavy cream
$1^{1}/_{2}$ cups diced boiled potatoes (from about $^{1}/_{2}$ pound boiling potatoes)
1 teaspoon salt, or more to taste
$^{1}/_{2}$ teaspoon freshly ground black pepper, or more to taste
2 slices bacon, fried until crisp, drained, and crumbled
$^{1}/_{4}$ teaspoon ground red chile
$^{1}/_{4}$ teaspoon dried oregano

———•———

1. In a stew pot, melt the butter over medium-high heat. When the butter stops sizzling, cook the onion, celery, green pepper, and mushrooms until soft and mushy, about 6 minutes.

2. Add the oysters and their liquor, the milk, cream, and potatoes and bring to a gentle simmer; the liquid should only be shimmering. The shucked oysters will presumably have been in the refrigerator and will be cold. Cook until the oyster edges have curled, 1 to 5 minutes, depending on their size. Add the salt, black pepper, bacon, red chile, and oregano. Stir and cook for 1 minute. Serve immediately.

———•———

Makes 4 to 5 servings

MARYLAND SEAFOOD STEW

MARYLAND'S MOST FAMOUS SEAFOODS are soft-shelled crabs, blue crabs, rockfish, and oysters. One never uses soft-shelled crabs for stew because they taste so good pan-fried. A hard-shelled Maryland blue crab is ideal here, plus the oysters and rockfish, which is the local Maryland name for striped bass (not the rockfish that is also called blue-mouth or ocean perch). Maryland-style crab soup is tomato based, so this seafood stew is quite traditional. The final stew is thick and not soupy.

¼ cup vegetable oil
1½ large onions, finely chopped
1 cup dry white wine
2 cups water
One 10-ounce can tomato puree
1½ teaspoons sugar
1½ teaspoons salt
½ teaspoon freshly ground black pepper
½ teaspoon dried oregano
1 tablespoon finely chopped fresh basil leaves
¼ cup plus 2 tablespoons finely chopped fresh parsley leaves
¾ pound striped bass fillets
½ pound crabmeat, picked over for cartilage and shells
18 oysters, washed well, soaked in cold water to cover mixed with 1 tablespoon baking soda for 1 hour, and drained

1. In a casserole, heat the vegetable oil over medium-high heat, then cook the onions, stirring, until translucent, 6 to 7 minutes. Add the wine, water, tomato puree, sugar, salt, pepper, oregano, basil, and parsley. Bring to a boil, then reduce the heat to low and simmer, uncovered, for 1 hour.

2. Return the liquid to a boil and add the fish, crab, and oysters and cook, covered, until the oysters open, about 12 minutes. Serve immediately. Discard any oysters that remain firmly shut.

Makes 4 servings

PINE BARK STEW

T HIS STEW FROM SOUTH CAROLINA HAS an unknown history, although one story goes like this: In 1675, two priests on a mission for the French explorer Robert Cavelier sieur de La Salle stopped in South Carolina's Low Country and were asked by the neighborly folks of one hamlet to stay for dinner. The priests watched the preparation of the meal, which the women commenced before the men returned from their hunting expedition for small game. One trick they engaged in was tying a net to the end of a pine sapling and bending the sapling into the river, where the net would fill with fish and, once the sapling was released, it would spring back with the catch. These fish went into the percolating stew pot filled with tomatoes, potatoes, and onions. On this occasion, as the priests delighted in this particular method, a piece of pine bark accidentally fell into the stew. But they loved the stew so much, pine bark and all, that they called it pine bark stew.

Another story behind the origin of the dish is that the name of the stew refers to the fact that it was prepared on the bank of the river where the fish were caught and where the pine bark was used to build a quick fire. The river in question might be the Pee Dee River about halfway between Charleston, South Carolina, and Wilmington, North Carolina. One recipe I looked at from that area also used curry powder and Worcestershire sauce. I've seen a number of recipes for pine bark stew, and there appears to be quite a bit of variation. These variations can be divided into two styles, restaurant style, which tends to be "fancier" and more enriched, and home style, which appears to be simpler, like this recipe.

The Shrimp Factory Restaurant in Savannah, Georgia, makes pine bark stew, which they call a kind of Southern bouillabaisse and make with a variety of fish and shellfish cooked in chicken broth. This particular recipe is adapted from a regional American cookbook published in the 1930s and from another recipe by Captain John A. Kelley of Kingston, South Carolina.

---

2 1/2 pounds boiling potatoes, peeled
2 cups fresh or canned crushed tomatoes
1 pound yellow onions, cut into chunks
1/4 pound thickly sliced bacon, cut into 1/2-inch pieces
1 quart water
1/2 cup ketchup
1 tablespoon Worcestershire sauce
1/2 teaspoon cayenne pepper
1 tablespoon plus 1 teaspoon salt
1 1/2 teaspoons freshly ground black pepper
1 1/2 pounds catfish fillets, each cut into halves or thirds

---

1. Put the potatoes, tomatoes, and onions in a food processor and process until mushy, but with minuscule chunks. Do this in batches if you must.

2. In a large cast-iron stew pot or Dutch oven, cook the bacon over medium-high heat until crisp, stirring, about 5 minutes. Add the vegetable mixture and water, and heat to a point where the broth begins to bubble. Reduce the heat to low and simmer, using a heat diffuser if necessary, until the potato chunks are very soft, about 3 hours, stirring frequently.

3. Stir in the ketchup, Worcestershire, cayenne, salt, and black pepper. Add the catfish and continue to simmer until the fish is cooked through, about 30 minutes. Correct the seasonings and serve.

Makes 4 to 6 servings

FLORIDA KEYS–STYLE LOBSTER STEW

WHEN FLORIDA CAME UNDER THE spotlight in late 2000 during the contested presidential election, Florida politicians were subjected to some caustic scrutiny. It was a sleazy affair, but none of this sleaziness should have surprised anyone who remembers the scene in the movie *Key Largo* when Edward G. Robinson says to Humphrey Bogart, "Let me tell you about Florida politicians. I make them. I make them out of a whole cloth just like a tailor makes a suit. I get their name in the newspaper, I get them some publicity, and get them on the ballot. Then after the election we count the votes and if they don't turn out right, we re-count them and re-count them again until they do."

Anyone who has been to south Florida and the Florida Keys knows that this kind of shadiness is somewhat alluring. In the Keys, in places like Key Largo, you feel as if you're on the lam, even if you're only there to snorkel for spiny lobsters. For many years my friend Boyd Grove and I would head down to the Conch Republic to lounge about and snorkel. Someone asked me once "What do you do there?" to which I responded, "Do? You don't *do* anything." This langorous life is typical in all the Conch Republic, a name, incidentally, born in 1982 as part of a secessionist movement in reaction to annoying roadblocks set up by the U.S. border patrol, which was looking for drug smugglers and illegal aliens. Secession ceremonies were held in Key West and were immediately followed, in true Keys' fashion, by surrender to the state of Florida and a wild party.

The food in the Keys also has a certain amount of irreverence born of this independent spirit and the region's location in the Caribbean. Take, for instance, this lobster stew, which I adapted from one by Mrs. J. W. Brody, found in the *Key West Woman's Club Cookbook*, published in 1988. It is made with the Florida Keys lobster, a crustacean without the heavy claws typical of a Maine lobster. They have ten spider-like legs, long antennae instead of claws, and a spiny head—hence their name, spiny lobsters. Diving for lobsters is a popular sport in the Keys, but they are not easy to catch because they are nocturnal and hide in crevices or coral outcroppings. The locals call these lobsters "bugs." In this recipe, as with so much Keys cooking, the Key limes used in the broth are important and the spicing is Cuban influenced.

6 live spiny lobsters, or five 1¼-pound live
   Maine lobsters, or 1¾ pounds lobster meat
¼ cup extra virgin olive oil
1 large onion, finely chopped
1 large green bell pepper, seeded and finely
   chopped
4 large garlic cloves, finely chopped
1½ quarts water
1½ cups fresh tomato puree
Three 6-ounce cans tomato paste
4 bay leaves
Juice from 4 Key limes (about 1 cup)
¼ cup cider vinegar
½ teaspoon freshly ground cumin seeds
¼ teaspoon dried oregano
1 teaspoon sugar
Salt and freshly ground black pepper to taste
Freshly ground cumin seeds for garnish
Finely chopped fresh parsley leaves for garnish

—————◆—————

1. In a large lobster pot or stockpot, bring 1 inch of water to a boil and steam the lobsters until the meat is firm, about 20 minutes. Remove and let cool. Remove all the meat from the lobster and cut into small pieces. Refrigerate until needed. Reserve any tomalley and coral for another purpose.

2. In a stew pot or large saucepan, heat the olive oil over medium-high heat. Cook the onion, garlic, and green pepper, stirring, until soft, about 7 minutes. Add the water, tomato puree, and tomato paste and stir until well blended. Add the bay leaves, lime juice, vinegar, cumin, oregano, and sugar and season with salt and pepper. Bring the mixture to a boil, reduce the heat to low, and simmer for 30 minutes.

3. Add the lobster, stir, and cook until thick, about 5 minutes. Serve immediately with a sprinkling of cumin and parsley.

—————◆—————

Makes 6 servings

DEVEINING SHRIMP

—————◆—————

Many cooks devein shrimp, which means removing its intestinal tract. The intestinal tract looks like a black thread running down the "belly" of the shrimp from its head just below the flesh. Kitchen supply stores sell shrimp deveiners for this purpose, but some cooks pinch the tract by hand. Personally, I find it unnecessary to devein shrimp smaller than extra colossal, which run about 8 to a pound (see page 248). Almost any shrimp labeled medium, large, and even jumbo have such small intestinal tracts that you will no more notice swallowing them than you would swallowing a gnat on a hot and buggy summer's night.

LOUISIANA SHRIMP STEW

A VARIETY OF SHRIMP ARE CAUGHT IN Louisiana, and they are consumed fresh locally and shipped both fresh and frozen to the East and West coasts. The shrimp have different names but it would take a real expert to tell the differences. In Louisiana, many cooks catch their own and these are the best for a shrimp stew. This Louisiana recipe is quite popular and is also made with local crayfish. Ideally the stew should made only be with fresh shrimp, not previously frozen ones. The stew begins, as does so much Cajun cooking, with a nut-brown roux made with equal amounts of vegetable oil and flour. The stew cooks quickly, so stay near the stove. This shrimp stew should be served with steamed rice.

———— ● ————

3 tablespoons vegetable oil

3 tablespoons unbleached all-purpose flour

1 cup chopped onions

$^{1}/_{2}$ cup chopped celery

$^{1}/_{2}$ cup seeded and chopped green bell pepper

1 large garlic clove, finely chopped

$^{1}/_{2}$ cup finely chopped fresh parsley leaves

1 teaspoon cayenne pepper

3 pounds fresh shrimp, heads removed and shelled, or 1$^{1}/_{2}$ pounds previously frozen headless shrimp, shelled

2 cups hot water

1 teaspoon salt

$^{1}/_{4}$ to $^{1}/_{2}$ teaspoon freshly ground black pepper, to your taste

$^{1}/_{4}$ to $^{1}/_{2}$ teaspoon freshly ground white pepper, to your taste

———— ● ————

1. In a heavy, enameled cast-iron casserole or a Dutch oven, heat the vegetable oil over medium heat. Add the flour and cook until golden brown, stirring constantly (be vigilant—if the roux is even a little bit burned, it will ruin the taste of the stew), 4 to 5 minutes.

2. Add the onion, celery, bell pepper, garlic, parsley, and cayenne and cook until the vegetables are soft, stirring frequently, 6 to 7 minutes. Add the shrimp, hot water, salt, and black and white pepper. Reduce the heat to medium-low and cook until the shrimp are very firm but the stew is not dry, 12 to 15 minutes. Serve immediately.

———— ● ————

Makes 4 servings

BAJA SEAFOOD STEW

‹leaf›

BAJA IS THAT PENINSULAR PORTION OF Mexico that resembles a tail swinging south of California. It is an arid and narrow spur of land surrounded by water. Fish cookery is evident in small ports and tourist resorts throughout Baja. A favorite catch is mahimahi and the cooking is hot and spicy. This seafood recipe is quite extraordinary and more so when one considers that I found it, unattributed, on the Internet. I have only changed it slightly, but wish I was able to credit the person who wrote it. It is excellent; the flavors of the shrimp, clams, crab, and fish give an intriguing twist to the palpable taste of fresh orange juice and chiles.

1/4 cup extra virgin olive oil

1 small onion, finely chopped

2 jalapeños, seeded and finely chopped

2 large garlic cloves, finely chopped

2 pounds ripe tomatoes, peeled, seeded, and chopped

1 1/2 cups fresh orange juice

2 cups dry white wine

1 tablespoon finely chopped fresh basil leaves

1 tablespoon finely chopped fresh coriander (cilantro) leaves

1/2 teaspoon dried oregano

1 tablespoon grated orange zest

1 teaspoon salt

1/2 teaspoon freshly ground black pepper

1 tablespoon sugar

24 soft-shelled clams (about 2 pounds, preferably) or littlenecks, soaked in cold water to cover mixed with 1 tablespoon baking soda for 1 hour and drained

6 ounces crabmeat, picked over for cartilage and shells

3 pounds fresh medium-size shrimp with their heads left on, or 1 1/2 pounds previously frozen headless medium-size shrimp, shelled

1 pound mahimahi (dolphinfish), yellowtail, cod, or sea bass fillets, cut into 1-inch pieces

—————●—————

1. In a large casserole or Dutch oven, heat the olive oil over medium-high heat, then cook the onion, jalapeños, and garlic, until the onion is translucent, stirring, 3 to 5 minutes. Add the tomatoes, orange juice, wine, basil, coriander, oregano, orange zest, salt, pepper, and sugar. Bring to a boil, reduce the heat to low, and simmer, uncovered, for 15 minutes.

2. Add the clams, cover, and cook until they open, 5 to 10 minutes. Discard any clams that remain firmly shut. Add the crabmeat, shrimp, and fish, carefully folding them into the broth. Bring to a boil, then reduce the heat to medium. Cover and cook until the shrimp are pink and the fish flakes easily with a fork, shaking the casserole rather than stirring, about 5 minutes. Serve immediately.

—————●—————

Makes 4 to 6 servings

VERACRUZ-STYLE CRAB STEW

THE MEXICAN PORT CITY OF VERACRUZ on the Gulf of Mexico has been described as riotous and festive and the cuisine of Veracruz to this day evidences Iberian traits. This crab stew, called *chilpachol*, comes from Veracruz, and some would say the taste is also a bit riotous. As is so typical in Mexican cooking, the stew begins with the roasting of vegetables, including the chile peppers. This then becomes the foundation of the stew and the crab and shrimp are added later. Because the size and type of crabs available vary, use your best judgment as to when you add them. In this recipe I use the commonly available cooked Dungeness crabs, but a smaller crab is more typical in Mexico, in which case you might need eight of them. This will be a messy stew to eat because you must pick the crabs up with your hands and crack their shells.

———————●———————

1 pound ripe but firm tomatoes
1 medium-size onion, quartered
2 large garlic cloves
3 canned chipotle chiles in adobo sauce, drained, rinsed, and seeded
1/2 jalapeño, seeded
1/2 cinnamon stick
3 black peppercorns
2 corn tortillas, fried in olive oil until crispy brown, then crumbled
2 1/2 tablespoons lard
3 cooked Dungeness crabs (about 4 1/2 pounds), split in two
1 pound fresh jumbo shrimp with their heads on or 1/2 pound previously frozen headless shrimp, shelled
1 quart water
Leaves from 1 leafy sprig fresh epazote, chopped
Salt to taste
Lemon wedges for garnish

———————●———————

1. Preheat the oven to 450°F. Mix the tomatoes, onion, garlic, chipotles, jalapeño, cinnamon, and peppercorns together in a roasting pan and roast until soft, adding a few tablespoons of water if it seems to be drying out, about 1 1/2 hours. Add the crumbled fried tortillas and continue to roast until the sauce is thicker.

EPAZOTE

————●————

I had never heard of epazote (*Chenopodium ambrosioides*) until I moved to Los Angeles. It is a pungent-smelling herb that grows to about two and a half feet. In Mexican cooking, where it is predominantly used, cooks add it to flavor black beans, moles, chile sauces, cheese quesadillas, stews, and shellfish. There is no direct substitute, but I would use sage leaves in its place.

2. Meanwhile, in a casserole, melt the lard over medium heat, then add the sauce from the roasting pan. Pour a little water into the roasting pan to deglaze it, scraping any browned bits from the bottom of the pan, then add to the casserole. Reduce the heat to medium-low and cook, covered, until the liquid has evaporated, about 30 minutes, stirring occasionally. Add the crabs and shrimp and cook for 5 minutes, turning frequently. Add the water and epazote and season with salt. Cover, increase the heat to high, and remove from the heat when it reaches a boil.

3. Serve with lemon wedges.

———————●———————

Makes 6 servings

STEWS WITH VEGETABLES

This chapter is filled with vegetable stews. Although most of these stews don't contain meat, some do because this chapter is not about vegetarian stews but vegetable stews, and many vegetable stews around the world sometimes use little bits of meat, either for its fat or as a kind of condiment. A favorite vegetable stew of mine is a recipe I collected years ago in Roussillon, a part of France on the border with Spain that was a part of historic Catalonia. This Bean and Cabbage Stew from the Roussillon (page 301) is called *l'ollada*, and it combines small white beans, leeks, savoy cabbage, potatoes, and chickpeas. When I traveled in North Africa, I came across many vegetable stews that I found unique, delicious, and substantial. For instance, Vegetable Stew from Tunisia with Rose Petals (page 319) begins with some olive oil and garlic seasoned with the famous chile pepper paste of North Africa known as *harīsa*, followed by the addition of tomato paste, cayenne, cinnamon, caraway, and black pepper. As the stew builds in flavor, the vegetables are added, namely cauliflower, green beans, Swiss chard, zucchini, tomatoes, and green bell peppers. Finally the last "secret" ingredient gets sprinkled on, the crushed rose petals that make this stew so special. There are also vegetable stews from Turkey, Greece, Bavaria, Italy, France, Spain, India, and the good ole USA, the source for a great succotash recipe (page 325) that will make you realize how poor those frozen packages really are.

CATALONIAN LENTIL STEW

THIS EARTHY CATALONIAN STEW, CALLED *olla amb llentilles*, is made with green lentils and is given body by the potatoes, color by the Swiss chard, and spicing by the saffron. It is particularly nice served with pork, although you can certainly eat it as a main course with a green salad and some bread. If you would like this dish to be stewy, use 5 cups of water, but if you would like all the water absorbed, use 4 cups in step 3.

1¹/₂ *pounds Swiss chard*
2 *cups (1 pound) dried green lentils, picked over and rinsed*
¹/₄ *cup extra virgin olive oil*
2 *teaspoons salt*
8 *small new potatoes (about ³/₄ pound total), peeled*
¹/₂ *teaspoon saffron threads, crumbled*
1 *quart plus 1 cup water*
¹/₄ *cup medium-grain rice, such as Calarosa*

---

1. Chop enough of the white parts of the Swiss chard stems to measure 1¹/₂ cups. Cut about 6 ounces of the leaves into strips, and cut again crosswise. Reserve any leftover Swiss chard for another use.

2. Place the lentils in a strainer and soak in a bowl filled with cold water to cover for 10 minutes. Drain.

3. In a large saucepan or casserole, heat the olive oil over medium heat with the chopped Swiss chard stems and salt. Cook until soft, about 10 minutes, stirring. Add the Swiss chard leaves, potatoes, saffron, and water. Cook over medium heat until the water reaches a boil, 6 to 7 minutes. Reduce the heat to low, and cook until the potatoes have a little resistance when pierced by a skewer, about 15 minutes.

4. Add the drained lentils and cook until *al dente*, about 50 minutes. Add the rice, pushing it down into the liquid. Cover and cook until the rice is tender, about 15 minutes. Serve immediately.

Makes 4 to 6 servings

SPICY CATALAN STEW OF HARICOT BEANS

THE ROLE OF DRIED BEANS IN THE CUISINE of Catalonia is unique in the Mediterranean. They play a central role in the staple diet, much as they do in Mexico. Although it's true that beans are a staple or near-staple everywhere in the Mediterranean, the Catalonian love of beans is reflected in the role of the *olla* (stew) from the time of Don Quixote. The bean in those early bean stews must have been the fava bean or hyacinth bean, because *Phaseolus vulgaris*—the common bean so closely associated today with the cooking of Catalonia—did not appear in Europe until after Columbus's second voyage to the Americas in 1493. One of the first references to this bean was in 1565 in Clermont-sur-Lauquet in France, where it was called *monges*. It seems that this word might have come from the Catalan, which would make sense, since the common bean had to move north from Seville, where it first appeared in the Mediterranean.

This very flavorful Catalonian stew using *mongetes*, common beans, is called *salpiquet de mongetes*, a dish that will remind you of a poor man's or quick-style cassoulet in taste. The caul fat required in the recipe can usually be found in supermarkets that make their own sausages and serve ethnic populations. The Spanish-style, semidry sausage can be ordered from La Española (see the sources listed in the back of the book).

―――― ● ――――

1¹/₃ cups dried white haricot beans (about 9 ounces), picked over, rinsed, soaked in water to cover overnight, and drained

1 bay leaf

1 head garlic, first layer of peel rubbed off, plus 4 large garlic cloves, finely chopped

2 teaspoons salt

1 tablespoon lard

1 slice lean salt pork (about 1¹/₂ ounces), diced

1 medium-size onion, chopped

3 tablespoons finely chopped fresh parsley leaves

2 ounces bacon, chopped

1 walnut-size chunk caul fat, chopped

2 tablespoons tomato paste

1 tablespoon extra virgin olive oil

5 thin slices Spanish-style semi-dry sausage, salami, or pepperoni, chopped

2 teaspoons freshly ground black pepper

CAUL FAT

―――― ● ――――

Caul fat is a typical ingredient used in much Mediterranean cooking. It is also called omentum, epiplöon, peritoneum, or mesentery (names you will never hear a butcher use). Caul fat is the large, fatty, and transparent serous membrane, or fold of peritoneum, that covers the intestines of cows, sheep, and pigs. It is sold at any supermarket that makes its own sausages or that has an ethnic clientele. It is very thin and fragile and is also used to wrap food for grilling, a particularly wonderful taste if you have never tried it. When shopping for it, call it caul fat because the other names are virtually unknown by butchers and cooks.

1. Place the haricot beans in an earthenware casserole with the bay leaf, head of garlic, and salt. Cover with cold water. Turn the heat to high, bring to a boil, then reduce the heat to low. Simmer, covered, until the outer cloves of garlic are very soft, about 30 minutes. Drain, return the beans to the casserole, and cover again with fresh cold water just to the top of the beans. Extract the garlic cloves from their skin, chop, and set aside. Discard the bay leaf.

2. In a small skillet, melt the lard over medium-high heat. Brown the salt pork in it until a little crispy, 2 to 3 minutes. Add the onion and cook, stirring, until soft, about 6 minutes.

3. Add the 4 cloves of raw, finely chopped garlic, the parsley, and bacon to the skillet.

Cook, stirring, until the bacon is a bit crispy, about 4 minutes. Add the caul fat and cook for 1 minute. Add this mixture to the beans and stir. Add the tomato paste, reserved simmered and chopped garlic, olive oil, sausage, and pepper and season with salt. Simmer until the beans are very tender and the broth is in between a stew and a soup in consistency, 2¹/2 to 3 hours. If necessary, add water from time to time so the beans are always covered.

Makes 4 servings

CATALAN-STYLE ONION, POTATO, AND EGGPLANT STEW

WHEN I WAS RESEARCHING MY CULI-nary history of the Mediterranean, *A Mediterranean Feast* (William Morrow, 1999), I was helped enormously by a Catalan woman and her husband who lived near me in Cambridge, Massachusetts, at the time. Both Bill Cole and his wife, Montse, knew a lot about the cuisine of Catalonia, but over the years I lost touch with them. Then, through the Internet, I received a fan letter from some-one in Virginia who knew Bill and informed me that they were living in Catalonia, where Bill was teaching at a university. We reestab-lished contact, and one of the first things we began to do was exchange recipes. This recipe

is from Bill, who is not only fluent in Catalan, but in Catalan cuisine. He simply calls this dish *cebas, patatas, i albergína*, "onions, potatoes, and eggplants." Don't let these humble ingredients fool you—this is a delicious stew. Bill serves the leftovers at room temperature with lemon juice and crusty bread.

1 cup extra virgin olive oil
1 pound onions, coarsely chopped
1 pound boiling potatoes
2 pounds eggplant, peeled, quartered lengthwise, and sliced
2 tablespoons tomato paste
2 tablespoons finely chopped fresh basil leaves
1 teaspoon salt, and more to taste
2 cups canned chickpeas, drained
Lemon wedges for garnish
Crusty Italian or French bread for an accompaniment

1. Place the potatoes in a large saucepan, cover with water by several inches, and bring to a boil over medium-high heat. Cook until tender but firm in the center when a skewer is pushed in, about 15 minutes. Drain, and when cool enough to handle, peel and dice.

2. In an earthenware casserole set on a heat diffuser, heat the olive oil over medium-high heat. Cook the onions, potatoes, and eggplant together until the eggplant is very soft, about 25 minutes. (Or use a nonstick skillet directly over medium heat and check for doneness sooner.) Reduce the heat to medium-low and cook another 20 minutes. Add the tomato paste, basil, and salt, and stir until the tomato paste is blended. Add the chickpeas, cover, and cook until the potatoes are completely soft, about 30 minutes. Sometime during this period, correct the salt.

3. Let cool until just warm in the casserole or skillet, then serve with lemon wedges and crusty bread.

Makes 4 to 6 servings

WHITE BEAN, RICE, AND POTATO STEW
FROM THE ARAGON PROVINCE OF SPAIN

IN MEDIEVAL TIMES, THE KINGDOM OF Aragon was joined to Catalonia and formed one of the mightiest of Mediterranean powers. Today Aragon is a region of Spain, and the food of Aragon is simple and rustic. This preparation is called *recao de Binéfar*, named after a small town northwest of Lerida. This stew should be somewhat soupy by the end of the cooking time, so if it isn't, pour in a little water. Some cooks also add slices of cooked sausage or cooked ham.

1 cup (¹/₂ pound) dried white beans, picked over, rinsed, soaked in water to cover overnight, and drained
1 quart water

1 medium–large onion, chopped
6 large garlic cloves, finely chopped
1 bay leaf
3 tablespoons extra virgin olive oil
³/₄ pound boiling potatoes, peeled and diced
2¹/₄ teaspoons salt
¹/₂ cup medium-grain rice, such as Calarosa
1 teaspoon sweet paprika

1. Place the beans in a large saucepan and add 3 cups of the water, the onion, garlic, bay leaf, and olive oil. Bring to a boil and then reduce the heat to low. Cover and simmer for 1 hour.

2. Add the potatoes and salt and cook until the potatoes are almost tender, about 20 minutes. Add the rice and paprika, bring to a boil, and return the heat to low. Cover and cook until the rice is tender, about 15 minutes. Add the remaining 1 cup of water to make the stew soupy, if necessary.

3. Remove the stew from the heat and let stand, uncovered, for 5 minutes before serving.

Makes 4 to 6 servings

PISTO MANCHEGO

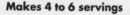

THIS FAMOUS VEGETABLE STEW FROM LA Mancha always contains tomatoes, bell peppers, and zucchini. There are versions of *pisto* all around Spain. Although the Spanish word *pisto* is related to the Italian *pesto*, the vegetables in this stew are not pounded into a pesto, although they do cook down into a kind of vegetable marmalade. The stew is more or less the same thing as the Andalusian *alboronía*, a dish that has a history going back to Islamic Spain and contains the same vegetables, but also includes eggplant. Some cooks like to add previously fried bacon chunks to turn the dish into a light supper. Alternatively, it is also very good with a couple of fried eggs on top. *Pisto* is also excellent at room temperature as a kind of tapas with small pieces of toasted bread, although my favorite way of eating it is at a slightly warmer temperature.

¹/₂ cup extra virgin olive oil

1 large onion, finely chopped

2 large garlic cloves, finely chopped

4 green bell peppers, seeded and cut into small pieces

1 pound zucchini, ends trimmed and cut into small pieces

1 pound ripe tomatoes, peeled, seeded, and chopped

2 tablespoon finely chopped fresh parsley leaves

¹/₄ teaspoon sugar

1 teaspoon salt

1. In a large skillet, heat the olive oil over medium-high heat. Cook the onion and garlic until translucent, stirring frequently so the garlic doesn't burn, about 5 minutes. Add the green peppers and cook until softer but still firm, about 10 minutes. Add the zucchini and cook until the pieces are also softer but still firm, about 15 minutes more.

2. Add the tomatoes, reduce the heat to low, and simmer, uncovered, until the juice of the tomatoes has evaporated, stirring occasionally, about 30 minutes. Stir in the parsley, sugar, and salt. Cook for another 5 minutes and serve.

Makes 4 to 6 servings

CHICKPEA STEW WITH SAFFRON FROM CÓRDOBA

A SPANISH *OLLA* IS AN EARTHENWARE POT used for making stews, and it also refers to the stew itself. There are as many *ollas* as there are families in Spain. This particular stew is known as an *olla Córdobesa*, a stew from Córdoba in Andalusia. The potatoes and chickpeas provide the body, while the cabbage and chile offer up color and flavor, and the saffron and bacon round the stew off, elevating it to a quite delicious preparation. Chickpeas are found in many Spanish stews. For example, in Majorca they make a chickpea stew called *cuirons escadins* with garlic, tomatoes, and *butifarron* and *longaniza* sausages.

Four 15-ounce cans chickpeas with their liquid (about 5 cups)
1 carrot, diced
³/₄ pound boiling potatoes, peeled and diced
1 fresh green chile, seeded and chopped
¹/₂ pound cured Irish or Canadian bacon, chopped
Large pinch of saffron threads
1 cup water
1 small head green cabbage (about 1¹/₄ pounds), damaged outer leaves discarded, cored, and chopped
Salt and freshly ground black pepper to taste

---

1. Place all the ingredients, except the cabbage, salt, and pepper, in a casserole or stew pot and turn the heat to medium-high. Once the water begins to shimmer, reduce the heat to low and cook for 1 hour.

2. Add the cabbage and simmer 1 hour more. Season with salt and pepper and serve.

Makes 6 to 8 servings

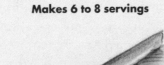

VALENCIAN RICE AND LENTIL STEW

A N *OLLETA* IS A POPULAR KIND OF Valencian stew made in a great variety of ways. Traditionally it is a housewife-style preparation originating from the mountains behind Alicante, in the Valencia province of Spain. This stew is properly called an *olleta de arroz con lentejas*, "a stew of rice with lentils," and it is particularly gratifying in the wintertime. The *ñora*, or dried bell pepper, called for in the ingredients list is not as exotic as it sounds; many supermarkets have them.

---

1 cup (¹/₂ pound) dried brown lentils, picked over and rinsed
1¹/₂ pounds Swiss chard, trimmed of the stalks and chopped
1 large potato, peeled and cut into 10 pieces
1 large turnip, peeled and cut into 10 pieces
2¹/₄ cups hot water
Salt and freshly ground black pepper to taste
¹/₂ cup extra virgin olive oil
1 dried red bell pepper
1 head garlic, with some peel pulled off
1 large, ripe tomato, peeled, seeded, and chopped
1 cup medium-grain rice, such as Calarosa

---

1. In a medium-size casserole or stockpot, cover the lentils, Swiss chard, potato, and turnip with the hot water. Season with salt and pepper, and bring to a simmer over medium heat. Cook for 20 minutes, then reduce the heat to low.

2. Meanwhile, heat the olive oil in a small skillet over medium heat and cook the dried red pepper, stirring, for 6 minutes. Remove from the oil, chop, and set aside. Add the head of garlic and tomato to the skillet and cook for 10 minutes, shaking the skillet occasionally. Transfer the tomato, garlic, and dried pepper to the casserole.

3. Cook the *olleta* for another 40 minutes over low heat, then add the rice and cook until the rice has absorbed the liquid and is tender, about 20 minutes. Discard the head of garlic and serve immediately.

Makes 6 to 8 servings

BEAN AND CABBAGE STEW FROM THE ROUSSILLON

THE FRENCH PROVINCE OF ROUSSILLON is part of historic Catalonia, and its most famous stew is called *l'ollada*, a very old dish whose name simply means "the stew." The word *ollada* derives from the Old French verb *aeuller*, meaning "to replenish the cask or cauldron," reflecting the idea that the cook continuously adds more water, beans, vegetables, or meat to the forever-simmering stew. These stews can contain any number of ingredients, such as chickpeas, turnips, leeks, and a host of other root and leafy vegetables, and in the Gerona and Barcelona provinces of Catalonia, various meats such as grapefruit-size meatballs, blood sausage, a variety of other sausages, or veal knuckle.

1/2 cup dried small white beans (about 1/4 pound), picked over and rinsed
6 quarts water
1 bouquet garni, consisting of several sprigs each fresh thyme and parsley and 1 bay leaf, tied in cheesecloth
3/4 pound leeks (white and light green parts only), split in half lengthwise, washed well, and sliced
6 ounces salt pork, cut into small dice
3/4 pound Savoy cabbage (about 1/2 small head), damaged outer leaves removed, cored, and sliced
1 pound boiling potatoes, peeled and diced
One 15-ounce can chickpeas, drained
Salt and freshly ground black pepper to taste
3 tablespoons rendered goose or duck fat (see page 348)

1. Put the beans in a stew pot and cover with the water. Bring to a boil over high heat, then add the bouquet garni, and boil for 1 hour, stirring occasionally.

2. Add the leeks and salt pork and cook for 30 minutes, stirring occasionally. Add the cabbage, potatoes, and chickpeas and cook until tender, stirring frequently, about 10 minutes. Season with salt and pepper, add the goose fat, and cook for 3 minutes more. Serve immediately.

———— ● ————

Makes 6 to 8 servings

VEGETABLE STEWS WITH MEAT IN THEM

———— ● ————

What, you might ask, is meat doing in a stew in the chapter on vegetable stews? Well, in the Mediterranean, especially, meat is used in small portions, almost like a condiment to flavor the stew, which is predominantly vegetables. This is, in fact, what a vegetable stew is traditionally; it is not a "vegetarian" stew. Because of the Mediterranean's historic poverty, there are very few vegetarians in traditional societies. (Vegetarianism has been an ethical choice historically made by members of relatively prosperous populations, and because of modernization and the accompanying increase in wealth, it is becoming more common.) One will often find stews, mostly in North Africa, the Middle East, and Greece and Turkey, that are considered vegetable stews but contain meat.

SPINACH BOUILLABAISSE

———— 🍃 ————

THIS RECIPE FROM PROVENCE, CALLED *bouillabaisse d'épinards*, is considered very local and rustic, a dish made by housewives. It is such a home preparation that I don't believe I've ever seen this dish on a restaurant menu in Provence. The designation *bouillabaisse* is often given to any dish in Provence that contains saffron. This preparation could equally be called a soup, but, because of its thickness, I think it is proper to consider it a stew—it certainly is a dish that you could have as a main course. The final cooking of the eggs will require some care. You want the yolks to be runny and the whites to be firm, so you need to watch closely and use the time suggested below only as a rough guide.

———— ● ————

2 pounds spinach, heavy stems removed, washed well, with rinse water left clinging to the leaves
3 tablespoons extra virgin olive oil
1 large onion, finely chopped
1 quart boiling water
Freshly ground black pepper to taste
Pinch of saffron threads, gently crushed in a mortar with 1 teaspoon salt
2 large garlic cloves, crushed
1 stalk fennel with its leaves, finely chopped
3 tablespoons finely chopped fresh parsley leaves
1 pound Yukon Gold potatoes, peeled and diced
4 large eggs
4 slices Toasted Bread (see variation on page 224)

Le Ragoût de Truffes

Here's a stew you or I are unlikely to make, unless we've won the lottery. A truffle stew sounds absurd, but apparently at one time, before the twentieth century, around Carpentras, in Provence, truffles were common enough for people to have made this. The famous French gastronome Curnonsky said that in a truffle stew a man could see his hometown, its monuments, and all the resources of his native soil.

To make the stew, some large truffles about two inches in diameter are brushed clean and peeled. The peels are crushed with a little olive oil in a mortar and then forced through a sieve. Meanwhile, a fine *mirepoix* of carrot, the white part of a leek, and an onion are seasoned with thyme and bay leaf and mixed with the truffle peelings. Thickened veal stock in poured into a saucepan and heated with the *mirepoix* and the truffles cut up in slices. The stew is simmered for 20 minutes, and finally half a cup of Châteauneuf-du-Pape is added. Each slice of truffle is served on a slice of bread fried in olive oil or butter.

1. Put the spinach in a large pot. Cook, covered, over high heat until the leaves begin to wilt, stirring occasionally, about 4 minutes. Drain well, pressing the water out with your hands, then chop.

2. In a 10-inch skillet, heat the olive oil over medium-high heat. Cook the onion until translucent, stirring, about 6 minutes. Add the drained spinach, stir, and add the water. Season with pepper and add the saffron and salt. Reduce the heat to low, and add the garlic, fennel, parsley, and potatoes. Cover and cook until the potatoes are soft, about 25 minutes.

3. By this time, the stew will be dense. Make 4 small indentations, or wells, with the back of a soup ladle. Crack 1 egg over each indentation and cook the 4 eggs until the whites are firm, 5 to 8 minutes.

4. Place 1 slice of bread in each individual bowl, and top with the spinach bouillabaisse and 1 egg per person. Serve immediately.

Makes 4 servings

GIANFOTTERE

T HIS RATHER IMPRESSIVE VEGETABLE stew from the southern Italian province of Calabria is meant to use typical seasonal vegetables in one grand preparation to feed lots of people. It is usually eaten piping hot, but I actually like it better when it is reheated or at room temperature. The recipe can easily be cut in half if you don't need to feed this many people. You will need two large casseroles for this dish, and it would be preferable if the one that is used to finish the stew is a wide and deep earthenware casserole shaped like a brazier.

2 red bell peppers
2 yellow bell peppers
2 green bell peppers
1$^{1}/_{2}$ pounds potatoes, peeled and cut into
  $^{1}/_{2}$-inch chunks
4 pounds eggplants, peeled and diced
2 tablespoons salt, plus extra for sprinkling the
  eggplant
1$^{1}/_{2}$ cups extra virgin olive oil
6 medium-size zucchini, ends trimmed, peeled,
  and sliced
2 cups peeled and diced winter squash, such as
  pumpkin, butternut, or acorn
1 pound diced, chopped, or shredded mixed
  seasonal vegetables of your choice, such as
  kale, mustard greens, celery root, broccoli rape,
  Swiss chard, spinach, or green beans
4 large onions, sliced and separated into rings
2 large garlic cloves, crushed
2 sprigs fresh rosemary

2 teaspoons dried oregano
Good-size pinch of saffron threads
2 large, ripe tomatoes, peeled, seeded, and
  chopped
1$^{1}/_{2}$ cups water
1 tablespoon freshly ground black pepper, or
  more to taste
2 tablespoons finely chopped fresh basil leaves
2 tablespoons finely chopped fresh parsley leaves

1. Preheat the oven to 425°F. Place the peppers in a baking dish with a little water or on a wire rack set over a baking sheet and roast until the skins are blistered black, 35 to 40 minutes. Remove the peppers from the oven. When cool enough to handle, remove the seeds, peel off the skins, and cut lengthwise into sixths. Set aside.

2. Put the potatoes in a large saucepan and cover with cold water. Bring to a boil over medium heat and cook until semihard, 10 to 15 minutes. Drain and set aside.

3. Lay the eggplant pieces on some paper towels and sprinkle with salt. Leave them to drain of their bitter juices for 30 minutes, then pat dry with paper towels.

4. In a large casserole, heat $^{3}/_{4}$ cup of the olive oil over medium-high heat. Cook the peppers for 5 minutes. Remove with a slotted spoon and set aside. Reduce the heat to medium, add the eggplant, zucchini, squash, and any other root vegetable you are using, such as celery root. Cook, covered, stirring occasionally, until soft looking, 20 to 25 minutes.

5. Meanwhile, in a large, deep earthenware casserole set on a heat diffuser, heat the remaining ³⁄₄ cup of olive oil over medium-high heat until smoking. Add the onions, garlic, rosemary, oregano, and saffron. Stir well, and cook until soft, stirring occasionally, about 15 minutes. Add the tomatoes and cook for 8 minutes. Add the water, reserved potatoes, and the eggplant, zucchini, squash, and other partially cooked vegetables, if using. Add the 2 tablespoons of salt and the pepper. Reduce the heat to low, and cook until the potatoes are completely soft, about 45 minutes.

6. Serve from the earthenware casserole after discarding the rosemary and garlic. Sprinkle the top with the basil and parsley and serve hot or at room temperature, if desired.

Makes 10 servings

PASTA FASOOL

ASTA FASOOL IS THE DIALECT EXPRESsion used by both Italian-Americans and southern Italians to refer to a famous bean-and-macaroni stew from southern Italy that is popular in the Campania region and Naples in particular, as well as in other southern Italian regions. Most Italian-Americans can trace their roots to southern Italy and Sicily; this is where the great majority of their ancestors came from in the late nineteenth and early twentieth centuries. They call this dish *pasta fasool* or *pasta e fasul*, which is nothing but *pasta e fagioli*, pasta and beans. It is also known in Naples by the dialect term *munnezzaglia*. Typically, it is not considered a stew but rather a thick soup, as they like it in Campania. White cannellini beans are usually used, but I like to use red beans too. The pasta used is always *pasta mischiata*, mixed pastas, such as *laganelle* (a flat, ¹⁄₂-inch-wide pasta), broken vermicelli, *mezzani* (macaroni), *tubetti*, *pennette*, and so forth, but usually a combination of thick and thin pastas.

2¹⁄₂ cups (about 1 pound) dried white cannellini, red borlotti, or speckled red kidney beans, picked over and rinsed
8 large garlic cloves, 4 crushed and 4 finely chopped
6 sprigs fresh parsley
¹⁄₄ cup plus 2 tablespoons extra virgin olive oil
1 celery stalk, including leaves, finely chopped
1 pound ripe tomatoes, cut in half, seeds squeezed out, and grated against the largest holes of a grater down to the peel
2 tablespoons tomato paste
¹⁄₂ teaspoon ground red chile
1 teaspoon freshly ground black pepper
¹⁄₂ cup water
1 tablespoon dried oregano
1 pound mixed short pasta

1. Place the beans in a medium-size saucepan of lightly salted and peppered water and add the 4 crushed garlic cloves and the parsley sprigs. Bring to a boil and cook until the beans are nearly tender, about 1¹/₂ hours, replenishing the water as needed. Drain the beans, discard the parsley and garlic, and save 2 cups of the cooking water.

2. In a large casserole, heat ¹/₄ cup of the olive oil over medium-high heat. Cook the *soffritto* of celery and chopped garlic until soft, stirring constantly so the garlic doesn't burn, 2 to 3 minutes. Add the tomatoes, tomato paste, red chile, black pepper, and water. Stir, reduce the heat to low, and simmer for 10 minutes. Add the drained beans and oregano and simmer for 30 minutes, stirring occasionally and adding 1 to 2 cups of the reserved bean cooking water while the beans cook, so they are slightly "stewy" looking.

3. Meanwhile, bring a large pot of abundantly salted water to a boil, cook the pasta until *al dente*, and drain. Transfer the pasta to the beans and cook until creamy, about 5 minutes. Check the seasonings, pour on the remaining 2 tablespoons of olive oil, and serve immediately.

Makes 8 servings

EGGPLANT AND ARTICHOKE STEW ALLA PANTESCA

A DISH COOKED *ALLA PANTESCA* MEANS it is cooked in the style of the cooking found on the island of Pantelleria off the southern coast of Sicily. It is a tiny island famed for its capers, and one finds an aromatic style of cooking that utilizes capers, raisins, olives, nuts, and blends of herbs and vegetables. This dish is quite wonderful as an antipasto the next day, so you may want to double it.

1 medium-size eggplant, peeled and cubed
Salt
1¹/₂ quarts olive oil or olive pomace oil for frying
3 tablespoons extra virgin olive oil
1 medium-size onion, thinly sliced and separated into rings
2 large, ripe tomatoes, peeled, seeded, and chopped
2 large garlic cloves, finely chopped
¹/₄ cup dry red wine
2 large artichoke hearts (preferably from fresh artichokes), coarsely chopped
4 salted anchovy fillets, rinsed
1¹/₂ tablespoons capers (preferably salted Pantelleria capers), drained, rinsed, and chopped if large
4 large imported Sicilian (Paterno) olives, pitted and chopped
1¹/₂ tablespoons golden raisins, softened in tepid water to cover for 15 minutes and drained

GETTING TO THE HEART OF THE MATTER— PREPARING ARTICHOKES

To prepare an artichoke heart or foundation, wash the artichoke and cut off the top half of the bracts (improperly called leaves) with a large, sharp chef's knife. Remove the little bracts at the stem. Cut the stem off near the bottom so the artichoke can stand up without tipping over. Many people throw away the stem, but the flesh inside is edible, so slice off the skin and reserve the stem flesh (this is much easier to do if the artichoke has been boiled whole first).

To extract the choke, peel, slice, or break off the little pale green bracts near the choke and discard them. Then, with a paring knife, slice off the woody parts surrounding the bottom. In a circular motion, cut out the hairy choke. Once the artichoke is cut, it will blacken, so you must always keep half of a lemon nearby and immediately rub the artichoke heart with the cut side of the lemon when you reach it. As you finish each artichoke, put the heart in a bowl of water acidulated with lemon juice or vinegar to keep it from blackening.

---

1 tablespoon water
1 dried chile
Freshly ground black pepper to taste
1/2 cup finely diced **caciocavallo** or **provolone** cheese
6 large fresh mint leaves, chopped

---

1. Lay the eggplant cubes on some paper towels and sprinkle with salt. Leave them to drain of their bitter juices for 30 minutes, then pat dry with paper towels.

2. Meanwhile, in a casserole or skillet, heat the extra virgin olive oil over medium heat, then cook the onion until translucent, stirring, about 6 minutes. Raise the heat to high and add the tomatoes, garlic, and wine and cook until most of the wine has evaporated, about 10 minutes. While the tomato and wine mixture is cooking, preheat the frying oil in a deep-fryer or an 8-inch saucepan fitted with a basket insert to 370°F. Reduce the heat to low under the casserole and add the artichoke hearts, anchovies, capers, olives, raisins, water, and chile and season with salt and pepper. Cook, stirring, for 5 minutes.

3. Deep-fry the eggplant cubes until golden brown, turning once, about 8 minutes in all. Drain on paper towels and add to the tomato sauce, mixing carefully by lifting and folding. Cook for 1 minute over medium-high heat, then add the diced cheese and mint and cook for 1 more minute. Remove from the heat. Serve warm or at room temperature as a relish, vegetable side dish, pasta topping, or as a main-course stew.

Makes 4 servings

SARDINIAN VEGETABLE STEW

THE FOOD OF SARDINIA IS INFLUENCED BY several factors, including the fact that it is an island and historically isolated from the main flow of trade. The food is simple, local, and emphasizes fresh vegetables and to a lesser extent fish, even though it is an island. This earthy vegetable stew called *stufato di verdure* has rich, aromatic flavors. It is based on a *soffritto* of finely chopped garlic and parsley that is like a pesto.

1 large garlic clove, peeled
Leaves from 1 small bunch fresh parsley (a
  good-sized handful)
¹/₂ cup extra virgin olive oil
1 pound small white onions
1 large, ripe tomato, peeled, seeded, and chopped
6 fresh basil leaves
Salt to taste
1 pound small new potatoes, peeled
1 pound green beans, ends trimmed

1. Pound the garlic and parsley together in a mortar with a pestle until it is a pesto.

2. In a casserole with high sides, heat the olive oil over medium-high heat. Cook the onions until yellow, stirring, about 4 minutes. Reduce the heat to low. Quickly stir in the garlic-and-parsley pesto so it doesn't burn from the still-hot casserole. Let it sizzle for 1 minute and stir in the tomato and basil leaves. Cook for 30 minutes, covered.

3. Salt the stew and add the potatoes and green beans. Cover and simmer until the potatoes are easily pierced with the tip of a skewer, about 1 hour. Serve from the casserole.

Makes 3 to 4 servings

RED BELL PEPPER AND BROCCOLI STEW

FIRST OF ALL, THE COLORS OF THIS *PEPER-oni rosso e broccoli in umido* are really wonderful. They are bright and vibrant, making this dish all the more appetizing. This all-vegetable stew appears so simple, but the taste is great. Although you could eat it alone, I like to serve it over *farfalle* (butterfly pasta) or rice. There is one part of this stew that you must pay careful attention to, namely, watch the broccoli, because broccoli, and all cruciferous vegetables, must not be overcooked. When they are, chemicals in the plant break down and release sulfurous compounds, such as ammonia and hydrogen sulfide, which interact with the chlorophyll in the plant, causing the broccoli to turn an unappetizing, brownish gray color and to have a very unpleasant smell. This recipe is how I do it when I'm pressed for time. If I've got the time, I'll roast and peel the peppers first.

2 tablespoons extra virgin olive oil
4 fleshy red bell peppers, seeded and cut into
   strips
1 medium-size onion, thinly sliced and
   separated into rings
2 large garlic cloves, finely chopped
1 bunch fresh broccoli (about 1 pound), broken
   into florets and stems cut into ½-inch pieces
Salt and freshly ground black pepper to taste

---

1. In a large skillet, heat the olive oil over medium heat. Cook the red peppers, onion, and garlic until soft, adding small amounts of water to keep the skillet from drying out and stirring from time to time, about 30 minutes.

2. Meanwhile, bring a saucepan of water to a boil, salt lightly, cook the broccoli stems for a few minutes, and add the florets. Cook the broccoli until tender but still bright green, about 10 minutes. Drain, break up slightly with a fork, and toss with the red bell pepper stew. Season with salt and pepper and serve immediately.

Makes 4 servings

MUSHROOM STEW FROM CALABRIA

MUSHROOM STEWS ARE PARTICULARLY popular in Italy, especially in the regions of Sardinia and Calabria, the toe of the Italian boot. Most of the mushrooms collected by Italian foragers are wood or forest mushrooms rather than the button (field) mushrooms popular with Americans. I think it's true that forest mushrooms are more flavorful than button mushrooms, but they are more expensive. Make this with field mushrooms but consider throwing in a good handful of some more exotic mushrooms such as portobello, lobster, trumpet, chanterelles, black trumpet, shiitake, oyster, cremini, and/or enoki. If you use the greater amount of olive oil called for in the ingredient list, the final dish will be richer and, of course, fattier. I think this stew is best when served with some garlic-rubbed crostini or spaghetti.

---

4 pounds mixed mushrooms from at least 5
   different types
¾ to 1½ cups extra virgin olive oil, to your
   taste
4 large garlic cloves, finely chopped
4 teaspoons dried oregano
Salt and freshly ground black pepper to taste
2 pounds ripe tomatoes, peeled, seeded, chopped,
   and drained
2 dried chiles
¼ cup plus 2 tablespoons finely chopped fresh
   mint leaves

1. Clean the mushrooms, if necessary, by brushing them and then trimming with a small knife, or by rubbing dirt off with a paper towel, not by washing. Slice into large pieces, including the stems. Leave the smaller mushrooms whole.

2. In a large casserole, heat the olive oil with the garlic and oregano over medium-high heat for 2 minutes, stirring so the garlic doesn't burn. Reduce the heat to medium-low, add the mushrooms, and season with salt and pepper. Toss the mushrooms so they are well coated with olive oil. Slowly cook the mushrooms for 15 minutes, tossing and stirring occasionally.

3. Add the tomatoes, chiles, and mint. Cook until the stew is thick and syrupy, about 30 minutes. Check the seasonings, remove the whole chiles, and serve.

Makes 6 servings

BAVARIAN VEGETABLE STEW

I N THE LATE 1960S AND THROUGHOUT THE 1970s, I traveled extensively in Germany. While I was there, I loved to have this kind of vegetable stew with sausages or really any kind of meat, but especially pork. It all sounds so simple and, in fact, seems like it wouldn't have a lot of flavor, but it does because the mix of vegetables is a good one, and the heavy casserole lid traps all the flavor. In Bavaria they call this preparation *Gemüsepichelsteiner.*

6 tablespoons ($^3/_4$ stick) unsalted butter
4 carrots, cut into $^3/_8$-inch-thick rounds
Salt and freshly ground black pepper to taste
$^1/_4$ cup finely chopped fresh parsley leaves
1 large celery root, peeled and sliced $^1/_4$ inch thick
1 parsley root, peeled and sliced $^1/_4$ inch thick
4 leeks, split lengthwise, washed well, and sliced
1 small head cauliflower (about 1 pound), broken into florets
$^1/_2$ pound sugar snap peas, tough strings removed
$^1/_2$ pound green beans, ends trimmed and cut into 1-inch pieces
$^1/_2$ head Savoy or green cabbage (about $^3/_4$ pound), damaged outer leaves discarded, cored, and thinly sliced
1 pound potatoes, peeled and sliced $^1/_4$ inch thick
$1^1/_2$ cups water

1. In a large casserole, melt 3 tablespoons of the butter over medium-high heat, then turn off the heat. Layer the carrots over the bottom of the casserole. Season with salt and pepper and sprinkle with a little parsley. Continue layering the vegetables in the order in which they are listed in the ingredients list, sprinkling each layer with salt, pepper, and parsley. The last layer should be the potatoes, sprinkled with parsley. Dot the top of the potatoes with the remaining 3 tablespoons of butter.

2. Pour the water over the vegetables, cover tightly, and bring to a boil. Reduce the heat to low and cook until all the vegetables are tender, about 1 hour.

———— ● ————

Makes 6 to 8 servings

TOURLU

A *TOURLU* IS THE GREEK VERSION OF THE Turkish vegetable stew called *türlü* (page 317). This Greek *tourlu*, sometimes called *youvetsi* or *briami*, is quite easy to prepare. You simply toss it all together and stick it in the oven. Strictly speaking, I suppose you can't call it a stew because it is baked, but the eating is purely stew—if you eat it hot. But many Greeks like to let it cool to room temperature before eating, or refrigerate it overnight before serving it at room temperature, sometimes as a *meze*, the kind of small tidbit eaten with a glass of ouzo or some wine. I've adapted this recipe from something similar that I ate when I was in the tiny village of Ía, on the northwestern portion of the island of Santorini (Thira), of Atlantis fame. Although the island is today totally given over to tourism, an enterprising traveler willing to search can find some non-tourist food.

———— ● ————

1 red bell pepper
1 yellow bell pepper
1 green bell pepper
1 pound ripe tomatoes
1 large parsnip, peeled and cut into bite-size chunks
3 medium-size zucchini or 2 zucchini and 1 yellow summer squash, ends trimmed and thickly sliced
1 medium-size red onion, cut into eighths
1 leek (white and light green parts only) split lengthwise, washed well, and cut into chunks
1/2 fennel bulb, including leaves, cut into bite-size chunks
2 large garlic cloves, finely chopped
3 tablespoons finely chopped fresh coriander (cilantro) leaves
1/8 teaspoon ground cinnamon
2 cups extra virgin olive oil
Salt and freshly ground black pepper to taste

———— ● ————

1. Preheat the oven to 425°F. Place the peppers and tomatoes in a baking dish with a little water or on a wire rack set over a baking sheet and roast until the skins on the peppers blister and turn black, 35 to 40 minutes. Remove the peppers and tomatoes and, when cool enough to handle, remove the seeds and peel off the skins of the peppers and peel the skins from the tomatoes.

2. Reduce the oven temperature to 375°F. In a large casserole, preferably an earthenware one, toss together the parsnip, zucchini, red onion, leek, fennel, the grilled bell peppers and tomatoes, the garlic, fresh coriander, cinnamon, and olive oil and season with salt and pepper. Place the casserole in the oven and bake, uncovered, until the parsnip is tender and portions of whatever vegetables are on top are beginning to blacken slightly, 1¹/₄ to 1³/₄ hours. Serve hot or let cool to room temperature before serving.

Makes 6 servings

BRIAMI

BRIAMI IS THE NAME OF A VARIETY OF different family-style vegetable stews found in Greek home cooking. This recipe is a variation on these stews, and on similar stews that are found in Turkey and the Balkans. What is unique is that the whole ensemble of vegetables is layered and baked until the entire dish melds together into one magnificent taste. Technically, it's hard to call this a stew, but it is, for want of a better word, "stewish." A lot of olive oil is used, and as a result, this actually feeds a lot of people. Everything is baked together in a mishmash and it becomes quite lovely and delicious.

1¹/₂ pounds mixed new Yukon Gold, Peruvian Purple, and red potatoes, halved
3 large carrots, thickly sliced
1 kohlrabi, without the leaves, peeled and sliced
3 beets, trimmed, peeled, and quartered
1 large red onion, sliced and separated into rings
1 large white onion, sliced and separated into rings
4 large garlic cloves, finely chopped
3 tablespoons chopped fresh dill

1 tablespoon dried oregano
1¹/₂ cups extra virgin olive oil
Salt and freshly ground pepper to taste
2 pounds ripe tomatoes, peeled, seeded, and sliced

---

1. Preheat the oven to 350°F.

2. Toss all the ingredients, except the salt, pepper, and tomatoes, together with 1 cup of the olive oil. Season with salt and pepper and arrange in an earthenware casserole. Cover the top with the tomatoes and pour the remaining ¹/₂ cup of olive oil on top. Bake until the potatoes and beets are tender and the tops of the vegetables are dark in places, about 1¹/₂ hours. Serve immediately.

Makes 6 to 8 servings

GREEK OKRA STEW

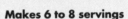

THIS GREEK VEGETABLE STEW, CALLED *bamies laderes*, which means something like "okra in olive oil," is often made for a Greek Lenten menu. The Lenten period in Greece often sees these kinds of vegetable stews, called *ladera* (which literally means "oily") being made. It is a Greek method of stewing vegetables that is also found in Turkey, where these foods are known as *zeytinyağlı sebze yemekleri*, "olive oil vegetable foods." There is a very specific way of making these vegetable stews in Greece. A copious amount of olive oil is poured into a pan with a little

OLIVE OIL

As a consumer, you need to know how olive oils are rated and categorized for sale. Because olive oils come from a wide variety of places and because of the variety of olive oils themselves, all with different flavors and colors, the "best" olive oil for you will depend on your own taste. The International Olive Oil Council, a United Nations body, has drawn up trade standards and has tried to standardize the language used for describing olive oils. The term *olive oil* means the oil extracted from the fruit of the olive tree, excluding oils obtained by using solvents or reesterification processes. It also excludes mixtures with other oils. Edible olive oils that don't need to be refined are categorized as follows: virgin olive oil is the oil obtained from the fruit solely by mechanical or other physical means under conditions that do not lead to the alteration of the oil. When virgin olive oil is intended for consumption in its natural state, it is designated *extra virgin olive oil* and has a maximum acidity of 1 percent. *Fine virgin olive oil* or *virgin olive oil* has a maximum acidity of 2 percent. *Ordinary virgin olive oil* has a maximum acidity of 3.3 percent. Olive pomace oil is a by-product of processed olives, mostly the dry material of the olives (skin, pulp seed, and pieces of stone). Cooks usually use olive pomace oil for deep-frying.

Most good cooks keep three or more different kinds of olive oils in their pantry: The first is a good quality, but relatively inexpensive extra virgin olive oil for sautéing. The second is a virgin or pomace oil kept for cooking at higher temperatures. The third is an estate-bottled, cold-pressed extra virgin olive oil that is almost never used for cooking and is drizzled on foods. It often is very distinctive in taste, and the cook chooses one suited to his or her liking.

---

water, and one or more kinds of vegetables are added, along with tomatoes or tomato sauce, an herb, and a spice. The vegetables are covered and cooked slowly, then salted at the end.

There appears to be an enormous amount of olive oil in this preparation, but remember that you *cook* in this amount of oil, you don't eat all this oil (although both Greeks and Turks will sop up everything with bread). This recipe derives from a taverna dish I had in Sparta that I thought particularly delicious.

---

1 pound fresh small okra, bottoms trimmed
1/4 cup red wine vinegar
Salt to taste
1 cup extra virgin olive oil
1 medium-size onion, chopped
1/4 cup finely chopped celery
1 Italian long green pepper (peperoncino), seeded and finely chopped
1/2 cup peeled and finely chopped eggplant
4 garlic cloves, finely chopped
3 cups fresh or canned crushed tomatoes with their liquid
1 tablespoon tomato paste
1 teaspoon sugar
Freshly ground black pepper to taste

1. Soak the okra in the vinegar with a sprinkling of salt for 1 hour.

2. In a large casserole, heat the olive oil over medium heat. Cook the onion, celery, green pepper, eggplant, and garlic until soft, stirring occasionally, 6 to 8 minutes. Add the tomatoes, tomato paste, and sugar. Stir well and cook for 10 minutes.

3. Drain the okra, and add it to the casserole. Season with salt and pepper and add more water, if necessary, to keep the okra moist instead of oily. Cover, reduce the heat to low, and simmer until the water has evaporated, about 4 hours. Serve warm, using a slotted spoon.

Makes 4 to 6 servings

GREEK LENTEN VEGETABLE STEW

IN EVERY REGION OF GREECE THERE IS A variety of Lenten stews, made without meat, of course. The variations are based on local produce and always fresh vegetables. Typically, a lot of olive oil is used in a vegetable stew, although I've cut the quantity down considerably in this recipe, called *yahni nistismo*, "Lenten stew." Cumin, pepper, coriander, allspice, and dried herbs are used in winter stews, while fresh dill, parsley, savory, thyme, and mint are used in the summer. Wine, vinegar, and lemon are used year-round. There are two types of island stew cookery: *Kavourthistá* always starts with the frying of meat and vegetables before they are put into a stew, making whatever is cooking richer in color but also heavier. *Yahnistá* starts with the gentle sautéing of onion before the addition of the remaining ingredients. I normally serve Greek-style vegetable stews at room temperature only because I prefer them that way, as the flavors steep and mingle better, I think.

2 tablespoons unsalted butter
1/2 cup extra virgin olive oil
1 large onion, chopped
2 potatoes, peeled and cut into large dice
3 zucchini, ends trimmed and cut into 2-inch lengths
1/2 pound green beans, ends trimmed and cut in half
4 large, ripe tomatoes (about 1 1/2 pounds), quartered
8 scallions (white and green parts), cut into 1-inch pieces
1 cup chopped fresh parsley leaves
2 tablespoons finely chopped fresh mint leaves
1 teaspoon dried oregano
1 teaspoon salt
Freshly ground black pepper to taste
1 bay leaf
2 cups water
1 pound spinach, heavy stems removed and washed well

1. In a casserole, melt the butter with the olive oil over medium heat. When the butter stops sizzling, cook the onion until soft, 5 to 6 minutes. Add all the remaining ingredients, except the water and spinach, and toss so everything is coated with butter and oil. Add the water, and bring to a boil. Reduce the heat to low, cover, and cook until the potatoes are tender, stirring occasionally, about 45 minutes.

2. Add the spinach, cover again, and once it wilts, after about 5 minutes, remove the pot from the burner. Serve hot or at room temperature with crusty bread.

Makes 6 servings

POTATO AND CARROT STEW FROM GREECE

THERE IS A CLASS OF VEGETABLE STEWS IN Greek cooking known as *ladera* (or *laderes* or *latheros*), a word that means "oily" and indicates that the vegetables are cooked in lots of olive oil. These can be eaten as a vegetable stew but are equally popular in Greece served at room temperature as a side dish or kind of *meze*. This stew has a cornucopia of vegetables, and is a little spicy hot because of the chile pepper, which is not always used in Greek cooking as generously as I use it here.

1 cup extra virgin olive oil
1 pound leeks, split lengthwise, washed well, and coarsely chopped
1 large onion, thinly sliced and separated into rings
4 large garlic cloves, finely chopped
1 fresh green chile, seeded and finely chopped
1 pound carrots, cut into rounds
1 tablespoon tomato paste
3/4 pound potatoes, peeled and cut into chunks
1/2 pound turnips, peeled and cut into chunks
1 cup water
1 tablespoon dried oregano
1/8 teaspoon ground cinnamon
Salt and freshly ground black pepper to taste

1. In a large earthenware casserole set on a heat diffuser, if necessary, or in a large skillet, heat the olive oil over medium heat. Cook the leeks, onion, garlic, chile, and carrots until the onion is translucent and the leeks are soft, stirring occasionally, 12 to 15 minutes.

2. Add the tomato paste, potatoes, turnips, water, oregano, and cinnamon and season with salt and pepper. Stir well to mix, and reduce the heat to low. Cover and cook for about 2 hours, or until the potatoes and turnips are tender, adding a few tablespoons of water when necessary to prevent the stew from drying out completely, although there should be no water left when it is fully cooked.

3. Serve hot or let cool in the skillet and serve at room temperature.

Makes 4 to 6 servings

GREEK GARDEN PEA AND OLIVE OIL STEW

THE GREEKS ARE QUITE FOND OF VEG-etables and even fonder of cooking them in lots of olive oil and a little water, always with the addition of some herbs, and sometimes a spice or two. This recipe, called *arakas latheros*, would typically be eaten as a main course, served with fresh crusty French- or Italian-style bread. Ideally, you will want to make this stew in the late springtime, when fresh garden peas in their pods begin to appear in markets. You can also use frozen peas, but don't use canned peas, which just won't work.

¾ cup extra virgin olive oil
3 medium-size onions, chopped
2 carrots, chopped
2 large garlic cloves, chopped
1 tablespoon finely chopped fresh parsley leaves
1 tablespoon finely chopped fresh fennel leaves
1 teaspoon finely chopped fresh mint leaves
6 cups fresh peas (from about 6 pounds pea pods)
Salt to taste
1 teaspoon paprika
1¼ cups water
1 tablespoon tomato paste

1. In a casserole or large skillet, heat the olive oil over medium heat. Cook the onions, carrots, and garlic until soft, stirring occasionally, about 15 minutes. Add the parsley, fennel, and mint, and stir, then add the peas, salt, paprika, and water. Reduce the heat to low, cover, and simmer for 30 minutes, stirring occasionally.

2. Stir in the tomato paste and cook until the stew is bubbling and almost no water is left, stirring occasionally, about 10 minutes.

Makes 4 servings

HÜNKAR BEĞENDI

THIS EGGPLANT STEW IS A CREAMY DISH that is so heavenly tasting the Turkish name, *hünkar beğendi* (pronounced HOONkar BAYendi), means "sultan's delight." It is traditionally an accompaniment to the spicy lamb stew called *tas kebabı* (page 128). There are two stories told about how this dish came about. The kitchens of the Ottoman sultans were famed for their culinary creations made to please the ruler, and this dish was said to have been created for Sultan Murad IV (circa 1612–40). Another story has the dish named after it was requested by Empress Eugénie, the wife of Napoleon III, when she visited the Topkapi palace in the mid-nineteenth century. The *kashkaval* or *kasseri* cheese can be found in Middle Eastern, Greek, or Armenian markets.

2 pounds eggplant
2 tablespoons fresh lemon juice
1/2 cup (1 stick) unsalted butter
1/2 cup unbleached all-purpose flour
1 1/2 cups hot milk
1 cup grated **kashkaval** or **kasseri** cheese
Salt and freshly ground black pepper to taste

———●———

1. Preheat the oven to 425°F. Roast the eggplant in a baking pan until the skins blister and turn black, about 40 minutes. Once the eggplants are cool enough to handle, remove the flesh from the charred skins and transfer to a strainer. Leave to drain for 30 minutes to leach them of their bitter juices. Transfer to a food processor, add the lemon juice, and process until smooth.

2. In a large, heavy casserole, melt the butter over medium-high heat. When it stops sizzling, stir in the flour to form a roux and cook for 2 to 3 minutes, stirring. Remove the casserole from the heat and whisk in the milk slowly until a thick, white sauce without lumps has formed.

3. Return the casserole to the burner. Stir in the pureed eggplant, reduce the heat to low, and simmer for 20 minutes, stirring occasionally. Stir in the cheese and beat well until smooth. Season with salt and pepper and serve.

Makes 4 to 6 servings

TÜRLÜ

ÜRLÜ, A KIND OF VEGETABLE RATA-touille or stew, is said to originate in the eastern Turkish city of Erzincan. It is a preparation known by the same name in Greece (*tourlu*) and by a similar one in Egypt (*turly*). *Türlü* is made in a summer and winter version, this recipe being the summer version. Some cooks also add bits of lamb or chicken to the stew. The *türlü* is made in an earthen-ware *marmite* or potbellied stew pot.

———●———

1 pound eggplant, peeled and cut into cubes
Salt
1 cup extra virgin olive oil
4 medium-size onions, chopped
2 garlic cloves, crushed
1/2 pound zucchini, ends trimmed, peeled, and sliced
3 green bell peppers, seeded and quartered
1/2 pound green beans, ends trimmed and cut in half crosswise
1/2 pound fresh small okra, bottoms trimmed
5 ripe tomatoes (about 1 1/2 pounds), peeled, seeded, and sliced
Freshly ground black pepper to taste
2 tablespoons finely chopped fresh parsley leaves
Paprika to taste

———●———

1. Lay the eggplant cubes on some paper towels and sprinkle with salt. Leave them to drain of their bitter juices for 30 minutes, then pat dry with paper towels.

2. In a large skillet, heat 1/2 cup of the olive oil over medium-high heat. Cook the eggplant cubes, stirring, until browned, about 8 minutes. Remove from the skillet and set aside.

3. Heat another ¼ cup of the olive oil in the same skillet and cook the onions and garlic over medium-high heat until the onions are translucent, stirring, about 6 minutes. Turn off the heat and set the skillet aside.

4. Preheat the oven to 350°F. In a large casserole, layer half of the eggplant cubes over the bottom. Cover this layer with half of the sliced zucchini, half of the peppers, and half of the green beans. Spread half of the onions over the beans, then half of the okra, and then half the tomatoes. Sprinkle with some salt, pepper, half of the parsley, and an abundant amount of paprika. Repeat the vegetable layers, finishing with the remaining sliced tomatoes. Sprinkle with more salt, pepper, the remaining parsley, and paprika. Pour the remaining ¼ cup of olive oil over all, cover, and bake until soft, about 1½ hours. Serve lukewarm.

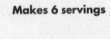

Makes 6 servings

TURKISH SUMMER VEGETABLE STEW

BURIED IN THE CROOKED WARRENS OF the city of Antalya, on Turkey's Mediterranean coast, is a little restaurant called the Huseyinin on Eski Sebzeciler İçi Sokak (the name means "Old Inner Street of the Greengrocers"), named after a narrow pedestrian passageway in this old city founded by Attalus II, king of Pergamum in about 150 B.C. Although Antalya is surrounded by snow-capped mountains on three sides, it sits on a fertile plain, which makes the city not only an agricultural hub for the region but commercially important because fresh fruits and vegetables are trucked to all parts of Turkey. This recipe is based on the very good meal I had at the restaurant; on the menu it was simply called *güveç*, a word that refers both to the earthenware casserole in which the stew is cooked and the stew itself. This particular version is a summer vegetable stew, while in the winter one would eat *güveç kiş*, a winter stew based on root vegetables.

½ cup extra virgin olive oil

1 medium-size onion, thinly sliced and separated into rings

2 pounds large, very ripe tomatoes, peeled, seeded, and chopped, with all their juices

1 fresh red chile, seeded and very finely chopped

4 Italian long green peppers (peperoncini), seeded and coarsely chopped

*3 large garlic cloves, pounded in a mortar with 1
teaspoon salt until mushy*

*1 medium-size Yukon Gold potato, peeled,
halved, and sliced ¼ inch thick*

*2 medium-size zucchini, ends trimmed, peeled
lengthwise in zebra stripes, and cut into
1-inch-thick rounds*

*2 cucumbers, peeled, seeded, and cut into 1-inch
chunks*

Salt and freshly ground black pepper to taste

1 cup fresh green peas

*¾ pound spinach, washed well and heavy stems
removed, if desired*

---

1. In a large earthenware casserole set on a heat
diffuser, heat the olive oil over medium-high
heat. Cook the onion until translucent, stirring, about 5 minutes. Add the tomatoes, chile,
green peppers, and garlic and continue to
cook, stirring, until the peppers begin to
soften, about 12 minutes. (If you are not cooking with earthenware and a diffuser, cook over
medium heat and check for doneness sooner.)
Add the potato and cook until it starts to look
soft, about 5 minutes. Reduce the heat to low,
add the zucchini and cucumbers, and season
with salt and pepper. Cook, covered, until the
potatoes are soft, about 40 minutes.

2. Add the peas and cook until they are tender,
about 10 minutes. Add the spinach and cook
until it wilts, 4 to 5 minutes. Let the stew rest
in the casserole for 15 minutes before serving.

Makes 6 servings

VEGETABLE STEW FROM TUNISIA WITH ROSE PETALS

THIS IS A TUNISIAN VEGETABLE STEW
called *maraqat al-khuḍra*. It can be made
with any seasonally available vegetables but
the ones I use here are pretty typical. You can
follow the principle given here in this recipe
and add whatever vegetables you want. I would
suggest keeping the Swiss chard or replacing it
with mustard greens or kale or collard greens.
The essential spice mix in the stew is the chile
paste known as *harīsa*, which you will have to
make first. Edible rosebuds for culinary purposes are, surprisingly, not that hard to find,
but you need to look. The best place is a
whole-foods or natural foods store. You could
also try ordering from Kalustyan (see the
sources listed at the back of the book). Serve
with warm Arabic flatbread.

---

*1 tablespoon **Harīsa** (page 34)*

½ cup water

1 tablespoon tomato paste

3 tablespoons extra virgin olive oil

3 large garlic cloves, finely chopped

½ teaspoon cayenne pepper

¼ teaspoon ground cinnamon

1 teaspoon freshly ground caraway seeds

Salt and freshly ground black pepper to taste

*1 small head caulifower, stalk trimmed away
and broken into medium-size florets*

*¼ pound fresh green beans, ends trimmed and
cut into 1-inch lengths*

1¼ pounds Swiss chard, trimmed of heavy
   white stalks, then cut crosswise into 1-inch-
   wide strips
4 small zucchini (preferably a cultivar that is
   mottled yellow and green), ends trimmed and
   cut into 1-inch-thick rounds
1 pound ripe tomatoes, cut in half, seeds
   squeezed out, and grated against the largest
   holes of a grater down to the peel
1 green bell pepper, seeded and cut into chunks
6 organic rosebuds, crushed

———●———

1. Mix together the *harisa*, water, and tomato
paste in a small bowl.

2. In a large earthenware casserole set on a heat
diffuser, heat the olive oil over medium-high
heat. Cook the garlic for about 30 seconds,
making sure it doesn't burn. Add the *harisa* and
water mixture, the cayenne, cinnamon, caraway,
salt, and pepper. Cook for about 3 minutes,
then add the vegetables and rosebuds. Cover
and cook until the Swiss chard wilts, about 5
minutes. (If you are not cooking with earthenware and a diffuser, cook over medium heat
and check for doneness sooner.)

3. Reduce the heat to low and simmer, covered, until the cauliflower is tender, 30 to 45
minutes. Serve immediately.

———●———

Makes 4 servings

MURSHĀN

THIS TUNISIAN VEGETABLE STEW, CALLED
murshān, is made with delicate young turnip
leaves steamed with Swiss chard and fava
beans. The name of the stew derives from the
root word meaning "to nibble." It is a preparation from the region of Sousse and is sometimes known as a *shakshūka*, a word that is
usually reserved for a kind of vegetable rata-
touille cooked with many eggs, but is sometimes used to refer to any kind of vegetable
stew. The greens in this stew more or less
disintegrate, but they take on a deliciously
"stewy," melted sort of texture.

———●———

¾ cup extra virgin olive oil
1 small onion, chopped
2 teaspoons granulated garlic
1 teaspoon cayenne pepper
2 teaspoons finely ground coriander seeds
Salt and freshly ground black pepper to taste
1½ cups dried fava beans (about ½ pound),
   picked over, rinsed, soaked overnight in water
   to cover, drained, and skins removed
1 to 2 pounds young turnip leaves, to your taste
1 pound Swiss chard leaves, trimmed of the
   lowest, thickest part of the stem

———●———

1. In a large earthenware casserole set on a heat
diffuser, heat the olive oil over medium-high
heat, then cook the onion until soft and
golden, about 5 minutes. (If you are not cooking with earthenware and a diffuser, cook over
medium heat and check for doneness sooner.)

2. Add the garlic, cayenne, coriander, salt, and pepper. Mix well, then add the fava beans, turnip leaves, and Swiss chard. Cover, reduce the heat to low, and cook until the fava beans are tender, about 2 to 3 hours, depending on how long the beans soaked. Check the seasoning and serve.

Makes 4 servings

TURNIP, TOMATO, CHICKPEA, AND SPINACH STEW WITH BEEF FROM TUNISIA

A LTHOUGH THIS STEW IS CALLED *LIFTIYYA* in Tunisia, meaning "turnip stew," it is, in fact, a beef or veal stew with turnips, the beef acting as a flavor for the star of the dish, namely the turnips. This is a different culinary philosophy than we are used to in the United States, where beef is often the center of the plate. This spicy hot stew of turnips is also flavored with several spice mixtures. It is very satisfying and best accompanied by a salad. The best turnips to use are new ones, about 1¹/₂ inches in diameter.

1 pound boneless beef or veal stew meat, trimmed of any large pieces of fat and cut into 1-inch cubes
2 tablespoons Tābil (page 37)

¹/₂ teaspoon freshly ground black pepper
¹/₄ cup plus 2 tablespoons extra virgin olive oil
1 small onion, chopped
1 pound fresh or canned tomatoes, peeled, seeded, and chopped
1¹/₂ cups water
2 teaspoons Harīsa (page 34)
¹/₂ cup canned chickpeas
2 teaspoons cayenne pepper
1¹/₂ pounds small turnips, peeled and quartered
²/₃ cup finely chopped fresh parsley leaves
10 ounces spinach, stems removed, leaves washed well, and cut into strips
2 teaspoons salt
Juice from 1 lemon

1. Roll the meat in the *tābil* and black pepper. In a casserole, stew pot, or the bottom portion of a *couscoussier*, heat the olive oil over medium-high heat. Brown the meat with the onions until coated with a syrupy gravy, 5 to 6 minutes. Add the tomatoes, 1 cup of the water, the *harīsa*, chickpeas, and cayenne, and bring to a boil, stirring. Reduce the heat to low, cover, and cook until the meat is tender, about 1¹/₂ hours.

2. Add the remaining ¹/₂ cup of water, the turnips, parsley, spinach, and salt, season with black pepper, and cook until the turnips are easily pierced by a skewer, about 1 hour. Stir in the lemon juice and serve.

Makes 4 servings

TUNISIAN-STYLE SPICY SWISS CHARD AND BLACK-EYED PEA STEW

THIS TUNISIAN VEGETABLE STEW IS A KIND of *murshān* (page 320), a vegetable ragout of turnip tops, Swiss chard, fava beans, and spices. Here it is a hot, spicy dish, with lamb used as a seasoning. Everything is rich and flavorful, making for a very satisfying and warm meal. The use of the pasta that the Italians call *tubetti* is not atypical of Tunisian cooking, as pasta is very popular in Tunisia.

––––––•––––––

1/4 cup extra virgin olive oil
1 medium-size onion, finely chopped
3 large garlic cloves, finely chopped
4 ripe plum tomatoes, peeled, seeded, and chopped
2 teaspoons freshly ground caraway seeds
2 teaspoons freshly ground coriander seeds
1 teaspoon freshly ground cumin seeds
1 teaspoon Tābil *(page 37)*
1 tablespoon Harīsa *(page 34)*
1 fresh red chile, seeded and finely chopped
1 pound boneless lamb stew meat, trimmed of any large pieces of fat and diced
Salt and freshly ground black pepper to taste
1 1/2 quarts water
1 pound Swiss chard stems
1/2 pound potatoes, peeled and cubed
Leaves from 1 bunch fresh coriander (cilantro), finely chopped
1/4 cup tubetti
3/4 pound fresh or frozen black-eyed peas

1. In a stew pot, heat the olive oil over high heat. Add the onion, garlic, tomatoes, caraway, ground coriander, cumin, *tābil*, *harīsa*, and chile and cook until the mixture looks like a paste, stirring frequently, about 5 minutes. Add the lamb, season with salt and pepper, and cook, stirring, until the lamb browns, about 5 minutes. Add the water, reduce the heat to medium-low, and cook until the lamb is somewhat tender, about 1 1/2 hours.

2. Add the Swiss chard and potatoes and cook for 1 more hour.

3. Add three-quarters of the fresh coriander, the *tubetti*, and black-eyed peas and cook until the pasta is soft, about 30 minutes. Serve with the remaining fresh coriander sprinkled on top.

––––––•––––––

Makes 4 servings

GREEN BEAN AND POMEGRANATE STEW FROM SYRIA

THIS RECIPE FROM ALEPPO, IN SYRIA, where they use a lot of pomegranate molasses, is called *lūbya bi'l-rummān* ("green beans with pomegranate"). I've adapted this recipe from one described to me by Lubaba al-Daker, a young student from Damascus whose aunt lives in Aleppo and is quite a good cook. Typically, it can also be made with lamb, in which case you would want to serve it with rice pilaf (page 125). Pomegranate molasses is usually found in Middle Eastern markets, although better supermarkets will carry it too.

———————

¹/₄ cup plus 2 tablespoons extra virgin olive oil
1 medium-size onion, chopped
1 tablespoon **Bahārāt** *(page 119)*
1 teaspoon ground cinnamon
One 6-ounce can tomato paste dissolved in 1 quart water
2 pounds fresh green beans, ends trimmed
Salt and freshly ground black pepper to taste
8 large garlic cloves, chopped
¹/₂ cup finely chopped fresh coriander (cilantro) leaves
2¹/₂ tablespoons pomegranate molasses
2 tablespoons fresh lemon juice

———————

1. In an earthenware casserole set on a diffuser, heat 3 tablespoons of the olive oil over medium-high heat. Cook the onion, *bahārāt*, and cinnamon until the onion is soft, stirring occasionally, 5 to 6 minutes. Reduce the heat to low, add the diluted tomato paste and the green beans, and season with salt and pepper. Cover and cook for 45 minutes.

2. Uncover and cook until the green beans are tender, not crunchy (taste one to see if it is done), another 30 to 45 minutes.

3. In a small skillet, heat the remaining 3 tablespoons of olive oil over medium-high heat.

Cook the garlic and coriander together for 1 to 2 minutes, stirring constantly and paying close attention to any possible acrid smell that would indicate that the garlic is burning. Stir the garlic and coriander into the bean stew. Add the pomegranate molasses and lemon juice, stir to mix well, and cook for 10 minutes. Serve immediately.

———————

Makes 4 servings

KERALA-STYLE VEGETABLE STEW

T HIS IS A TYPICAL AND CLASSIC HINDU vegetarian stew called *avial* (or *aviyal*) from the Indian state of Kerala, on the south-western tip of the subcontinent, which is known for its spicy foods. But this recipe is not spicy (although it could be, if you wanted to add a fresh green chile) and in fact, since the final stew is somewhat sweet because of the mango, it is best served with a hot and spicy dish. Some cooks also use tamarind pulp for the stew. Typically, one would serve some rice pilaf (page 125) on the side. Do not add the yogurt to the stew until the end; it will separate if it cooks.

1 small eggplant, peeled and cut into 1-inch
   cubes
Salt
1 tablespoon coconut oil or grapeseed oil
1 small sweet potato, peeled and cut into 1-inch
   cubes
1/2 cup shelled fresh or frozen green peas or 1 cup
   sugar snap peas, tough strings removed
1 cup green beans, ends trimmed and cut into
   1-inch lengths
1 carrot, sliced
1 small onion, sliced
1/2 cup seeded and chopped green bell pepper
3/4 teaspoon turmeric
1/4 teaspoon freshly ground cumin seeds
1 cup water
1 medium-size, ripe tomato, peeled, seeded, and
   diced
1/2 green mango, peeled, seeded, and diced
1/3 cup unsweetened grated coconut
1 cup high-quality, full-fat, plain cow's milk
   yogurt
1 tablespoon unsalted butter at room
   temperature

1. Lay the eggplant pieces on some paper towels and sprinkle with salt. Leave them to drain of their bitter juices for 30 minutes, then pat dry with paper towels.

2. In a stew pot, combine the oil, eggplant, sweet potato, green peas, green beans, carrot, onion, green pepper, turmeric, and cumin. Add the water and 1 teaspoon of salt, bring to a boil, reduce the heat to low, and simmer, uncovered, until the vegetables are soft and very little water remains, 1 to 1 1/4 hours.

3. Add the tomato, mango, and coconut. Stir and simmer until they blend into the stew, about 15 minutes.

4. Remove from the heat, stir in the yogurt and butter, correct the seasonings, and serve.

Makes 4 to 6 servings

SPICY INDIAN EGGPLANT STEW

THIS RECIPE CAME TO ME ABOUT THIRTY years ago when I first became fascinated with Indian cuisine. There weren't very many Indian cookbooks around at that time, and Indian restaurants seemed to serve the same standard Americanized dishes over and over again, in the same way that Chinese restaurants do in America. I realized that for the real thing I needed to go to India, not an Indian restaurant in America. Or I had to be lucky enough to be invited into an Indian home, as I was, thanks to my friend Chitrita Banerji. Chitrita is Bengali, and at her table I certainly learned something about the taste I hoped to achieve in my own cooking. This is not her recipe, but I know this spicy eggplant stew will be enjoyable. Typically, you would serve this over some rice pilaf (page 125).

3 small eggplants (about 3 pounds total), peeled,
   sliced lengthwise, then cut crosswise into
   ¹/2-inch-thick slices
1 teaspoon salt, plus extra for sprinkling
¹/2 cup plus 2 tablespoons vegetable oil
3 large onions, thinly sliced and separated into
   rings
4 large garlic cloves, finely chopped
1 tablespoon freshly ground coriander seeds
1 teaspoon ground red chile of your choice or
   cayenne pepper
¹/4 teaspoon turmeric
1 fresh green chile, seeded and finely chopped
¹/2 cup unsweetened grated coconut
Juice and pulp of 1 small lemon, seeds removed
1 bay leaf
1 teaspoon sesame seeds, toasted in a dry skillet
   over medium heat until fragrant, then crushed
1 cup water
1 teaspoon brown sugar
1 teaspoon black mustard seeds, toasted in a dry
   skillet over medium heat until they begin to
   pop
2 tablespoons finely chopped fresh coriander
   (cilantro) leaves

1. Lay the eggplant pieces on some paper towels and sprinkle with salt. Leave them to drain of their bitter juices for 30 minutes, then pat dry with paper towels.

2. In a large skillet, heat ¹/4 cup of the vegetable oil over medium-high heat. Brown half of the eggplant pieces on both sides, about 6 minutes in all. Remove from the skillet and set aside. Add another ¹/4 cup of the oil to the skillet, and once it is heated, cook the remaining eggplant in the same way and set aside.

3. In a large casserole or stew pot, heat the remaining 2 tablespoons of oil over medium-high heat. Cook the onions, garlic, coriander seeds, red chile, turmeric, and fresh chile until soft, stirring a few times, about 5 minutes. Add the coconut and cook, stirring, another 2 to 3 minutes. Add the lemon juice and pulp, the remaining 1 teaspoon of salt, the bay leaf, sesame seeds, and water. Stir, add the eggplant, and cover. Reduce the heat to low, and simmer until the eggplant is very tender and the sauce thick, about 1¹/2 hours.

4. Add the brown sugar and mustard seeds, stir, and cook for 5 minutes. Stir in the coriander leaves and serve.

Makes 6 servings

SUCCOTASH

AS A KID I HATED SUCCOTASH, AND AS AN adult I found out why: we never had it freshly made. Frozen packages of tasteless succotash, usually with bits of red bell pepper in it, was all we ate. Unfortunately, many others have been led away from what should be the natural appeal of succotash by the major food companies who have produced packages of tasteless frozen versions of the dish. These hardly even intimate how delicious the real thing is. A modern version of succotash is simply a vegetable stew containing mostly fresh lima beans and fresh sweet corn, but sometimes kidney beans instead of lima beans. Luckily, frozen lima beans are really pretty good, so go ahead and use them if you can't find fresh, which are, after all, pretty hard to find. This recipe is a very simple one, which is the way I like it; there is no need to keep adding things.

———————●———————

Salt
2 cups fresh sweet corn kernels, scraped from 2 large ears of corn
2 cups frozen lima beans
2 tablespoons unsalted butter
1/2 cup heavy cream
1/2 teaspoon paprika
Freshly ground black pepper to taste

———————●———————

1. Bring a large saucepan of water to a boil, salt lightly, and cook the corn and lima beans for 12 minutes.

2. Drain the corn and beans, return to the saucepan, and add the butter, cream, and paprika, and season with salt and pepper. Turn the heat to medium, and once the mixture starts bubbling, cook for 5 minutes. Serve immediately.

———————●———————

Makes 4 servings

JAGASEE

THIS RECIPE IS ADAPTED FROM A COOK-book published by the Harwichport Library Association in 1934 called *From Cape Cod Kitchens*. It is meant to feed a large group of people and was once made regularly for church picnics and such. The original recipe calls for two quarts of dried lima beans and three cups of raw rice, an amount that would serve twenty-five people. I've scaled this recipe down to feed about six people, and I use frozen lima beans since dried lima beans are not too common. If you can get dried lima beans, soak 1/2 cup of them overnight in water to cover, then drain before cooking in boiling water for 1 1/2 hours.

I don't know where the name *jagasee* comes from, but it is true that nineteenth-century Cape Cod cooks, and New England cooks in general, had a proclivity for giving made-up and fanciful names to their creations.

———————●———————

One 2-ounce piece salt pork
1 medium-size onion, chopped
2 cups frozen lima beans
1 1/2 tablepoons ketchup or 1/4 teaspoon paprika
3 tablespoons chopped celery
Freshly ground black pepper to taste
1/2 green bell pepper, seeded and chopped
1/2 cup long-grain rice, rinsed in a strainer under running water
1 teaspoon salt
1/2 cup water

1. In a heavy, cast-iron casserole or Dutch oven, brown the salt pork over medium heat until browned on all sides, 8 to 10 minutes. Add the onion and cook until golden, about 4 minutes.

2. Add the lima beans, ketchup, celery, black pepper, bell pepper, rice, salt, and water. Cover and simmer over very low heat, using a heat diffuser if necessary, until the rice is tender, 7 hours. Serve.

Makes 6 servings

XONEQUI

XONEQUI (PRONOUNCED "SHUNEky") is the Mexican name for a kind of green, leafy vegetable, also called tannier spinach, belembe, and Tahitian taro (*Xanthosoma brasiliense* [Desf.] Engler), a member of the Araceae, the same family that taro is in. This vegetable is also prominent in a West Indian stew called *callaloo*. It may be possible to find it in a farmer's market in California or Florida, but it can be replaced with spinach.

If you look at the amount of chile peppers used in this recipe, you would think it is spicy hot, but the final stew is not. It has a delicate taste, but is substantial because of the black beans. As strange as it may seem, I once tested this recipe just before testing the Swedish Salmon Stew from Växjö (page 256) and served them both to my friends Billy and Laurie

Benenson and their family and we all went crazy over the unlikely combination, it was so good. *Xonequi* is served with corn flour dumplings; you'll find directions for these in step 5. Serve with tortillas if you want to skip the dumplings.

2 cups (about 1 pound) dried black beans, picked over and rinsed
4 quarts plus 3 1/2 cups water
1 1/2 teaspoons salt, or more as needed
2 pounds tannier spinach or spinach, heavy stems removed and washed well
5 tablespoons lard
1 small onion, finely chopped
1 large garlic clove, finely chopped
2 fresh ancho or pasilla chiles, seeded and chopped
5 dried red chiles
1 cup masa harina (corn flour)
2/3 cup crumbled Mexican queso fresco, ricotta salata, or cow's milk feta cheese
2 tablespoons chopped fresh coriander (cilantro) leaves

1. Put the beans in a large saucepan filled with 4 quarts of the water, add 1 teaspoon of the salt, and bring to a boil. Cook until the beans are tender, about 1 1/4 hours. Drain, saving 1/2 cup of the cooking liquid.

2. In a large saucepan, bring 2 cups of the remaining water to a boil, plunge the spinach in the water, and cook, covered, until it wilts, 3 to 4 minutes. Drain, saving 1/2 cup of the spinach cooking liquid.

3. In an earthenware casserole set on a diffuser, melt 3 tablespoons of the lard over high heat. Cook the onion, garlic, fresh chiles, and dried chiles, stirring, for 2 minutes. (If you are not cooking with earthenware and a diffuser, cook over medium-high heat.) Add 1 cup of the remaining water, reduce the heat to medium, and cook until the chiles are soft and the onions are translucent, 25 to 30 minutes.

4. Add the beans and their reserved $1/2$ cup of broth and the spinach and its $1/2$ cup of broth. Cook until the broth is bubbling and the spinach looks "suspended," about 10 minutes.

5. Meanwhile, in a small bowl, mix the masa harina with the remaining 2 tablespoons of lard, the remaining $1/2$ cup of water, the cheese, the remaining $1/2$ teaspoon of salt, and the coriander. Form the mixture into balls the size of a golf ball. Once the broth is bubbling, add the dumplings carefully. Cover, reduce the heat to low, and cook without looking or lifting the cover for 20 minutes. Serve immediately.

Makes 6 servings

STEWS WITH MIXED MEATS

This chapter is one of my favorites because it's where all the stews that mix up different meats are. Just as a good seafood stew will have a variety of fish and shellfish, so too a great stew often has a variety of meats. The Catalan Escudella (page 334) is a stew of impressive tastes, made with flavorings that come from chicken feet and gizzards, a lamb foot and shank, a prosciutto bone, and beef marrow bones, all cooked with some vegetables and a huge, grapefruit-size meatball made of ground pork, sausage, garlic, and parsley. A wildly luscious stew that begs to be made on a cold winter day is one from the Lombardy region of Italy, *ragù d'anitra con luganega e castagne*, or Duck, Sausage, and Chestnut Stew (page 350), which is as rich as it sounds.

I love classic stews, such as the French *pot-au-feu*. My recipe is in the style of Carcassonne, a medieval walled city in the Aude department of the Languedoc in southwestern France. This *pot-au-feu à la carcassonnaise* (page 339) cooks all day, and the smells that waft through the house are very enticing, especially when you come back indoors after some time in the cold. The meats used include a variety of sausages, beef ribs, bacon, lamb neck, and veal marrow bones, as well as vegetables such as cabbage, onions, white beans, tomatoes, carrots, celery, and shallots, all seasoned with summer savory and a fragrant bouquet garni. The *pot-au-feu* cooks until the meats are falling off the bone, about seven hours. I've also got three recipes for cassoulet. The first is the authentic cassoulet of Castelnaudary (page 342), which is quite a project and perhaps not for the novice. The second is an easier cassoulet (page 347), which everyone will enjoy and is not too difficult to make, although all cassoulets are time-consuming because there is a lot of preparation and simmering. The third is a kind of faux cassoulet (page 349) that does not skimp on taste, but is so much easier to make.

A stew I was quite surprised at—surprised because it tastes so good—is the famous Russian stew called *Solyanka* (page 362). It's a "pickly" stew with veal shoulder, kielbasa, ham, duck breast, and turkey thigh, and what seems like a zillion other ingredients. *Solyanka* is garnished with lemon slices and sour cream, and that really puts this stew over the top. If you go for hot and spicy, Louisiana-style Cajun gumbos, you'll go crazy over Roast Duck, Oyster, and Andouille Sausage Gumbo (page 365). Although the recipe is involved, I think the combination of duck and oysters is just a drop-dead wonderful taste, and you won't be disappointed.

A SPANISH STEW FROM MADRID

SPANISH STEWS ARE VARIOUSLY KNOWN by the words *olla, olleta, callo, cassolo, estofado, calderata,* or *cocido.* This stew, known in Madrid in the province of Castile as *callos a la madrileña,* is a kind of *menudo,* or tripe stew, of which one might find variations throughout Spain. The cooking of tripe is not that popular anymore in America, although it once was very much so. To properly prepare tripe, so that you can see what you are missing, read the boxes on page 7 and page 333 and the introduction to Tripe à la Mode de Caen on page 6. *Butifarra* sausage is a Catalonian-style sausage that can ordered from La Española (see the sources listed at the back of this book). You can also get the Spanish-style chorizo sausage through this company.

———————●———————

2 3/4 *pounds beef honeycomb tripe*
1/2 *cup distilled vinegar*
5 *quarts water, plus more as needed*
1 *large onion, cut into chunks and separated into layers*
1 *head garlic, unpeeled*
4 *bay leaves*
10 *black peppercorns*
1/4 *cup extra virgin olive oil*
1 *medium-size onion, chopped*
1 *large garlic clove, finely chopped*
One 6-ounce *piece cooked ham or Canadian bacon, cut into 4 or 5 pieces*
1 *pound* **butifara** *sausage or Polish kielbasa*

1 *pound Spanish-style chorizo sausage or hot Italian sausage*
One 1/4-pound *piece Irish bacon, cut into 6 pieces*
1 *tablespoon paprika*
3/4 *pound beef marrow bones*
4 *cups canned chickpeas, drained*
Salt and freshly ground black pepper to taste
1 *teaspoon cayenne pepper*
1 *pound Swiss chard, cut up*

———————●———————

1. Soak the tripe in the vinegar and water to cover overnight in the refrigerator. Drain.

2. Put the tripe in a large stockpot along with the water, cut-up onion, head of garlic, 3 of the bay leaves, and the peppercorns. Bring to a boil and cover. Reduce the heat to medium-low, and cook until the tripe is tender (so taste a little bit of it now and then) about 3 to 5 hours. Add more water if it is evaporating quickly. Drain the tripe, saving 2 cups of the broth. Cut the tripe into bite-size portions.

3. In an earthenware casserole set on a heat diffuser, heat the olive oil over medium-high heat (or use a stew pot directly over medium heat). Cook the chopped onion and garlic until translucent, stirring frequently so the garlic doesn't burn. Lightly brown the ham, *butifara* sausage, chorizo, and bacon, about 3 minutes. Add the paprika and stir. Add the marrow bones, reserved cooking broth, tripe, chickpeas, and the remaining bay leaf and season with salt, black pepper, and the cayenne. Reduce the heat to low and cook until the sausage meats are almost tender, 1 1/2 to 2 hours.

PREPARING AND COOKING TRIPE

Tripe refers to any of the stomachs of cud-chewing animals. The tripe usually available in American supermarkets is beef honeycomb tripe. Although the tripe you buy will already be cleaned, there are some steps you will want to take to ensure a properly cooked tripe. Remove any fat that may still remain on it, then place the whole tripe in a bowl with 1/2 cup distilled white vinegar and cover with cold water. Let

this sit, covered, in the refrigerator overnight.

When it's time to cook the tripe, bring some water to a boil with another 1/2 cup vinegar and gently boil the tripe until it is the right texture, anywhere from 4 to 7 hours. After cooking, tripe should have the texture of cooked squid—ever so slightly chewy but not tough or impossible to chew. Check the tripe by cutting off a small portion and tasting it.

4. Add the Swiss chard and cook until the leaves are wilted and the white stalks are tender, about 40 minutes. Serve immediately, cutting up the sausage into serving-size portions.

Makes 6 servings

SPANISH-STYLE CHORIZO SAUSAGE AND PEPPER STEW

S PANISH-STYLE CHORIZO IS VERY DIFFERent from Mexican style, which tends to be hotter. You can order Spanish-style chorizo from La Española (see the sources listed at the

back of the book), or you could use the Portuguese-style *chouriço* that is found in supermarkets wherever there are concentrations of Americans of Portuguese heritage, especially on the East Coast. The pork skin in this recipe might seem superfluous, but it is an essential flavor; you can use the skin from a piece of salt pork if you like.

2 tablespoons extra virgin olive oil
One 2-inch square piece pork skin
1 small onion, chopped
1 green bell pepper, seeded and chopped
2 garlic cloves, finely chopped
1 pound ripe plum tomatoes, peeled and seeded
1/2 cup dry white wine
1 teaspoon paprika
Salt to taste
1/4 pound lean ground beef
1/2 pound Spanish- or Portuguese-style chorizo sausage, cut up

1. In a large saucepan or casserole, heat the olive oil over high heat. Cook the pork skin, onion, bell pepper, and garlic until soft, stirring constantly, about 4 minutes.

2. Add the tomatoes, wine, and paprika and season with salt. Cook for 2 minutes and add the ground beef and chorizo. Cover and cook over low heat until the sausages are cooked through, about 1 1/2 hours.

Makes 2 to 3 servings

ESCUDELLA

E SCUDELLA IS THE NATIONAL STEW OF Catalonia. Although I find it magnificent, it is nothing but a big family stew-soup, whose full name is *escudella i carn d'olla*, literally "bowl of stew meat." It is usually made at Christmas. All the bones and feet provide the gelatinous flavor for the rough vegetables, such as cabbage and turnips, that make this stew so substantial. This recipe comes from my friend Montse Contreras, who lives in Sitges but is originally from the Bergueda region of Catalonia. This recipe is how her mother makes it. The classic Catalonian sausage is called *botiffara*, which can be ordered from La Española (see the sources listed at the back of the book). Commercially made chicken sausage is pretty close in taste to *botiffara* (*butifarra* in Spanish), which is made with pork or

veal. The giant meatball you'll make in step 2 is fun to eat when the stew is served. Remember to use all the bones and feet called for in the ingredients list, otherwise you will wonder why I'm so enthusiastic about this stew. You may have to allow yourself a few weeks to find all this stuff—the bones and whatnot—but it's worth it and you can just toss everything in the freezer until you decide to wow everyone with this dish.

---

2 chicken feet, skinned
1 chicken gizzard
1 lamb foot and ankle
1 1/3 pounds lamb shank
1 ham or prosciutto bone (about 2 pounds) or one 1/4-pound piece prosciutto with its fat
2 pounds beef marrow bones
5 quarts water
1 slice stale French bread, crust removed
1 large egg, beaten
1/2 pound ground pork
1/2 pound **botiffara** or chicken sausage, casing removed and meat crumbled
2 garlic cloves, finely chopped
1/4 cup finely chopped fresh parsley leaves
Salt and freshly ground black pepper to taste
1/4 cup fresh bread crumbs (optional)
1 potato, peeled and cut into chunks
1 carrot, cut into chunks
1 pound Swiss chard, stems discarded and leaves chopped
Unbleached all-purpose flour for dredging

---

1. Place the chicken feet, gizzard, lamb foot and ankle, lamb shank, ham bone, and marrow bones in a large stew pot. Cover with the water and bring to a boil. Boil, uncovered, for 2 hours, turning the meat occasionally. Replenish the water if necessary. Turn the heat off and remove the bones with a slotted spoon. Remove the marrow from the soup bones with a knife and small spoon and set aside. Remove the meat from the lamb shank, cut it up, cut up the prosciutto if using, and set aside. Strain the broth through a cheesecloth-lined strainer to remove all particles, then return the broth to the stew pot along with the marrow and shank meat. Discard all the bones.

2. Soak the slice of bread in water. Squeeze out the water and place the bread in a medium-size bowl with the beaten egg. Add the ground pork, *botiffara*, garlic, and parsley and season with salt and pepper. Form the meat into a single large ball; if it doesn't hold together well, add some bread crumbs. Set aside in the refrigerator.

3. Bring the broth in the stew pot to a boil and add the potato, carrot, and Swiss chard. Season to with salt and boil for 10 minutes. Dredge the meatball evenly in flour, tapping off any excess, and add it to the broth. Boil until firm, replenishing the water if necessary, 20 to 25 minutes. Serve immediately. The meatball can be divided so there is a portion for each diner.

Makes 6 servings

COCIDO

THIS ANDALUSIAN STEW, OR *COCIDO Andaluz*, is sometimes called the national dish of Spain. A chickpea stew found throughout Spain in hundreds of versions, it is also known by the name *olla podrida*, a name made famous by Cervantes's *Don Quixote*. Traditionally, *cocido* is served as two, and even three, courses as the important midday meal. Some cooks strain the broth and serve it as a first course with rice or *fideos*, a vermicelli broken into 1-inch lengths. The second course consists of the meat and vegetables, or the vegetables can be saved for yet a third course, served with whatever sausages are in the pot.

One Spanish culinary authority proposed that *cocido* was invented in the late fifteenth century when the Marranos, converted Jews, in order to convince their Christian neighbors of the sincerity of their conversions, began substituting pork for cooked eggs in a traditional, long-simmering Jewish dish known in Spain as *adafina* (see page 78). But the dish may have even earlier roots, as reflected in a recipe in an anonymous thirteenth-century Hispano-Muslim cookbook.

This recipe, which I collected in Andalusia, is typical of a *cocido* to be found around Granada. One can order Spanish-style chorizo and the prosciutto-like cured ham known as *jamón serrano* from La Española (see the sources listed at the back of the book).

3 cups dried chickpeas (about 1½ pounds), picked over, rinsed, soaked in cold water to cover overnight, and drained

1½ pounds oxtails

One ½-pound piece **jamón serrano**, domestic prosciutto, or slab Canadian or Irish bacon, cubed

1 ham bone or one ¾-pound beef shank

1 quart plus 1 cup cold water

1 garlic clove, peeled

4 black peppercorns

Pinch of saffron threads, crumbled

½ teaspoon cumin seeds

2 ripe plum tomatoes, peeled, 1 chopped and 1 left whole

½ pound green beans, ends trimmed and chopped

4 chicken legs (about 1 pound total)

1 Spanish-style chorizo sausage or Polish kielbasa (about 1 pound), cut into 1-inch-thick rounds

1 boiling potato, peeled and diced

Salt to taste

1. Put the chickpeas, oxtails, *jamón serrano*, and ham bone in a large stew pot with 1 quart of the water. Bring to a simmer slowly, about 30 minutes, then cook over low heat for 1 hour, skimming the foam off the surface occasionally.

2. Meanwhile, in a mortar pound the garlic, peppercorns, saffron, and cumin together until mushy. Add the whole tomato and continue to pound until the mixture is homogeneous. This step can also be done in a blender or food processor.

3. Add the green beans, chicken legs, chorizo, potato, and the chopped tomato to the stew pot along with the remaining 1 cup of water. Carefully stir the stew and salt lightly. Add the tomato-spice mixture to the pot and stir carefully to blend well. Cook over very low heat for 2 to 4 hours, checking doneness occasionally after 2 hours. The *cocido* is done when the meat is falling off the chicken legs and the potato has lost its crunch, but before the potato begins to fall apart. Taste and correct the seasonings.

Makes 6 servings

SPANISH-STYLE CHORIZO

A Spanish chorizo sausage is not as hot as the Mexican sausage of the same name. It is best to replace it with a Portuguese *chouriço* sausage, a Polish kielbasa, or a mild Italian sausage if you don't order it as suggested in the headnote.

ANDALUSIAN CHICKPEA AND VEAL TRIPE STEW

THIS HEARTY TRIPE STEW, OR *CALLOS*, from Granada, in the southern Spanish province of Andalusia, is typical farmhouse fare and cooks for a long time. Most of the tripe sold in this country is beef, so it might take a trip to a real butcher to find veal or lamb tripe, but it's worth it. Tripe usually comes already cleaned, but it still needs to be boiled a long time to make it tender. This stew is incredibly satisfying. I would soak the tripe Saturday night and put the stew on the stove on Sunday morning, then sit everyone down for a late lunch about 5 P.M. on a cold winter day. One can order Spanish-style chorizo through La Española (see the sources listed at the back of the book). You may find it helpful to read the notes on tripe elsewhere in the book (pages 6–9, and 333).

---

3 pounds veal or lamb tripe
1 cup white wine vinegar
Salt to taste
¼ cup extra virgin olive oil
2 large onions, finely chopped
2 garlic cloves, finely chopped
¼ pound cooked ham, chopped
5 ripe tomatoes (about 1¾ pounds total),
*   peeled, seeded, and chopped*
¼ pound Spanish-style chorizo sausage or
*   Polish kielbasa, thinly sliced*
1 cup Chicken Broth (page 181)
½ cup dry white wine
2 cups canned chickpeas, drained
Freshly ground black pepper to taste

---

1. Soak the tripe in cold water and the vinegar to cover overnight in the refrigerator.

2. Drain and rinse the tripe under cold running water, and cut into 2-inch pieces. Place the tripe in a large stew pot and cover with fresh water by several inches. Add some salt and bring to a boil. Reduce the heat to medium-high and boil until tender but a little chewy, anywhere from 3 to 7 hours, replenishing the water and salt when necessary. I'm giving this range of time because I don't know if you will be using beef or veal tripe and because the time can be that variable, depending on the product used. So after about 3 hours, cut off and taste a small corner of the tripe to see if it is cooked to the texture you like. Drain or continue cooking. In any case, I don't think anyone has ever overcooked tripe.

3. In a large, nonreactive casserole, heat ¼ cup of the olive oil over medium-high heat. Cook the tripe until it is sticking to the pot a bit, stirring, 3 to 4 minutes. Remove the tripe with a slotted spoon and set aside. Add the remaining ¼ cup of olive oil to the casserole along with the onions, garlic, and ham and cook until the onions are golden and soft, stirring occasionally, about 8 minutes. Add the tomatoes and cook until the mixture is reduced a little, 6 to 8 minutes. Add the sausage and stir, then add the tripe and stir well to mingle all the flavors. Cook for 1 minute, then stir in the chicken broth and wine. Reduce the heat to low, stir in the chickpeas, and season with salt and pepper. Cover and simmer until the sausages are tender and cooked through, about 30 minutes. Serve from the casserole.

Makes 4 to 6 servings

IBERIAN LINGUIÇA AND CHICKEN STEW

THIS POTPOURRI OF A STEW IS A RIOT OF wonderful flavors. The chicken melts off the bone, the spicy linguiça sausage adds sparkle, the potatoes provide body, and the collard greens are healthy. You could replace the linguiça sausage, if you can't find it, with kielbasa. It is a stew with rich and hearty tastes, mainly because it uses collard greens, which hold up so well during long cooking, and it is seasoned with fragrant saffron. There is also pasta in this stew, and I've chosen to use *fregula*, a typical pasta on the island of Sardinia; it is not an Iberian pasta, but rather one made with semolina, water, and saffron and then roasted slightly before drying thoroughly. For years it was impossible to get in the United States, but lately one can find it sold at Italian markets and through Gallo Brokerage (see the sources listed at the back of the book). If you decide to use *ditalini* instead, you will find this small macaroni, usually used in soup and stews, in Italian markets.

FOR THE BROTH:

One 2-pound chicken
1 medium-size onion, quartered and separated into layers
2 carrots, 1 sliced and 1 cut into chunks
1 celery stalk
15 white peppercorns
1 bouquet garni, consisting of 1 tablespoon each dried oregano, summer savory, and thyme, and 1 bay leaf, tied in cheesecloth
4 quarts water

FOR THE STEW:

1 pound linguiça sausage or hot Italian chicken or turkey sausage
1 pound boiling potatoes, peeled and quartered
1 dried red chile
1½ pounds collard greens, the lower, heavier parts of the stems removed, then washed well and cut into ½-inch-wide strips
½ cup fregula or ditalini
Pinch of saffron threads, crumbled
Salt and freshly ground black pepper to taste

1. Place the chicken, onion, sliced carrot, celery, peppercorns, and bouquet garni in a stew pot and cover with water. Turn the heat to high, and before the water starts to bubble, reduce the heat to low. Poach the chicken until the meat almost falls off the bones, about 2½ hours. Remove from the pot, and when cool enough to handle, remove the meat, shred it, and set aside. Discard the bones and skin. Strain the broth and return 3 quarts of it to the stew pot.

2. Add the linguiça sausage, potatoes, carrot chunks, chile, and collard greens to the pot.

Turn the heat to high, and when the broth comes to a boil, reduce the heat to low. Cook until the potatoes are nearly tender, about 1 hour. Add the pasta and saffron, season with salt and pepper, and cook until the pasta is nearly tender.

3. Return the reserved chicken meat to the stew, and once it is heated, serve.

——————●——————

Makes 6 servings

POT-AU-FEU
IN THE STYLE OF CARCASSONNE

T HE MEDIEVAL WALLED CITY OF CAR-cassonne in the Aude department of the Languedoc in southwestern France is an architectural marvel that tourists descend upon today. It is an old town where even the "new city" dates from the thirteenth century. In the farmlands around Carcassonne, one finds cooks making famous dishes such as cassoulet and *pot-au-feu*. This *pot-au-feu à la carcassonnaise* is very enticing because the simmering aromas permeate the house for hours. You assemble everything in the morning and let it cook all day, unattended.

——————●——————

1 head green cabbage (about 1¹/₂ pounds), damaged outer leaves discarded

1¹/₂ pounds Saucisse de Toulouse (page 346) or ³/₄ pound mild Italian sausage, removed from its casings and crumbled
4¹/₂ pounds beef ribs
One 6-ounce piece slab bacon, sliced ¹/₄ inch thick
1¹/₂ pounds mutton or lamb neck or shoulder, trimmed of any large pieces of fat and cut into small pieces
1 pound veal marrow bones
1 large onion, chopped
2 celery stalks, sliced
2 carrots, sliced
3 scallions or shallots, chopped
6 large garlic cloves, crushed
³/₄ pound ripe tomatoes, peeled, seeded, and chopped
1¹/₂ cups dried white beans (about ³/₄ pound), picked over and rinsed
Salt and freshly ground black pepper to taste
1 tablespoon dried summer savory or thyme
1 bouquet garni, consisting of 15 sprigs fresh parsley, 10 sprigs fresh tarragon, 3 sprigs fresh sage, and 2 bay leaves, tied in cheesecloth
1¹/₂ quarts water

——————●——————

1. Bring a pot of water to a boil and cook the whole head of cabbage until the leaves can be peeled off easily, about 10 minutes. Drain, and when cool enough to handle, core and separate the leaves. Stuff each leaf with 1 heaping tablespoon or more of sausage meat by placing the meat at the stem end of the leaf and rolling it up, tucking in the sides. Set aside.

2. Preheat the oven to 275°F. Arrange the beef ribs, bacon, mutton or lamb, and marrow bones on the bottom of a large earthenware casserole (preferably) or enameled cast-iron casserole. Put the onion, celery, carrots, scallions, garlic, tomatoes, and white beans on top of and in between the meats. Season with salt and pepper and summer savory, and place the bouquet garni in the center. Pour in the water. Arrange the stuffed cabbage leaves on top with the remaining 1/2 pound of sausage meat. Press down with a heavy, ovenproof lid, pie pan, or small baking stone (if it fits). Place in the oven and bake until the meat is falling off the bones and the beans are tender, 6 1/2 to 7 hours.

Makes 6 servings

EARTHENWARE

Earthenware cooking vessels can very much improve the flavor of a stew, but they are hard to find in kitchen stores and require some patience to use. Most earthenware casseroles cannot take a direct flame, and therefore one must use a heat diffuser. This will mean that the heating-up process is much slower, and you should be aware of that when you look at suggested cooking times in the recipes. Once you've used your earthenware several times, you'll have a good idea of how it performs. Also, make sure you never put a hot earthenware stew pot or casserole on a cool counter surface or it might crack. Good sources for earthenware casseroles are La Española, Chef Walter Potenza, and Sur La Table (see the sources listed at the back of the book).

VEAL AND VEAL KIDNEY STEW WITH CREAM

I RARELY SEE *ROGNONS DE VEAU* ON A restaurant menu in the United States, but when I do, my eyes light up, for I just love the taste of veal kidneys when they are perfectly cooked. This rich, country-style stew combines veal shoulder and veal kidneys and is served in puff pastry cups called *vols-au-vent*, which are made by Pepperidge Farm and can be found in the frozen food section of most supermarkets. This stew is creamy, rich, and perfect for a bitingly cold evening. Don't forget to defrost the *vols-au-vent* before beginning.

2 tablespoons extra virgin olive oil
1 small onion, finely chopped
One 1/8-inch-thick slice pancetta, chopped
3/4 pound boneless veal stew meat, trimmed of any large pieces of fat and cut into small cubes
1 cup dry white wine
1 1/2 pounds oxtails
2 cups veal broth or Beef Broth (page 3)
1 bouquet garni, consisting of 8 sprigs each fresh parsley and thyme and 1 bay leaf, tied in cheesecloth
Salt and freshly ground black pepper to taste
2 tablespoons unsalted butter
1/2 pound veal kidney, cut into quarters
1/4 cup medium-dry sherry
1 cup heavy cream
4 vols-au-vent, defrosted and baked according to the package instructions

1. In a casserole or stew pot, heat the olive oil over medium heat. Cook the onion and pancetta until golden, stirring, about 6 minutes. Add the veal pieces and brown, about 10 minutes, stirring. Add the wine and cook until it is reduced by half. Add the oxtails, beef broth, and bouquet garni and season with salt and pepper. Bring to a boil, then reduce the heat to very low, using a heat diffuser, if necessary. With a skimmer, remove the foam that has formed on the surface. Cover and cook for 2 hours.

2. In a small skillet, melt the butter over medium heat. When it stops sizzling, cook the kidney until firm, about 4 minutes. Add the sherry and continue to cook for another 8 to 10 minutes. Remove the kidney and set aside, and scrape the sauce into the veal stew pot.

3. Strain the broth, discarding everything but the veal pieces, pancetta, if you can retrieve any, and oxtails. Remove the meat from the oxtails and set aside with the veal and kidney. Boil the strained broth until it is reduced to 1 cup, scraping down the sides occasionally. Add the cream, return the meat to the pot, and simmer for another 20 minutes over low heat.

4. Ladle the stew into the *vols-au-vent* and serve.

———— ● ————

Makes 4 servings

GRAS-DOUBLE SAFRANÉ À L'ALBIGEOISE

———— 🍃 ————

YOU MIGHT NOT KNOW IT, BUT THIS saffroned tripe stew from Albi is quite famous in France. When I was in the Haut Languedoc, in the southwestern portion of France, keeping an eye peeled for typical local dishes, one well-known chef suggested I try the local classic from Albi, capital of the Tarn region in the Haut Languedoc, called *gras-double safrané à l'albigeoise*. He didn't serve it in his fancy restaurant because it's just a family stew. But he did know a little restaurant in Albi where they made it, and he added that theirs was the best.

The diminutive, subterranean L'Auberge Saint-Loup made a very satisfying tripe stew with ham, veal shank, carrot rounds, and parsley in a brown ragout flavored with saffron. The dish is cooked all day, and is traditionally accompanied by boiled potatoes covered with capers and some cornichons (gherkins) on the side.

———— ● ————

2½ pounds beef or lamb tripe
½ cup distilled white vinegar
2½ pounds veal or pig feet, split, and lamb feet, left whole
3 tablespoons lard
½ pound fresh uncooked ham steak
1 pound veal shank
1 bouquet garni, consisting of 10 sprigs each fresh parsley and thyme and 1 bay leaf, tied in cheesecloth

1 leek (white and light green parts only), split in
  half lengthwise, washed well, and chopped
3 large carrots, cut into ¹/₂-inch-thick rounds
1 large onion, halved
1 head garlic, first layer of peel rubbed off
¹/₄ cup extra virgin olive oil
Salt and freshly ground black pepper to taste
2 cups dry white wine
2 quarts veal broth or Beef Broth (page 3)
2 pinches of saffron threads (about ¹/₂ teaspoon),
  crumbled
3 tablespoons tepid water

———————•———————

1. Soak the tripe in the vinegar and water to cover in the refrigerator overnight. Drain.

2. Bring a large pot of water to a boil and blanch the tripe and feet for 5 minutes to remove any particles or scum. Drain and set aside.

3. Rub the bottom of a large stew pot or casserole with the lard. Arrange the veal or pig's feet on the bottom. Place the tripe in one piece on top. Next add the ham, veal shank, lamb feet, bouquet garni, leek, carrots, onion, and head of garlic in one layer. Drizzle with the olive oil, and sprinkle with some salt and pepper. Pour in the wine and broth. Cover and cook over very low heat, using a heat diffuser if necessary, until the meat is tender but still attached to the bone, about 6 hours.

4. Remove the ham from the pot and cut into pieces. Set aside. Continue to cook the other meats until the tripe is soft, but with a little bite to it, and the other meats are falling

off the bone, another 2 to 4 hours. You can test for doneness during this period of time by cutting off a tiny piece of the tripe and tasting to see if it has a soft bite—it should have the texture and feel of cooked squid; if it is very chewy, continue cooking. Remove the veal shank and tripe and cut both into pieces. Discard all the bones, the bouquet garni, and onion. Transfer all the meats to the pot to reheat.

5. Meanwhile, steep the saffron in the tepid water for 30 minutes. Stir the diluted saffron into the casserole. Remove all the meats with a slotted spoon to serving bowls.

———————•———————

Makes 6 servings

CASSOULET

CASSOULET IS A FAMOUS BEAN STEW cooked in an earthenware casserole from the Languedoc region of France. This recipe is the true and authentic one, and as a result, involves quite a bit of effort. The effort is well rewarded, but the Simple Mock Cassoulet on page 349, though not as authentic, may be better suited to some cooks. Two of the most important ingredients in a cassoulet are items that cannot be bought fresh in this country, so this recipe instructs you how to make your own preserved duck, *Confit de*

Canard (page 345), and fresh Toulouse sausage, *Saucisse de Toulouse* (page 346).

Experts usually refer to three cassoulets when they speak of this dish, the cassoulet of Castelnaudary, a village in the Aude along the Canal du Midi, east of Toulouse, and the cassoulets of Carcassonne and Toulouse. Although there are small differences between the three, all are equally good. It's something of a sport to claim that one has found the "best" cassoulet, and every cook seems to have a different opinion about how to make a perfect one. I think it is all a bit nonsensical because you can make the perfect cassoulet in your own home if you follow this recipe and a few rules. The water used for a good cassoulet is quite important, and that is why I recommend bottled spring water. It should be hard and calcareous, which allows the beans to maintain their shape better. Also, patience is required because of somewhat involved preparations and a long cooking time, but the result is an incredibly strong, luscious, and fatty flavor. The pancetta in the ingredients list is not authentic, and is meant to replace the traditional *petit salé*, a lean salt pork, used by French cooks. You will notice that I ask you, at the end of the cooking, to break the bread crumb crust that has formed seven times. This is an old folkloric tradition that I find charming, and for all I know, it contributes to the excellence of cassoulet.

My recipe is a rich, authentic, full-bodied feast best served to your friends around two in the afternoon on a very cold winter day. Cassoulet is heavy, but it is a forgiving preparation, and even if you mess up you'll be rewarded.

2 pounds ham hocks, salted with 1 cup coarse salt (see Note 1 on page 345)

4 cups medium-size dried white haricot or Great Northern beans (about 2 pounds), picked over, rinsed, soaked overnight in water to cover, and drained

2 pounds Confit de Canard (page 345)

½ pound salt pork (brisket cut), with its skin

One ¼-pound slice pancetta

1½ pounds Saucisse de Toulouse (page 346)

1¾ pounds boneless pork shoulder, trimmed of any large pieces of fat and cut into smaller pieces

1½ pounds boneless mutton or lamb shoulder, trimmed of any large pieces of fat and cut into smaller pieces

2 medium-size onions, peeled and each studded with 2 cloves

1 large carrot, sliced into rounds

1 pound ripe tomatoes, peeled, seeded, and finely chopped

3 tablespoons tomato paste

10 garlic cloves, crushed

1 bouquet garni, consisting of 10 sprigs each fresh parsley and thyme and 2 bay leaves, tied in cheesecloth

2 quarts bottled spring water

1 pound fresh pork skin (see Note 2 on page 345)

Salt and freshly ground black pepper to taste

2 cups fresh bread crumbs made in a food processor from a French baguette with its crust

———————●———————

1. Prepare the salted ham hocks.

2. Bring a large pot of water to a boil and blanch the beans for 5 minutes. Drain and let them soak in cold water to cover for 1 hour.

Set the terrine or casserole with the duck confit in a pan of hot water so the duck fat softens.

3. Bring a large saucepan of water to a gentle boil and blanch the salt pork and pancetta for 10 minutes. Drain and slice the skin off the salt pork. Slice the salt pork and dice the pancetta. Set aside. Reserve the salt pork skin.

4. In a 6- to 8-quart casserole or stockpot, melt 5 tablespoons of the duck fat from the *confit* terrine over medium heat. Measure out 3 more tablespoons of duck fat and set aside. Puncture the *saucisse de Toulouse* with corn cob holders or toothpicks so it doesn't burst while cooking. Brown the sausage, turning occasionally, about 10 minutes. Remove the sausage and set aside. Brown the pork shoulder in the same casserole, 8 to 10 minutes. Remove and set aside. Brown the ham hocks, about 5 minutes. Remove and set aside. Brown the mutton shoulder, 8 to 10 minutes. Remove and set aside. Brown the salt pork and pancetta, about 4 minutes. Remove and set aside. Brown the duck confit, about 4 minutes. Remove and set aside with the other meats.

5. Add the clove-studded onions and sliced carrot to the casserole and cook until the onions turn color, stirring occasionally, 4 to 5 minutes. Add the tomatoes, tomato paste, garlic, bouquet garni, and bottled water and season with some salt and pepper. Return all the meats, including the duck, to the pan, along with the fresh and salt pork skins. Bring to a boil, and reduce the heat to medium-low. Cover and simmer until the meats are tender, about 2 hours.

6. Remove the ham hock, salt pork, Toulouse sausage, pork shoulder, mutton shoulder, and duck. Cut the meat off all the bones. Chop the salt pork. Slice the sausage into thick rounds. Remove the bones from the duck.

GAME PLAN FOR MAKING CASSOULET

Making an authentic cassoulet is quite involved, although that's only because we're not in France, where one can buy the sausages and preserved duck needed for the stew. An American cook will have to make it all from scratch, and that's what the recipe on page 342 instructs you to do. You will begin this process about 2 months before making the cassoulet.

First, collect as much duck fat as you can by roasting a duck or two in the weeks before you make the *Confit de Canard* (page 345).

Second, make the *confit*, for which you will need all that fat, about 6 weeks before you make the cassoulet. That's how long it needs to be preserved before you can use it.

Third, make the sausages as described on page 346, before you begin the cassoulet.

Finally, salt the ham hocks for the cassoulet 2 days before you plan to begin the recipe (see Note 1 on page 345).

Discard the bones and remove any fat from the meat, reserving the fat from the ham hocks. Strain the broth through a colander or conical strainer, discarding the vegetables and saving the broth.

7. Preheat the oven to 275°F. Line the bottom of a heavy 6- to 8-quart casserole (it can be the same one you just used, thoroughly washed and dried) with the pork skins, fat side down, and the fat from the ham hocks. Pour in half the beans, then layer the meat from the pork shoulder, ham hock, mutton shoulder, duck confit, salt pork, pancetta, and the sausages on top. Cover with the remaining beans. Pour enough of the reserved broth into the casserole so that it just reaches the top of the beans. Sprinkle the top with the bread crumbs and dot or drizzle with the reserved 3 tablespoons of duck fat. Bake, uncovered, until the crust is golden brown, breaking the crust 7 times by pushing down slightly with the back of a ladle, about 4 hours. Serve immediately after the seventh time.

Makes 12 servings

Note 1: Roll the ham hocks in the coarse salt and arrange in a glass or ceramic bowl or tray. Leave in the refrigerator for 2 days. Wash off the salt before using in step 4.

Note 2: The fresh pork skin is an essential flavoring for cassoulet. If you are unable to get it from your butcher, use the rind from a piece of fatback. Blanch the rind for 5 minutes in boiling water to soften it and remove the salt.

CONFIT DE CANARD

Confit de Canard is fat-preserved duck. It is an old method of preserving duck in its own rendered fat. This recipe comes from Odile Lacarrière, my father's neighbor in the southwest of France where he lives part of the year. Making *confit de canard* is easy, although you do need quite a bit of duck fat, which you can get by roasting a couple of ducks in the weeks beforehand and saving all the rendered fat. Alternatively, you can buy duck fat through mail order.

One 5-pound duck
¹/₂ cup salt
¹/₂ teaspoon freshly ground black pepper
1 teaspoon dried thyme
1 bay leaf, crumbled
4 to 5 cups rendered duck fat (see Note on page 346)
1 cup Freshly Rendered Lard (page 154)

1. Separate the duck with a heavy cleaver or poultry shears into 2 thighs, 2 wings, 2 legs, and 2 breast halves. Divide each of the breast halves in two. Rip away and pull off all the fat and skin. Chop the fat into small pieces and set aside.

2. Mix together the salt, pepper, thyme, and bay leaf and toss with the duck pieces in a large bowl. Arrange the duck pieces in a ceramic or glass baking dish and let marinate for 24 hours, covered, in the refrigerator.

3. Preheat the oven to 300°F. Put all the cut-up duck fat and skin in a medium-size casserole and place in the oven for 1¹/₂ hours. Pour off the liquid fat and let cool. Add to the rendered duck fat listed with the ingredients.

4. In a medium-size heavy casserole or saucepan, melt all of the rendered duck fat over very low heat, about 25 minutes. Rinse the duck pieces and dry with paper towels. Add the duck thighs to the completely melted duck fat so they are covered. If you do not have enough fat, cook in batches. Cook the duck thighs for 30 minutes, then add the remaining duck pieces and cook for 1 hour, making sure all the pieces are covered with fat. Turn off the heat and let everything cool and solidify.

5. Sprinkle salt on the bottom of a ceramic or glass casserole or terrine. Skim off the top layer of duck fat and cover the bottom of the casserole or terrine with it. Place the pieces of duck over the fat. Melt the remaining duck fat again and pour it over the duck to cover, making sure you do not include any meat juices. Let it cool until solid. Melt the lard again and cover the duck fat layer with a ¹/₄-inch layer of lard. Cover with plastic wrap and leave in the refrigerator for 4 to 6 weeks before using in cassoulet.

———•———

Makes 1 *confit* of duck

Note: Rendered duck fat is merely the fat collected in the baking pan after roasting a duck. Pour off the fat slowly and carefully, making sure you don't collect any of the meat juices. Let cool, then refrigerate until needed. It will keep indefinitely.

SAUCISSE DE TOULOUSE

Saucisse de Toulouse is simply a fresh country sausage. This recipe comes from the sausage maker José Crestou of St. Germain-du-Bel-Air, a neighboring and slightly larger village than the hamlet where my father owns a farmhouse in southwestern France. This is the sausage used in cassoulet, but you can also just take the sausage and stew it in some wine, tomatoes, olive oil, and thyme. To make your own sausage, you will need a mixer with a sausage attachment (such as a KitchenAid) or a meat grinder/sausage stuffer (such as a Moulineux). Hog casing is sold in any supermarket that makes its own sausage, but you may need to ask for it.

———•———

6 pounds boneless pork butt (preferably) or shoulder, with its fat, cut into small cubes
2 pounds pork fatback, rind removed and fat cut into small cubes
2 tablespoons salt if using salted pork fatback, 3 to 4 tablespoons if using unsalted pork fat
2 tablespoons freshly ground black pepper
2 teaspoons freshly grated nutmeg or ground mace (optional)
About 25 feet of hog casing

———•———

1. In a large bowl, toss the pork butt and fatback thoroughly with the salt and pepper. Chill the mixture in the refrigerator for at least 4 hours or overnight so the flavors blend.

2. Coarsely grind the meat by pushing it through a meat grinder, using the blade with the largest holes, or process in short pulses in a food processor until the mixture has a consistency somewhere between ground and chopped.

3. Open one end of the hog casing, fit it over the faucet in your kitchen sink, and place the remainder of the casing in a medium-size bowl in the sink. Turn the water on gently to wash out the casing. The casing is sold cleaned; you are merely washing away preserving salts and residue. Now you are ready to start stuffing.

4. Affix one end of the casing over the funnel attached to the sausage-stuffing attachment of a stand mixer or meat grinder. Push the entirety of the casing onto the length of the funnel (it will contract and fit fine), leaving about 2 inches dangling from the end. Tie this end in a double knot.

5. Turn the grinder or mixer on, and as the sausage stuffing begins to flow into the casing, it will push the casing off the funnel. Have a large bowl or platter ready to catch the sausages. Twist or tie off with kitchen twine to make links, or leave to make several very long sausages. Do not overstuff the sausage, otherwise it will burst, either then and there or during cooking. Also, be careful that the sausage stuffing enters the casing continuously and evenly and that no air bubbles develop. If air bubbles do occur, it is better either to cut the sausage at that point and start a new one by tying the end off, or to prick the air bubbles with a toothpick.

6. Refrigerate the sausage for 24 to 48 hours before cooking or freezing. The sausages can be divided into portions of different or identical weights, and frozen for later use in freezer bags for 2 to 4 months.

Makes 8 pounds sausage

Note: To cook the sausages in dishes other than cassoulet, place them in a large pot and cover with water. Bring almost to a boil. Just as the water begins to bubble, reduce the heat to below a boil, and poach the sausages for 10 minutes if you will be grilling or frying them, or 40 minutes if serving them boiled.

CASSOULET MÉNAGÈRE: AN EASIER CASSOULET

THE FAMOUS CASSOULET OF SOUTH-western France, made properly, is a time-consuming but wonderful dish. The recipe for the authentic cassoulet is on page 342. This recipe, which I call *cassoulet ménagère*, or housewife's cassoulet, is an easier and more approachable cassoulet. I adapted it from the one made by Odile Lacarrière of Frayssinet, a little farming hamlet in the region of Lot, where my father lives part of the year. Odile and her husband, Robert, are my father's neighbors, and they raise several hundred head of sheep and some ducks in order to make their own foie gras. Odile makes a rough-and-ready, everyday type of cassoulet as it should be, with a pound of dried white beans, not too small, she says, *collet de mouton* (mutton neck), *poitrine fumée* (smoked pork breast), *échine de porc* (pork back), *saucisse de Toulouse* (pork sausages from Toulouse), and *confit de canard* (fat-preserved duck). She simmers the meats in water flavored with garlic, tomatoes, onions, and carrots on the stove top until done.

This recipe is my interpretation of hers, emphasizing ease of preparation, although the cooking time will still be nearly as long as the authentic, full-blown cassoulet. *Confit* is not used here; just duck and any garlic sausage will do.

* * *

3 tablespoons rendered duck fat taken from **Confit de Canard** *(preferably, page 345) or* **Freshly Rendered Lard** *(page 154)*

3 ounces lean salt pork, diced

1 pound boneless lamb or mutton shoulder, trimmed of any large pieces of fat and cut into smaller pieces

One ¹/₂-pound piece smoked bacon, cut into quarters

2 pounds pork baby back ribs, cut into 4 pieces

1 pound mild Italian sausage or any garlic sausage (about 4 links)

1³/₄ pounds cut-up duck (2 breast halves, 2 thighs, and 2 legs), skin removed from the breast halves

2 medium-size onions, chopped

2 garlic cloves, finely chopped

2 carrots, chopped

1 tablespoon unbleached all-purpose flour

One 6-ounce can tomato paste diluted in 1 quart water

1 cup mutton or pork broth (optional; see page 99 or 171)

1 bouquet garni, consisting of 10 sprigs each fresh parsley and thyme and 2 bay leaves, tied in cheesecloth

4 cloves

2 teaspoons salt

1¹/₂ teaspoons freshly ground black pepper

2 cups (about 1 pound) dried medium-size white beans, picked over, rinsed, soaked overnight in water to cover, and drained

One 5-inch square piece fresh pork skin

* * *

1. In a large casserole, melt the rendered duck fat with the salt pork over medium-high heat until the salt pork begins to get crispy. Brown the lamb, about 4 minutes, and with a slotted spoon, remove it and the salt pork to a platter. Brown the bacon, pork, sausage, and duck in that order, about 4 minutes for each, transferring the meats, as they finish cooking, to the platter with the lamb.

2. Preheat the oven to 275°F. Add the onions, garlic, and carrots to the casserole and cook until the onions are translucent, about 7

HOW TO RENDER FAT

* * *

Fat is rendered when you have solid pieces of fat from the animal and you want it in liquid form. Place the piece of fat in a baking dish and place in a preheated 250°F oven until you have as much liquid fat as you need. This fat, from beef, veal, pork, duck, goose, chicken, or other animals, can be collected and stored for months in the refrigerator or indefinitely in the freezer.

minutes. Add the flour and stir to combine. Pour the tomato paste and water mixture into the casserole along with the broth, if using, and stir in the bouquet garni, cloves, salt, and pepper. Return the browned meats to the casserole, pushing them down into the broth and add the beans, pushing them down into the broth as well. Place the piece of pork skin on top. Cover the casserole, place in the oven, and cook until the meat and beans are tender, 4 to 4 1/2 hours. Correct the seasoning and serve.

Makes 6 to 8 servings

SIMPLE MOCK CASSOULET

THERE ARE THREE FAMOUS CASSOULETS, as I've explained in the authentic cassoulet recipe on page 342. But because a cassoulet can be so individualized, one might say there are a thousand cassoulets, each made according to the whims of the cook. A true cassoulet is an amazing thing to taste, as is the simpler Cassoulet Ménagère ("housewife's cassoulet," page 347). The cassoulet featured here is a bit lower on the rung. The tastes are great, but it is much easier to prepare than the authentic cassoulet and should not be compared with it. I hesitate to call this a quick cassoulet, because it cooks for almost twelve hours. But the day I made this, I said to my son Ali, who was ten at the time, that I wanted to have something that cooked all day. So we cooked this most of one winter day and were very pleased.

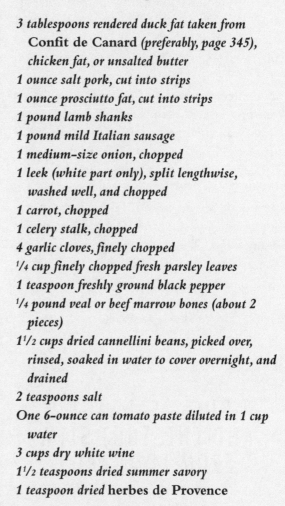

3 tablespoons rendered duck fat taken from **Confit de Canard** (preferably, page 345), chicken fat, or unsalted butter
1 ounce salt pork, cut into strips
1 ounce prosciutto fat, cut into strips
1 pound lamb shanks
1 pound mild Italian sausage
1 medium-size onion, chopped
1 leek (white part only), split lengthwise, washed well, and chopped
1 carrot, chopped
1 celery stalk, chopped
4 garlic cloves, finely chopped
1/4 cup finely chopped fresh parsley leaves
1 teaspoon freshly ground black pepper
1/4 pound veal or beef marrow bones (about 2 pieces)
1 1/2 cups dried cannellini beans, picked over, rinsed, soaked in water to cover overnight, and drained
2 teaspoons salt
One 6-ounce can tomato paste diluted in 1 cup water
3 cups dry white wine
1 1/2 teaspoons dried summer savory
1 teaspoon dried **herbes de Provence**

1. In an enameled cast-iron casserole, Dutch oven, or an earthenware casserole set on a diffuser, melt the duck fat over medium-high heat. Cook the salt pork and prosciutto fat until almost crispy, stirring, about 5 minutes.

Remove and set aside. Brown the lamb and sausages on all sides in the hot fat, about 5 minutes. Remove and set aside. Cook the onion, leek, carrot, celery, and garlic until soft and the onion is translucent, stirring frequently, 8 to 10 minutes. Return the salt pork and prosciutto fat to the pan, stir in the parsley and black pepper, and add the marrow bones.

2. Preheat the oven to 220°F. Place the beans on top of the cooked vegetables in the casserole. Season with the salt and put the lamb shanks and sausage on top. Pour in the diluted tomato paste and and sprinkle with the savory and *herbes de Provence*. Push any beans that are visible under the liquid. Taste a little of the liquid and adjust the salt. Cover, place in the oven, and cook until the beans are tender and the meat is falling off the bone, 11 to 12 hours.

———◦———

Makes 4 servings

DUCK, SAUSAGE, AND CHESTNUT STEW FROM LOMBARDY

I N LATE FALL OR EARLY WINTER, AS THE weather gets colder and I can see my breath, I think about making this rich duck and sausage stew that is known in Lombardy as a *ragù d'anitra con luganega e castagne* (duck ragout with Luganega sausage and chestnuts). My recipe is adapted from one by Luigi Carnacina, an Italian chef of the mid-twentieth century who is thought of by many as the Escoffier of Italy. The sausage used in the dish, *luganega*, is a very simple and relatively plain, thin sausage made in a variety of ways in Lombardy and the Veneto. You can replace it with a mild Italian sausage or a fresh garlic sausage. This recipe involves blanching a number of ingredients. Simply place the food in boiling water until partially cooked.

———◦———

¼ cup chopped duck fat, removed from the duck
One 5-pound duck, cut into 10 serving pieces
    with a cleaver, with fat removed and reserved
    (as much as possible)
½ cup diced salt pork, blanched in boiling water
    for 15 minutes and drained
1 medium-size onion, coarsely chopped
1 large carrot, sliced
2 garlic cloves, crushed
1 cup dry red wine
2 cups Chicken Broth (page 181)
1 cup Quick Tomato Sauce (recipe follows)
1 bouquet garni, consisting of 5 sprigs fresh
    parsley, 3 sprigs fresh thyme, and 1 bay leaf,
    tied in cheesecloth
3 tablespoons burro maneggiato (see Note)
1 pound luganega sausage (see page 155) or
    commercially made mild Italian sausage,
    blanched in boiling water for 10 minutes,
    drained, cooled, and sliced
15 baby carrots, blanched in boiling water for 7
    minutes and drained
20 chestnuts, peeled (see page 351), blanched in
    boiling red wine for 15 minutes, and drained
Salt and freshly ground black pepper to taste

1. Chop enough of the duck fat to measure ¼ cup and discard the rest. In a large casserole, brown the salt pork and duck fat together over medium-high heat, stirring occasionally, about 5 minutes. Remove the salt pork with a slotted spoon and set aside.

2. In the fat remaining in the casserole, brown the duck pieces on all sides, about 10 minutes, and remove them with a slotted spoon. In the remaining duck fat, cook the onion, carrot, and garlic cloves, stirring frequently until the onion is soft, about 5 minutes. Remove the vegetables from the casserole with a slotted spoon and set aside. Pour off the duck fat and discard.

3. Return the vegetables and duck to the casserole and heat over medium-high heat, stirring occasionally. Pour in the wine and boil until it has almost evaporated, 12 to 15 minutes. Add the chicken broth, tomato sauce, and bouquet garni and bring to a boil. Reduce the heat to low and simmer, partially covered, for 1½ hours.

4. Remove the duck pieces from the casserole with a slotted spoon and refrigerate. Discard the bouquet garni and push the broth and vegetables through a strainer or food mill, discarding the leftover vegetable pulp. Transfer the broth to a ceramic bowl and place in the refrigerator. Let cool until the fat forms a layer on top, about 6 hours, then discard the fat.

5. Return the defatted broth to the casserole and heat over medium heat. Stir in the *burro maneggiato*, and once it has melted, stir in the reserved salt pork, duck pieces, sausage, baby carrots, and chestnuts. Reduce the heat to low, cover, and simmer for 1 hour. Check the seasonings and serve.

Makes 4 to 6 servings

Note: *Burro maneggiato*, or *beurre manié* as the French call it, is butter mixed with flour used as a binder for sauces and stew. Mix 1½ tablespoons of unsalted butter at room temperature with 1½ tablespoons all-purpose flour until it forms a paste, and then use as directed.

HOW TO PEEL CHESTNUTS

Place each chestnut on a surface with the rounded side up and the flat side down. Make an "x" on the rounded side with a small sharp paring knife. Place on a baking sheet and roast in a preheated 425°F oven until the shells are brittle, 35 to 40 minutes. Remove, and once the chestnuts are cool enough to handle, peel off and discard the brittle shell and skin.

QUICK TOMATO SAUCE

This easily made tomato sauce is required for Duck, Sausage, and Chestnut Stew from Lombardy (page 350), but it is also very nice as an all-purpose sauce for pasta.

3 tablespoons extra virgin olive oil

1 garlic clove, crushed

1 small onion, finely chopped

1½ pounds ripe plum tomatoes, peeled, seeded, and chopped, or one 28-ounce can crushed tomatoes

Salt and freshly ground black pepper to taste

1 sprig fresh basil (optional)

———————●———————

In a sauté pan, heat the olive oil over medium-high heat with the crushed garlic clove. Discard the garlic as it begins to turn light brown and add the onion. Cook until it turns translucent, stirring frequently, about 4 minutes. Add the plum tomatoes, season with salt and pepper, and cook over medium heat for 20 minutes. Add the basil, if desired, during the last 5 minutes of cooking.

———————●———————

Makes about 2½ cups

MINESTRONE WITH BEANS, CABBAGE, SQUASH, AND PESTO

◗

I N ITALY, A *MINESTRONE*, WHICH MEANS "big soup," is usually served as a first course. But because they are so hefty and satisfying—they are big after all—I consider them stews and therefore include a few in this book. This hearty minestrone, loaded with all kinds of vegetables and flavors, is inspired by some *minestre* I was introduced to in Tuscany, the Veneto, Liguria (where they do, in fact, stir pesto into their minestrone), and other regions in northern Italy.

———————●———————

½ cup extra virgin olive oil

2 ounces salt pork, chopped

1 medium-size onion, chopped

1 leek (white and light green parts only), split lengthwise, washed well, and chopped

4 garlic cloves, finely chopped

1 celery stalk, chopped

½ pound beef chuck on the bone, trimmed of any large pieces of fat

½ small chicken (about 1½ pounds), halved lengthwise, or 1 Cornish game hen

1 bouquet garni, consisting of 6 sprigs fresh parsley, 3 sprigs fresh basil, and 1 sprig each fresh rosemary and thyme, tied in cheesecloth

1 medium-size, ripe tomato, peeled, seeded, and chopped

2 quarts water

1 large parsnip, peeled and cut into chunks

1 large carrot, cut into chunks

1 large turnip, peeled and cut into chunks

1 medium-size boiling potato, peeled and cut into chunks

³/4 pound hubbard or other squash, peeled, seeded, and cut into chunks

¹/4 cup dried red kidney beans, picked over and rinsed

¹/3 cup dried black beans, picked over and rinsed

¹/2 pound mustard greens, heavy stems removed and cut into strips

¹/2 pound green cabbage, damaged outer leaves removed, cored, and cut into strips

Salt and freshly ground black pepper to taste

¹/2 cup Pesto (recipe follows)

1. In a large stew pot or casserole, heat the olive oil with the salt pork over medium-high heat. Cook the onion, leek, garlic, and celery until translucent, about 10 minutes. Add the beef, chicken, bouquet garni, tomato, and water. Bring to a boil, skim the surface of foam, and reduce the heat to low. Partially cover and cook until the meats are slightly tender, about 1¹/2 hours.

2. Add the parsnip, carrot, turnip, potato, squash, red and black beans, mustard greens, and cabbage. Season with salt and pepper and simmer on low heat, partially covered, until everything is tender, about 3 hours.

3. Meanwhile, make the pesto. Stir a spoonful of it into each individual bowl and serve.

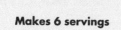

Makes 6 servings

PESTO

Pesto alla genovese, as it is known, is fresh basil pounded together with garlic, cheese, pine nuts, and olive oil to form a paste. It is native to the city of Genoa and found in cooking throughout Liguria. Pesto is traditionally tossed with a kind of pasta called *trenette* (also called *bavette*), which is like fettuccine, and it also finds its way into lasagne and minestrone.

Leaves from 1 bunch fresh basil (about 80), washed

2 large garlic cloves

Pinch of salt

2 tablespoons pine nuts, toasted in a preheated 350°F oven until golden

3 tablespoons freshly grated Parmigiano-Reggiano cheese

3 tablespoons freshly grated pecorino cheese

³/4 to 1 cup extra virgin olive oil, plus extra for storing pesto

1. The basil leaves used for making pesto must be completely dry. Use a salad spinner to remove the water from the washed basil, then pat dry with paper towels. Leave the basil leaves spread out on top of paper towels for 1 hour to dry thoroughly.

2. Place the basil, garlic cloves, salt, and pine nuts in a large mortar and begin gently pushing with the pestle. Once the basil begins to mush, pound it more, pressing the leaves clinging to the sides down into the center of the mortar. Pound gently so that you turn the pesto into a paste, not a liquid. Slowly add the cheeses, about 1 tablespoon at a time every minute, and continue pounding. You will be pounding 9 to 12 minutes.

3. If your mortar is not very large, scrape the pesto, once it is a thick paste, into a large, deep, heavy ceramic bowl and slowly begin pouring in the olive oil, stirring constantly with the back of a wooden spoon, or continue to use the pestle gently. The pesto can be used immediately or stored, topped with more olive oil, in a tightly covered jar in the refrigerator. Always retop with olive oil as you use it. It will keep for 6 months in the refrigerator as long as you continually replenish the olive oil as you use the pesto.

———————●———————

Makes 1¹/₂ cups

BOLLITO MISTO

BOLLITO MISTO ("MIXED BOIL") IS THE famous stew of the Piedmont, in particular, where it is also known as *gran bui*, but it also made in Lombardy and Emilia. It consists of mixed meats that are boiled and is served with a green sauce based on parsley, or a red sauce based on tomato or, in its place, *mostarda di Cremona*, a jarred sweet-and-sour fruit relish, recommended here. You can get the Dondi brand from Formaggio Kitchen and other good Italian markets and gourmet stores or order the Sperlari brand directly from the company (see the sources listed at the back of the book).

Traditionally, in the Piedmont *bollito misto* consists of beef, veal and/or veal tongue, chicken, *cotechino* sausage, available from Molinari Brothers, and half a calf's head, which will have to be specially ordered if you decide to use one. *Bollito misto* is a special preparation, and most recipes, unlike mine, are designed to feed large groups of people. Restaurants will make it with a good variety of vegetables on the side. To make it special, arrange all the boiled meats attractively on a large serving platter after they are cooked.

———————●———————

2 celery stalks, cut up
1 large onion, peeled and studded with 3 cloves
1 large, thick carrot, cut into chunks
3 quarts water
1 veal tongue
One 2-pound beef brisket
1 Cornish game hen, rinsed
¹/₂ beef foot
1 pig foot
One 6-inch square slice fresh pork skin (see Note 2 on page 345)
¹/₂ calf's head (optional)
1 cotechino sausage or 6 mild Italian sausages, pricked all over with a corn cob holder or the tip of a skewer
Dijon mustard for serving (optional)
Mostarda di Cremona *for serving (optional)*
FOR THE GREEN SAUCE:
¹/₄ cup plus 2 tablespoons extra virgin olive oil
¹/₄ cup finely chopped fresh parsley leaves
2 salted anchovy fillets, rinsed and finely chopped

1 tablespoon capers, drained, rinsed, and finely
  chopped
1 large garlic clove, finely chopped
¹/₂ teaspoon Dijon mustard
¹/₂ teaspoon red wine vinegar

---

1. In a 16- to 20-quart stockpot, put the celery, onion, and carrot and cover with the water. Bring to a boil.

2. Add the veal tongue and beef brisket, return to a boil, and reduce the heat to low. Simmer for 1 hour, covered, skimming off the foam rising to the top of the broth. Remove the tongue, let cool, and, with a paring knife, peel off the outer layer of skin. Trim away all the fat and gristle and return to the pot.

3. Add the game hen, beef foot, pig foot, pork skin, calf head, if using, and *cotechino*. Return to a boil, cover, and reduce the heat to low. Cook until all the meats are tender, about 3¹/₂ hours. You can serve now or leave the meats in the broth over very low heat to serve later.

4. While the meat is cooking, stir together the ingredients for the green sauce in a serving bowl.

5. When it is time to serve, remove each of the meats from the pot and slice, discarding bones and skin, and arrange the meat attractively on a serving platter. Ladle some broth over everything and serve with Dijon mustard, *mostarda di Cremona*, and the green sauce.

Makes 6 servings

SCOTTIGLIA

*S*COTTIGLIA IS THE EQUALLY ANTIQUE AND famous meat version of *Cacciucco* (page 239), an old seafood stew found in Leghorn (Livorno) and along the Tuscan coast. This *scottiglia* is from Arezzo in Tuscany and is also known as *cacciucco di carne*. The Italian culinary expert Giovanni Righi Parenti tells us in his book *La cucina toscana* that *scottiglia* is "a masterpiece among the stews." He admits that the stew has a remote origin and that it appears to have imported some Spanish elements, although Parenti doesn't go on to explain what elements these might be, to the frustration of his readers. One writer claims that the name of the stew comes from the fact that there are up to seven different kinds of meats used, but there is nothing intrinsic to the name that would account for that explanation. Another food writer suggests, more probably, that the name comes from the verb *scottare*, "to burn." In the medieval Latin culinary language of Verona in 1276 we know that the word *scotare* meant "to boil over a fire," so it seems that it's true that the word *scottiglia* may have this origin.

It is important that you use at least five different meats, because the intermingling of many flavors is what makes the stew so special. The cured pork jowl (*guanciale*) called for in the ingredients list is still difficult to find in this country, so you can substitute pancetta. This stew is meant to be accompanied by a robust Chianti wine.

THREE ITALIAN CURED PORK PRODUCTS

There are three pork products that you will come across in much Italian cooking and they are flavorings that give a traditional dish its authentic taste. These are all forms of *salume*, cured products.

Pancetta is pork belly, the cut used for making bacon. It consists of layers of fat and meat. Pancetta is hung in a dry and airy place to cure for 20 days. It is flavored with cloves and black pepper. Most of the pancetta you will come across in Italian markets is a rolled up product called *pancetta arrotolata*. *Pancetta stesa* is more or less what the belly looks like in its natural state. Although both are used for cooking, the rolled-up pancetta is also thinly sliced and eaten as a component to an antipasto.

Guanciale is cured pig's jowl, and it is cured more or less the same way as pancetta, which it looks like. It is not readily found in Italian markets in this country. You can use salt pork or pancetta in its place.

Lardo is the layer of hard fat on a pig's back nearest to the skin. It is flavored with herbs, salt, and lots of pepper and used in stew cookery and in the making of an initial *soffritto* for sauces and ragouts. Replace it with pork fatback rubbed with freshly ground black pepper, salt, dried oregano, and ground cloves. Let it sit for 1 week in the refrigerator in that mixture, then use it in slices for cooking.

$^1/_2$ cup extra virgin olive oil

1 large onion, finely chopped

1 large carrot, finely chopped

1 celery stalk, finely chopped

3 large garlic cloves, finely chopped

1 dried red chile, seeded and crumbled

3 tablespoons finely chopped fresh parsley leaves

6 large fresh basil leaves, finely chopped

$^1/_2$ pound boneless beef stew meat, trimmed of any large pieces of fat and cut into 1$^1/_2$-inch cubes

$^1/_2$ pound boneless pork shoulder, trimmed of any large pieces of fat and cut into 1$^1/_2$-inch cubes

1 pound veal shank or shoulder on the bone, cut into 4 pieces

$^3/_4$ pound rabbit legs (about 2)

1 squab or Cornish game hen (about 1$^1/_2$ pounds), halved lengthwise

$^3/_4$ pound hot Italian sausage

6 ounces guanciale (cured pork jowl) or smoked lean slab bacon, cubed

Juice of 1 lemon

1 cup dry red wine

1 pound ripe tomatoes, peeled, seeded, and crushed

1 cup Beef Broth (page 3)

Salt and freshly ground black pepper to taste

$^1/_2$ loaf Italian bread, sliced and toasted, for serving

1. In a large earthenware casserole set on a diffuser, heat the olive oil over medium-high heat. Cook the onion, carrot, and celery until soft, stirring, about 5 minutes. (If you are not cooking with earthenware and a diffuser, cook over medium heat and check for doneness

sooner.) Add the garlic, chile, parsley, and basil. Stir, then gradually add the beef, pork, veal, rabbit, squab, sausage, and *guanciale* and brown them evenly, turning the pieces occasionally, about 12 minutes. You may need to do this in two batches.

2. Add the lemon juice and let it evaporate, about 3 minutes. Add the wine, reduce the heat to low, and let the wine evaporate, about 20 minutes. Add the tomatoes and broth and season with salt and pepper. Stir, cover, and cook over very low heat, using a heat diffuser if necessary, until all the meats are very tender, 3 to 3½ hours. Serve immediately with the toast on the side.

Makes 6 servings

CORSICAN RAGOUT OF MUTTON, DUCK, AND SAUSAGE

THE CUISINE OF CORSICA IS A POTPOURRI of Italian, Provençal, Ligurian, Spanish, and Arab influences. Corsica was once ruled by the Genoese and is today a part of France. Even with all the culinary influences impinging on Corsican food, there are still distinctive Corsican dishes. But it should be remembered that Corsica was always a poor island, so cooking meat was an indication of an elevated social class. In a traditional Mediterranean society the copious use of meat is a luxury reserved for special occasions, especially Christmas or Easter. The primary meat of Corsica is goat and is eaten around Christmastime. Lamb and mutton are the second choices. This Corsican-style ragout is a rich dish that I love to make in the winter. As you can see by the ingredients list, it is chock-full of hearty tastes like turnips and red kidney beans. The chile pepper is not typical of Corsican cooking, but I like to add it here.

4 duck legs (about 1 pound total)

2 lamb arm or shoulder chops (about 1 pound)

3 tablespoons extra virgin olive oil

1 small onion, finely chopped

1 carrot, chopped

1 celery stalk, chopped

2 garlic cloves, crushed

1 fresh green chile, seeded and chopped

1 pound fresh garlic sausage or Polish kielbasa

1 bouquet garni, consisting of 5 sprigs each fresh parsley and thyme, 2 sprigs fresh rosemary, and 1 sprig each fresh tarragon and sage, tied in cheesecloth

2 tablespoons tomato paste diluted in 2 cups water

2 cups dry red wine

1 pound turnips, peeled and cut into 2-inch cubes

1 cup dried red kidney beans, picked over, rinsed, soaked in water to cover overnight, and drained

Salt and freshly ground black pepper to taste (optional)

1. Preheat the oven to 400°F. Place the duck legs and lamb on a wire rack in a roasting pan and roast in the oven for 35 minutes. Remove from the oven and discard the fat.

2. In a casserole, heat the olive oil over medium-high heat. Cook the onion, carrot, celery, garlic, and chile until soft, about 5 minutes. Reduce the heat to low, add the duck legs, lamb, sausage, bouquet garni, diluted tomato paste, and wine, and stir well to combine. Cover and cook for 1½ hours.

3. Check the seasonings, and add salt and pepper, if desired. Add the turnips and beans and continue to cook the ragout until the turnips are easily pierced with a skewer, about 1 hour. Cut up the sausage and serve.

Makes 4 to 6 servings

BIGOS

ONE POLISH COOKBOOK DESCRIBES bigos as one of "the most precious jewels" of Polish cuisine. Bigos is a hunter's stew made of previously cooked meat, cabbage, sauerkraut, apples, and prunes, although recipes have traditionally varied depending on what was left over. That is, in fact, the key to the dish; it was originally a stew for leftovers. The more types of sausage and meats used, the better the stew will be. Long ago bigos would be cooked for hours and then stored in wooden casks or great stoneware pots. It was then reheated multiple times, which, it is said, made it even better. It was a food that could be quickly heated up for unexpected guests, or taken along for a hunting party, where it was reheated in a kettle hung over a field fire. It was traditional in the hunting lodges of the old Polish nobility, when the men would return ravenous from a day of hunting, to eat bigos accompanied by oceans of ice-cold vodka and rye bread. A cask of bigos was often taken by travelers on their journeys. Some cooks still insist that bigos be served only after it has been reheated three times, and I have been told that seven times is perfect.

The various sausages, roast pork, ham and smoked bacon called for in this recipe are most easily found in a Polish or East European delicatessen, which are all over this country. Because the sauerkraut is an important part of this stew, I recommend the Vavel brand of kapusta kiszona (sauerkraut), imported from Poland by Adamba Imports, because it tastes good and is very thinly sliced (see the sources listed in the back of the book).

One 4-pound duck

One 1-pound pork loin

¾ pound Polish hunter's sausage or kielbasa sausage

¾ pound Cracow sausage or any German-style pork sausage

1 cup water

1 head green cabbage (about 1 pound), damaged outer leaves removed, cored, and cut into wedges

2 pounds sauerkraut, drained

4 Granny Smith apples, peeled, cored, and sliced
1 bay leaf
4 allspice berries, crushed
2 tablespoons unsalted butter
2 ounces smoked slab bacon, diced
2 ounces dried porcini mushrooms, soaked in
   tepid water for 30 minutes and drained
2 tablespoons lard
2 large onions, finely chopped
20 pitted prunes, cut into strips
Salt and freshly ground black pepper to taste
1 teaspoon freshly ground caraway seeds
1 teaspoon sugar
$^3/_4$ cup Madeira wine
$^1/_2$ pound cooked ham, cut into bite-size cubes
1 tablespoon tomato paste

━━━━━●━━━━━

1. Preheat the oven to 350°F. Place the duck on a wire rack in a roasting pan and roast until golden, about 1$^3/_4$ hours. Roast the pork loin at the same time in a separate pan until it reaches an internal temperature of 140°F, about 1$^1/_4$ hours. Remove and discard the skin and fat from the duck. Remove the meat from the bones and dice. Then dice the pork loin as well.

2. Place the sausages and water in a large enameled cast-iron casserole and cook over medium heat until cooked through, about 20 minutes. Remove the sausages and cut into large dice. Save the cooking water.

3. Bring a large pot of lightly salted water to a boil, then plunge the cabbage wedges in the water to scald them and immediately drain. Transfer the cabbage to the casserole in which

the sausage cooked and add the sauerkraut. Stir well, and cook, uncovered, over low heat until softer, about 30 minutes. Add the apples, bay leaf, and allspice. Stir well to mix and cook, covered, for another 30 minutes.

4. In a small saucepan, melt the butter over medium heat. Cook the bacon until much of its fat is rendered, stirring occasionally, about 12 minutes. Transfer the bacon to the casserole with the cabbage. Cook the mushrooms in the bacon fat for 2 to 3 minutes, stirring. Remove the mushrooms with a slotted spoon, slice, and add to the casserole.

SEARCHING THE INTERNET FOR FOOD

━━━●━━━

Don't you wish there were a site that listed where you could buy a particular food product? Well, we're not there yet, if you've ever tried to use a search engine for that purpose. As a test, I've tried several times to find East European delicatessens that sell Crakow sausages and I came up with nothing, even though I regularly buy my Crakow sausages at a local Polish deli a few blocks away from where I live in Santa Monica, California. When using search engines, you need to be a little clever in your wording. For example, rather than asking for "East European delicatessens" try searching for the particular food, or brand of food, you're looking for, plus other information, such as "Cracow sausages + Polish delicatessens + mail order." No guarantees, but you never know, because the Web changes every day.

5. In a large skillet, heat the lard over medium-high heat. Once it has melted, cook the onions until lightly browned, about 15 minutes. It will take this long to cook the onions because there will be a lot of juice that must evaporate before they start to brown. Add the onions to the stew and stir well to mix. Add the prunes, season with salt and pepper, and add the caraway, sugar, and Madeira. Stir again to mix well and cook over medium heat, covered, for 30 minutes, reducing the heat if the mixture is percolating too much.

6. Add the pork loin, duck, sausages, ham, and tomato paste and cook, covered, over low heat until everything is hot and has been bubbling for a while, about 1¹/₄ hours. Let the stew cool and then refrigerate.

7. The next day, reheat the stew over low heat, covered, until bubbling, stirring and turning the stew every 15 minutes, about 1¹/₂ hours all together. Let cool again and then reheat for a third time, also for 1¹/₂ hours over low heat, covered. Serve very hot.

Makes 8 servings

BOSNIAN STEW

IN SERBO-CROATIAN, THE LANGUAGE spoken in Bosnia and Serbia, *glineni lonac* refers to a potbellied earthenware stew pot made of soft terra-cotta with two handles and a tight-fitting lid. It was originally used for slowly braising in the embers of a fire. This stew is known as *Bosanski lonac*, or "Bosnian stew"; it is cooked for a long time in a slow oven and then served in smaller, individual replicas of the larger *lonac*, called *lončiće*. Maria Kaneva-Johnson, in her superlative work *The Melting Pot: Balkan Food and Cookery*, tells us that according to Alija Lakišić's *Bosanski Kuhar* ("Bosnian Cookbook"), this stew had its inception during the Middle Ages as a miner's one-pot stew. The miners put the few ingredients available to them in large communal clay pots, marked on the outside with symbols to identify which group of workers it was meant to feed. The pots were sealed, put in a fire, and left to stew while the miners worked deep below ground. This stew is typically varied, depending on seasonal availability and the preferences of the cook. One is therefore likely to find many different recipes, depending on the family and the time of year. This recipe is adapted from Ms. Kaneva-Johnson's book.

¹/₂ *cup finely chopped fresh parsley leaves*
¹/₄ *cup finely chopped fresh celery leaves*
1 *teaspoon salt*
3 *ounces pork fatback, finely chopped*
1¹/₂ *pounds boneless beef chuck, trimmed of any large pieces of fat and cut into 3-inch cubes*
2 *pounds boneless pork shoulder, trimmed of any large pieces of fat and cut into 3-inch cubes*
1¹/₂ *pounds boneless leg of lamb, trimmed of any large pieces of fat and cut into 3-inch cubes*
6 *small new potatoes (about 1¹/₂ pounds), peeled and left whole*

*3 medium-size onions, sliced 1/4 inch thick and
    separated into rings*
2 carrots, cut into 1/2-inch-rounds
*1 bouquet garni, consisting of 2 teaspoons black
    peppercorns, 4 cloves, 4 allspice berries, and
    2 heads garlic, cloves separated and left
    unpeeled, tied in cheesecloth*
1/2 cup dry white wine
Flour paste rope (see page 9)

1. In a small bowl, mix together the parsley, celery leaves, salt, and pork fatback. Put the beef chuck, pork shoulder, and lamb in a bowl and toss with half of the parsley and fatback mixture. Put the potatoes, onions, and carrots in another bowl and toss with the remaining parsley and fatback mixture.

2. Preheat the oven to 250°F. Layer the bottom of an earthenware casserole with half the vegetables, place the meat on top, and then top with the remaining vegetables. Push the bouquet garni into the meat and pour in the wine.

3. Place the lid on the casserole and seal them together with the flour paste rope. Place the casserole in the oven and bake for 8 hours.

4. Break open the seal and serve from the casserole.

Makes 6 to 8 servings

GREEK FAVA BEAN STEW

THIS IS REAL PEASANT FARE, A SIMPLE STEW typical of Greek mountain cooking and reminiscent of the way poor people might have cooked some fifty years ago. Fava beans have been popular with Greeks since the days of Homer and earlier. In fact, it is thought that the plant originated in the Near East and was introduced to agriculture in the late Neolithic period. The fava bean's earliest known appearances in Greece were at two late Neolithic sites, Sesklo and Dimini. In this preparation, all those bones will make a very delicious-tasting meal, so don't skimp on them.

*2 cups dried fava beans, picked over, rinsed,
    soaked overnight in water to cover, and drained*
*1/2 cup dried chickpeas, picked over, rinsed,
    soaked overnight in water to cover, and drained*
2 pounds lamb bones with some meat on them
1 pound veal bones with some meat on them
1 pound pork bones with some meat on them
2 cups peeled, seeded, and chopped ripe tomatoes
5 scallions, cut up
20 black peppercorns
8 cloves
15 sprigs fresh parsley
8 garlic cloves, crushed
1 cup dry red wine
2 quarts cold water

1. Boil the fava beans in water to cover for 5 minutes and drain. Boil the chickpeas in water to cover for 20 minutes and drain.

2. Put the fava beans, chickpeas, and remaining ingredients in a stew pot and bring to a boil. Reduce the heat to low, and skim the surface of foam. Simmer, partially covered, until the beans are very soft and the meat on the bones flakes off, 4 to 5 hours. Discard the bones before serving.

⎯⎯⎯ ● ⎯⎯⎯

Makes 4 servings

SOLYANKA

T HE NATIONAL STEW OF RUSSIA, *SOLYANKA* (also transliterated as *solianka* and *soljanka*) is a word that means "confused" in Russian. Some experts say the word derives from the word *sol* (salt) because of the addition of the salty pickles, olives, and capers. Others say that the original name was *selianka*, which is related to *selo* (village), making it a typical village dish. The origin of this stew is said to come from the large potluck dinners villages would have. Everyone would bring something to throw into the common cauldron, which simmered all day. A *solyanka* could be one of three kinds, made of meat, fish, or mushrooms.

This recipe is an amalgam adapted from the classic Russian cookbook of the nineteenth century by Elena Molokhovet, *A Gift to Young Housewives*, published in 1861 and translated into English and edited by Professor Joyce Toomre, and from Anya von Bremzen and John Welchman's *Please to the Table: The Russian Cookbook*. Molokhovet includes cabbage, cucumbers, several kinds of mushrooms, chicken, goose, and boiled beef in her stew. All the previously cooked meats used in the stew, as you can see by the ingredients list, are best if cooked first, then cut up.

Darra Goldstein, author of *A Taste of Russia: A Cookbook of Russian Hospitality*, tells me that Russian sour cream is very different from ours. It's thicker than the Swedish *gräddfil* (see page 257), and when it is spooned into a soup or stew, it swirls beautifully rather than breaking up. The flavor is like an earthy *crème fraîche*.

⎯⎯⎯ ● ⎯⎯⎯

6 tablespoons (³/₄ stick) unsalted butter

3 large onions, sliced and separated into rings

¹/₂ head green cabbage (about 1 pound), damaged outer leaves removed, cut into wedges, and cored

1 cup diced cooked veal shoulder meat (from about ¹/₂ pound boneless veal, see Note)

1 cup diced cooked Polish kielbasa sausage (from about ¹/₂ pound kielbasa, see Note)

1 cup diced cooked ham (from about ¹/₂ pound ham, see Note)

1 cup diced cooked duck breast meat (from about ¹/₂ pound duck breast, any skin and fat removed; see Note)

1 cup diced cooked turkey thigh meat (from about ¹/₂ pound turkey thigh, any skin and fat removed; see Note)

³/₄ ounce dried wild mushrooms (about 12), soaked in tepid water for 15 minutes and drained, soaking liquid reserved

2 quarts Beef Broth (page 3)

1 bouquet garni, consisting of 2 bay leaves and 10 black peppercorns, tied in cheesecloth

2 medium-size dill pickles, drained and diced,
   plus ¼ cup pickle juice from the jar
2 tablespoons capers, drained, rinsed, and
   chopped if large
12 marinated mushrooms from a jar, drained
One 16-ounce can crushed tomatoes
2 tablespoons tomato paste
1 tablespoon unbleached all-purpose flour
12 pitted imported green olives, drained
¼ cup finely chopped fresh dill
¼ teaspoon dried marjoram
3 large garlic cloves, finely chopped
2 teaspoon hot Hungarian paprika
Salt and freshly ground black pepper to taste
Lemon slices for garnish
Sour cream for garnish

———•———

1. In a large casserole or stew pot, melt 4 tablespoons of the butter over medium-high heat. Once it stops sizzling, add the onions, cabbage, veal, kielbasa, ham, duck, turkey, and rehydrated mushrooms. Reduce the heat to medium-low, and cook for 10 minutes, stirring occasionally. Add the beef broth and mushroom soaking liquid, bring to a boil, and cook at a boil for a few minutes. Reduce the heat to low, add the bouquet garni, pickles, capers, and marinated mushrooms. Stir, cover, and cook for 10 minutes.

2. Meanwhile, in a medium-size skillet, melt the remaining 2 tablespoons of butter over low heat. Add the tomatoes and tomato paste and cook for 7 to 8 minutes, stirring. Add the flour and cook, stirring, until thick, a few minutes more. Add the olives, dill, marjoram, garlic, ¼ cup of pickle juice, and paprika.

Season with salt and pepper, stir, and cook, covered, for 10 minutes.

3. Turn the tomato sauce into the stew pot with the cabbage and continue to cook for 10 minutes. Turn off the heat and let stand, covered, for 10 minutes before serving. The stew will look like a thick minestrone and the broth will be soupy. Serve with a couple of lemon slices and a few dollops of sour cream in each bowl.

———•———

Makes 6 servings

Note: Making *solyanka* requires small amounts of a number of cooked meats. The best and easiest way to do this is all at once. In a large casserole, bring several quarts of water to a boil. Reduce the heat until the water is just bubbling gently, and add the whole pieces of veal, kielbasa, ham, duck breast, and turkey thigh. The meats will all come out at different times as they finish cooking. The times suggested are guidelines, so remove the meats once they are all firm: the kielbasa after about 15 minutes of cooking, ham after about 20 minutes, duck breast after about 45 minutes, veal after about 1¼ hours, and turkey thigh after about 1½ hours.

DUCK, SHRIMP, ANDOUILLE SAUSAGE, AND OKRA STEW WITH RICE

SOME OF THE MOST EXTRAORDINARY cooking in America comes out of the bayou country of south Louisiana. In the eighteenth century, settlers of New Orleans and Acadiana, the swamps and waterways to the west and south of New Orleans, developed two then distinct styles of cooking. Over the years they have blended together. This mix of Creole and Cajun cooking is what we know today. One of the standard techniques of this style of cooking is the preparation of a roux, which is the beginning of a gumbo and other local dishes.

Gumbo, mostly associated with the cooking of Louisiana but also known along the Gulf coast from Tampa to Texas, is a stew-soup thickened with okra or powdered dried sassafras leaves, better known as gumbo filé. Gumbo also contains various meats or seafood and vegetables, most importantly okra. The word *gumbo* is of African origin, brought over by African slaves and similar to the word *ochinggombo*, meaning "okra" in the Umbundu language, or perhaps deriving from the *nkombo*, the word for "runaway slave" in Kongo, a Bantu language. This gumbo is turned into a kind of jambalaya, the Louisiana version of paella, with the addition of rice.

1 teaspoon vegetable oil or rendered duck fat (page 348)
2 jumbo shrimp, peeled
1 pound duck legs and thighs
2 tablespoons unsalted butter
2 tablespoons unbleached all-purpose flour
1/2 green bell pepper, seeded and chopped
1 fresh red chile, seeded and chopped
2 serrano chiles, seeded and chopped
1 small onion, chopped
1/2 celery stalk, chopped
2/3 cup dry white wine
1 teaspoon garlic powder
1/2 teaspoon onion powder
1 teaspoon Cajun seasoning (see Note)
1/2 pound fresh small okra, bottoms trimmed
2 andouille sausages (about 12 ounces total), cut into thick rounds
2 cups Chicken Broth (page 181)
Salt and freshly ground black pepper to taste (optional)
3/4 cup long-grain rice, rinsed

1. In a large skillet or casserole, heat the oil over medium heat just until it films the pan. Cook the shrimp for 1 minute. Remove and set aside. Add the duck and brown on all sides, about 20 minutes. Remove and set aside. Discard all but 1 teaspoon of duck fat from the skillet. Add the butter and flour to the skillet and cook, stirring constantly, to form a golden roux, about 2 minutes. Add the bell pepper, chiles, onion, and celery and cook for 2 to 3 minutes, stirring. Add the wine, garlic powder, onion powder, and Cajun seasoning and cook until the wine has evaporated, scraping the bottom of the skillet as you stir.

2. Return the duck to the skillet and add the okra, sausages, and chicken broth. Stir, and add salt and pepper, if necessary. Cover, reduce the heat to low, and simmer for 1¼ hours. Add the rice, cover, and cook for 15 minutes. Turn off the heat. Place a paper towel under the lid to absorb moisture and let the casserole sit for 30 minutes before serving.

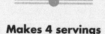

Makes 4 servings

Note: To make your own Cajun seasoning, mix together: 1 tablespoon salt, 1 teaspoon freshly ground black pepper, 1 teaspoon freshly ground white pepper, 1 teaspoon garlic powder, ½ teaspoon cayenne pepper, ½ teaspoon hot paprika, ½ teaspoon onion powder, ¼ teaspoon freshly ground coriander seeds, ¼ teaspoon freshly ground cumin seeds, ⅛ teaspoon dried basil, ⅛ teaspoon dried oregano, and ⅛ teaspoon dried thyme. Store in a sealed container with your other spices.

ROAST DUCK, OYSTER, AND ANDOUILLE SAUSAGE GUMBO

THIS GUMBO IS A LITTLE DIFFERENT THAN the previous one. I think the combination of duck and oysters is just a drop-dead, wonderful taste. This recipe is a little involved, because you have to roast the duck first and then open oysters, but I just can't imagine you will be disappointed. I always drink beer with gumbo, but a light red wine or a rosé, something to go with the spiciness, is nice too. Serve with rice or cornbread.

One 4- to 5-pound duck
1 leek (white and light green parts only), halved lengthwise, washed well, and chopped
2 quarts water
2 cups finely chopped onions (about 1 large onion)
1 cup finely chopped celery (about 2 stalks)
2 cups seeded and finely chopped green bell pepper (about 2 peppers)
1 jalapeño, seeded and finely chopped
6 large garlic cloves, finely chopped
½ cup finely chopped fresh parsley leaves
2 bay leaves
½ teaspoon dried thyme
¼ teaspoon dried oregano
½ teaspoon freshly ground white pepper
½ teaspoon freshly ground black pepper
2 teaspoons salt
1 teaspoon cayenne pepper
2 pounds andouille sausage or Polish kielbasa, sliced
½ cup vegetable oil
½ cup unbleached all-purpose flour
24 oysters, washed well, soaked in cold water to cover mixed with 1 tablespoon baking soda for 1 hour, drained, and shucked, plus the oyster liquor (about 1 cup liquor)
1 teaspoon gumbo filé (see page 366)

GUMBO FILÉ

———•———

Gumbo filé is a spice used in the Creole and Cajun cooking of Louisiana. It is made from the dried and powdered leaves of sassafras (*Sassafras albidum*). It is used both as a thickening agent in stews and gumbos and as a flavoring, providing a mild and musty taste. A good gumbo filé to look for is one made by Zatarain's, which is available in most supermarkets.

1. Preheat the oven to 350°F. After pulling off as much fat as possible, set the duck on a wire rack in a roasting pan and roast until golden brown all over, about 1 3/4 hours. Let the duck cool, and remove all the meat, cutting the pieces so they are a little bigger than bite-size. Set aside in the refrigerator until needed.

2. Put all the duck bones in a stockpot or large saucepan with the leek. Cover with the water, and bring to a boil. Reduce the heat to low and simmer for 2 hours. Strain through a cheesecloth-lined strainer, discard the bones and leek, and reserve the broth.

3. In a large bowl, mix together the onion, celery, bell peppers, jalapeño, garlic, and parsley. In a small bowl, mix together the bay leaves, thyme, oregano, white pepper, black pepper, salt, and cayenne.

4. Put the duck, sausage, and reserved broth in a pot. Bring to just below a boil, and cook

for 30 minutes. Drain, set aside the meat, and reserve 3 cups of the broth.

5. In a large casserole or stew pot, heat the vegetable oil over high heat until smoking. Add the flour and cook until it forms a chocolaty dark brown roux, whisking constantly with a long-handled wire whisk and being careful not to splash any hot oil on yourself, about 4 minutes or a little less. Watch it carefully; if the roux burns even a little, it will affect the taste of your gumbo. Remove the casserole from the heat and add the mixed chopped vegetables, stirring. Add the spice mixture, stirring constantly. Once it is well blended, return to the heat, reduce it to medium, and continue to cook until the vegetables are soft, about 5 minutes. Add the reserved duck and sausage, 2 1/2 cups of the reserved broth, and the reserved oyster liquor (but not the oysters). Bring to a boil, reduce the heat to low, and simmer until the gumbo is not so liquidy and the sausages are very tender, about 2 hours.

6. Add the oysters and cook until they firm up and their edges curl, 3 to 8 minutes (keep checking). Check the seasoning, add the gumbo filé, and stir. Serve immediately.

———•———

Makes 6 servings

ANDOUILLE SAUSAGE, SHRIMP, AND OYSTER GUMBO

A GUMBO IS A WHOLE MEAL IN LOUISIANA. It's hard to say how gumbo was invented, although its connection to Africa is not in doubt (see page 364). According to one legend, it came about when okra was introduced to Mobile, Alabama, in 1704 by twenty-five French mademoiselles known as the Cassette girls, who arrived in search of husbands. They came by way of the West Indies, where they had acquired okra from African slaves, who called the plant gumbo and used it in stews, also called gumbo. Today a gumbo does not have to contain okra to be called gumbo. The most popular ingredients used in a gumbo are sausage, andouille, shrimp, oysters, crabs, duck, and chicken. Backwoods cooks are known to throw alligator, squirrel, venison, and nutria (a water rat that populates the bayous) into the pot. I'm quite wild about gumbos, especially when they mix meats with seafood, as this recipe does. Serve over rice.

2 tablespoons vegetable oil

1 pound andouille sausages or Polish kielbasa, sliced

1/4 cup unbleached all-purpose flour

1 small red bell pepper, seeded and chopped

1 small green bell pepper, seeded and chopped

1 medium-size onion, thinly sliced and separated into rings

1 1/2 quarts cold water

1 bay leaf

2 tablespoons salt

1 1/4 pounds fresh shrimp with their heads on or 10 ounces previously frozen headless shrimp

24 oysters, washed well, soaked in cold water to cover mixed with 1 tablespoon baking soda for 1 hour, drained, and shucked, plus the oyster liquor (about 1 cup liquor)

One 14-ounce can Italian plum tomatoes, with their juices

1/2 teaspoon dried thyme

1/2 teaspoon dried oregano

1 teaspoon cayenne pepper

Freshly ground black pepper to taste

1/2 teaspoon Tabasco sauce

1/2 cup sliced shallots

2 tablespoons finely chopped fresh coriander (cilantro) leaves

1. In a large skillet, heat the vegetable oil over medium heat. Brown the sausages, about 8 minutes. Transfer to a platter with a slotted spoon and set aside. Pour off all but 2 tablespoons of the fat and make a roux by adding the flour, stirring with a whisk or wooden spoon, almost constantly over medium heat until dark golden brown, about 45 minutes. Lower the heat if the roux is cooking too fast.

2. Add the bell peppers and onion. Reduce the heat to low and cook until the vegetables are soft, stirring every once in a while, 6 to 10 minutes. Add a few tablespoons of water to deglaze the pan, scraping up any browned bits on the bottom.

3. In a medium-size saucepan, bring the 1¹/2 quarts of water to a boil with the bay leaf and salt. Drop the shrimp into the boiling water with their shells on, and boil for 2 minutes. Remove the shrimp with a slotted spoon, reduce the heat to low, and let the water simmer for 15 minutes. Meanwhile, peel the shrimp, throwing the shells and heads back into the simmering water. Strain the shrimp water immediately, discarding the shells and bay leaf. Pour the shrimp stock into a large clean pot and bring to a boil. Stir in the roux mixture, sausage, oyster liquor, tomatoes, thyme, oregano, cayenne, black pepper, Tabasco, and shallots. Reduce the heat to low, and simmer for 2 hours, stirring occasionally.

4. Stir in the shrimp, oysters, and coriander and cook until the shrimp are pink or orange and the edges of the oysters have curled up, 3 to 8 minutes (keep checking). Serve immediately.

***

Makes 4 servings

KENTUCKY BURGOO

THE FAMOUS BURGOO IS *THE* STATE STEW of Kentucky. Burgoo is traditionally served on Derby day, at political rallies, and horse sales—namely at huge outdoor events with thousands of people. In a cookbook from the 1930s, a recipe for burgoo by Mr. J.T. Looney of Lexington, Kentucky, yielded 1,200 gallons of the stew and called for 2,000 pounds of potatoes. This recipe is a scaled down version that will feed fifteen people (feel free to cut it in half, if you like). I based the recipe on several others, including J. T. Looney's and another called Dead Heat Kentucky Burgoo from *The Kentucky Derby Museum Cookbook*, published in 1988.

The word *burgoo* is of unknown origin but since it originally referred to a thick oatmeal gruel (according to William Ellis, author of *The Country Housewife's Family Companion*, published in 1750), it appears to be related to loblolly, which was always a kind of nautical meal, a meal prescribed by a ship's doctor for medicinal reasons. Some conjecture that the word *burgoo* is related to burgood, an archaic word meaning "yeast."

In some recipes I've looked at, the cook will also add cabbage and Worcestershire sauce. If you can manage it, include a mix of Fordhook lima beans and speckled butter beans instead of just frozen lima beans, which will make the stew all the more interesting. Just so you know, this recipe is developed with the goal of capturing the essence of a traditional burgoo in mind. Therefore, you may want to add more salt, pepper, and chile pepper to spice up the final dish at the end of the cooking. Serve hot with baking powder biscuits for a truly great meal.

***

One 3-pound broiler chicken
2 pounds beef shank
3 quarts water
Salt and freshly ground black pepper to taste

6 slices thickly cut bacon

4 pounds ripe tomatoes, peeled, seeded, and
    chopped, with all their juices

1 cup peeled and cubed potatoes

2 cups coarsely chopped carrots (about 2 carrots)

1 cup chopped onions

1 cup chopped celery

1 cup seeded and chopped green bell pepper

2 tablespoons packed brown sugar

1/2 teaspoon red pepper flakes, or more to taste

4 cloves

1 large garlic clove, finely chopped

1 bay leaf

Corn kernels scraped from 4 ears

2 pounds fresh or frozen lima beans, or half
    Fordhook lima beans and half speckled butter
    beans

10 ounces fresh okra, bottoms trimmed

2/3 cup unbleached all-purpose flour

1/4 cup finely chopped fresh parsley leaves

---

1. In a 10-quart Dutch oven or stockpot, put the chicken, beef shank, and water and season with salt and pepper. Bring to just below a boil, skim any froth on the surface, then reduce the heat so the water is only shimmering. Cook until the chicken is tender, about 1 hour. Remove the chicken and beef from the broth. Remove all the meat from the chicken and the shank and discard the chicken skin and all the bones. Cube the beef and chicken and set aside. Reserve the broth separately.

2. In a skillet, cook the bacon until crisp. Remove, drain on paper towels, and crumble into a bowl. Leave the bacon fat and drippings in the skillet.

3. Add the cubed beef, crumbled bacon, tomatoes, potatoes, carrots, onions, celery, green pepper, brown sugar, red pepper flakes, cloves, garlic, and bay leaf to the stockpot with the broth. Cover and bring to a boil. Reduce the heat to low, and simmer for 1 hour, stirring often.

4. Discard the bay leaf and add the cubed chicken, corn, lima beans, and okra. Return to a near boil and reduce the heat to low. Cover and simmer until the okra is tender, stirring occasionally, about 30 minutes.

5. Heat the bacon fat reserved in the skillet over medium-high heat. Add the flour and cook, scraping and stirring, until homogenized into a roux. Stir into the stew. Cook the stew over low heat until the stew thickens, about 20 minutes. Correct the seasonings by adding more red pepper flakes, if desired, and salt and black pepper. Sprinkle on the parsley and serve.

Makes 15 servings

PLYMOUTH SUCCOTASH

IN JANUARY 1769, A GROUP OF SEVEN young men from Plymouth, Massachusetts, met to form a club they called the Old Colony Club. In December of that year, they decided to hold their annual meeting on the anniversary of the 1620 landing on Plymouth Rock. This celebration was first observed on December 22, 1769, and called Forefather's Day; the use of the term "pilgrims" for the early colonists had not yet come into use. The annual Forefathers' Day dinner was a succotash and, ever since the first dinner in 1769, a traditional succotash has been prepared, often in a special bowl and with much fanfare.

A proper succotash is debated with as much enthusiasm and contentiousness as any Texan would discuss a true chili con carne (page 49). The original succotash is a descendant of the local Native American cooking, namely a meal based on a corn soup made with beans, unripe corn, and various meats, especially bear, or else fish. Over time it has evolved into a kind of boiled dinner with corned beef, chicken, salt pork, white Cape Cod turnips, potatoes, hominy, and boiled beans with some salt pork. Originally, the beans used were dried peas, but over time lima beans have become popular. The word *succotash* derives from Narragansett, a branch of the Alqonguin language, the original word being *msiquatash*, a word that may mean boiled corn kernels.

Hominy are kernels of corn that have been treated in a special way, usually soaked in a caustic solution and then washed to remove

the hulls. There are different kinds of hominy, with different tastes. The kind used in Plymouth would have been rather bland. I like to use the Mexican-style hominy sold as *nixtamal*, which, although not strictly authentic, gives a very earthy flavor to the succotash.

1/2 cup dried green peas or split peas, picked over and rinsed
1 potato
1 small turnip
2 cups whole-kernel hominy (nixtamal)
One 1 1/2-pound Cornish game hen, halved lengthwise, or 2 chicken thighs and legs
1 pound beef brisket
One 2-ounce piece salt pork
1 cup water
Salt and freshly ground black pepper to taste

1. Place the peas in a pot with cold water to cover by several inches. Bring to a boil and cook until very tender, about 3 hours. Drain and pass through a food mill or mash until it looks like mashed potatoes. Set aside until needed. While the peas are cooking, boil the potato and turnip separately in water to cover until tender. Drain, peel, dice, and set aside.

2. Bring a medium-size saucepan filled with water to a boil and add the hominy. Cook over medium-high heat until it is half cooked, about 3 hours. Drain and set aside, saving 2 1/4 cups of the cooking liquid.

3. Place the game hen, beef, salt pork, and hominy in a large casserole and cover with the reserved hominy cooking water and the 1 cup of water. Season with salt and pepper, bring to just below a boil, and simmer, uncovered, until very tender, about 4 hours, adding small amounts of water if it looks like it's drying out. The water should never reach a boil.

4. Add the pea puree and stir so all the fat is absorbed. Add the potato and turnip, stir, and cook until the potato is very soft and the hominy fully cooked, about 1 hour more. Do not boil at any time. Serve hot.

Variation: To make a quick vegetable succotash, combine 2 cups defrosted frozen lima beans, 2 cups freshly cooked corn kernels scraped from the cob, 1/2 teaspoon salt, 2 tablespoons unsalted butter, a dash of paprika, freshly ground black pepper to taste, and 1/2 cup heavy cream in a large saucepan. Cook for about 5 minutes until bubbling hot, and serve.

Makes 4 servings

PUERTO RICAN BEEF, PORK, MALANGA, AND PLANTAIN STEW

THIS PUERTO RICAN STEW IS A SIMPLE vegetable stew called *sancocho*. It has some ingredients that you may have difficulty finding, although I didn't, once I looked closely at the produce section of my supermarket. If you've never heard of malanga (*Xanthosoma sagittifolium*) or seen it, you might not realize that it is used in Caribbean cooking, and many supermarkets carry it for their Latino customers. Malanga is pear shaped and looks like a root vegetable (actually it's the corm of a plant related to taro). It can be replaced with yautia, another taro-like plant found in markets in Florida, or taro.

One 1-pound beef flank steak, cubed
1/2 pound boneless pork shoulder, trimmed of any large pieces of fat and cubed
2 ounces sliced ham, chopped
1 medium-size onion, chopped
2 large, ripe tomatoes, peeled, seeded, and chopped
2 green bell peppers, seeded and chopped
1 fresh green chile, seeded and chopped
1 leafy sprig fresh coriander (cilantro)
1 tablespoon salt
2 quarts water
1/2 pound malanga, peeled and cut into 1-inch cubes
1/2 pound pumpkin, peeled, seeded, and cut into 1-inch cubes
1/2 pound yams, peeled and cut into 1-inch cubes
1/2 pound small boiling potatoes, peeled and halved
1 ripe green plantain, peeled and cut into 1/2-inch-thick rounds
1 ripe red plantain, peeled and cut into 1/2-inch-thick rounds
Fresh corn kernels scraped from 2 ears

1. Put the beef, pork, ham, onion, tomatoes, bell peppers, chile, coriander, and salt in a large casserole. Cover with the water and bring to a boil. Reduce the heat to low and simmer, uncovered, until the meat is somewhat tender, about 1 hour.

2. Add the malanga, pumpkin, yams, potatoes, plantains, and corn and continue to cook over low heat, uncovered, for 1¼ hours. Cover, increase the heat to medium, and cook until the meat and vegetables are tender, about 30 minutes. Uncover, and if there is a lot of liquid left, boil for 8 minutes to evaporate it a bit. Reduce the heat to low and cook until you have a thick stew, about 40 minutes.

Makes 6 to 8 servings

FEIJOADA

FEIJOADA IS SAID TO BE THE NATIONAL dish of Brazil, and black beans are the indispensible ingredient in this stew. It might be impossible to list all the ingredients that go into a *feijoada*, because every region does something a little different, but the standard ingredients are the black beans, a variety of sausages, jerked beef, pork, cured meats, bacon, tongue, and the ear, foot, and tail of a pig. In Bahia, pumpkin and kale might be included, and orange juice as well. There is no record of this dish existing before the nineteenth century, but it is nevertheless a very popular Brazilian preparation that is almost ritualistic in character. The meats are separated from the beans and served attractively on a platter. It is a festive and ceremonial dish that is conveyed in the meaning of the word *feijoada*, which can roughly be translated as "bean-o-rama," and ultimately derives from the Greek word for bean, *phasolus*, through the Latin.

Various traditional accompaniments come with the final dish, including *arroz brasileiro*, rice and onion fried in lard and then cooked with tomatoes. Another traditional accompaniment is *farofa de manteiga*, manioc meal cooked with eggs and onion. Kale cooked in bacon fat can be served too, along with sliced oranges and/or bananas.

This recipe is adapted from Margarette de Andrade's *feijoada* recipe, published in the *Washington Post* on February 7, 1963. To simplify serving this stew, feel free to mix the meat and beans thoroughly. You can order fresh chorizo sausages from La Española (see the sources listed in the back of the book). If you can't get a pig tail and ears, double the number of pig feet.

1 pound unflavored jerked beef pieces (not stick form)
1 small smoked (preferably) or unsmoked beef tongue (about 2½ pounds)
½ pound Canadian bacon
5 cups dried black beans (about 2½ pounds), picked over and rinsed
1 pound fresh Spanish- or Portuguese-style chorizo sausages
1 pound pork spareribs

1 pound smoked or cooked Portuguese linguiça
    sausages or andouille sausages
2 pig feet
2 pork tails
2 pig ears
One 1-pound piece lean stew beef (see page 29),
    trimmed of any large pieces of fat and halved
1/4 pound lean slab bacon, cut into strips
Salt to taste
1 tablespoon lard
2 large onions, chopped
3 garlic cloves, crushed
1 medium-size, ripe tomato, peeled, seeded, and
    chopped
1 tablespoon finely chopped fresh parsley leaves
1 dried chile

---

1. In four separate bowls, soak the jerked beef, tongue, Canadian bacon, and beans overnight in water to cover. Drain.

2. Place the drained beans in a large stockpot and cover with water by several inches. Bring to a boil and cook, uncovered, until tender, adding water as needed, 50 to 60 minutes. Drain, reserving 2 1/4 cups of the bean cooking water.

3. Meanwhile, as the beans are cooking, prepare the jerked beef. Place in a medium-size saucepan of cold water, bring to a boil, reduce the heat to low, and simmer until fork-tender, about 1 hour. Drain, cut into 1-inch-wide strips, and set aside.

4. In a large saucepan, place the tongue in boiling water and cook until the skin can be removed, about 1 1/4 hours. Once the tongue

is cool enough to handle, slice off the skin and set the tongue aside.

5. Puncture the fresh sausages with a toothpick or corn cob holder and blanch in gently bubbling water until firm, about 15 minutes. Drain, cut in half crosswise, and set aside.

6. Bring a large stockpot filled with water to a boil, reduce the heat to medium, and blanch the Canadian bacon, spareribs, smoked linguiça sausages, and pig feet, tails, and ears until the feet are falling apart, about 1 1/2 hours. Drain, reserving 2 cups of the broth, and set aside the fresh pork sausages separately.

7. Put the remaining blanched meats, the beef, and the slab bacon in a very large stockpot. Cover with tepid water, slowly bring to a boil, and reduce the heat to medium-low. Simmer until the meats are falling-apart tender, about 2 hours. Drain, discard the feet, tails, and ears, and add the rest of the meat to the beans along with the blanched fresh pork sausages. Simmer until the meats are very tender and the beans are soft enough to mash easily, about 1 hour. Season with salt.

8. In a large skillet, melt the lard over medium-high heat. Cook the onion and garlic until translucent, stirring so the garlic doesn't burn, about 8 minutes. Add the tomato, parsley, and chile. Add about 2 cups of the beans and mash with a wooden spoon. Stir in 2 cups of the reserved bean cooking water and simmer until the mixture thickens, about 20 minutes. Return the mixture to the pot containing the beans and meat. Simmer 1 more hour, adding the reserved 2 cups of pork broth, if necessary, to keep it moist and stewing. Correct the seasonings and add the remaining ¼ cup of bean cooking liquid if the stew is too dry.

9. Remove all the meats and cut into small portions so everybody gets some of each. Traditionally, the tongue is placed in the middle of a large platter with the meats served around it. The beans are served separately in a deep serving dish.

———— ● ————

Makes 12 to 14 servings

CLIFF'S NO-NAME STEW

THIS STEW IS THE LAST STEW. NOT ONLY IS this the last stew in the book, it is the last stew I tested for this book, and the way it came about was by emptying my freezer and refrigerator, going to the farmer's market, dumping everything into a large stockpot, and cooking it nearly forever. It was a heavenly stew, and I was fortunate to eat it with my friends Sarah Pillsbury, Bill and Laurie Benenson, Bill Grantham and Martha Rose Shulman, Steve Monas and Maggie Megaw, Kimba Hills and John Truby, and two of my children, Dyala and Seri. A great discussion arose as to what to call this stew, since it had no name. Not everyone at the table could believe all these ingredients were actually in my freezer. I lied. Some suggestions for a name were Cliff's last stew stew, everything-but-the-kitchen-sink stew, don't ask don't tell stew, the night has a 1,000 eyes stew, blind date stew, get me outta here stew, roadkill stew (there is no roadkill in it, though), off the cliff stew, over the cliff stew, LOOK OUT stew, last date you'll ever have stew, Wright's folly stew, don't call me I'll call you stew, I know where you live stew, PETA nightmare stew, and if you eat this stew… stew. Anyway, it's a great stew with no name. You'll need a 20- to 22-quart stockpot to make it, though.

———— ● ————

2 pounds beef honeycomb tripe
¼ cup distilled white vinegar
2 pounds beef chuck flanken–style ribs, cut up to separate the ribs
2 pounds fresh chorizo or andouille sausage, cut into thick rounds
½ pound hot Italian sausage, cut into thick rounds
½ pound prosciutto bones
½ pound lamb shoulder, trimmed of any large pieces of fat and cut up
¼ pound ham fat, chopped
¾ pound ham bone
½ pound smoked slab bacon, cubed
1¾ pounds boneless, skinless chicken thighs
1¼ pounds goat meat on the bone, trimmed of any large pieces of fat
1¼ pounds beef or veal marrow bones
¼ pound Parmigiano-Reggiano cheese rinds
½ cup pearl barley
¼ cup dried red kidney beans, picked over and rinsed
¼ cup dried white beans, picked over and rinsed
2½ pounds fresh fava beans in the pod, shelled (see page 129)

½ cup fresh or frozen lima beans

½ cup fresh or frozen peas

1 small head green cabbage (about 1½ pounds), damaged outer leaves removed, cut into wedges, cored, and each wedge cut into 3 thinner wedges

3 large carrots, cut into chunks

1 very large parsnip (about 1¼ pounds), peeled and cubed

6 ounces fenugreek leaves (optional)

1¼ pounds Swiss chard (both leaves and stems), cut up

1 large turnip (about ½ pound), peeled and cubed

1 pound pumpkin, peeled, seeded, and cubed

1 large leek (white and light green parts only), split lengthwise, washed well, and cut up

4 heads fresh garlic (preferably) or 3 heads garlic, first layer of peel rubbed off

1 celeriac (celery root; about 3 pounds), peeled and cubed

20 black peppercorns

Salt to taste

1 bouquet garni, consisting of 1 bunch each fresh basil, thyme, and dill, 15 sprigs fresh Italian parsley, and 2 bay leaves, tied in cheesecloth

1 pound beef feet

2 pounds pig feet

1. Soak the tripe in the vinegar and water to cover in the refrigerator overnight. Drain and cut up.

2. Put all the ingredients in a 20-quart stockpot, placing the feet on top. Cover with cold water and bring to a boil over high heat. Reduce the heat to low, using a heat diffuser, if necessary, and simmer until all the meats are disintegrating, about 8 hours.

3. Remove and discard the feet, bones, garlic heads, and bouquet garni before serving.

Makes 18 servings

Sources

ADAMBA IMPORTS
585 Meserole Street
Brooklyn, NY 11237
www.adamba.com
(718) 628-9700; fax (718) 628-0920
Vavel brand of kapusta kiszona *(sauerkraut)*

CACIQUE
14923 Proctor Avenue
La Puente, CA 91746
(626) 961-3399, ext. 505 (customer service);
fax (626) 369-8083
www.CaciqueUSA.com
Mexican queso fresco

CAFÉ ANATOLIA
24 Market Square, 2nd Floor
Pittsburgh, PA 15222
(412) 261-3890; fax (412) 201-5609
www.cafeanatolia.com
Turkish sausages

LA ESPAÑOLA
25020 Doble Avenue
Harbor City, CA 90710
(310) 539-0455; fax (310) 539-5989
www.donajuana.com
Spanish paprika, longaniza *sausage, Spanish-style
semidry sausage*

ESPERYA USA
1715 West Farms Road
Bronx, NY 10460
(877) 907-2525; fax (718) 860-4311
www.esperya.com
Italian food, especially salted anchovies

ETRURIA CLASSICA GASTRONOMIA
286 Atwells Avenue
Providence, RI 02903
(800) 344-6311; fax (401) 273-6879
www.chefwalter.com
Earthenware by Chef Walter Potenza

FORMAGGIO KITCHEN
244 Huron Avenue
Cambridge, MA 02138
(888) 212-3224
www.formaggiokitchen.com
Mostarda di Cremona

FRONTIER NATURAL PRODUCTS COOPERATIVE
Norway, IA
(800) 669-3275; fax (800) 717-4372
www.frontierherb.com
Herbs and spices

GALLO BROKERAGE
93 Willow Street
Wilkes-Barre, PA 18702
(570) 822-9743; fax (570) 822-6622
Fregula

THE GREAT AMERICAN SPICE COMPANY
P.O. Box 80068
Fort Wayne, IN 46898
(888) 502-8058; fax (260) 420-8117
www.americanspice.com
Spices

JAMISON FARM
171 Jamison Lane
Latrobe, PA 15650
(800) 237-5262; fax (724) 837-2287
www.jamisonfarm.com
Lamb

KALUSTYAN CORPORATION
855 Rahway Avenue
Union, NJ 07083
(908) 688-6111; fax (908) 688-4415
www.kalustyan.com
Spices

P.G. MOLINARI & SONS, INC.
1401 Yosemite Avenue
San Francisco, CA 94124
(415) 822-5555; fax (415) 822-5834
www.molinarisalame.com
Cotechino *and other sausages*

PENZEYS
19300 West Janacek Court
P.O. Box 924
Brookfield, WI 53008
(800) 741-7787; fax (262) 785-7678
www.penzeys.com
Spices

SALUMERIA ITALIANA
151 Richmond Street
Boston, MA 02109
(800) 400-5916
www.salumeriaitaliana.com
Salted anchovies

SUR LA TABLE
1765 Sixth Avenue South
Seattle, WA 98134
(800) 243-0852; fax (206) 682-1026
www.surlatable.com
Earthenware

THE VERMONT COUNTRY STORE
RR1, P.O. Box 231
North Clarendon, VT
(802) 775-4111
www.vermontcountrystore.com
Common crackers

WILLIAMS-SONOMA
P.O. Box 7456
San Francisco, CA 94120
(800) 541-2233
www.williams-sonoma.com
Kitchenware and earthenware

ZEN SHEEP FARM
Tom and Nancy Zennie
7723 Quincy Street
Zeeland, MI 49464
(616) 875-7811
Lamb

Index